Lost Boys
The Beulah Home Tragedy

JACK HOBEY

Lost Boys: The Beulah Home Tragedy, written and edited by Jack Hobey. Produced by Harbor House Publishers, Inc. Manufactured in the United States of America. While every effort has been made to ensure the accuracy of the information presented, the author and the publisher do not guarantee accuracy and are not liable for any omissions or errors. Please report any new information to the author.

Harbor House Publishers, Inc.
221 Water Street, Boyne City, Michigan 49712 USA
800-491-1760 • harbor@harborhouse.com • www.harborhouse.com

DEDICATION

Dedicated to all the boys who lived at The Buffalo Newsboys and Bootblack's Home, The Chicago Children's Temple Home, The Leoni Beulah Land Farm, and The Boyne City Beulah Home.

1893-1913

CONTENTS

PROLOGUE

The Boyne City Affair

Herman Swift's supporters termed this period the "Time of Troubles" and his critics termed it the "Boyne City Affair." Whichever side you ultimately may take in this story, the drama began to unfold at roughly nine o'clock the morning of November 30th, 1909. And rather predictably, simply given the sensational accusations, that day would mark the peak of Mr. Swift's fame and notable career.

Swift was general manager and treasurer of the Beulah Land Farm for Boys, an orphanage in Boyne City, a town in the northwest corner of the lower peninsula of Michigan. He took his motto from English author Samuel Coleridge: "It were better to gain the prayer of a fatherless child than to secure the favor of an emperor" and the Beulah Home was known as "The Greatest Life Saving Station on the Great Lakes." By 1909, Herman Swift was well known around the state of Michigan. He was one of the most popular and important people in Boyne City, and the Beulah Home was the city's most famous institution.

The morning of November 30th, 1909, a boy named Kent drove a team of two gray horses pulling a farm wagon toward Horton Bay, a small village located some four miles northwest up the shore of Pine Lake from the Beulah Home. Sidney Jones sat next to Kent. Jones had worked as farm superintendent at the Home since June. The farm work for the season was finished and now he assisted Swift's efforts to construct a grand new building on the Beulah Home property. This represented Swift's great dream to build a facility to serve an additional one hundred homeless boys. They broke ground for the building in July of 1909. Fig.1 is a photo of Beulah Home boys working on the foundation.

On Monday, November 29th, 1909, Sidney Jones had advised Swift that the Horton Bay quarry contained a blue-gray stone, stone superior to that they currently were utilizing in the foundation for the new building. On November 30th, two Beulah Home boys, Simon Mack and Earnest Wardell, were assigned to assist Jones in gathering stone. The two boys rode in the back of the wagon.

Two Teachers

The Beulah Home boys identified themselves as members of two groups: the "big boys" and the "little boys." Adults at the Home termed the boys "older boys" and "younger boys." Miss Mable Hardy taught the older boys and Miss Leonora Ferris taught the younger boys. Mable

At work on the new building (Fig. 1)   PHOTO: Edward Beebe

Hardy would support Herman Swift throughout his entire Time of Troubles, while Leonora Ferris was the woman who initiated the Boyne City Affair.

Two Beulah Boys

Both Simon Mack and Earnest Wardell were "older boys." Simon was a "little boy" and Earnest was a "big boy" but Simon drove the conversation that Sidney Jones overheard coming from the back of the farm wagon as they drove toward the quarry.

Simon Mack was born in Grand Rapids, Michigan on July 10th, 1896. He lived with his parents in a rented home at 85 4th Avenue, a tough neighborhood near the river. Simon's father John's parents emigrated from Ireland to Canada. John emigrated from Canada to Grand Rapids where he worked as a railroad brakeman. Simon's mother's maiden name was Mary Zylstra. Both of her parents had come to Grand Rapids from the Netherlands. John called Mary, "Minnie." Minnie Mack died of pneumonia on September 23rd, 1902. Simon was only six. Three years later, John Mack either died or disappeared. He left three orphans: Mammie, age 16; Arthur, age 13; and Simon, age 9.

In August of 1905, Arthur and Simon Mack were sent to the Beulah Home for Boys. Three months later, Arthur walked out of the Home and disappeared, probably returning to Grand Rapids. Simon was only nine, but he was street-wise when he arrived at the Beulah Home. He was not old enough to leave the Home on his own, however, and Arthur elected not to take him along.

In November of 1909, there were around fifty boys living at the Beulah Home and Simon Mack probably had been there as long as any of them. Simon was small and still considered a "little boy," but he was crafty and wily. He knew the routine at the Home and knew how to manipulate it. He had the ability to lead most any of the boys, whether they were "little" or "big." By

November of 1909, Simon's sister Mammie had advanced to become a librarian at the Grand Rapids Public Library. Some of the Beulah boys claimed Simon had plans to escape the Home, go live with Mammie, and "chase girls in Grand Rapids."

Grand Rapids ranked second to the City of Detroit in terms of population of Michigan cities. In the early 1900's, it continued to be a significant lumbering center and had become the country's major center for the production of fine furniture. Grand Rapids' population approached 100,000 as thousands of immigrants arrived looking for work in the furniture industry. Simon Mack grew up in the Dutch ghetto down near the large river, the Grand River that curled through the city. Huge log piles lined the river and ghetto boys played, smoked, drank, and schemed within those piles. Ultimately, at least six other boys would leave this Grand Rapids neighborhood and join Simon Mack as inmates at the Boyne City Beulah Home.

Herman Swift attempted to civilize boys like Simon Mack and by 1909 Simon had the benefit of over four years of Swift's teachings and schooling. But rough edges remained and Simon spoke with a residue of urban, ghetto slang and dialect, dropping "t's" off the beginnings of words, sounding like a Dickens' boy absent the English accent.

Sidney Jones rode in a farm wagon traveling down a rough twin rutted trail toward a stone quarry in Horton Bay. Simon Mack sat in the back of the wagon and he spoke quickly, earnestly. It wasn't that easy to understand Simon, but Jones clearly deciphered a series of explicit, sensational accusations of abuse of boys at the Home by Herman Swift. Simon recited specific instances of abuse against specific boys and Earnest Wardell did not say anything. All Sidney Jones heard from Earnest was a series of "uh huhs" and "yahs."

Earnest Wardell had been at the Beulah Home almost as long as Simon Mack. Earnest grew up in the Village of Mancelona, a town on the North-South Mainline of the Grand Rapids & and Indiana Railroad and twenty-eight miles south of Boyne City.

Antrim Iron Works operated a large blast furnace in Mancelona and loggers harvested hardwood trees in the area to provide charcoal for that furnace. As the trees in the area were harvested, they were not replaced. Lumberjacks moved north and now the area attracted farmers. It was a rural setting and Earnest's father was a farmer. He also was a drayman.

Earnest was born in 1896 and he either was the youngest of seven children or the second youngest of eight. Earnest's mother Melina Jane Wardell died of bilious fever on March 1, 1905. She was only forty-four.

Mancelona is located in Antrim County. The Village of Bellaire is the county seat. On June 29, 1905, the *Bellaire Independent* carried the following obituary:

"Wardell, W.J., fatally injured at Mancelona last week. He was delivering from the depot a large wooden pulley weighing 430 pounds, the wheel being balanced crossways on his dray and he was steadying it with one leg and one arm while holding the lines in his other hand. His team became frightened while crossing the track and the wheel went off, Mr. Wardell being underneath. His exterior wounds being dressed, he remained unconscious, and the next day it was ascertained that he had ruptured a blood vessel at the base of the brain. He died during the early hours of Sunday morning, never having regained consciousness."

William James Wardell, age forty-seven, died on June 24, 1905. He was a widower, his wife Melina Jane having died three months earlier. William left behind seven or eight orphaned children. Some of the children already had left home. Mancelona residents took in some of the others. The youngest son Earnest became an inmate at the Beulah Home in Boyne City, arriving right around the time that Simon Mack arrived.

Earnest was only a little older than Simon, but Earnest was tall, much larger than Simon. And Earnest adapted very well to the discipline and instruction provided at the Beulah Home. Herman Swift invested a great deal of time in teaching the Beulah Home boys singing and public speaking. The boys put on performances in the hall on the fourth floor of the Home and in churches and theatres in Boyne City and surrounding towns. During the summer Swift toured the state with a quartette of boy singers and speakers. These were the most skilled performers among the boys at the Home. Earnest Wardell may well have arrived at the Beulah Home speaking in the dialect or slang English spoken by the lumber camp kids who attended the Mancelona public school. But by 1909 he had earned a place in the Beulah boys quartette. In the initial days of the Boyne City Affair Earnest opposed Herman Swift, then he changed his mind, something that Simon Mack did not do.

Two Laborers

William J Allison was a stonemason who lived in Montcalm County, Michigan, some one hundred fifty miles south of Boyne City. Allison became the mystery man in the Boyne City Affair. He worked a short time, just four and a half days, on the construction of the foundation of the new building at the Beulah Land Farm. At Herman Swift's trial, Allison would testify on behalf of Swift, becoming the key witness in a conspiracy defense. He testified that he rode along on that wagon that went to the stone quarry on November 30, 1909. He also testified that he heard Sidney Jones and Simon Mack plotting against Swift, a plot that entailed getting little boys to falsely charge Swift with abuses, thereby getting rid of Swift and leaving Jones to run the farm and Simon to return to Grand Rapids and chase girls.

At Swift's trial, Sidney Jones would testify that having reached the stone quarry, he confronted Simon Mack and Earnest Wardell and they both volunteered to him details about Swift's abuses. Jones claimed he could not recall ever meeting Allison.

Jones, Mack, Wardell, Kent, and perhaps Allison loaded the farm wagon with stone and proceeded slowly back to the site of the new building construction. Mack and Wardell attended classes late that afternoon and after dinner they returned to the construction site. At the site, Sidney Jones instructed the two boys to tell George Snell what they had told him. Jones already had provided details to Snell.

George Snell left Canada and moved to Michigan in 1898. He was twenty-eight years old when he arrived in Empire, a small town in the Leelanau Peninsula, twenty-five miles west of Traverse City. Sometime between 1900 and 1904, Snell moved from Empire to Boyne City. The Federal Census of 1910 would report that Boyne City was the fastest growing town in the United States. Snell worked as a carpenter, but then established a contracting business. He became the most prominent contractor in town, building many commercial retail buildings and then in 1906 building the beautiful Presbyterian Church. The Church was constructed of orange Boyne City brick over a cut stone foundation and may well have been designed by Isaac Erb or based on an Erb design. Herman Swift placed Snell in charge of the construction of the new building at the Beulah Home.

Isaac Erb was born in Thedford, Lambton County Ontario, Canada in 1855. He was a religious man, a member of the Methodist Church, and a famous architect who designed houses and commercial, public, or fraternal buildings. Perhaps the most noted of his designs was the basis for the construction of the First Presbyterian Church at 811 Wall Street in Port Huron, Michigan. The construction was completed in 1895. The style is Romanesque Revival and includes an orange brick exterior over a cut stonewall foundation.

Isaac Erb was the man who designed the plans for the new building at the Beulah Home for Boys in Boyne City. The building's location was on Silver Street just east of the Beulah Home. Erb also provided a landscape design to tie the new building into an appropriate relationship with the Home and the surroundings. Based on his understanding of Herman Swift's good works, I imagine Erb provided both designs as his contribution to the Home.

The design for Swift's grand new building almost certainly anticipated an orange brick exterior rising above a cut blue-gray stone foundation, just like the Presbyterian Churches in Port Huron and Boyne City and the Methodist Episcopal Church in Eaton Rapids, Michigan. The Boyne City Brick Company was located very close to the Beulah Home. The company produced over 300,000 orange bricks per day and it is easy to imagine Herman Swift beseeching the owners for support for his new building.

Swift anticipated that the building would represent the peak of architectural excellence in northern Michigan. The building must have represented a tremendous challenge for George Snell. Swift and Erb both were perfectionists and dreamers. The building probably included a number of intricate design features. Snell was expected to construct it with local labor. Compounding the challenge was Swift's insistence that Snell use the inmates of the Home to work on the construction. Fig.1 in fact is staged to show only boys on the construction site.

Erb visited Boyne City in July of 1909 and laid out the plans for the new building as well as the landscape design. By the end of November, however, Snell still was working on the foundation and winter fast was approaching. Snell was not in a good mood on the afternoon of November 30th when Sidney Jones confronted him with the accusations of abuse by Swift. There was something about Jones that troubled Snell a bit. Jones was rough and in the past he had made critical comments about Swift. Furthermore, Jones professed great knowledge and interest in land and farming. But in fact, before Swift hired him to supervise the Beulah Home farm in the spring of 1909, Jones had not farmed but rather had spent seventeen years operating a lathe and turning out wooden handles in a lumber mill in Harbor Springs, a town on the shore of Lake Michigan's Little Traverse Bay. In spite of all this, Snell felt he best not ignore the accusations and that afternoon of November 30th he asked Jones to direct Simon Mack and Earnest Wardell to him.

As the two boys approached Snell he motioned them over to a spot away from the work site, a far enough distance to prevent other boys or laborers from hearing the conversation. Snell asked the two boys to tell him what they had told Jones, but only if it was the truth. Simon Mack led the discussion describing Swift's abuses of a number of boys. Earnest Wardell added a number of details. Neither Simon nor Earnest indicated that Swift had abused them. Snell was both amazed and appalled by the accusations.

At the end of the workday the evening of November 30th, Snell and Jones mounted their horses and rode down Charlevoix Street away from the Beulah Home. They turned left on Michigan Avenue toward town. They did not speak. At Lake Street they turned south along the row of factories. First were the Boyne City Chemical Plant on the left and the Charcoal Iron Plant on the right. Twelve tall stacks poked up from the Chemical Plant. That plant produced wood alcohol, acetic acid, and charcoal from waste hardwood. At the time it was the largest charcoal production plant in the United States. The charcoal production was transferred across Lake Street to the Charcoal Iron Plant. There it was utilized to produce pig iron. A smoke stack some 135 feet tall poked up from the Charcoal Iron Plant. That plant lay along the shores of Pine Lake, running south to a point where it met the north boundary of the Von Platen Lumber Mill. The Von Platen Mill covered eight acres along the lake, but it seemed small once you passed by it and reached the property of the next lumber mill that ran south and covered most all the Boyne City waterfront. That mill was White's Lumber Mill No.1, "the Big Mill." And the Big Mill seemed small when looking past it and observing the property of William Sutherland Shaw's Tannery Complex that ran up Pine Lake along the opposite shore from the Beulah Home. This was one of the largest tanneries in the world. When the wind blew the wrong way, the smells of the Chemical Plant, the Charcoal Plant, the lumber mills, and the tannery wafted over the Beulah Home.

Snell and Jones passed by the large factories, the football field sized piles of waste wood, pig iron, and logs, and entered the commercial district of Boyne City. They rode to the city building and tied their horses. They entered the building and met Richard Beach.

Richard W. Beach became Chief of Police of Boyne City on April 9, 1909. Beach lived with his wife Marie and seven children in a small home on Pine Street. From his front porch Beach could peak around the far south end of the Big Mill and glimpse the lake. He was not in the high rent district, but he owned the home. Beach had achieved some success at several jobs, but did not have police experience prior to becoming Chief of Police. I picture him as a large man, wearing a long black coat and either a cowboy-style or bowler hat. He wore a large brass badge on his coat and seemed imposing, intimidating and a bit impetuous.

Beach listened carefully and with some excitement to the accusations Simon Mack and Earnest Wardell had made against Herman Swift. George Snell did most of the talking. Snell kept Sidney Jones in the background and Jones' contribution consisted largely of a series of vigorous head nods of agreement.

Snell carefully repeated the accusations at the request of the Police Chief. The Chief made no demand for written statements from either Snell or Jones. He indicated that he would pursue the matter. Snell and Jones left the city building. Snell turned his horse south for home and Jones turned his horse north.

Richard Beach sat for a few moments and pondered what course he should take. Herman Swift was the second most famous and probably the most highly respected man in Boyne City. But Beach personally did not care too much for Swift. Since his appointment as Chief of Police,

Beach also had been given responsibilities as City Water and Street Commissioner. In his capacity as Street Commissioner he had several occasions to visit Swift at the Beulah Home. He found Swift to be small and pompous, rather a milk-toast man with a bossy attitude.

In Herman Swift's trial, Richard Beach testified that for three days he pondered the accusations against Swift laid out by George Snell. The truth was that on the very next morning, December 1st, 1909, Beach set off to meet with City Attorney, Arthur Urquhart.

That same morning, Simon Mack recognized trouble was brewing at the Beulah Home. He grew very concerned and then he ran away, following on foot the path that Snell and Jones had taken the prior afternoon, and quickly arriving at the city building. Simon ended up in the office of Justice of the Peace Elisha Shepherd. He never returned to the Beulah Home.

Richard Beach arrived at Arthur Urquhart's office about the same time that Elisha Shepherd called. Beach waited impatiently while Urquhart listened to Shepherd. Shepherd advised Urquhart that a boy had run away from the Beulah Home and was there with him at the city building. The boy had made claims of abuse against Herman Swift. Shepherd told Urquhart he'd like to see him immediately and hung up. Urquhart was not happy. He had a schedule that day and it did not include dealing with accusations against Swift. Urquhart had been through this on several prior occasions. The most recent had occurred two months earlier and involved a Beulah Home boy from Sault Ste. Marie named Franklin Haley. Franklin had stolen candy from a local Boyne City establishment and once apprehended took the position that he had been abused by Herman Swift. Urquhart trapped the boy in a web of lies and returned him to the Home. He knew there were a number of tough boys at the Home, most wanted to leave, and many of those understood that claims of abuse might either get them or Swift out of the place.

Arthur Urquhart was born in April of 1880 on a farm in Wyocena, Wisconsin, a small rural community near Madison. He was admitted to the practice of law in the State of Michigan in Lansing on June 16, 1903. A year later he moved to Boyne City where he established a law practice, dealt in real estate, and sold fire insurance, a crucial requirement for any business in town. He was active in the Republican Party and served as a Circuit Court Commissioner for Charlevoix County. He also served as Supervisor of the Fourth Ward of the City. In April of 1908, Arthur Urquhart was appointed unanimously to serve as Boyne City's City Attorney. His pay was fifty dollars every three months. He was only twenty-eight.

The city did not pay Urquhart enough to deal with the issue that Justice Shepherd and Richard Beach brought him the morning of December 1, 1909. Beach described the abuse accusations disclosed to him by George Snell as he and Urquhart walked to the City Building to meet Justice Shepherd. Urquhart explained to Beach that in all likelihood it was the case of a tough boy trying to get even with Swift for something. He told Beach he did not think it would take long to make the boy retract what he had said about Swift.

Urquhart later wrote that when he and Beach arrived at the Justice Office he confronted Simon Mack and: "tried to find the motive for making the accusation and went after him so severely that Justice Shepherd accused him of trying to cover up the case against Swift. After questioning him for some time he decided that the boy was either telling the truth or that he was a most clever liar."

Urquhart then called the prosecuting attorney for Charlevoix County, Alfred B. Nicholas. Nicholas lived in East Jordan some ten miles southwest of Boyne City. Nicholas said he would not be able to deal with the Swift matter for another week, but he told Urquhart: "in fairness to Swift the charges should be examined at once." Nicholas felt relieved. He had been pestered in the past with charges against Herman Swift and here was an opportunity to get to the bottom of the matter without being directly involved. He told Urquhart to take the Chief of Police and a deputy up to the Beulah Home and investigate the accusations. As a precaution, Shepherd signed an arrest warrant for Herman Swift.

Urquhart, Beach, and the deputy left the Justice Office, reached Lake Street, and proceeded past all the factories, through the din and smoke. A Michigan December rain fell, trying to turn to snow. At Michigan Avenue they turned left, following the lake. Urquhart's steps slowed. He repeated to himself: "You must be very careful about this!" At John Street they turned right and walked up the hill to the steps to the Beulah Home. Urquhart looked up at the lights in the windows of the large Victorian structure and followed the large man up the steps. He jumped when Richard Beach banged hard on the lower level door.

The very next day Alfred Urquhart and Richard Beach returned to the Beulah Home and arrested Herman Swift. So began the Time of Troubles or the Boyne City Affair depending where you stood on the matter. And neither Urquhart nor Beach knew the arrest would lead to the Michigan Supreme Court and through the offices of two Michigan state governors; and drag them along for over three years and beyond.

Lumber Barons Once Operated Own 'Boystown' Here in Lush Lumber Era

"Mention 'Boys Town' to almost anyone and instantly they'll think of Father Flanagan's Boys Town in Douglas County, Nebraska. Yet few people realize that Boyne City had a Boy's Town going strong as early as 1904, thirteen years before Father Flanagan's Boys Town was started.

Boyne's Boys Town was located one mile from the city, and it was known as the Beulah Land Farm. Situated on a high plateau overlooking Pine Lake, the large four-story building...housed the homeless boys from Grand Rapids, Detroit, and Chicago. The building, originally intended for a hotel, with its farm of 160 acres, belonged to homeless lads through the generosity of the then local lumber barons...

Herman Lee Swift, manager of the Beulah farm, was their Father Flanagan. Showing kindness and sympathy—something that the ragged urchins had not experienced in the big city—Swift soon won and kept their confidence...

With the decline of the lumber industry in Northern Michigan went the decline of Northern Michigan's Boy's Town."

Boyne Citizen, July 13th, 1950

Lost Boys: A band of boys who were lost by their parents and came to live in Neverland.

–Peter Pan, J.M. Barrie, 1904

I

The Farmer-Soldier and the Preacher's Daughter

The conclusion of the War of 1812 and the end of hostilities in areas west of the Appalachian Mountains marked the beginning of a massive wave of emigration from the state of New York to the state of Michigan. Later a second wave of emigrants would seek lumbering or mining jobs in Michigan. Then a third wave would seek manufacturing jobs in cities like Detroit or Flint. But the first wave of settlers principally sought fertile, cheap land.

Elizabeth F. Elliot wrote a book titled *Pioneer Women of the West*. Scribner published the book in 1852 and at that time Michigan was indeed a western state. Harriet Noble's diary is included in the book. The diary describes a tedious, harrowing, and discouraging relocation from western New York, across Lake Erie, through the rough frontier town of Detroit to a homestead near Ann Arbor. The diary begins: "My husband was seized by the mania," a reference to pulling up stakes in New York, leaving established towns, schools, and churches, and moving to the frontier, the swamps, forests, the uncleared lands in Michigan.

Harriet Noble referred to the phenomena as a "mania." Others termed it frenzy. Whatever the case, in the state of New York, families were large and farmers' sons grew older and were pushed to emigrate by the growing scarcity of tillable land. They were pulled by the lure of cheap land. In 1845, the state of Michigan employed an agent in New York. They provided him with pamphlets and advertising support. His sole job was to attract settlers to Michigan.

One of the men persuaded to emigrate was Thomas Ashley Swift. His father Samuel had served his country as a private in the Connecticut militia during the Revolutionary War. Thomas married Eliza Mattison in 1833 and on December 6th, 1833, Eliza gave birth to a son they named Hoyt Ashley Swift. Hoyt apparently is a name derived from the English word "hoit" meaning a long stick. The name became a nickname for thin boys. Hoyt Swift was thin, and I believe he grew up to become a straight-laced, tough man, like a hickory stick.

Hoyt Swift was born in the town of Batavia, New York, the county seat for Genesee County. Genesee County, Michigan was organized in 1836, one year prior to Michigan gaining statehood. The county is located in southeastern Michigan and its major city is Flint. It was given its name in order to attract settlers from Genesee County, New York. In 1840, Thomas Ashley Swift moved his family from New York to Michigan, almost certainly to Genesee County. At an early age, Hoyt Swift began work as a farm laborer.

Lucy Ann Sutton (Fig.2)

Richard Sutton and his wife Sarah moved to Michigan from the state of New York in the late 1830s. Their daughter Lucy Ann Sutton was born in Livingston County, Michigan on September 1st, 1840. Shortly after this, Richard moved the family north to Argentine a small town in Genesee County.

In 1845, the Wesleyan Methodist denomination established a college in Leoni, a small town east of Jackson, Michigan. They named the college the Leoni Seminary and Lucy Sutton attended that school for four years. Lucy was an excellent student and when she left the seminary she possessed the equivalent of a college degree, a most unusual accomplishment for a woman in 1858. The Leoni Seminary will reappear in a curious fashion later in this story.

Lucy Sutton married Hoyt Swift on March 3rd, 1858, when Lucy was seventeen and Hoyt was twenty-seven. They almost certainly were married in a Methodist-Episcopal or M.E. Church. In the early days, the Michigan M.E. Church was part of the Genesee County, New York Conference. This probably is what brought Richard Sutton and his family to Michigan. Richard Sutton was an M.E. Church clergyman. That fact and the Methodist Episcopal Church would play major roles in the lives of Lucy and Hoyt and in the life of their son, Herman Swift.

In 1776, only nineteen percent of the citizens of the United States were members of the Baptist or Methodist churches. By 1850, this number had climbed to fifty-five percent. The movement of people to these two protestant movements and away from the established protestant churches: the Lutheran, Reformed Anglican, Presbyterian and Congregational, was termed the Second Great Awakening. It represented a move toward a more emotional and experience-based religion and away from a theological and intellectual-based religion.

The Methodist Episcopal and Baptist Churches placed emphasis on revivalism and evangelism. Revival or tent camp meetings were very common in frontier Michigan. Revivals often were termed Union Revival Services and took on religious/social/political goals of fighting for emancipation and prohibition. But the principal goal of the revival meeting was personal conversion, the born again experience. And men converted in one of those meetings became candidates for a ministry that required no formal academic training. Evangelism represented the obligation to convince more people to respond to the message of the church. The character of the evangelical churches appealed to the people of the west, or frontier, and spurred fast growth in those areas. That growth also was aided by the shortage of academically qualified ministers to serve traditional protestant churches in places like Michigan.

We may guess that Richard Sutton's ministry was based more on emotion and experience than on academic background and we can be quite certain that his daughter, Lucy Swift, grew up in a busy environment of revivalism and evangelism.

Eaton Rapids: Herman Swift's Birthplace

In December of 1858, Hoyt and Lucy Swift moved to the town of Eaton Rapids in Eaton County in south-central Michigan. By this time men had harnessed the power of the Grand River that runs through the town and cheap power supported the growth of a number of man-

Lucy Sutton Swift (Fig.2)   Hoyt Swift (Fig.3)

ufacturing companies. In 1852, a dry goods storeowner drove down a well and struck a free flow of mineral water. Professors at Michigan Agriculture College, now Michigan State University, tested the water and found it contained high levels of magnesia, potassium sodium, silica acid and lime. Entrepreneurs quickly drilled another fourteen wells and attracted visitors with claims that the mineral water would cure any ailment. Hoteliers built a number of fancy hotels and six passenger trains daily delivered wealthy visitors. They called the town of Eaton Rapids the Saratoga of the West.

When Hoyt and Lucy Swift arrived in Eaton Rapids, Main Street would have been a very busy and exciting place. The heart of Main Street for the Swifts, however, lay at 600 S. Main, the site of the Methodist Episcopal Church.

On March 3rd, 1859, Lucy gave birth to the Swift's first child, a daughter they named Hattie. Lucy focused on the Church and raising Hattie and Hoyt focused on his work as a farm laborer.

Like most Michigan counties, Eaton County contains sixteen townships. Each township contains thirty-six sections and each section represents one square mile or 640 acres. Ever since 1815, Michigan farmers have bought, sold, and traded properties located and measured in terms of sections. A quarter of a section or a "quarter" represents 160 acres. The United States Homestead Act of 1862 in effect blessed this as the number of acres required by a farmer to prosper. Farm prosperity depended upon many factors: the farmer's knowledge and strength, the richness of the soil and the percentage that was tillable. But putting these factors aside, the Michigan farmer strove to acquire at least a "quarter." Later we shall see that Hoyt's son, Herman Swift, successfully strove and acquired a "quarter" and then fought with great vigor to retain it.

Hoyt Swift (Fig.3)

Many of the counties among the three southern-most rows of Michigan counties were named after members of Andrew Jackson's presidential cabinet. Eaton County was named after John H. Eaton who became Jackson's first Secretary of War. This would prove prophetic for Hoyt Swift.

Hoyt enlisted as a private in Company G of the state of Michigan's 20th Infantry Regiment on August 2nd, 1862. This regiment was one of a number raised by the state of Michigan in response to President Lincoln's famous Civil War call for "three hundred thousand more." Company G was raised in Eaton Rapids and that is where Hoyt enlisted.

The *History of the 20th Infantry Regiment* identifies the regiment's chaplain as Joseph Jones from Eaton Rapids. Jones was a Methodist Episcopal preacher. John Wesley founded the Methodist Church in England and laid down the *General Rules of the Society* published on May 1, 1743. Hiram Mattison, a famous abolitionist M.E. Church preacher, wrote a book titled: *The Impending Crisis of 1860 or the Present Connection of the M.E. Church with Slavery and Our Duty in Regard to It.* In that book, Mattison quoted Wesley's rules: "These rules forbid: 'doing harm' and require 'doing unto others as we would have them do to us.' It is certain these rules forbade slaveholding."

In 1862, Eliza Mattison Swift lived in Eaton Rapids with Hoyt and Lucy. It is almost certain that the three Swifts sat in the Eaton Rapids M.E. Church and listened to Pastor Joseph Jones preach the words of Wesley and Mattison against the evils of slavery. And it is equally certain that when Hoyt set off for war all three Swifts believed he was fighting for the country, but more than that he was fighting for God and Christ.

20th Infantry Regiment volunteers gathered at a camp in Jackson, Michigan, arriving from July 26, 1862 to August 18, 1862. They left Jackson on September 1st and traveled by train to Washington D.C. In 1863, the Regiment was deployed to the Western Front. Under General Grant's leadership they fought on the front-line in battles across Mississippi, Kentucky, and Tennessee. They spent the winter of 1863/1864 at a place called Blane's Cross Roads, a very small town in Eastern Tennessee near Knoxville. The men of the regiment would refer to this experience as "Valley Forge." The Regiment traveled east in March of 1864. They crossed the Rapidan River into Virginia on May 5th, 1864. From that date they were not "out of range of an enemy bullet for more than a few days, until April 3, 1865." During what they termed the "battle summer" of 1864, the Regiment lost more men to death and wounds than its total strength at the start of the war. Hoyt Swift never forgot that battle summer and never forgot Blane's Cross Roads.

Hoyt fought in twenty-seven battles, was engaged under fire for 390 days, and was severely wounded. He reenlisted at least once and was present at the end of the Civil War when the 20th Michigan Infantry Regiment participated in President Lincoln's Grand Review of troops in Washington D.C. on May 23, 1865. He served in the Civil War for two years, nine months, and twenty days. Chaplain Joseph Jones served that time right along with Hoyt.

The Regiment returned to Jackson, Michigan and was disbanded on June 4th, 1865. Hoyt Swift and the other men were paid the final installment of bounties or bonuses they had earned serving in the Union Army, seventy-five dollars held over from their original enlistments plus any reenlistment amounts. Hoyt returned home to Lucy. Nine months later, on March 17th,

1866, Lucy gave birth to a second girl. They named the baby Belvia.

On August 13, 1867, Hoyt and Lucy Swift purchased a home and an adjoining lot in the town of Eaton Rapids. They paid one hundred and twenty dollars and acquired the property from a farmer named Silas Crittenden. It totaled only a little over one and a half acres and this appears to be the only property that Hoyt Swift ever owned. Initially, I researched property records in Eaton County with the thought that I would find 160 acres owned by Hoyt Swift and thus prove my theory that his son Herman pushed to acquire 160 acres in order to match his father's accomplishment. The only property I found was the home and lot acquired on August 13, 1867. The property was located on Plain Street at the corner of West Street. West Street marked the boundary of Eaton Rapids and to the west stretched farmland and wood lots. The railroad ran behind the Swift home and, much more importantly, the Methodist Episcopal Church sat at 600 Main Street, only five blocks away.

The Homestead Act of 1862 allowed United States citizens to acquire up to 160 acres of public land at no cost if they homesteaded the land and met other requirements for a period of five years. Civil War veterans were allowed to apply the time they served on active duty to this residency requirement. This means Hoyt Swift might have acquired 160 acres through a land grant under the Homestead Act simply by homesteading the property for a little over two years.

Three million acres in Michigan were transferred through land grants, but by 1865 most of that land lay to the north of Eaton County. Hoyt Swift may have been in no condition to move north. He had spent considerable time in the hospital during the Civil War. I am not sure what wounds or illnesses he may have suffered, but on September 18, 1872, the Federal Government determined him to be an "invalid" and he was granted a pension for his service in the Civil War. Hoyt never moved north and never acquired 160 acres and his son Herman did both. But Herman was never a soldier.

The Civil War played a great role in Hoyt Swift's life. Perhaps the most significant event in Lucy Swift's life began with the birth of a third daughter on January 8, 1869. Lucy and Hoyt named the baby Beulah. They would have five children and Beulah was the only one of the five given a biblical name. The name Beulah has a Hebrew origin and means either "bride" or "married." But I do not believe that this is where Lucy Swift found the name "Beulah."

John Bunyan served as an early minister in the Baptist Church in England during the seventeenth century. He is the author of *Pilgrim's Progress*, an allegorical story of a man named Christian as he moves "from this world to that which is to come." As protestant evangelists toured the Midwest in the mid and latter portions of the 1800s, they became known as the preachers of tents and tracts. Tracts are written religious works, often printed in pamphlet form and always preaching the message of Jesus Christ. Evangelists set the foundation for a tract more frequently upon a portion of *Pilgrim's Progress* than on any other book aside from the Bible. Bunyan's book was very important to Lucy Swift and would become very important to her son Herman. Both probably at some point memorized the work. Regardless of this, Lucy was well aware that toward the end of *Pilgrim's Progress* Christian arrives in the: "Land of Beulah, a lush garden area, just before crossing the River of Death into Heaven." Lucy Swift's third baby girl died of lung fever on February 3rd, 1869. She was only twenty-six days old. It may well be that Lucy named her Beulah the day that she died.

Hoyt and Lucy Swift's fourth child was born in Eaton Rapids on November 26th, 1870. They named the boy Thomas Lee Swift after Hoyt's father Thomas Ashley Swift. Sometime before 1880, they renamed the boy Herman, and Herman would be their only son. Ironically, the name Herman is of German origin and means "soldier."

A fifth and final child, a daughter named Blenn, was born to the Swifts in Eaton Rapids on January 22nd, 1874. Blenn is a very unusual name. I believe Lucy may have formed the word as a contraction of the words: "Beulah in heaven."

His sister Hattie was twelve years older than Herman, Belvia was four years older, and Blenn was three years younger. Through his life all three sisters supported Herman, but he would gain most support from his younger sister Blenn and inspiration from the sister he never met, Beulah.

Herman Swift was a small boy. My guess is that his father was tough and that he pushed Herman toward the land and toward farming. In 1912, a woman named Ethelyn Dyer allegedly wrote a book titled *The Victories of a Boy*. One of the book's chapters is titled "The Growth of an Idea." It is a story about Herman Swift, but also about Hoyt Swift, and it begins: "Something less or more than forty years ago, a small boy lived in Eaton Rapids, Michigan. A boy with bright, fearless, honest eyes; the forehead of a dreamer, and a hint of that quality which will bring dreams to pass. Even then his boyish philanthropy showed itself in unaccountable, unlooked for ways. For example, at one time the father of the boy had been making a strawberry bed.

The little fellow, quite naturally, wanted one too. He was given a small bit of ground with permission to set therein some of the newly purchased plants. To his father's disgust the little fellow took his basket instead to the railroad embankment and there from amid the weeds and grasses filled it with wild strawberry plants. Trudging home with them he met opposition from his father. He wanted to know, 'What are you going to do with those wild plants?' 'Well, they had no chance where they were, and I am going to see what they will do if I give them a chance.' 'I never knew you meant to do such a thing,' exclaimed the puzzled father; 'didn't I tell you to take all you wanted of the good plants?' The boy looked squarely up, spurred to the defense of his protégé. 'Papa, it's my strawberry bed isn't it? You gave it to me and it's my very own.' 'Well, I suppose I did,' was the grudging answer, 'but I never thought you would do a foolish thing like this.' 'Well, I am going to give these plants a chance. They never had any yet.'"

His father pushed Herman to farm, while his mother Lucy pulled him toward the Methodist Episcopal Church. At night, Herman lay there in the small home on Plain Street. He listened to the trains passing by and he dreamed of becoming a preacher, just like his grandfather, Richard Sutton. And he thought about his mother's memory of the baby sister that he never met, Beulah.

On August 22nd, 1890, the Eaton Rapids Journal carried the following article: "Died: On Monday, August 18, 1890, Mrs. Hoyt Swift, after months of intense suffering. Her malady seemed to be beyond the reach of the physician's skill, and for weeks her life has been despaired of. The funeral was held on Wednesday at 4 o'clock, attended by a large number of sympathizing friends. A beautiful tribute was paid to her memory by the floral offerings. At the foot of the casket was a design with "Lucy" in white, on a background of green. At the head was another beautiful design: "Rest, Mother, Rest."

On August 29th, 1890 the *Eaton Rapids Journal* carried Lucy Swift's obituary. The obituary reads in part: "In June, 1888, she was accidentally injured in the arm, from which she never recovered. Since October 1889, she has been an invalid, suffering intensely at times, until death came slowly to her relief August 18, 1890...During her long and painful illness, Mrs. Swift displayed a rare spirit of fortitude, patience, and unselfishness, and was greatly sustained by a steady and strong Christian faith. In the death of this lady the community has lost a valuable member. She had the genius of industry, and her executive ability, coupled with tenacity of purpose, won for her the admiration of those who knew her. Her unselfish and uncomplaining spirit prominent through her continued illness has been noted by many."

Very shortly after Lucy's death, Herman Swift left home. Hoyt Swift died almost exactly four years later on August 17th, 1894. On February 29, 1896, Blenn Swift sold the little house on Plain Street. The four surviving Swift children shared sale proceeds of seven hundred fifty dollars. Only Herman would one day return to Eaton Rapids.

II

The Mission

Somerset Center

In the summer of 1888, Herman Swift graduated from the 12th grade in the Eaton Rapids public schools. The commencement exercises were held in the Methodist Episcopal Church. Shortly after his mother's death in August of 1890, Herman departed Eaton Rapids and moved to Somerset Center, a small southern Michigan town located amidst lakes, rolling hills, and farmland in Hillsdale County. There Herman worked as a telegraph operator at the train depot. He almost certainly attended the Somerset Center Methodist Episcopal Church located on the Detroit-Chicago Turnpike that ran through town. He lived with his older sister Hattie and her husband Frank Rose.

Herman Swift probably left Eaton Rapids because his mother died. But there is a curious allegorical sense to Swift's move to Somerset Center and as a youth highly exposed to religion, he may have been aware of that. The bible includes many allegorical references to rivers and the "Source of the River." Preachers have interpreted a passage from Ezekiel (47:9.12) to mean that the source of the river comes from the sanctuary of God and flows through his followers. The source of the Grand River, the most significant natural feature in Eaton Rapids, lies some fifty miles southeast, natural springs that rise up near Somerset Center.

Swift spent only one year working and pondering life in Somerset Center. In 1891, he traveled by train to the City of Chicago.

Chicago

Chicago, Carl Sandberg wrote, is "the place where all the trains ran." Between 1871 and 1884 the population of the City of Chicago doubled, reaching over six hundred thousand citizens. By 1891, it had doubled again and Chicago was the world's largest rail hub. Trains entered and departed the city on all sides. In the neighborhoods a complicated network of cable cars, some machine powered and some horse driven, transported citizens from blocks of two story, brick multi-family dwellings to places of work or shopping. Stately hotels like the Palmer House lined the downtown streets. The Home Insurance Building constructed in 1885 was the world's first building erected around a steel skeleton, the world's first skyscraper. By 1891, many skyscrapers framed the Chicago skyline.

Within the city millionaires like Armour, Palmer, Field, and McCormick built beautiful mansions of stone and brick, homes with gables, stained glass windows, curving hardwood staircases, filled with Tiffany and Steuben. But in Chicago, next to the people in the mansions lived the working-class people in the two story brick flats and the wood framed, drafty houses, and next to them lived the poor people in the slums, thousands of them. Ethnic and class tensions stewed as if in a pot in the city, occasionally coming to a boil.

Anarchists jumped into the pot. Their goal was to destroy the rich. The bomb-throwing anarchist who killed the police and ignited the Haymarket riot (businessman's view) or Haymarket massacre (working man's view) in Chicago in 1885 came to symbolize their actions.

Progressives jumped into the pot. Their goal was to diminish the rich. They fought against the doctrine of Social Darwinism, the premise that economic success should flow entirely to the strongest. Jane Addams and Ellen Gates Starr founded Hull House in 1889. It was among the first settlement houses in the United States. Addams saw Social Darwinism as inhumane and unfair. She pushed to achieve immigrant assimilation. Hull House offered free classes in literature, art, history and domestic activities such as sewing. Addams also pushed to improve public health and transportation. She fought against child labor and dangerous working conditions. Like other progressives, she turned for assistance to the government and not to the rich.

Christians also jumped into the pot. The most significant of these was a man named Dwight Lyman Moody. Some experts consider him to have been a progressive, but Moody cultivated his support among the rich and not at city hall.

Herman Swift enrolled in the Moody Bible Institute in Chicago on March 19, 1892. On his application to the school, he cited experience as a telegraph operator and experience teaching Sunday school classes and managing a "mission" Sunday school. And on the application he listed only one "reference," a man named "Hiram Walker" who "works as an M.D. in Eaton Rapids." I spent some research time searching for a man named Hiram Walker who lived in the town of Eaton Rapids in 1892. No one will ever find this man, but in 1892 Hiram Walker did live in Walkerville, Ontario, Canada, across the river from Detroit. He placed his name on the bottles of a famous beverage of the day, Hiram Walker's Canadian Club Whiskey. It is said that Hiram Walker once established a church for his distillery workers. He closed it when the preacher began to preach against the evils of alcohol. This Herman Swift "reference" on a very important document suggests a sense of irony and a feeling of confidence on the part of a small rural man who was only twenty-one.

Dwight Moody was America's leading 19th Century evangelist, the Billy Graham of the era. He campaigned for Christ around the world. In 1876, his east coast campaign filled arenas in Brooklyn and Philadelphia. In New York City, that campaign filled the Hippodrome with 14,000 people per night for ten weeks.

When Moody was only four years old, his father died. To support the family, Dwight and his brothers were sent off to live with and work for more prosperous families. Later, Dwight preached about these experiences, the good and the bad, and he preached about his decision to move to the city when he was seventeen. The city was Boston and Moody achieved commercial success there and then moved to Chicago where he experienced even greater success selling shoes, trading real estate, and lending money. By 1860, Moody was out of debt and had over $7,000 in savings. Later he would preach about that and about the conflict in his life between commerce and religion.

Dwight Moody never received formal ministerial training. He gained his theological education through bible study and Church attendance. He attended church meetings six nights per week. He pursued his first religious mission in the "Sands." The Sands or "Little Hell" was located just north of the Chicago River along the Lake Michigan shore. This was a miserably poor area that was home to thousands of unemployed adults and thousands of street waifs. Most of these waifs were boys and folks called them "wharf rats" for their practice of living under wharfs. Christian missionaries, and even the police, avoided the area. But Dwight Moody rented a vacant saloon and initiated a "Sabbath School" in the Sands. Every Sunday night he walked alone through the Sands, entered that saloon, and by the light of a kerosene lamp read from the Bible and led the wharf rats in songs. Initially, few boys attended the Sabbath School and those that did were prone to engage in loud and rowdy behavior. People thought Moody's efforts were bound to fail, but he did not give up. He rewarded the boys with candy and pennies and attendance increased. He applied tough, but kind discipline and behavior improved. Folks thought Moody was insane to enter the Sands at night, but most admired his sacrifice and determination. Christians began to take notice of him.

As Moody aged, his fine speaking skills continued to improve. But he placed a higher value on his mission to educate than on his revival campaigns. In 1877, Reverend W.H. Daniels wrote a book titled: *Moody: His Words, Work, and Workers*. From a letter, Daniels quotes Moody referring to his schools as: "the best work I have ever done."

Dwight Moody saw the need for two types of schools. The first would serve the needs of disadvantaged children and the second would develop evangelists, people who were equipped to carry on the mission of the church, particularly in urban areas. Moody established the Northfield Seminary for Young Ladies and the Mount Hermon School for Boys near his hometown in Massachusetts. Mount Hermon is the highest mountain in the Holy Land area. I believe the religious importance of Mount Hermon led Herman Swift to change his name to Hermon Swift.

Both the Northfield Seminary and the Mount Hermon School took on the task of providing Christian based education and building successful economic and social futures for underprivileged children. Through donations, Moody amassed large land holdings both at Northfield and Mount Hermon. Mount Hermon included 750 acres and the boys were encouraged to work on the school's large farm.

The Moody Bible Institute on North LaSalle Boulevard in Chicago represents Dwight Moody's principal effort in his second area of scholastic focus, the arena of educating evangelists. Moody founded the institute in 1889. Initially, his goal simply was to develop evangelists for downtrodden urban neighborhoods by attracting young men and exposing them to an intense sixty-day experience of biblical lectures, home visitations, and evening revival meetings.

By 1892, the Moody Bible Institute had achieved significant success and recognition. When Herman Swift enrolled, he entered a school that had passed well beyond its initial goals. He almost certainly absorbed the writings and experienced the preaching of Dwight Moody, but during this period Moody spent most of his time in Massachusetts. He had convinced Reverend Reuben Torrey to run the Bible Institute. Torrey graduated from the Yale Divinity School in New Haven, Connecticut in 1878. He was a man with a strong academic religious background. Under Torrey's leadership, the Bible Institute began to identify students with promise and encouraged them to stay beyond sixty days to gain more formal training.

Herman Swift left the Moody Bible Institute on May 17th, 1892, exactly sixty days after the day he entered. His Institute personal folder includes the following notation upon his departure: "Fair abilities, a little unstable, enthusiastic. Left to engage in work among boys in New Haven, Connecticut."

Swift left Chicago in 1892, missing the 1893 Chicago World's Fair, perhaps the greatest world's fair. He took with him lessons from Torrey and more importantly, lessons from Moody. He poured over Moody's sermons, carefully read his books, and examined his life. He knew the man had "over $7,000" before he began his religious work. He knew he possessed great farm properties. He knew he began his ministry working with underprivileged boys. Importantly, Herman Swift learned the benefits of cultivating the rich and the folly of ignoring or attempting to destroy them. He learned of the Armours, the Palmers, the Fields, the McCormicks, and the Farwells; and of the Steuben and Tiffany. He learned that any good sermon contains at least three messages: repent for your sins, do more good, and give more money.

New Haven

John C. Collins graduated from Yale University in 1875, the same year Reuben Torrey graduated. Collins and Torrey both graduated from the Yale Divinity School in 1878. Dwight Moody held a one-month revival campaign in New Haven in 1878. Both Collins and Torrey were touched strongly by that campaign.

The *Modern History of New Haven* published by S.J. Clarke in 1918 includes a biography of John Collins. That biography describes Collin's singular ambition to be: "that of assisting in the mental, moral and religious training of young boys." The biography points out that he had founded the New Haven Boy's Club in 1874. This was one of the first clubs of its kind and Collins had yet to graduate from Yale.

John Collins convinced The International Christian Worker's Association to authorize him to establish boys' clubs throughout New England. By 1892, he had established twenty-five clubs serving 25,000 boys. Collins laid the groundwork for the organization known today as the Boys and Girls Clubs of America. In 1892, John Collins, probably at the suggestion of Reuben Torrey, selected Herman Swift to serve as Superintendent of the New Haven Boys Club (later Swift would refer to it as the Yale University Boys Club) on Crown Street in New Haven.

Collin's boys clubs rented rooms in urban centers. The rooms were equipped with reading materials, games, light gymnastics equipment, and bathrooms. J.A. Spalding in the *Illustrated Popular Biography of Connecticut* published in 1891 wrote that Collins placed: "Young Christian men in charge of the rooms as superintendents." The superintendent opened the room every evening during the colder months of the years. He was responsible for attracting boys to the facility and managing and teaching them while they were there. During the day and during warmer months, superintendents visited boys in their homes, in jail and at police court.

In his role as Superintendent of the New Haven Boys Club, Herman Swift gained experience in managing unruly street boys. He preached from the bible. He taught the boys to sing. He implemented John Collin's penny savings bank program that encouraged poor boys to save money. He learned how to manage vocational training programs. He provided a written report on his activities to Collins every week. Herman Swift only stayed ten months in New Haven and then he moved to Buffalo arriving early in 1893.

Buffalo

Buffalo in many respects was a smaller eastern twin to the City of Chicago. It was a major rail hub and was located at the far western end of the Erie Canal and the far eastern end of Lake Erie. Great Lakes shipping lines began in Buffalo and ended in Chicago. Buffalo like Chicago was home to a huge stockyard and heavy industries. It was a major lumbering center. It was the largest steel-making center in the world. Thousands of immigrants: Italians, Germans, Jews, African-Americans, and others arrived each year. The city would be the eighth most populous in the country by 1900.

And as in Chicago, industrious men became millionaires in Buffalo. They built stone and brick mansions with curving hardwood staircases, tile and marble and filled them with Steuben and with Tiffany. The small wealthy neighborhoods stood amidst the working class neighborhoods, the blocks and blocks of the "twin houses," the two story brick duplex houses they built for the workers and their large families. And next to the working class neighborhoods stood the slums. Here thousands of poor lived in wooden tenement houses or lived on the streets. Ethnic and class tensions stewed as if in a pot in the city and occasionally boiled over. And in Buffalo, as in Chicago, Christians attacked, progressives harnessed and anarchists stirred these tensions.

On Thanksgiving Day of 1872, the Young Men's Association of the Buffalo Grace Methodist Episcopal Church held a dinner for boys who worked as newsboys and bootblacks and lived on the streets of the city. The adults who attended were moved by the plight of the street boys as well as by their great thanks for the dinner. This one dinner then led to the establishment of the Buffalo Children's Aid Society whose articles of incorporation established the objectives of: "the protection, care, shelter and saving of friendless and vagrant children in the City of Buffalo; furnishing them with food, raiment, and lodging; aiding and administering to their wants; providing them with suitable occupation; instructing them in moral and religious truths and in the rudiments of education; and, with such means as the society can properly employ, endeavoring to make them virtuous and useful citizens."

By 1893, the Children's Aid Society operated a facility called the Newsboys and Bootblack's Home in a two-story brick building with a basement and a dormer attic located at No. 29 Franklin Street near the rail-yards in south Buffalo. Herman Swift was hired as Superintendent of this Home, a nice promotion from his position in New Haven.

In Buffalo, Swift managed a staff including an assistant superintendent William Crawford, a matron Mary McPherson, a cook, a laundress, and a maid. He managed a building that included a dining room, kitchen and laundry in the basement; a classroom, playroom and lavatory on the first floor; apartments for the staff, a parlor, sewing room, and hospital room on the second floor; and two large sleeping dormitories in the attic.

Swift reported to a fifteen-man board of Trustees and to a large board of Lady Managers. The Lady Managers included Sabina Morris, a leading progressive—Buffalo's Jane Addams; and Mary Purdy, the wife of Andrew Purdy, minister of the Asbury Methodist Episcopal Church, a large downtown church that Herman Swift joined.

Charitable donations covered sixty percent of the expenses of the Buffalo Newsboy and Bootblack's Home in 1893. The boys living at the Home earned the money to cover the remaining annual expenses, over fifteen hundred dollars. St. Paul preached: "those who do not work, shall not eat." Herman Swift certainly cited that scripture as he preached to the boys. Each of them who earned money paid one or two dollars per week to stay at the Home. Swift carried over Collin's New Haven Home money saving program and each of the Buffalo Home boys placed the money they saved into their own savings box at the Home.

As Herman Swift began his work in Buffalo, the American economy entered what has been termed The Depression or The Panic of 1893. National unemployment surged from 3% in 1892 to 19% in 1894. This was the greatest economic crisis the country had faced since its founding and the crisis hit particularly hard in urban areas like Buffalo. Like any good charitable organization manager, Swift realized his fortunes lay with his Board of Trustees and the Board of Lady Managers. For the most part, these were members of Buffalo's high society. They were rich and had a rich network of friends and it paid Swift to cultivate his relationships with these people.

Swift held church service for the boys every Sunday at 9:00 A.M. Attendance was not mandatory, but most of the boys did attend. Swift often took the occasion to invite Trustees and Lady Managers to the services. He also invited local protestant ministers to attend and at times to preach.

Younger boys at the Home attended public school. Weekday evenings, Swift spent the hour of 7:00 to 8:00 P. M. educating all the boys in the Home's classroom. Subjects included spelling, reading, writing, arithmetic, history, and physiology. This was followed by singing, games, Bible reading and prayer. Swift enjoyed hosting Trustees and Lady Managers at his evening school hour and at singing, speaking, and piano performances by the boys of the Home.

In January of 1894, the *Buffalo News* published an article reporting on the annual meeting of the Buffalo Children's Aid Society (the Newsboy and Bootblacks Home.) This meeting covered Herman Swift's first year as Superintendent of the Home. The article was titled: "Newsboy's Happy Home" and subtitled "How Life Wags for the Little Waifs at the model institution on Franklin Street." The writer notes that: "the boys are not ruled by the rod but rather by kindness coupled with extreme firmness and in that way are led on from one step to another in the scale of discipline and duty until they become obedient, thrifty, cleanly, studious boys."

Finally, the writer notes the efficient work of Superintendent Herman Swift and recites a number of successes: "During the year 132 boys were admitted to the Home and every one of them helped in some way...144 letters were written to boys who have gone from the Home, to strengthen and encourage them in well doing. One hundred and thirty-three visits to Police Court and stations were made in search of friendless and unfortunate boys...Not one of the boys of the Home was arrested during the year and the police no longer regard them as 'suspects.' The boys who held situations worked all through the heated term without a vacation, although the monotony was occasionally broken by 14 picnics and excursions; the different steamboat companies always kindly donating the tickets."

On August 24th, 1894, the *Eaton Rapids Journal* published the following obituary:

"Swift—On Friday, Aug. 17, 1894, at his late home in the second ward, Hoyt Swift, at the age of 61 years, after a six months serious illness with Bright's disease...

Mr. Swift enlisted in the Twentieth Michigan Infantry... and served over three years in the war. He was a brave soldier... He was severely wounded and contracted in the service ailments from which he always afterward suffered... After the war he was extensively engaged in the bee business and was well known as an expert apiarist...

Mr. Swift, residing as he did in the house in which he died for 28 consecutive years, was well known to all Eaton Rapids people. He was universally respected for his high character, his consistent Christian life and for his unceasing warfare upon everything he believed to be wrong."

Hoyt Swift survived farming a small one and one half acre plot of land by raising bees and selling honey. He died of "Bright's" disease, a disease of the kidneys brought on by, among other things, exposure to cold and wet conditions, like those conditions Hoyt experienced in the winter of 1863/1864 at Blane's Cross Roads, "Valley Forge."

On August 24th, 1894, the *Eaton Rapids Journal* also published the following article: "Hermon L. Swift, who has been here for several weeks by reason of his father's fatal illness, returned to Buffalo, N.Y. today. Mr. Swift is there engaged in an important work as superintendent of the newsboys' home and school. The association, which owns the $30,000 building used as the school, have just unanimously reelected him to his old position at an annual salary of $1,200, besides board and apartment. Mr. Swift is popular with the newsboys and is highly successful in his work to improve their condition."

The Moody Bible Institute in Chicago continued to maintain a personnel file on Herman Swift. The file contains the following notation: "Swift went to Buffalo as Supt. News Boys Home and School." On March 2nd, 1895, someone added the following notation: "Buffalo, New York, doing well." Sometime in 1896, someone wrote in the file: "As above, results very gratifying." Finally, the file contains two important letters received at the Moody Bible Institute in 1896.

On May 11th, 1896, the Reverend John C. Collins wrote a letter as secretary, on the stationary of The International Christian Workers Association, to the Reverend Reuben A. Torrey in Chicago, Illinois. The letter reads as follows: "Dear Torrey: Had a letter from Mr. Farwell the other day asking about Swift who was with me in the boy's work at one time and has since been in Buffalo. I do not know whether Swift was in the Bible Institute or not. Think he was. Mr. Farwell was thinking some about having him to work in connection with boys' work and wanted to know what I thought of him. This morning I had a letter from Swift asking me to give him a recommendation. I think possible he may strike you in the same way and so feel that I ought to let you know why he left Buffalo. I was there the other day and it is stated that he was arrested for evil practices with the boys, pled guilty in the city court, fined and ordered to leave the city immediately, which he did. He also pledged he would not go into boys' work. I do not know how true the charges are, of course, nothing about them, only these are the facts reported to me by people who know all about it. They rather thought that he was not guilty but that he should not have left the way he did. But as the stories were told to me it looked pretty suspicious. Thought you ought to know about it if he advertised his connection with your Bible Institute. Fraternally, John C. Collins"

John Farwell, the man referred to in Collins' letter, was one of Dwight Moody's best friends as well as his most significant financial supporter. Farwell was one of those wealthy Christians who take to heart the story of Lazarus and believe that charity is not a voluntary part of his religion. Herman Swift must have met John Farwell when he attended the Moody Bible Institute in 1892. Farwell was a major supporter of the Institute. His financial support allowed Moody to practice a free tuition policy for students, a policy still practiced today.

Herman Swift returned to Chicago when he was forced out of Buffalo in 1896. He turned to John Farwell for assistance in gaining a position working with underprivileged boys. Farwell must have looked down on the small man, listened to his scandalous story, then offered to investigate the matter and see if he might be of help. Farwell met with Reverend Reuben Torrey and suggested that he write letters seeking the opinions of Christian leaders who had worked with Swift in New Haven and Buffalo. Torrey addressed one of those letters to Pastor Andrew Purdy in Buffalo. Purdy was unable to respond, but his wife Mary did and this is the second important letter in Herman Swift's Moody Bible Institute file.

Mary Purdy mailed the following letter from the Asbury M.E. Parsonage on October 16th, 1896: "Mr. Torrey, Dear Sir, Your letter of inquiry in regard to Br. Swift came this morning, and I hasten to answer you, for what I say in regard to him will be most heartily, sincerely, and gladly. First, however, I must tell you why I answer this instead of my husband, Br. Swift will probably hear, that he is no more with us, but has been taken to his home in Heaven. Our hearts are nearly broken, and we are, oh, so lonely, but I know just how he would answer your letter, for he thought very much of Br. Swift and had great confidence in him.

We visited the Home often, and always admired the sweet Christian spirit he manifested there. The boys were never so good and orderly at home or in church as there. Three of the matrons there while he was, were members of our church. Two of them were formerly deaconesses, elderly women, and I have heard them both say, that Mr. Swift was one of the noblest Christian characters they ever saw. His patience with the boys was wonderful, and he never punished one of them only for their good, and when he thought it must be done for the honor of the home. Dr. Purdy esteemed him as one of the brightest and best of the young men of our church, and this church would give him a license to preach now as quickly as ever. He did not leave Buffalo in disgrace! He is respected as much as ever, and if he should return today, our church would receive him gladly. He was wronged, fearfully wronged, and it is a pity that the devil has his own way so many times. Some of his imps there in the home, (because they were rebuffed for their vileness by one who they knew was pure and good,) managed to carry out their evil designs, and Mr. Swift's pure sensitive nature could not endure the trials and unwisely, he went away. The matron who was there at that time told me that Mr. Swift had been quite ill and was still feeling very poorly. She thought that if he had been well, he could have endured the persecutions and come off (as he had a right) victorious.

Br. Swift had not a single bad habit. He despised everything that was not honest and true. He obeyed the rules of our church to the letter and kept his boys from everything that would have a tendency to lead even their thoughts from the right. He is one of the grandest young men we ever saw...

I hope this will be as satisfactory as if Dr. Purdy had written you for I know that he would have said as much for Br. Swift and perhaps more. He certainly esteemed him highly. We know that he was a great power for good in that Home and none can say one word against him, and tell the truth. If you wish to ask any more questions feel free to do so. All that knew Mr. Swift would tell you the same that I have.

Sincerely, Mrs. Andrew Purdy"

Pastor Torrey received Mary Purdy's letter on October 21st, 1896. He must have found her letter to be persuasive. In early 1897, Herman Swift was hired as manager of the Children's Temple Home of Chicago.

III

The Grower of Boys and Beans

"Life of William: As Written By Himself"

"I was born May 24th, in the year 1885, in an old fashioned log house in Monterey, Ohio. The house is now tore down. I spent the first six years of my life with my father, but it lacked twenty-two days of my being six when my mother died. I then left my father and my brothers and went to live with my grandfather. I stayed there a little over three years. In that time my father married again, and he married my mother's sister.

Now I must state that I had three brothers. The younger stayed at my grandmothers (on my mother's side) ever since my mother died. He was a cripple and always will be. The next to the youngest brother is also crippled as my stepmother beat him so hard that he got the hip disease.

The next oldest brother is well as far as I know now. My stepmother then left my father and he went to work in a sawmill, then I did not have any place to stay. All this time I had been having a hard time. I finally went to Ohio City to my aunt's where I stayed two weeks when I got on a freight train and went to Bluffton, when in about two weeks I heard that my uncle was coming after me and I got on a freight train and come to Chicago. I had been lying, stealing and going with the worse toughs of Chicago about three months when a detective got hold of me. I lived in a Police Station for the next month and a half when I came to this Home (Children's Temple Home) and here I expect to stay.

I came here the last of September and I have been giving up swearing and trying to keep from lying. I now expect to lead a better life. I hope I will go to the farm (Leoni Beulah Land Farm) when the next ones go. With God's help I can give up all these bad things and be a better boy than I have been."

William's "life story" was included in *Give the Boy a Chance,* a little promotional green hardbound book published by Herman Swift and the Children's Temple Home, Chicago, Illinois in 1900. The book runs ninety-one pages and consists of personal testimonials in support of Herman Swift's missionary work, newspaper articles supporting that work, life stories written by boys living under Swift's supervision in Chicago and Leoni, Michigan, photographs of those boys, and finally a short concluding contribution written by Swift and titled "Credit Where Credit Is Due:"

"It was my purpose not to contribute a line to this little volume, but have every thought and word from others interested in the work. I am compelled, however, in justice and right to give credit where credit is due.

First. To our Heavenly Father who has so graciously blessed us with every needed thing and opened the hearts of His children to so royally support the efforts put forth.

Second. To the noblest and most self-sacrificing men and women who have volunteered their services, without salaries, and are living day and night right with these little waifs brought from the streets and alleys of the city. If there be any special honor or credit for the success of this work let it be to Miss M.E. Richards, Mr. Alfred B. Parry, Mr. Radcliff W. Groves, Mrs. Board-man, and Miss Jennie H. Stevens for without them the work could not have been such a success.

Let me say to the reader that if you ever intend to help this work in this world, in the name of the Master do it right now. Thousands of children are perishing for what we so long to give them but soon the opportunity will be lost forever. Yours for His service, Hermon Lee Swift."

Herman Swift had arrived back in Chicago sometime in 1896. Shortly after his arrival, the *Chicago-Times Herald* introduced an article titled "Saving the Waifs" with the following: "How many people in Chicago know the number of friendless and neglected boys arrested and thrust into jail during the last year? Incredible though it may seem the records show that 16,000 home-less and neglected lads in this city were confined behind prison bars for trying to steal the most miserable living the world ever owed to human beings." Having defined the scope and depth of the problem, the article continues: "But the tremendous balance in which so many futures weigh is being tilted the right way by Hermon Lee Swift. 'What will save these children?' he would ask himself. And there seemed but one answer: 'Parental love, Christian influence, and home envi-ronment.'" The article continued with a description of Swift's plans and actions to personally provide those necessities to the street boys of Chicago

With only eighteen dollars in his treasury, Swift initially rented a small building at 79 Larrabee Street. Here, in a very tough neighborhood along the river in north central Chicago, he opened a mission called the Children's Temple. I believe this mission operated much like Dwight Moody's original Sabbath School in the Sands. Swift invited street boys to attend evening serv-ices at the Children's Temple. The services included bible readings, singing, and games, but most importantly he provided the boys with free food and clothing.

Herman Swift brought with him from Buffalo the knowledge and ability to raise money from wealthy supporters. Now back in Chicago, to reduce his dependence on wealthy institutions like the Moody Church and on wealthy individuals, he introduced the "dime book" which would remain a staple of his fund raising activities. Swift promoted the dime book to people of modest means and particularly to children in Sunday schools. Christians across the country mailed postcards request-ing Herman Swift's dime books. They then dutifully filled the books with ten dimes and returned them to the "Children's Temple Home, Care of Hermon L. Swift, Manager and Treasurer."

Herman Swift's fund raising activities proved successful, and on November 5th, 1897, he closed the Larrabee Street mission and opened the Children's Temple Home in a rented house at 6 Washington Place. This was in a nice neighborhood of two story brick-homes in central Chicago. Mrs. Roswell G. Bogue lived at 5 Washington Place, right behind the Children's Temple

Home. Lucy Bogue was a sixty year old widow who had lived in her home for almost thirty years when she wrote a letter to Herman Swift. That letter is reprinted in *Give the Boy a Chance* under the title "My Impressions of the Home." The letter reads: "Two years ago one winter's evening, I happened to glance out of my back window and found myself looking into a lighted room in another house where many boys were gathered around a table apparently ready to eat supper.

It was a pretty sight! Though the room was plain and the table simple, the good cheer that filled all the faces seemed to turn the supper of bread and milk to an almost regal repast. This was my introduction to the Children's Temple Home…

Through inquiry and watching, we soon learned more of the Home and it became a familiar sight to see Mr. Swift with four or five boys clustered around him at the window, deep in a story or a talk…Never was there any quarreling or squabbling in their play, that seemed to be entirely relegated from their midst, though at the first all the faces showed signs of former hardness and bitterness, which could easily have cropped out under other influences.

We grew very fond of them in our midst, and when Mr. Swift decided it was best to move farther North, we really missed them…That underneath every ragged jacket is a warm little heart that is hungry to lift itself into light and right if but given half a chance, the Children's Temple Home proves beyond a doubt, but that half chance we must give to those who are born without it, and Mr. Swift and his helpers have found the way to give it…

It is a work that I am deeply interested in, this of saving our boys through loving care. Is not this a better and more Christ-like way of doing than shutting them up and separating them from all loving influences? I want to see the necessary funds supplied freely for this work that those who are giving their lives, without salary, may not have to beg the bread…

Will you not have a share in spreading such a work? And your own little boys and girls who are blessed with a mother's and father's love let them too share in helping to enlarge the Home and the Beulah Land Farm that more boys may be rescued.

Mrs. Roswell G. Bogue, 5 Washington Place, Chicago, Illinois"

By 1900, Swift had relocated the Children's Temple from 6 Washington Place, moving several miles north to a building at 734 Wells Street. This is the move "farther north" that Lucy Bogue refers to in her letter. The Wells Street building was located in the midst of the Moody Empire, between the Church and the Bible Institute. Swift took advantage of volunteers from the Moody Church. The *Chicago-Times Herald* reported that: "Miss Harriet Lampherd of the Moody Church Christian Endeavor gives sewing lessons (at the Children's Temple Home) once a week."

The 734 Wells Street building was a four-story brick structure. Fine curtains draped all the windows. Bold white letters reading "Children's Temple Home" sat above the large wooden front doors. A chubby speckled cat lay in the sun in the parlor bay window next to those doors. The home included a fine library stocked with over one thousand books. Each of the boys was assigned certain household tasks. They attended morning and evening church services in the Home. Swift taught the boys to sing and encouraged them to memorize hundreds of bible verses. The boys displayed these skills at churches across North Chicago, promoting the Home and raising money.

In Chicago, Herman began the curious practice of petitioning probate court and gaining guardianship of the boys in his care. In *Give the Boy a Chance* he claimed this was: "necessary so that the boys cannot be taken back by their parents when their regeneration has been partially accomplished, and they will be thrown back into the way of sin again."

The twelfth census of the United States, completed in 1900, lists only seventeen boys living at the Children's Temple Home. The boys ranged in age from eight to fifteen. Each was labeled an "Inmate" of the Home. The three boys who were over thirteen years old all worked, two as messengers and one as a jeweler's assistant. The other boys attended the LaSalle School, a public school located within a few blocks of the Home. Swift later would encounter trouble in sending his boys to public schools, but this does not appear to be the case in Chicago. Most of the Wells Street "inmates" were born to immigrant parents and all came from rough backgrounds, but they probably fit in well with the other children at the LaSalle School.

In 1900, roughly at the time of the publication of *Give the Boy a Chance*, Herman Swift received another piece of very important promotional support. This came in the form of a six-page article published in the twenty-ninth volume of *The Sunday Magazine*, a magazine published in London. A journalist named Harold J. Shepstone wrote the article titled: "A Commonwealth of Waifs." The first half of the article describes the Children's Temple Home in Chicago. The second half describes the "Commonwealth," the Beulah Land Farm.

As early as his days as Superintendent of The Newsboy and Bootblacks Home in Buffalo, Herman Swift had outlined the goal of securing a home in the country in order to place street boys into a setting more conducive to Christian development. The "Newsboys' Happy Home" article in a January 1894 edition of the *Buffalo News* noted: "The report of Mrs. C.H. Utley, secretary of the Women's Board, spoke of the need of better facilities at the Home and advocated the purchase of land in a different locality, where the surroundings would be entirely changed and more beneficial for the boys and where a more commodious building can be erected."

Leoni Beulah Land Farm

On April 27th, 1899, Herman Swift achieved his goal. That day Wesley Sears, Register of Deeds for Jackson County, Michigan recorded the transfer of the southeast corner of the southwest corner of Section 36, Leoni Township. The property was a forty-four acre fruit and vegetable farm. Ebenezer Sherman, his wife Harriet, Ellen Welsh, and Nattie Sweet in exchange for $2,000 sold the property to "Beulah Land Farm for Boys, Herman L. Swift, Trustee." I believe that this property had been the site of the Leoni Seminary. The seminary had been closed in 1859. Oxen carts hauled the contents of the library east to the town of Adrian, Michigan and the Leoni Seminary became a part of the newly founded Adrian College. In 1859, the little town of Leoni bore the nickname of "whiskey town" and this reportedly played a part in this move. Whatever the case, it seems that Herman Swift established his first boys' farm on or near the site where his mother Lucy had studied for four years back in the 1850s.

Now Herman began to refer to himself as a "grower of boys and beans." And he called the farm the "Beulah Land Farm." This was the first time that Herman Swift used the word "Beulah." And I believe that Herman named the Beulah Land Farm remembering the garden in *Pilgrim's*

Progress and in honor of his baby sister Beulah.

Harold Shepstone wrote of Herman Swift's acquisition of the Beulah Land Farm: "The 734 Wells Street, Chicago, building quickly proved to be inadequate for the numbers who applied. Then again, it was by no means advisable for the boys to be kept in idleness and as country homes could not be found fast enough to meet the demand, it was decided to purchase a farm that should be devoted to homeless boys for all time. After many negotiations, a fruit and vegetable farm was purchased in Southern Michigan. This property is recorded at the Registrar's Office as the Beulah Land Farm for homeless and neglected children, specifying that no man or body of men shall ever utilize it for any different purpose. To raise the necessary funds the following novel subscription plan was adopted. Cards that contained blank spaces for ten dimes were distributed to the children in the various Sunday Schools and places of worship in Chicago, and for each filled card a certificate was given of stock in the farm—a case of children helping children. Furthermore, the farm belongs to the boys, a fact that could not be disputed by law, and is referred to in Chicago as the 'only junior commonwealth in the world.'"

Herman Swift's first Beulah Land Farm was located in Leoni Township near the small town of Grass Lake in Jackson County, Michigan. In 1899, Leoni had a little depot at mile marker 217 on the Michigan Central mainline. The mainline ran between Chicago, 217 miles to the west and Detroit, 68 miles to the east of the Leoni Depot. Swift took up residence at the Leoni farm shortly after he acquired it in 1899. His title was "Manager and Treasurer, Beulah Land Farm." Mary Richards served as Matron of the farm. Ernest Corbin served as farm manager, teaching the boys to perform the various tasks at the farm.

The 1900 United States Federal Census lists Swift, Richards, and Corbin as residents and twenty-one boys as inmates of the Beulah Land Farm in Leoni. Swift had taken a number of homeless girls into the Children's Temple Home, but had quickly handed them over to relatives or foster parents. He believed that orphaned or neglected boys faced much greater odds of being cast off to the streets than did girls and facts on the streets supported this belief. "Homeless boys are expected to shift for themselves, and to earn their own livings. It is different in the case of the motherless and fatherless girl; she will probably be taken care of by a kindly neighbor or friend, but not the boy," wrote Herman Swift.

Boys living at the Children's Temple Home were allowed to transfer to the Beulah Land Farm if over a period of time they displayed good behavior and an ability to live within the strict discipline parameters established by Herman Swift. "To go to the farm and become a member of the junior commonwealth is the sole desire of the boy after he has entered the Temple Home, where its golden prospects and interesting life are constantly retold," wrote Harold Shepstone.

Herman Swift promoted his Leoni Beulah Land Farm as the only junior commonwealth in the world. Swift claimed that the boys created the laws that governed the farm. Each fall they elected officers to represent them in management of the farm. Perhaps most importantly, as Shepstone wrote, Swift promoted the claim that the farm belonged to the boys and that the property was legally recorded in such a way that no man or body of men could ever use it for any purpose other than as a farm for homeless and neglected boys.

Of the twenty-one boys living at the Leoni Home in 1900, eleven were born in Illinois and only two were born in Michigan. They ranged in age from nine to fourteen. All of them attended a nearby public school. The 1900 Federal Census of the residents of the Leoni Beulah Home includes Herman Swift's claim that "nothing is known of the parents of these boys." That claim largely was untrue.

Within several months of that census, Swift faced two major problems in Leoni Township. First, a number of residents objected to the influence of the Beulah Home boys in the public school. Swift overcame this problem by establishing a school at the Home. Second, there was a fear that the Home might fail financially leaving the street waifs in the care of the community. In 1900, the Michigan State Legislature passed a bill requiring the incorporation of all institutions "carrying on the business of receiving or maintaining minor children in homes of indenture."

Herman Swift's Leoni Township Home was not incorporated. Acting at the request of the county's prosecuting attorney, who was supported by the Michigan State Attorney General's office, on October 17th, 1900, the Jackson County board of supervisors ordered Herman Swift to close the Beulah Home and to remove himself and the boys from the State within sixty days. In response to this, Swift quickly organized a public defense.

The *Jackson Evening Press* reported: "... But the time is drawing near when the man who has done so much in so short a time for society must take his boys from the farm which he has purchased, and which he has told them was their property. That is, he must if he obeys the mandate of the law. 'Get out by December 17 or go to jail,' is the ultimatum of Prosecuting Attorney Smith. That gentleman saw what was being done, prated of the admirable and noble work—and made that recommendation to the board of supervisors, who surely acted hastily and without knowledge of the facts.

Mr. Swift will not get out. If he is arrested he will have no difficulty in obtaining half the responsible men of Jackson on his bail bond. (Author's note: this exact claim would be repeated during the Time of Troubles in Boyne City.) The prosecution of a man for doing this work is a travesty on our civilization. Why, in the name of decency, did not the prosecutor, if he must make a pretense of law enforcement, request Mr. Swift to incorporate, as the statute provides? The supervisors listened to very poor advice, and in consequence find themselves in a position repellant to their sense of right, justice and decency. The original cause of complaint, the attendance of the boys at the Leoni School, has been removed. Separate instruction is now given them at the farm."

An October 31st, 1900 *Detroit Free Press* article reads in part: "'I will sink $1,000 personally rather than see the Beulah Home driven out of the state by stupid legislators and lawyers,' promised a prominent Christian citizen of Detroit yesterday to Hermon Lee Swift, the treasurer and general manager and originator of that worthy institution of practical charity that is located at the quiet little village of Leoni, in Jackson county...In addition to the recruiting station or branch establishment now conducted in Chicago, it is expected to establish a similar one in this city, for Detroit boys form no inconsiderable element in the home at present."

Finally, just prior to the December 17th deadline, the *Jackson Daily Patriot*, within an article titled: "The Beulah Land Farm is Incorporated and Will Stay," reported: "With the news of the incorporation of the Beulah Land Farm by Mr. Swift, with a board of trustees containing such well known names as L.H. Field and Richard Waldron of this city and L.M. Bowen Treasurer of the D.M. Ferry Seed Company of Detroit, the only objection, even under an absurd and narrow statute, to the carrying on of this splendid work is apparently surmounted."

Herman Swift did not refer to the board of the Leoni Beulah Land Farm as a "Board of Trustees," but rather as a "Board of Incorporation and Management." Mary Richards served as secretary of the board. Swift served as Manager and Treasurer. L.H. Field served as president. Leonard H. Field opened a general merchandise business in Jackson, Michigan in 1869. By 1900, the L.H. Field store or "Field's" was the most notable department store between Detroit and Chicago. Field's flagship store on the corner of Main and Jackson Streets occupied 22,000 square feet and Leonard Field had the most public and famous name in Jackson.

Richard Waldron served as auditor of the board. Waldron was a real estate broker. He lived with his family and two servants in a mansion on West Trail Street in Jackson.

Lemuel W. Bowen served as Vice-President of the board. Bowen worked for the D.M. Ferry & Co. seed company. D.M. Ferry owned the seed company and also was the President of the First National Bank of Detroit. Lemuel Bowen referred to himself as a seedsman. He and his family lived in a mansion on Woodward Avenue in Detroit. Bowen was one of Henry Ford's original financial backers and in 1905 became one of two founders of the Cadillac Automobile Company. He had grown up in Grass Lake in Jackson County. I imagine that he and Waldron helped Herman Swift acquire the land in Leoni Township and that Bowen was the "prominent Christian citizen" who promised to sink $1,000 into the Leoni Beulah Land Farm if necessary to overcome the attack by the county board of supervisors.

Herman Swift required all the boys at the Children's Temple Home and the Leoni Beulah Land Farm to write "life stories." A number of these were published in *Give the Boy a Chance* and Harold Shepstone included William's story at the end of his article. Swift also promoted his mission through use of photography. He had learned well the Bible's message to seek money from the wealthy and talent from the tradesmen. For Herman Swift, photographers represented perhaps the most important tradesmen. Fig.4 is a professional photograph of Swift featured at the beginning of the Harold Shepstone article. It suggests the importance of formality and appearance to Swift, but in this latter regard falls far short of the power of the "before" and "after" photographs which Swift featured in his promotional efforts. Fig.5 is perhaps the most famous of these paired photographs. It is titled: "Give the Boy a Chance" and shows a boy "in the city" and then "in the country" under the influence of the Beulah Home. Swift used this image in the book of the same title and later used it in postcard form to support fund raising. Harold Shepstone utilized it as an illustration in his article. Herman Swift possessed a machine that allowed him to project life sized images of the before and after photos. Ruby Stanleigh, in *Give the Boy a Chance*, writes that this was done to the "delight of the boys."

Fig.6 is a photograph of William, the boy who wrote the life story that introduced this chapter. He wears a lapel button that represents his position as an inmate at the Children's Temple Home. G. Lissau took the photograph in his studio located at the northwest corner of the intersection of Clark Street and Chicago Avenue, close to the Home. He catered to a wealthy clientele

Herman Swift c. 1898 (Fig.4)

and I believe he donated his talents to Herman Swift. Lissau probably created cabinet card photographs of all the boys who stayed a period of time at the Children's Temple Home.

Fig.7 is a photograph of a boy named Oscar Weber. It was taken the day he arrived at the Children's Temple Home in 1898. I have not seen an "after" photograph of Oscar. Herman Swift reported that Oscar's parents had both died when he was very young. Thrown onto the streets of Chicago, he struggled to make a living as a bootblack and newsboy. In the winter he slept on the sidewalk next to the big steam wheel, a noisy feature of the city's transportation system. When the wheel was turned off later in the night, Oscar "kept from freezing by walking the streets," reported the *Jackson Daily Patriot* in an article under four headlines: "Life Transformed; The Story of an Ex-street Arab of Chicago; He Is Now A Model Boy; And Much Taken Up With His Life at the Beulah Land Farm in Leoni, Mich."

Oscar Weber arrived at the Leoni Beulah Land Farm with the first group of boys that were sent from the Children's Temple Home in Chicago. In the election for the first president of the Beulah Land Farm "Junior Commonwealth," Oscar received all the votes but three. He served as the first and probably last president. In that capacity, Oscar wrote a letter that reads in part: "To everybody, —I want to tell you about our farm and the first thing I will tell you is about the location, which is very beautiful. We are surrounded by linden trees and if you stood on our front porch you would have a wonderful sight before your eyes, for just down the hill is a beautiful lily pond...

Then if you turn your face toward the East you can see the Church steeples in Grass Lake three miles away, and if you look North the first thing that will meet your eyes will be our apple orchard, and then the wheat, corn and potato fields and back of them all our 'Park Beulah' where

Before and After (Fig.5)

the huckleberries grow and where the wintergreens are thicker than hair on a dog. Fishing, swimming, and skating are some of our delights. God has so prospered us that we have a Billy Goat. We have also a dog, cat, chickens, cows, horses and such things. Each boy has a garden and we raise radishes, peas, lettuce, onions and about a hundred other things. We played ball with the Grass Lake nine and beat them 18 to 1.

When we first came to the farm I was elected President and the next night we celebrated by having a big bonfire and speeches. You see it is this way. We boys own this farm and everything on it. We call it the Junior Commonwealth...The people of the United States run themselves and we do the same. We work the farm and get paid for every hour we work. If we don't work we don't get no pay. We have school right in the home from 9 to 4 o'clock every day except Saturday and Sunday, but Sunday we always go to Church and Sunday-school.

Besides the school we have Bible class, Singing School, Debating Society, and Sewing School which meets nights after supper. We have a telegraph which runs to other farm houses and some of the boys are learning how to telegraph, and some are learning short hand and how to run a type writer; but I should like to learn to play the piano more than anything else. We have a good piano and when I earn money enough I am going to hire a teacher to learn me.

I don't know how any one could find a better place in the world to live than this farm and all the boys are so happy even if they ain't President. Yours Truly, Oscar Weber, President, 'Junior Commonwealth.'"

The Beulah Land Farm for Boys operated for only a very short time in Leoni. I don't believe that Herman Swift ever had a chance to incorporate the place. In early 1901, he became entangled

William (Fig.6)   PHOTO: G. Lissau   Oscar Weber (Fig.7)

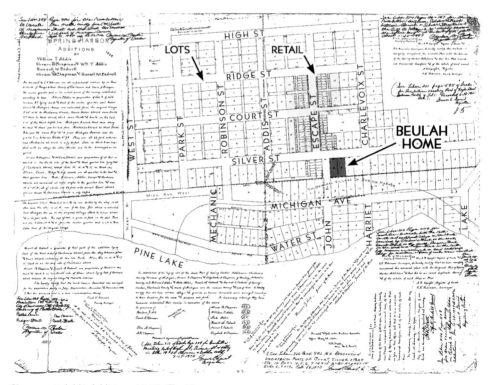

Chapman & Addis Addition - 1883 (Fig.8)

in a scandal that replicated the scandal that forced him to depart Buffalo. This scandal involved charges of abuse by Swift in both Leoni and Chicago. Years later he would claim that he had never faced charges in Chicago and claim that he had been found innocent of the charges in Leoni. Both these claims may or may not be true. Whatever the case, as he had done in Buffalo, Herman Swift elected not to face the charges of abuse and to move on to a new location. It appears that the three outside Leoni Beulah Home Board members believed in Swift's innocence. But wishing to avoid scandalous publicity over the charges, they met with Swift and agreed to facilitate his move out of Jackson County.

Board member Richard Waldron at various times listed his occupation as "loaning money," but in 1900 he referred to himself as a "real estate broker." I believe Richard was related to Charles Waldron. Charles had been involved with a failed investment in a rambling hotel on Silver Street in the town of Bay Springs in northern Michigan. It seems that Richard gained information about that building from Charles and he suggested that the Leoni Beulah Home Board help Herman Swift investigate this property.

Leoni Board President Leonard H. Field owned a northern Michigan cottage near Bay Springs. I believe he agreed to assist Herman Swift in investigating and perhaps acquiring the Silver Street building. Leoni Board Vice-President Lemuel Bowen agreed to assist Swift in disposing of the Leoni Beulah Home property. Herman Swift immediately plunged enthusiastically into the mission of starting up a new Beulah Home for Boys.

On April 9th, 1903 Herman Swift sold the Leoni Beulah Land Farm for two thousand four hundred dollars, banking a four hundred dollar profit on the transaction. He sold the property to a man named Frank O. Strickland. Strickland boarded in a house at 36 Butternut in Detroit. He did not have the money required to purchase the property from Swift, but his boss did. Strickland worked as a foreman at the D.M. Ferry seed company. Bowen had attempted for over two years to sell the Leoni Beulah land, but finally used Strickland as a straw man and purchased the property himself. In doing this, Bowen assisted Swift in his plans to open a new boys home in northern Michigan. Later, on August 18th, 1908, Strickland transferred the Leoni Farm property to Anna. E. Hunt in exchange for $1.00. That same day Hunt transferred the property back to Strickland for $1.00. Anna E. Hunt was deputy register of deeds for Jackson County. This transaction suggests that Lemuel Bowen was concerned about Herman Swift's title to the property.

The *Chicago Street Directory* for 1900 contains a listing for the "Children's Temple Home" at 734 Wells Street. The 1901 *Directory* contains no listing for the Children's Temple Home. It appears that both that Home and the Beulah Home in Leoni were closed sometime in early 1901.

When Herman Swift sold the Leoni Beulah Land Farm property, he signed the deed transfer as "Beulah Land Farm for Boys, Herman Swift, trustee, of Bay Springs, Charlevoix County, Michigan." The boys who were inmates at the Leoni Beulah Land Farm allegedly owned the property, but when the property was sold they received none of the proceeds. Over a year earlier, Herman had committed the funds to the acquisition of a new Beulah Land Farm in Bay Springs in Charlevoix County in northern Michigan.

IV

Chapman's Folly

Hiram Chapman and his wife Elizabeth lived in Reading, a Village in Hillsdale County in south central Michigan. Hiram worked as a farmer. He understood land values and was very successful. By 1880, Chapman was describing his occupation as capitalist and he was worth over $50,000. In early 1882, he made an acquisition of fifty acres of land just north of the Village of Spring Harbor, Michigan. Spring Harbor was located at the base of the larger arm, the eastern arm, of Pine Lake in Charlevoix County.

Between July and December of 1882, surveyors completed a survey of Chapman's property (Fig.8). The register of deeds titled this plat: "The Chapman and Addis Addition to Spring Harbor," but Chapman's vision was a new village. He named the village Bay Springs and planned a great resort. The key to Chapman's vision he imagined in Block 1, for there he would construct a wonderful large resort hotel. The hotel formed the foundation for his speculation on the property. Chapman assumed that visitors to the hotel would purchase the lots, shop at the stores, and play in the park. Like all property developers, he assumed he had selected the proper location.

Chapman's hotel was called "The Tourist Home," and was located at the southeast corner of Silver and John Streets. Hiram, Elizabeth, and their six children lived at 84 Silver Street in Reading Village. John Street almost certainly comes from the name John Miller. John Miller and his wife Harriet are credited with being the first white settlers in the area. In Fig.8, Harriet Street is a short street running parallel to John Street. John and Harriet Miller had lived in a cabin near the point where Lake Street meets the Pine Lake shore (Fig.8). They lived alone there between the deep blue lake and a virgin forest of pine and hemlock trees. A river entered Pine Lake just south of the cabin and John named it the Boyne River, remembering the river near his boyhood home in Ireland. As settlers arrived in the area of the river, they formed a village and named it Boyne Village (later Boyne City). In May of 1873, under the Homestead Act of 1862, John Miller successfully staked his claim to his property and platted Spring Harbor. Bay Springs sat on a bluff above Spring Harbor.

Block 1 in Bay Springs offered Hiram Chapman a fine view of Pine Lake, but as he began construction of his wonderful hotel in 1883 he speculated on something else, the ability to move tourists by rail and ship to his hotel.

In 1873, the Grand Rapids and Indiana Railroad (GR&I) completed a line that ran from Grand

Rapids in the south to Petoskey, a village on Lake Michigan's Little Traverse Bay. The GR&I had located a depot in Boyne Falls Village, some seven miles southeast of Bay Springs. Chapman's partner William Addis developed a plan to run a narrow gauge railroad, the Spring Harbor and Boyne Falls, from his lumber mill in Spring Harbor to the GR&I depot in Boyne Falls. In May of 1883, the S.H.&B.F. initiated passenger service. Now tourists had rail access to Chapman's dream resort.

In 1877, the Federal Government had initiated a dredging project to create a navigable channel that would run from Lake Michigan through Round Lake and then into Pine Lake. In 1883, they completed this project and now Great Lakes tourist steamers had access to Chapman's dream resort.

Chapman's hotel was built of virgin pine boards. The exterior boards were thick and over ten inches in width. The hotel rose up four floors, with the first floor built into the bluff on one end and opening up in a walkout style toward the lake on the other. The first floor included a kitchen, a number of large rooms, and an indoor swimming pool, the first in northern Michigan. The second floor included a number of large guest rooms and the third floor included many smaller guest rooms. The fourth floor housed a large ballroom and stage.

Hiram Chapman had committed a large amount of capital to the hotel, but the resort failed to attract many visitors. The Tourist Home Hotel in Bay Springs quickly became known as "Chapman's Folly." A few residential lots were sold to speculators, but no cottages were constructed and no retail businesses were established in Chapman's resort. 1884 was not a time of economic recession. Resorts in Charlevoix, Harbor Springs, and Petoskey experienced rapid growth. The failure of Chapman's resort may largely have been due to the conversion of the Boyne Village and Spring Harbor area into a major manufacturing center. Factories spread like a flood across the Pine Lake shoreline. Retail stores sprung up along Lake and Water Streets in Boyne Village, established there to serve hundreds of factory workers. Up in Bay Springs, not much was going on. There was not much to do, not like in Charlevoix, Harbor Springs, or Petoskey. And even in 1885, one could look over the bluff in Bay Springs and see sawmills, brick plants and lumber-carrying vessels. A prospective cottage owner may have objected to the additional inconvenience in traveling to Bay Springs, but more significantly, it seems to me that they sensed the place was more blue-collar than blue-blood, more Flint than Palm Beach or Charlevoix.

H.B. Chapman recognized his problems with the Bay Springs property and understood the need to cut his losses. His hotel's occupancy was low in the summer and negligible in the winter when the lake froze and travel by ship was impossible. Addis' railroad folded and Addis had left town. Now winter travel was restricted to a seven-mile stagecoach ride to reach the G.R.&I. depot in Boyne Falls. The hotel had a steam boiler furnace on the first floor, but visitors froze in the drafty building, particularly those who chose to save money and stay on the third floor. Chapman endured the losses of the winter of 1884/1885 and then did what any smart speculator will do. He turned to his banker, Charles Waldron.

On November 14th, 1885, Hiram Chapman sold block 1 of the Chapman Addis Addition (the "Tourist Home Hotel Property") and a number of adjoining properties to Charles Waldron for twelve thousand dollars. To finance the acquisition Waldron took on a ten thousand dollar loan from the 3rd National Bank of Detroit. The bank recently had been organized by a number of wealthy Detroit businessmen. The members of the board of 3rd National were a conservative group, but not board member William H. Stevens. Stevens served as the first president of the bank. They called him Captain Stevens and he had returned to Detroit in 1885 as a wealthy man. He made his money mining silver in Colorado. Captain Stevens approved the large loan to Charles Waldron. Waldron changed the name of the Tourist Home Hotel to the Waldron House. During the summer of 1886, the hotel hosted a number of balls in the fourth floor ballroom. Unfortunately, this did not occur often enough and never occurred in winter.

Waldron recognized his financial problems with the Waldron House as early as the summer of 1886. On June 25th, 1886, Waldron used a quitclaim deed to transfer half interest in the Hotel Property to Captain Stevens. Stevens took on responsibility for half of the ten thousand dollar bank loan.

On August 30th, 1888, Charles Waldron appointed Ephraim Shay of Bay Springs, Michigan his sole and legal attorney, granting him power of attorney to sell and dispose of property, including: "all of my stock of general merchandise and all household goods now stored in the frame hotel building and in the barn adjoining, both situated on Block 1 of Chapman & Addis Addition to Bay Springs, Michigan. Also, to rent the above described hotel and barn and also any dock at Bay Springs, Michigan." Ephraim Shay ran a lumber mill on the lake shore below the Waldron House. He became one of northern Michigan's most famous people as the inventor of the Shay Locomotive that revolutionized lumbering operations around the world.

Two days earlier, on August 28th, 1888, the 3rd National Bank of Detroit had foreclosed on the hotel property owned by Charles Waldron and Captain Stevens. The purchase price or consideration in this transaction was stated as seven thousand dollars, suggesting that Waldron and Stevens had paid off three thousand dollars of the original ten thousand dollar mortgage.

From 1888 through 1892, the United States economy steadily grew and the Boyne Village economy grew, but aside from the weeds that grew up around the vacant Waldron House hotel, not much changed in Bay Springs. The hotel sat there rising up amidst the vacant lots and farmers in wagons passed by on Charlevoix Street and shook their heads over Chapman's Folly. Then the Panic of 1893 struck the United States economy leading to collapses in the stock market and the banking business. 3rd National Bank of Detroit was one of the banks that collapsed.

Joseph L. Hudson lived in a mansion on Woodward Avenue and was the leading retail merchant in Detroit. Aside from Henry Ford, his name would become the most recognizable in the city as he grew his retail empire, the J.L. Hudson Company. When 3rd National Bank collapsed, Hudson was a board member and served as vice-president of the bank. He personally paid out two hundred and sixty five thousand dollars to deal with all the liabilities of the failed bank. Then he merged the assets of the bank into First National Bank of Detroit, the bank owned by his friend, D.M. Ferry. The assets included the mortgage on the large Silver Street building and the adjoining properties in Bay Springs.

In 1893, the Chapman & Addis Addition continued to lie right at the outskirts of Boyne Village/Spring Harbor/Bay Springs, right at the edge of civilization. West Street, on the far left of the Fig.8 survey, where Michigan Avenue ended, marked the border, and continued to do so in 1910. Given the weak economy and the lonely, stark circumstances of the location, selling the Waldron

House had proven a very difficult challenge. But finally on December 30th, 1893, a local farmer named Alverado Boise purchased the property for $7,000, totally representing an assumption of the bank mortgage. The deed of sale covered the hotel property and a number of adjoining properties and I will refer to these as the "Boise properties." The man who signed the deed for the seller was: "J.L. Hudson, President, First National Bank of Detroit."

As the 1890s progressed, lumber related manufacturing companies in the Boyne area again began attracting a steady flow of workers. Boise attempted to take advantage of this by converting the rambling old hotel to transient apartments, but this plan failed and Boise lost the "Boise properties" to a bank foreclosure in 1897. Joseph L. Hudson continued to hold Boise responsible for the mortgage.

Bay View Association

Leaders of the Michigan Methodist Church met in Jackson, Michigan on November 9th, 1875 with the goal of organizing a northern Michigan summer campground. One of the leaders present that day was a Methodist preacher named Seth Reed. He had given up early plans to become a lawyer and instead became one of the very early ministers in the Michigan Methodist Church. Reed was appointed as one of eight committee-members responsible for establishing the summer camp. Within a year they had selected a site on a beautiful forested bluff overlooking Little Traverse Bay two miles north of the town of Petoskey. Reverend Reed named the location Bay View.

By 1885, Bay View included 131 summer cottages, a chapel, two railroad depots, a dormitory, a dining room and a hotel. During the summer, the Association hosted Sunday school sessions, ministerial training, and devotional meetings. Reverend Reed and other leaders elected to add a "Chautauqua," a secular program that would include schools of music, elocution, cooking, art, and literature. Reed at this point served as Pastor at the Court Street Methodist Church, the oldest church in Flint, Michigan. He suggested one of his Flint parishioners, a lawyer named John M. Hall, to lead the Chautauqua. Hall would serve twelve years as superintendent of the Bay View Assembly and Bay View Summer University. Reverend Seth Reed is known as one of the creators of Bay View. Hall is known as one of its principal builders.

John M. Hall owned a beautiful cottage called Wayside located on lot 1, block 11, on the first terrace of the Bay View Association. Leonard H. Field, the President of the Leoni Beulah Land Farm board, owned the cottage just two lots north of Wayside.

On September 2nd, 1901, the *Petoskey Daily Resorter* published the following article in its "Bay View Breezes" section: "Rev. W.S. Sly spoke twenty minutes in behalf of the Rocky Beach Orphanage Association of which he is president."

I believe that John M. Hall assisted Leonard Field in relocating Herman Swift to northern Michigan. George F. Brown and his company The Flint Land Co. acquired the "Boise properties" in Bay Springs through a tax sale on August 14th, 1901. Brown was a real estate developer and, like Hall, he was a lawyer from Flint. Brown lived four blocks away from the Court Street Methodist Church. I believe that Brown, John M. Hall, and Reverend Seth Reed were good friends.

On April 28th, 1902, George F. Brown sold the "Boise properties" to Lucena Green. Lucena and her husband Edward C. Green ran a clothing store on Main Street, just down the street from the L.H. Field department store in Jackson. Edward had learned the clothing business working for Leonard H. Field. Edward and Lucena Green were well acquainted with both Field and John M. Hall. The Green's owned a cottage on lot 16, block 39, of the Bay View Association.

On August 4th, 1902, the *Petoskey Daily Resorter* in the "Bay View Breezes" section reported: "Hon. Wm. J. Stine, Judge of Probate of Eaton County, is the guest of Mrs. M.A. Cook. Judge Stine is to read a paper at the meeting of the judges of probate to be held later in August in Petoskey."

While Herman Swift's move to Bay Springs probably was in motion as early as August 1901 when George Brown acquired the "Boise properties," this *Daily Resorter* article suggests that some men at Bay View still were performing background checks on Herman. Shortly after the date of this article, in August of 1902, Herman established his mission in the Silver Street building in Bay Springs. From that point forward, Chapman's Folly would be known as the Beulah Home for Boys.

V

~

The Promoter

On October 17th, 1902, Lucena Green sold the "Boise properties" back to Alverado Boise. The tax sale of the properties to George Brown, the sale by Brown to Lucena Green, and the sale by Green to Boise all were recorded at the Charlevoix County Register of Deeds Office on November 10th, 1902. Three days earlier, on November 7th, the *Boyne Citizen* in a front-page article reported:

"The Beulah Land Farm Home for Boys is now at Bay Springs. The Trustees of this incorporation have purchased the Bay Springs Hotel, "Chapman's Folly," with 120 acres of land. The hotel is 180 feet long, built in the form of an 'L' and is said to have cost $40,000. The first story is brick and the other three frame surrounded by verandas. It has 64 rooms, well adapted for home and school purposes. One is a theater, 90 feet long, for entertainments and lectures. Financial help is needed. The Bay Springs property was bought for $5,000. It is under the direction and loving care of Herman Lee Swift."

On July 18th, 1903, Alverado Boise sold the "Boise properties" to Herman Swift. Boise signed the deed transfer in Tennessee. Swift was in a position to finance this transaction because he had sold his Leoni Beulah Home property on April 9, 1903. On the deed transferring the Leoni property he declared that he lived in Bay Springs, Michigan. On the deed transferring the Silver Street property Swift identified the purchaser as "Herman L. Swift as sole trustee for the Beulah Land Farm for Boys of Leoni, Michigan." So Herman was "sole trustee." There was no group of "trustees of incorporation" as the *Boyne Citizen* had reported. And Herman was from Bay Springs on April 9, 1903 and from Leoni two months later on July 18th, 1903. Herman cleverly structured the two real estate transactions to insure that he captured the proceeds of the Leoni property sale and personally gained title to the "Boise properties." They also were structured in such a way that, aside from Edward Green who witnessed the deed of sale from his wife to Alverado Boise, no other names of members of the Leoni Board or the Bay View Association appear on the documents. Herman Swift paid five thousand and five hundred dollars for the "Boise properties" suggesting that another fifteen hundred dollars had been paid down on the seven thousand dollar bank mortgage. I believe small portions of the five thousand and five hundred dollar payment went to The Flint Land Company and to Alverado Boise and the major portion then went to Joseph L. Hudson.

Each time that Herman Swift traveled from Leoni to Bay Springs to investigate, structure or complete the movement of his orphanage, he traveled over two hundred eighty miles. The trip required a one hundred and two mile ride west on the Michigan Central Railroad from the little depot in Leoni to Grand Rapids, then a one-hundred seventy mile ride north on the Grand Rapids and Indiana Railroad to Boyne Falls, and finally a seven mile stagecoach or train ride northwest to Boyne City or Bay Springs.

For a number of reasons, Boyne City would prove to be a fine base of operations for Herman Swift. But I think the thing that brought him to the site was the Silver Street building and importantly, the land surrounding the building. In Leoni, he had acquired forty-four acres, but he had not achieved his dream of owning a "quarter," one hundred sixty acres.

The day that Herman Swift purchased the Silver Street property he also acquired one hundred twenty acres of surrounding land in the Chapman and Addis Addition. The title transfer states that Swift paid five thousand five hundred dollars for the building and the land. Presumably, two thousand four hundred dollars of that money came from the sale of the Leoni property. The source of the remaining three thousand and one hundred dollars and the ownership of the Boyne City Beulah Home property would become very important issues in 1909.

Herman Swift traveled to Boyne City as early as the summer of 1901. He stepped off the train, walked to the corner and placed his bags in the dust of Park Street. Looking just south down Park Street he could see the Methodist Episcopal Church. Herman became a member of that church shortly after his move to Bay Springs. Kitty corner from the depot Swift could see the Public School building, one of the first brick buildings in town. They were in the process of adding on to the building in order to accommodate the addition of a twelfth grade. Herman Swift took note of the building and, remembering his experience in Leoni, he planned to quickly build a good relationship with the top man in the school.

Right across Park Street men were in the process of constructing a most unusual tower. They were building the tower on a two-story building that housed the fire station and town jail. Wooden shingles covered the tower and it rose up in the form of a continuously shrinking square. Firemen used the tower to dry out fire hoses, but that was not its primary function. The tower held a very fine clock mechanism manufactured by the Howard Clock Company of Boston. The mechanism kept excellent time on clocks positioned on each of the four sides of a cupola at the top of the tower. Town citizens set their watches by the village clock and if they were not in a position to see the clock they could still hear it as it loudly chimed every half hour. Up on the bluff in the north part of the city, Herman Swift would have a fine watch and other than setting that watch, he did not pay that much attention to the village clock tower. The boys at the Beulah Home, however, would depend on the chimes of that clock to manage their time, their works, and their schemes.

Herman waited until a carriage arrived. I imagine that a man from Bay View drove the carriage. The man helped Swift place his bags in the rear of the carriage and then the two men set out for the large Silver Street building. They turned left down Park Street. At the first corner they turned left down Water Street, heading down toward the lake. Water Street was lined with many commercial buildings. It was a wide dirt street and most of the buildings were constructed of wood at that time. The driver noted the growth of the village and pointed out new businesses as they traveled down Water Street. Water Street runs parallel to Main Street, but for some reason the town's commercial activity has always been centered on Water Street. It seems as if they named the wrong street Main Street.

Water Street, not surprisingly, ends at a point where it meets Lake Street. Watson's Drug Store occupied the northeast corner at Lake and Water Streets, probably the prime retail location in the town. John Watson was Irish and a bit of a rebel. The sign on the side of Watson's store read: "This is the Place. You can get what you want and get it Right!" He sold alcohol in a number of "medicinal" forms in his drug store and probably would not turn into a strong supporter of Herman Swift's. But that would not have been clear to Swift as the carriage turned right on Lake Street and proceeded to follow the shore of the lake toward the large Silver Street building.

As the driver guided the carriage north on Lake Street they passed a number of saloons on their right. Herman Swift took note of the names on the saloons. It is important to identify your enemies.

In 1901, William White and Godfrey Von Platen each operated large lumber mills on the shores of Pine Lake in Boyne City, but some of the shoreline in the town remained open. Swift eyed the lake, but as they reached the end of Lake Street and turned on Michigan, for some reason he turned his head right and noted the empty lot on the corner. In 1905, the Baptists built a church on that lot. Boyne City annexed Silver Springs and Bay Springs and those two towns became Ward 1 of the City, an area known as North Boyne. And two of the three notable buildings in North Boyne were the Beulah Home for Boys and the Baptist Church. The leaders of that church would prove to be among Swift's most important supporters.

Herman Swift and the boys under his guardianship took up residence in the rambling home on the bluff in Bay Springs in August of 1902. I imagine the fall was a splendid season, but when winter arrived cold drafts blew through the home. In spite of this, the home seemed warm enough to boys who had experienced winter living in boxes and barrels on the streets of Chicago. Swift quickly began to promote his endeavors to salvage forsaken boys in his new boys home in northern Michigan. His efforts brought in donations from downstate Michigan and importantly from the local Boyne City churches. Swift and his charges survived that first winter.

The large hotel that Hiram Chapman constructed for $35,000 converted very nicely into an orphanage. The lowest level of the Beulah Home building contained a heated swimming pool, a shower room, and a large open area. The Beulah Home boys referred to this floor as the "basement" even though it opened up to the outdoors on the side of the building that faced the lake. Swift converted the open area in the basement into one large classroom. A series of support beams split the classroom in half down its length. The little boys occupied desks on one side of the beams and the big boys occupied desks on the other side. The boys shared some instruction, but for the most part one teacher instructed the little boys and another instructed the big boys.

The first or ground floor of the Beulah Home contained a kitchen, a dining room, an office and a lavatory. The lavatory contained eight white porcelain basins donated by a Detroit plumber. Hot and cold water ran to each basin. Along the lavatory walls, the boys each hung a towel and a toothbrush beneath plaques containing their individual names. Swift converted one other room on the first floor into a chapel and, of the sixty-four rooms in the building, the chapel and the classroom were the most important. Swift made the chapel available to the congregations of the Methodist Episcopal and Baptist Churches in Boyne City.

At an early time in the history of the Beulah Home, Reverend W.J. McCune and his wife traveled from their home in Petoskey to spend a day with the Swifts. Herman and Grace Swift met the McCunes at the depot in Boyne City. They rode to the Home in a farm wagon pulled by two large horses and driven by Herman Swift. Later Reverend McCune wrote about that visit: "The boys assemble in Chapel every evening for prayers and a few words of council, admonition, and helpfulness from Mr. Swift. Oh, how they sing! It is worth a long trip to hear them. We have never heard such a splendid Boy's Chorus. They sing with their might and for the very joy of it. They must be a happy lot to sing as they do."

Herman Swift converted the guest rooms on the second and third floors into rooms for the boys. Each room was heated by a radiator and contained an electric light. Each boy had a small desk, a chair, a bed and a storage box. The fourth floor contained several additional boys' sleeping rooms, but the bulk of it contained a large and very well equipped gymnasium. There were roughly fifty-five sleeping rooms in the Beulah Home. Swift advertised that it was the only boys home in the United States with private rooms rather than dormitories.

On February 6th, 1903, the *Boyne Citizen* reported that: "Protracted meetings were led by the Rev. Reed at the Beulah Home this week." *Citizen* readers were very aware that this referred to Reverend Seth Reed, one of the founders of the Bay View Association.

On August 23rd, 1903, the *Boyne Citizen* reported that: "The Rev. A.R. Keillor has been holding services at the mission established at the Beulah Home in Bay Springs a year ago and to show their appreciation the boys on Sunday made him a present of a purse of fifty dollars which they had earned in various ways... Rev. Keillor accepted the token gracefully and on Tuesday forwarded the same to Miss R. Nellie Cunningham of Matanzas, Cuba to be used for the benefit of an industrial school for boys there of which she has charge." Reverend Alexander Keillor was minister of the Boyne City Methodist Episcopal Church. The *History* of that church includes a note that: "Rev. Keillor initiated a preaching schedule at the 'Beulah Home for Unfortunate Boys' in December 1902." The August 23rd article indicates that Herman Swift had established his Beulah Home in Bay Springs in August of 1902. It describes a donation by the Beulah boys to a mission in Cuba. Swift ultimately would develop correspondence relationships with boys homes in Cuba and the Philippines. He recruited at least three Cuban boys to the Chicago Children's Temple Home and at least one Cuban boy to his Boyne City Beulah Home.

In August of 1904, the *Beaver Island News* (Beaver Island lies in Lake Michigan west of Charlevoix) reported that: "The Beulah farm boys, twenty-five in number, spent the week camping on the shores of Beaver Island last week. In command of the boys was foster father Mr. Hermon Lee Swift and his helpers. The boys created a very good impression while on the Island by their well bred manners and gentlemanly ways." Herman Swift implemented a military basic training type discipline over much of the life at the Beulah Home. The boys marched into the dining room for meals. At a softly spoken command they took assigned seats. When the meal was over they responded to soft commands to stack dishes, then stand, and then march off to place their dishes at the sink in the kitchen.

Instruction took place in three areas: the chapel, the schoolroom, and the farm. Swift accepted boys of any or no religious background. He advertised that religious instruction at the Beulah Home was non-denominational, but Christian based. From the outset, Swift provided in-house schooling for the boys at the Boyne City Beulah Home. School instruction was compulsory. The annual school year covered six days per week for forty weeks.

Boyne City constructed a large brick public school to serve the children of North Boyne in 1905. That building, along with the Baptist Church and the Beulah Home, constituted the three major buildings in North Boyne. The school was located just to the northwest of the Beulah Home. While the Beulah boys did not attend that school, they received a good deal of support from the children that did.

Herman Swift knew a great deal about farming. He had learned this from his father Hoyt. There was significance to the fact that Swift referred to the orphanage as The Beulah Land Farm for Boys. He held great belief in his ability to civilize a boy by bringing him out of the urban ghetto, removing him from the harmful temptations of that environment and placing him in a rural, agricultural setting. The Beulah Home boys worked at various tasks in the home, but principally they worked on the farm. They raised beans, corn, potatoes, and various fruits. It was reported that the boys planted over one thousand fruit trees the first year that Swift owned the farm. Each boy was assigned to one of the teams responsible for a particular crop. In addition, each boy was given his own small plot of land. Swift promoted the fact that each boy "had his own room and his own plot of land" and promoted the benefits this provided in terms of building a sense of responsibility. The individual plots also encouraged entrepreneurial development. One of the boys constructed a chicken coop on his plot. Another boy raised goats.

In addition to religious, educational, and agricultural instruction, Herman Swift provided instruction in self-government. He had introduced this concept in Leoni, but in Boyne City he took it to a higher level. When he chose to promote this element of his management approach he referred to the Beulah Home as "The Beulah Land Commonwealth for Boys." The word commonwealth has a number of meanings, but Swift focused upon the word's reference to a political or governmental system in which the body of citizens (the boys at the Home) had the power to elect people to represent them as well as the power to create the laws and rules that governed them.

Each year during Thanksgiving week the Beulah Home boys met as a group and elected officers for the following year. These included a President, a Treasurer, a Secretary, a Poor Commissioner, and several Inspectors. The boys voted on proposals by Manager Swift, including items as minor as adding a fence on the property or purchasing a pig. They also voted on any newly proposed rules or regulations for the Home. Among the Commonwealth's most important rules were rules that no boy was to enter another boy's room unless invited and no boy was to be in the area of the bedrooms during the school or work day unless given permission. The fine for breaking these rules was one dollar, a large sum for the Beulah Home boys. The Inspectors, usually bigger boys, were tasked with enforcing the rules and regulations. This involved identifying rule breakers to Herman Swift who then dealt out the prescribed punishment.

Each of the boys had a bank account. They were allowed to work for employers during the summer months. Their employers paid Swift who deposited the amounts to the boys' accounts. The boys earned a "credit" for each twenty minutes of work in the Home or on the farm. For every ten "credits" a boy earned a "merit" and for every ten "merits" he earned a "share." During Thanksgiving week Swift informed the boys of the farm's "profit." The farm's main objective was to provide food for the Home. Profit represented sales of surplus food less the costs of operating the farm. The value of a "share" was determined by dividing the profit by the total number of earned "shares." Each boy's bank account was credited with the value of his "shares."

The boys used money from their bank accounts to purchase items that had been donated to the Beulah Home, including clothing, shoes, and books. This money went into the "poor fund." The "Poor Commissioner" then used the money to acquire shoes and clothing for new arrivals that had no money to make purchases. Herman Swift promoted this as a system that taught thrift, self-reliance and humanity.

With few exceptions, the Beulah Home served boys between the ages of eight and sixteen. Most boys were placed with adoptive families or returned to parents or relatives before they reached the age of sixteen. If they were not placed, however, at age sixteen they were pushed out. Herman Swift promoted the fact that the average boy left the Home with between twenty and thirty dollars. He also promoted the fact that the boys owned the Home and the farm and this would return to haunt him.

On February 2nd, 1906, in the most prominent part of the paper, the center top of the front page, the *Boyne Citizen* published the following article under the headline: "APPRECIATIVE TRIB-UTE, To H.L. Swift from His Boys: Our Dear Mr. Swift:

As you are about to leave us for a while we must stop to think of all the things you have done for us in the past. No doubt many of us would be behind prison bars if it were not for the interest you took in us all. Whatever good there is in us you have made. We were thinking of getting you a present but though we are all poor in money, we are not poor in love. We want, every one of us, to give you our best wishes, and we want you to have a very pleasant trip and a hasty return. We also want to send our very best wishes and love to the one who will soon be our mother as you have been our father. We want you to take good care of yourself, for if you should get hurt or die there would be no one else to take such care and interest in us as you have taken. You may be sure we will remember and think of you all the time until you return.

With the kindest love and wishes, YOUR BOYS.

The above was composed by a committee of three, selected by the boys at one of their meetings and then signed by every boy at the Beulah Land Farm. No doubt this real testimony of appreciation and love is more highly valued than any gift which Mr. Swift could possibly receive."

Grace Munson Swift

Grace Munson was born in Toledo, Ohio in August of 1882. Her mother Mary Kurtz Munson died in October of that same year. Her father Wallace Munson worked at a wagon-making factory in Toledo and raised Grace and her sister Anna until his death in March of 1889. Grace became an orphan at the age of six. In 1900, Grace and her sister lived with their maternal grandmother Rose Kurtz in a home at 1461 Milburn Street in Toledo. Grace worked as a dressmaker. She was twenty-three and Herman Swift was thirty-five when they married at the home on Milburn Street on January 31st, 1906.

On February 9th, 1906, the *Boyne Citizen* carried the following article:

"The many friends of the groom have received announcements of the marriage of Miss Grace Munson of Toledo, O., to Mr. Hermon L. Swift, at the home of the bride's grandmother on Wednesday Jan. 31. They will be at home after the first day of April. All will join *The Citizen* in wishing them a long and happy life together."

Finally, on Friday, April 12th, 1906, the *Boyne Citizen* reported:

"Mr. and Mrs. H.L. Swift returned last Friday from their wedding trip. A large number of townspeople, augmented by numerous friends from Charlevoix and Petoskey, met them at the train and proceeded to the Home with them, where the afternoon and evening were spent most pleasantly. During their absence, the ladies of Boyne have been making window shades, curtains, and floor coverings for the various rooms, and the big mansion was certainly home-like upon their arrival."

Grace Swift was young but she successfully filled the role as "mother" for the Beulah Home boys. Herman took part of the basement at the Home and created a sewing room for Grace. Grace joined Herman as a member of the Boyne City Methodist Episcopal Church. As years passed, she took on administrative responsibilities and in effect became assistant manager of the Home. Grace would be Herman Swift's greatest supporter until the day he died and beyond.

On May 10th, 1907, the *Boyne Citizen* printed the following small article: "Never in the history of Boyne City has interest in spiritual matters equaled the high stage at present. Beginning last April 18th, the Kerr brothers have held union revival services in the Presbyterian and Methodist churches." Herman Swift felt very at home in this atmosphere. On May 31st, 1907, the *Citizen* published another small article that reads: "The county Sunday School Association is holding an interesting convention in the Presbyterian Church...The boys of the Beulah Home sang for those assembled, 'Christ is that Sunny Side of Life.'"

In July of 1907, the staff at the *Boyne Citizen* produced a fine promotional piece for The Boyne City Board of Trade. The piece contained a key insert, a one-page description of The Beulah Land Commonwealth for Boys. They titled the insert: "The Greatest Life Saving Station on the Great Lakes."

In the introduction, the author of the insert, probably the editor of the paper with major input from Herman Swift, describes his view of the Beulah Home: "Lads utterly homeless, neglected and forsaken are received into this Boys' Paradise and given a fighting chance in life. These little street waifs of our large cities have not been given a square deal by any means and are terribly handicapped by inheritance and environment...When it is taken into consideration that these boys are taken from the very slums of the cities and the lower walks of life, some of the boys even sleeping in barrels and boxes and under sidewalks and obliged to either steal or starve, and then in a very short time are made to appear like little gentlemen because of the refining influence of the Home; boys of tender years who have known nothing but lives of crime and vice, that being all they have seen about them, then one can realize somewhat of the wonderful work being done."

The author then describes several boys who achieved success following their time at the Home. One of these is a boy from Detroit: "whose father is in Jackson Prison and whose mother is an evil woman." While living at the Beulah Home this boy worked for the *Boyne Citizen* and learned to set type and run printing presses. Herman Swift found a family in Boyne City who took the boy into their home. The author adds that: "the boy is in eleventh grade and has just finished complete algebra and began work in geometry. He is also reading in Caesar and has rhetoric, physics and German."

The author makes several pleas for readers to provide financial support to Herman Swift and the Beulah Home. He includes a letter written by Reverend Louis Grosenbaugh minister of the Boyne City Methodist Episcopal Church from 1905 to 1908: "For nearly three years I have been in close personal touch with the work done in Beulah Home. The work done here by Mr. and Mrs. Swift has been a revelation and a surprise to me. I had always thought that little could be done for boys taken from bad parentage and impure environment, but I am now fully assured that the management of Beulah Home succeeds in making good and trustworthy boys of nearly all the homeless and friendless lads that come under its care. I am personally acquainted with many of these boys; I often see them in church, Sunday School, and on the streets of Boyne City. I can truthfully say that they are fully as correct in their habits and quite as attractive in personal appearance as the boys that are brought up in our best homes (letter dated May 23, 1907.)."

The Boyne City Beulah Home Board of Directors

On February 1st, 1912, a banquet was held to dedicate the opening of a fine new hotel in Boyne City, the Wolverine Hotel on Water Street. The reception list included the most important people in the city, and the first positions on the list were occupied by William and Louise White. William was President and General Manager of the W.H. White Lumber Company, the largest business in Boyne City. White Lumber owned logging rights over thousands of acres in northern Michigan. They operated three lumber camps employing over two hundred men and cutting over 135,000 feet of logs daily during the timbering season. Logs were transported over a rail system financed and built by William White.

Aside from his lumbering interests, William White also had an ownership interest and served as First Vice President of the Boyne City Chemical Company. He was Secretary of the Elm Cooperage Company, Treasurer of the Michigan Maple Company and President of First National Bank, the major bank in Boyne City. White owned a major interest in the bank.

White's second wife, Louise Reeder of Lake City, Michigan, was very religious and prior to the marriage she had planned to become a missionary. William and Louise were members of the Boyne City Methodist Episcopal Church. Louise signed her membership card: "M. Louise Reeder White." She was a confidant, forceful person and I believe a major supporter of Herman Swift and the Beulah Home for Boys. Her husband William H. White was a trustee of the Boyne City M.E. Church and was first on the list of Beulah Home Board Members. He served as President.

William S. Shaw was President and Treasurer of Boyne City Tanning. He served as President of Boyne City Chemicals, President of Boyne City Clay Products, and Vice President of First National Bank of Boyne City. He also served on the Beulah Home Board. Shaw imported hides from Argentina and treated them with chemicals derived from hemlock bark, a waste product from White's lumber mills. He produced excellent shoe leather in what was one of the largest tanneries in the world. He described himself as a "manufacturer of soles," a term Herman Swift might have used to describe himself.

John M. Harris was born in Canada in 1861. He moved to the Boyne City area in 1881. He was admitted to the practice of law in the State of Michigan in Charlevoix County on May 4th, 1893. By 1900, Harris was prosecuting attorney for Charlevoix County. In 1907, he worked as a lawyer in partnership with E.A. Ruegsegger. In April of 1907, Boyne City gained a fourth class city charter and John Harris was elected the first mayor of the city. Ruegsegger became city clerk.

John Harris wore his hair slicked back and his eyes were set back and penetrating. My guess is that he was a tough character and that he served as William White's personal attorney. John and Nellie Harris had five children. John served as secretary of the Boyne City School Board and Judge of Probate for Charlevoix County. Herman Swift dealt with probate courts across the state of Michigan. Parents or courts or guardians granted guardianships to Swift for most of the boys committed to the Home. That was one of the reasons that Herman Swift placed Judge Harris on the Board of the Beulah Home. Another was that John and Nellie were prominent members of the Boyne City Methodist Episcopal Church. John was a trustee of the church. Finally, Swift picked Harris because he was an outspoken supporter of the prohibition of liquor. Interestingly, Harris was one of the few people who had speculated by purchasing property in the Chapman and Addis Addition. He had purchased portions of two blocks and had platted lots on the property. He never sold any of those lots and ultimately donated them to Herman Swift.

Godfrey Von Platen was another member of the Beulah Home board of directors. Von Platen owned and operated a large lumber mill located just north of White's Big Mill on Pine Lake. He was a shareholder in Boyne City Chemical, a major supporter and supplier to the Tannery and the Charcoal Iron Company, and a charter member and investor in the First National Bank of Boyne City. Von Platen seems to be one of those rare leaders who are tough and get away with it, a man who in 1905 travels with his family on a lengthy European cruise then returns to Boyne City and agrees to serve as "farm inspector" for the Beulah Home for Boys. I imagine that Godfrey took the job seriously. He lived right around the corner from the Home and probably visited frequently. Arthur White in his 1926 book *White's Old Grand Rapids* wrote that Godfrey Von Platen: "was known to go to Chicago and return with two suitcases full of candy for the mill children and other children in Boyne City." The "other" children certainly included the Beulah Home boys.

A fifth member of the Beulah Home board of directors was Hubert E. Bell. Hubert was born in 1876 in Union City, a small town in southeastern Michigan. He was teaching in Union City when he was offered the school superintendent's position in Boyne City. He was only twenty-four when he accepted the job and he and his wife Lizzie moved over two hundred and fifty miles to the frontier in northern Michigan.

In 1901, the Boyne City teaching staff totaled four people, including Hubert who also was Superintendent. Rapid growth in the city's manufacturing sector and in its population drove rapid growth in the school system. By 1907, Hubert was managing a staff of twenty-two teachers, nine hundred students, and an annual budget of seventeen thousand dollars. He served as a steward of the Boyne City M.E. Church. "Prof. H.E. Bell" also held the important position of "auditor" on the board of directors of the Beulah Home for Boys.

A sixth member of the Beulah Home board in 1907 was Samuel C. Smith. S.C. Smith was a large man, stern and serious with a high forehead and a Roman nose. He favored high-collared, starched white shirts and dark suits. He had a charitable nature, but was critical, skeptical, and demanding. In 1905, Samuel was working as a bookkeeper in a Petoskey bank when William H. White offered him the position of Cashier of the new First National Bank of Boyne City. Smith jumped at the opportunity. From an operational point of view, in 1905 the "cashier" was the most important person in the bank. He was responsible for cash receipts and disbursements, for cash flow. He was the general manager of the bank.

Samuel C. Smith also served as Treasurer of the Boyne City Board of Trade. On January 12, 1908, the editor of the *Boyne Citizen* wrote: "There isn't a reason why every business man, every manufacturer, every professional man in Boyne City should hesitate a moment in becoming a member of an organization having for its object the promotion of the material interests of Boyne City." The Beulah Home attachment to the brochure the *Boyne Citizen* produced to promote the Board of Trade included the following observation: "Boyne City is proud of the fact that it is the scene of one place (the Beulah Home) of effort to give these boys a chance and people from far and near will realize that this place has something more than great mills and factories for money getting and that its citizens are men of sentiment and philanthropy who give as well as receive."

 Samuel Smith served as Sunday School Superintendent of the Boyne City M.E. Church. His religious background, his leadership position on the Board of Trade, and his outspoken support for the prohibition of alcohol, all encouraged his enthusiastic service on the Beulah Home board. He was Cashier of the First National Bank and knew that Swift maintained a large deposit of money at the bank. But curiously, given Smith's educational background in accounting and his financial job, he served as "secretary" of the Beulah Home board of directors and Hubert Bell, the school superintendent, served as "auditor." Neither man understood the flow of money into and out of the Home. Later both would regret this.

The seventh and last member of the Beulah Home board of directors was Peter F. McIntire, who served as Vice-President. McIntire, like White and Harris, served as a trustee of the Boyne City M.E. Church. He also taught a Sunday evening Bible class at the Church. In 1907, McIntire was sixty-three years old, fifteen years older than the next oldest member, William H. White. Godfrey Von Platen and William S. Shaw were only thirty-seven and forty, respectively. Peter McIntire operated a hardware store on Water Street and also served on the Boyne City School Board. His kind face, charcoal eyes, and long white beard made him look like Santa Claus.

Herman Swift had attracted a group of ambitious, successful, important, and distinguished

Boyne City citizens to serve on the Beulah Home board. Five of the seven board members were prominent figures in the Boyne City M.E. Church. This was a group that would help Swift promote the Home and most importantly would help him raise money. Peter McIntire was least distinguished and important among the group, but he would be the only board member to stick with Herman Swift through the Boyne City Affair.

On November 2nd, 1908, the *Boyne Citizen* reported on Herman Swift's plan to raise money for the grand new building at the Beulah Home. In an article titled: "Beulah Home Raising Building Fund" the *Citizen* reported: "In a grand attempt to raise $5,000 before Thanksgiving Day, Manager Swift of the Beulah Home took his boys quartette to Petoskey Sunday and entertained one of the largest audiences which was ever gathered in that city at the Presbyterian church and as a result the collection amounted to $400. At the close of the service Mr. A.B. Klise, a public spirited citizen, presented the boys with a check for $1,000 while Mrs. Klise gave them another $60 making the total $1,460.

The boys must raise $400 before Thanksgiving Day in order to make the $5,000 which if they succeed will be the means of receiving another $5,000 donation to be used in the erection of another large building to accommodate a large number of boys who are constantly seeking admission to the home.

At present there are 80 boys in the home and the new building which is to be 60 by 60 feet square and three stories high will afford room for many homeless waifs. The boys expect to be able to do much of the building work themselves the raw material being close at hand and they will do as much of it as possible under the supervision of a master builder. The work of saving the homeless waifs is a very deserving one and should meet with the hearty support of everyone especially at this time of year."

As early as 1908, Herman Swift met a man who would make significant contributions to the promotion of the Beulah Land Farm for Boys. This man was a tradesman, a photographer named Edward Beebe. Beebe lived in Kalkaska, a gritty northwestern Michigan lumbering and railroad town located on the G.R.&I. main line some thirty-two miles south of Boyne Falls. By 1908, he had exhausted most of the photography opportunities in Kalkaska and was rapidly expanding his territory, traveling by rail and capturing photographs in places like Beaver Island, Leland, Elk Rapids, Suttons Bay, and Boyne City.

On September 23rd and 24th of 1908, Beebe attended the Charlevoix County Fair in East Jordan. He may well have arrived on the lake steamer that carried Herman Swift, his assistants, and the Beulah Home boys from Boyne City to the Fair. Fig.9 is a Beebe photo postcard showing the: "Beulah Home Boys at East Jordan Fair '08." The photo includes fifty-one boys. The man standing without a hat, the fourth standing figure from the right side of the picture is Herman Swift. The woman to Swift's right is almost certainly Grace Swift.

The horses and carriages in the photograph no doubt belonged to kind East Jordan citizens who provided transportation to carry the Beulah boys from the dock to the Fair. In 1908, Charlevoix County contained three principle towns: Charlevoix, Boyne City and East Jordan. This is still true today. Charlevoix lies at the top of Lake Charlevoix (Pine Lake in 1908), Boyne City lies at the bottom of the long East Arm of the lake, and East Jordan lies at the bottom of the other long arm, the South Arm. East Jordan, like Boyne City, was a blue-collar town, while Charlevoix, at least during summer, was a blue-blood town. All three towns play roles in this story.

On March 11th, 1909, the *Kalkaskian*, one of Kalkaska's two weekly papers, printed the following small article: "E.L. Beebe has just completed a large order of pictures for Beulah Home. There were 2300 postcards and 300 large views." I have never seen an example of the "large views." This is unfortunate because these views undoubtedly better represented both the pictures of the Beulah Home and Edward Beebe's photographic art. Search in antique stores, flea markets, and at postcard shows, and it is possible to find examples of Beebe's Beu-lah Home postcards. Eastman Kodak introduced photographic postcard stock in 1902. This stock allowed a photographer to print a photograph on postcard sized heavyweight paper. On one side the paper contained a preprinted postcard form and the other side was coated with a photosensitive material. The stock allowed Beebe and other photographers to participate in what is known as the "Golden Age of Postcards," a period running roughly from 1904 to 1915. People mailed millions of postcards and by 1909 postcard collecting was the biggest hobby in the United States. Both Edward Beebe and Herman Swift recognized this fact. Over the course of his mission career, Swift had made good use of photography, including the fine cabinet cards produced by G. Lissau in Chicago, to promote his cause and to raise money. By 1908, Swift had abandoned the cabinet card and had turned to the postcard. And when he commissioned a series of Beulah Home postcards he did not turn to an excellent local photographer named Russell Leavenworth, but rather to Beebe whose reputation he believed would boost the sales of the postcards across the State of Michigan and across the country. These Beulah Home post-cards play a significant role in this story.

In late February or early March of 1909, Edward Beebe traveled the Grand Rapids and Indi-ana railroad from Kalkaska to Boyne Falls. There he changed trains and traveled northwest to the depot in Boyne City. Herman Swift met him at the depot and together they traveled in a horse drawn farm wagon to the Beulah Home. Beebe took a wonderful series of photographs at the Home. Five of these are interior views. Fig.10 is a photo of Beulah boys swimming in the heated pool in the basement. Fig.11 is a photo of the boys seated in the large school classroom in the basement. Fig.12 is a photo of the boys washing up in the first floor lavatory. Fig.13 is a photo of the boys seated in the first floor dining room. Herman Swift sits in the far right background of this photo. I believe that the woman to the far right and in the middle of the photo is Mable Hardy and the woman to Mable's right is Leonora Ferris. Fig.14 is a photo of the boys posed with floor hockey sticks in the large gymnasium located on the top floor of the Home.

Beebe took at least two pairs of "before" and "after" photos at the home. Fig's 15 and 16 show the boys first posed on four sleds preparing to slide down the hill toward the lake and next the resulting "mix up" following their slide.

Fig's 17 and 18 show a boy in a barrel. I am not certain of the identity of the boy, but I believe that he is a nine-year-old named Jimmy or Jimmie Fair. And I believe that Jimmy was an orphan and that perhaps Herman or Grace Swift gave him his name. These pictures carry significant symbolism that comes directly from a popular Herman Swift sermon as he preached of saving boys, waifs who struggled to survive "living in barrels on the streets of Chicago." The first of these pictures shows the boy sleeping in the barrel and is titled: "Where we found Jimmy—Your little brother and mine." The second shows the boy as he departs the barrel. This picture is titled: "Good Morning – This is the day I depart for the Beulah Land Farm for Boys in Boyne City." "Good Morning" was a title Beebe used in other photographs. There is an inference that the barrel photos were taken in Chicago, but Beebe took them at the Beulah Home in early 1909, probably at a point where a shed met the brick exterior of the Home's basement.

Herman Swift placed the Beebe Beulah Home postcards in a large suitcase that he carried along to the various sites where he and the boys performed across the State of Michigan. He sold the cards individually and probably in the form of a package. The first card in the package would have been the card shown in Fig.19. Many photographs were taken of the Beulah Home, but this is the finest. It captures the architecture of the building as well as the scale, displaying the entire front or lakeside as well as the entire west side of the building. Boys are posed standing on the first floor porch as well as on the first floor railing.

As Beebe worked on his Beulah Home postcard series, he also completed a series of Boyne City postcard views. Fig.20 is card "302" in the series, a photograph of the little Boyne City, Gaylord, and Alpena (B.C.G.&A.) railroad depot in Boyne City. A number of the Beulah boys stand in the foreground of the picture.

Local Option

Supporters of prohibition lost a Michigan statewide election in 1887. Largely in response to this, the Michigan Local Option Law was passed by the state legislature in 1889. The law allowed Michigan counties to establish their own regulations in a number of areas, but the principal feature was a provision allowing individual counties to make it unlawful to manufacture or sell intoxicating liquors when a majority of the county electors voted in favor of prohibition. Within a few years the term "local option" came to represent a vote on the issue of prohibition and dry counties were termed local option counties. By the spring of 1908, only eleven of Michigan's eighty five counties had adopted the local option, but the prohibition forces were gaining strength spurred on by efforts of church groups, particularly the Baptists and the Methodist Episcopalians, and spirited actions by the Women's Christian Temperance Union. Twenty-nine Michigan counties, including most of those in the northern Lower Peninsula, would vote on the local option in the spring elections of 1909.

Local option articles dominated the front pages and editorial sections of northern Michigan newspapers in early 1909. In February that year, petitions for a local option vote were presented to the Charlevoix County Board of Supervisors. Attorney John M. Harris and his partner L.F. Knowles appeared on behalf of the local option committee. Charlevoix attorney Lisle Shanahan appeared on behalf of a man named Len Adams. Leonard Adams ran a saloon in the town of Charlevoix. Shanahan sought to void the petitions on the basis of a number of creative arguments. Among these were the facts that a number of voters had signed the petitions using initials rather than full names, the petitions were not the proper color, and the local option represented illegal seizure of property and was unconstitutional under the laws of the United States and the State of Michigan. These arguments failed and the Board of Supervisors unanimously approved a local option vote as part of the Charlevoix County spring election to be held on April 5th, 1909.

On March 23rd, 1909, the *Boyne Citizen* reported: "The Beulah Home boys were present at a mass meeting held in Petoskey (Petoskey is the county seat in neighboring Emmet County) Sunday in the interests of the local option. It was a rousing meeting, and reports from Petoskey are to the effect that Emmet County will be in the dry column."

Herman Swift promoted his mission through support of a number of progressive causes. For example, Fig.21 is a photograph of Swift, the Beulah Home boys, and a group of ladies from the Anti-Cigarette League posed on the steps and porch on the west side of the Beulah Home. But aside from his general appeal to Christian groups, Swift found his greatest promotional opportunity in participating in the prohibition or local option movement.

The local option mass meetings must have carried Herman Swift back to the revival meetings he had experienced as a boy in Eaton Rapids and as a young man in Chicago and Buffalo. They provided a tremendous stage for the Beulah boy speakers and singers. For Herman Swift they provided an ideal venue for a sermon combining a message of the importance of his mission to save street waifs with a message of the evils of alcohol.

Swift certainly viewed the local option meetings as exceptional fund raising opportunities, but he also carried a strong belief developed over a number of years that parental alcohol abuse was the principal cause of homelessness for street boys. *Give the Boy a Chance* provides short life stories of a number of the boys at the Children's Temple Home, including: "Lee, Herbert and Fred, ages 14, 12, and 10 years. Father a hopeless paralytic brought on by sin and drink." "Willie, age 9. Mother died from abuse and neglect of a drunken husband." "Otto (midget), age 7. Mother dead and father a drunkard. The father would compel the boy to accompany him to saloons and sing for money and drinks." Finally: "James, age 6. He and his mother were picked up from the streets half famished, by the police and taken to the Station. James says he hopes he will never see her again as she used to get drunk and beat him so hard." Herman Swift's powerful stories of boys whose lives had been damaged or threatened by alcohol abuse raised support for the local option and for the Beulah Home.

Elisha Clink

The *Charlevoix County Herald* was a newspaper published each Saturday in the town of East Jordan. On March 27th, 1909, the *Herald* carried an article titled: "Option Rally at Opera House." East Jordan attorney Elisha N. Clink figured prominently in that article. Clink had served as postmaster in East Jordan and then was admitted to the practice of law in that city in 1890. In 1909 he was forty-nine years old and an imposing man with a strong voice. He had served a term as prosecuting attorney but now was considered the pre-eminent defense attorney in Charlevoix County.

Elisha Clink gave one of the most persuasive and spirited speeches at the Option Rally. Among other things, he said: "The problem of the liquor traffic is one of the greatest the American people were ever called upon to solve; yet we are capable of solving it, and we will settle it right. The people are awakening as never before. Saloon keepers have brought it upon themselves. No sooner do they get a license than they provide a gambling outfit also and deprive a man of his money. During my term as county prosecuting attorney every saloon keeper arrested for violation of the law said, 'Why don't you arrest the other fellow also.'" Elisha Clink and Herman Swift were well acquainted as a result of their common interests in fighting for the Local Option.

Acquiring the "Quarter"

Over the course of March and April of 1909, Herman Swift accomplished one of his major life goals, ownership of a piece of property totaling 160 acres, a "quarter." Herman had acquired 120 acres when he acquired the Beulah Home and adjoining properties in the Chapman and Addis Addition from Alverado Boise back in 1903. In following years, kind citizens, including William Addis and his wife Jean, had donated lots in the Addition to "Herman Swift, sole trustee of the Beulah Home." Swift also acquired parcels seized by the State of Michigan for nonpayment of taxes. He paid one dollar for each of these parcels. Herman never paid property taxes and this would become a legal issue at a later date. Judge John M. Harris and his wife provided one of the last pieces to Swift's 160-acre dream when they donated their 19 lots in the Chapman and Addis Addition to "Herman Swift, sole trustee of the Beulah Home" on March 16th, 1909.

Herman Swift's important mission at the Beulah Home was interrupted by the tragic death of his sister Belvia on April 15th, 1909. Belvia was only forty-three. She had been a strong supporter of Herman's. I believe Belvia visited the Beulah Home on a number of occasions, staying for rather lengthy periods in a private room in the basement. Fig.22 is a cabinet card photograph of Herman's sisters Belvia and Blenn. G. Lissau took this photograph on an occasion when the two sisters visited Herman in Chicago. Belvia is on the right side of the photograph and Blenn on the left.

Herman now had lost two sisters, Belvia and Beulah. Two sisters remained, Blenn and Harriet, and he would lean heavily on these women as he passed through the Boyne City Affair.

On April 5th, 1909, Charlevoix County residents voted on the Local Option. In East Jordan, church ladies rented a downtown building and began providing free food at seven A.M. As folks ate, the ladies sang prohibition songs to the accompaniment of an orchestra. Church bells in town rang every hour to remind people to vote for the Local Option. Charlevoix County residents passed the Option by a margin of over twelve hundred votes. At eight P.M. all the factory whistles in Boyne City blew simultaneously in celebration of the vote. The sound could be heard all over the county.

Charlevoix County was one of nineteen Michigan counties to vote in the Local Option on April 5th, 1909. Thirteen saloons in Boyne City closed their doors the end of that month. Herman Swift was happy about this result, but it deprived him of a major fund raising vehicle. This may have been one of the factors that spurred Herman to refocus his attentions on the grand new building. Over the spring and summer of 1909, he accelerated his efforts to raise money for the building. The Beulah boys performed across the state. Grace sold glass, ceramic, and pressed metal novelties imported from Germany (Fig.23). Swift continued to promote his dime books. And he promoted and sold "cocoa cereal." Fig.24 is a postcard advertising this product. The boy pictured in the postcard was a Beulah Home boy who Herman and Grace called "Sunbeam." "Tickled to Death," says Sunbeam, "because we have cocoa cereal to drink at Beulah Land Farm for Boys." The postcard closes with a reference to the "H.L. Swift Cocoa Cereal Co., Boyne City, Michigan."

A monthly newsletter, *The Youths' Outlook*, represented another Herman Swift promotion and fund raising venture. The newsletter contained two subtitles: "For Boys and Girls Under Seventy," and the Coleridge quotation: "It were better to gain the prayer of a fatherless child than to secure the favor of an emperor." Herman Swift served as editor and publisher of the newsletter. It was mailed monthly from the Boyne City post office suggesting that it was printed by one of the Boyne City newspapers. The newsletter carried an annual subscription price of fifty cents. Advertising rates were one dollar per inch and Swift boasted of a circulation that ranged from twenty thousand to forty thousand copies.

Herman Swift provided the following notice to readers of the January 1911 issue of *The Youth's Outlook*: "If you find a large 'O' on the margin of your paper it is to notify you that your subscription to 'The Youth's Outlook' has expired. The paper is sent regularly to its subscribers until a definite order to discontinue is received and all arrears paid. Kindly renew by sending us 50 cents for another year.

If you find a large 'F' on the margin of your paper it is to remind you that you are forgetting the month of your pledge to the Beulah Land Farm. Kindly remit as soon as possible that this good work may be pushed to the limit. We are depending on you and are sure you will not fail us.

If you are paid up in full and a Beulah Boy has made a mistake in stamping an 'F' or 'O' on your paper just turn to your wrapper and see the date and if it is stamped 9-11 it means that you are paid in full and so credited on our records to the ninth month-September, 1911. Boys are nearly as bad as men in making blunders and therefore pay no attention to the big 'O' or 'F' if you do not deserve it.

Kindly remember that when it is your heart's desire to help Mr. Swift in his boy saving proposition, that there should not be a dozen different ways to make out money orders. All checks or orders should read to Hermon L. Swift or to his wife, Mrs. Grace Swift and envelopes so addressed and in care of 'The Youth's Outlook,' Boyne City, Michigan, in order to have it properly credited and amount of gift acknowledged in this paper."

The scope and success of Herman Swift's fund raising activities are illustrated in a front page *Boyne Citizen* article published on July 2nd, 1909. The article is titled: "At Beulah Home, Many of the Boys Received Gifts from the Excursionists:" It reads:

"The *Citizen* told last Tuesday of the big excursion to the Beulah Home from Traverse City and the following anent (regarding) the excursion is taken from the *Traverse City Record*.

Two hundred and seventy-five people took in the excursion to Beulah Home at Boyne City yesterday, where the ground was broken for the new building which Mr. Swift is to build for his boys.

There are 85 boys at the home and after the prayer by the Rev. Demas Cochlin these boys treated the visitors to singing which was wonderful and impressed the hearers of the good and great work which Mr. Swift has accomplished. Some of the lady visitors took shovels and tossed a few shovels of the sand into the wagon.

The boys at the home had been looking forward to the coming of the excursionists and while some of them were a little disappointed that there were not books enough to go around they all enjoyed the books the other boys received. A great many of the ladies in the crowd gave small change to the boys who did not receive books.

Mr. Swift is very proud of his boys and the visitors noticed the affection which exists between Mr. Swift and the boys, which is very apparent. There is a large swimming pool in the basement of the building where the boys can splash all they want to in the winter time, steam pipes all around the room keeping it at the right temperature for swimming.

The excursionists all came home feeling that they were amply repaid for their trip and are very enthusiastic over the school and the work.

Mrs. Arvilla Gardner was among the passengers on the *Chequamegon*. A great number of the passengers carried books for the boys there and a peculiar incident took place when Mrs. Gardner took her book to the home. The drive from the dock to the home was some distance and when the passengers arrived at the home they were glad to seek the shelter of the building. Mrs. Gardner was seated by the window holding the book which she had taken in her lap and had written across the front page of the book: 'This book is for a boy named Georgie' and had told Mr. Swift that if there was a boy there by the name of George that he should have the book, as George had always been a favorite family name with her. She had scarcely become seated when a small boy appeared with two tin cups filled with cold water and asked her if she would like a drink. Being somewhat warm she took the water and thanked him for it after which she asked him what his name was. To her complete surprise the boy said his name was George Gates, whereupon she immediately presented him with the book and he was a very much surprised boy and very delighted with the book.

The home was recently presented with an acylindrical sliding fire escape from some parties in Detroit that are interested in the home. The fire escape cost $1,000 and is greatly enjoyed by the boys, who can start at the top (of the Beulah Home building) and without stopping slide to the bottom within two feet of the ground. Some of the lady visitors also took a trip down the fire escape and pronounced it a good thing."

Arvilla Gardner was a widow who lived by herself in a home on Park Street in Traverse City. Following her trip as an excursionist, I believe she continued to look after the welfare of George Gates. George was a small ten-year old boy when he met Arvilla. He was born in Mancelona, Michigan and lived there with his mother, father, and older brother Nelson. George's mother died of heart disease when he was only five. His father William was a barber in Mancelona, but at some point it seems that William left town. When he left he placed his oldest son Nelson with a family in Mancelona and he placed his younger son George in the Beulah Home. At the Home, George shared a room on the second floor with a boy named Elliot Fay. Elliot would play a leading role in the Boyne City Affair while George would play a minor role. Apparently one of the people who had Arvilla's favorite family name was a nephew named George Gardner who lived in Newburg Township down in Cass County, Michigan. George worked as a laborer. His friend

W.R. Clendening operated a livery stable in the township. In the Federal Census taken in the spring of 1910, George Gates did not live at the Beulah Home, but rather lived in Newburg Township, Cass County. He lived as a "ward" of W.R. and Luella Clendening, there in the home where Arvilla had placed him at the beginning of the Boyne City Affair.

As years passed, when one asked North Boyne City old-timers about their recollections of the Beulah Home, they happily would recall the times as children when they visited the Home and joined the Beulah boys sliding down the fire escape. They always discussed the fire escape, but they preferred not to recall the Boyne City Affair, the Time of Troubles.

Beulah Home Boys at East Jordan Fair - September 1908 (Fig.9)

Swimming Pool (Fig. 10)

Classroom (Fig. 11)

Lavatory (Fig.12)

Dining Room (Fig.13)

Gymnasium (Fig. 14)

Winter Sport (Fig. 15)

A mix-up (Fig.16)

"Where We Found Jimmy" (Fig.17)

Good Morning - This is the day I depart for the Beulah Home (Fig. 18)

Boyne City Beulah Home (Fig. 19)

B.C.G.&A. Railroad Depot (Fig.20)

Anti-Cigarette League at Beulah Home (Fig.21)

Blenn and Belvia (Fig.22)

Beulah Home Novelties (Fig.23)

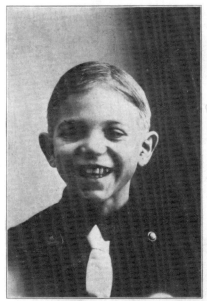

Cocoa Cereal (Fig.24)

VI

⟨⟩

Into the Time of Troubles

One might argue that Herman Swift's missionary career peaked close to that day the excursionists visited from Traverse City. The Beulah Home's next appearance in the *Boyne Citizen* came in a September 7th, 1909 article titled "Runs Away" and subtitled "A New Beulah Home Boy Gets Into Trouble." The article reads:

"Probate and Juvenile Judge (John M.) Harris held juvenile court at the Beulah Home yesterday, and two boys were tried, found guilty and sentenced.

One night last week Anderson's Club House, the Eagle Club, on Glenwood Beach, was broken into and about $12 worth of candy and a lot of gum was stolen. Suspicion pointed to Beulah Home boys as the guilty ones. Supt. Swift discovered the guilty parties to be Franklin Haley a recent arrival at the home from the Soo, and Frank Hall, another recent arrival. Juvenile Judge Harris was communicated with and yesterday he held court at the Home. The boys confessed to the robbery and were sentenced to receive lashes on the back at 4 o'clock this afternoon, and to be locked up alone until that time, and the judge designated Supt. Swift to administer the beating, which he refused to do.

After the trial the Haley boy ran away from the home and was caught at Boyne Falls yesterday by Deputy Sheriff Meeker, who brought the boy to the Beulah Home in this city. As a punishment for running away and to keep him from repeating the performance, a whiffletree chain was locked to his right ankle. In this way he spent the night last night. This morning when he got up he again ran away, and went to the home of Mrs. Thomas Burdick, who gave him his breakfast and notified Chief of Police Beach. When the officer found the boy he broke the lock and released the chain and brought him to City Attorney Urquhart's office, where the boy told a pitiful story of alleged cruelty, but he was caught in several lies, and it was evident the fear of the whipping he was to receive was the cause of his running away. Supt. Swift was communicated with and he came after the boy with the horses and while Mr. Swift was attending to some business, and while the rig was stationed in front of the post office, the boy ran through the post office and out into the alley and again made his escape. Two Beulah Home boys were sent after him, but at last accounts he had not been captured.

This is only one of many similar experiences with boys when they come to the home. They are only boys and they get home-sick or lonesome and imagine they are in prison and immediately resolve to escape. Especially is this true with boys of vicious habits and temperaments, who have not yet seen the bright side of a good home. The Haley boy claimed his mother works in a laundry at the Soo and that his father is dead, and evidently by his talk he has been mixed up in many scrapes from that part of the state where he came from.

Supt. Swift stated to the *Citizen* that none of his old Beulah boys who had been there had ever taken a cent wrongfully from anyone in Boyne City. The boys seem to think the world of Mr. Swift and he exercises a firm but parental care of them."

Frank Hall

Frank Hall was born in Big Rapids, Michigan in the spring of 1900. His mother's maiden name was Lula Breyford. Lula married a man named James Hall in 1895. She was only seventeen. By 1900, Lula and James had two daughters and then Frank was born and then James left. Lula lived with her mother and father, five siblings and three children in a small house in Big Rapids.

Several years later, Lula and James got back together. They had two more sons. One of their daughters married. James worked as a switchman on the railroad. And for some reason, in the summer of 1909, they placed Frank in the Beulah Home. Shortly after the candy theft incident, when the Time of Troubles arose at the Home, Lula and James arranged for Frank to leave. I believe he was placed with the Dilille family in Boyne City. Joseph Dilille worked as an engineer at Boyne City Chemical. He and his wife Lucinda lived at 401 Silver Street, a block away from the Beulah Home. In the spring of 1910, Frank Hall did not live with his parents and he did not live at the Beulah Home. A ten-year old boy named Frank did live with the Dililles.

Franklin Monroe Haley

Were it not for the article about the stolen candy, we would not know that the residents of the Beulah Home included Frank Hall and Franklin Haley. Franklin Haley must have been an interesting boy. The word "Soo" in the *Boyne Citizen* article refers to Sault Ste. Marie, a town located at the far eastern edge of the Upper Peninsula of Michigan, some eighty-seven miles northeast of Boyne City. The town's name means rapids of St. Mary's in Old French. It sits along the rapids of the St. Mary's River that connects Lake Superior with Lake Huron. The first lock in the river was constructed in 1855. Since then locks have been added, improved, and expanded in size to allow passage of large ships between the two lakes.

The famous Soo Locks are among the busiest in the world. They were busy in 1899 and Sault Ste. Marie was a busy, rambunctious, and tough town. The sidewalks bustled with the passage of loggers and sailors and laborers. Between Main Street and the river they constructed buildings from the beautiful rock pulled from the river bottom as they dug the locks. Amidst these buildings they constructed large, rambling wooden boarding houses. And further away from the river, up the hill, they constructed wonderful Victorian mansions for the shipping and lumber barons.

Franklin Monroe Haley was born in Sault Ste. Marie on October 19th, 1899. The *1899 Return of Births in the County of Chippewa* submitted to the "Honorable Secretary of State of Michigan" provides limited but interesting details about Franklin's birth. Franklin's mother was named

"Euphemia" and she was born in "Massachusetts." Franklin's father was "unknown" and "dead" and clearly one of these claims was untrue.

Euphemia Haley was born Louisa R. Vigeant in January of 1881. Her father Seraphim Vigeant was a sales agent for pianos. Her mother Elenore ran a boarding house. The stereotype for the father of a Beulah boy was a "drunkard." The stereotype for the mother was a "laundress." Herman Swift wrote in *The Youth's Outlook*:

"Among the scores of appeals received at the Beulah Farm for us to receive boys, come three most pitiful letters from widows. Two of these widows have four children each and the third has five, which they have been obliged to support for years. They have kept up this cruel and unequal struggle for a mere existence by washing clothes. There is so much competition among poor wash women who can find no other work which will leave them at home with their children that the price is pitifully small. The rich lady is shocked if she is obliged to pay two dollars for a two days' big washing and ironing and the wash women furnish the soap. Is it not asking enough for a poor woman to stand as both mother and father to a little flock of five even if all the means are provided and someone hired to do their washing for them? There is no question but what it is impossible for a frail woman to properly care for her children and also earn their living, pay for rent, fuel and clothing from washing of clothes.

Picture to yourself two rooms for a family of five and then with one of these rooms most every day of the week steaming with vapor from boiling clothes and lines strung about the stove on stormy days that clothes may be dried in time.

What refining or helpful home influences could ever be exerted over children in such a surrounding even by the best of mothers? No wonder the boys seek the streets and evil places of resort. The following letter is just one of many which the mails bring into the Beulah Farm:

'Dear Mr. Swift: Will you find one more unfortunate boy a home? He is eleven years old, his father is dead, and myself, his mother, has to wash for the support of five.

Please help me with this boy. I know I am asking a great deal, but if you will only take this boy for a couple of years, at least, I will try and help clothe him and help in all the ways I can.

I will give you five dollars cash toward his keep this winter and furnish the quilts for his bed. Yet we are so very poor and we have no home of our own. I cannot manage the boy at all, for he will swear at me and has got so he will lie and steal and cause me no little trouble. I am just heartbroken over him. If it is impossible for you to take him what shall I do or could you give me the address of some place where they would have him; but, Mr. Swift, take him if you can, for our home is so cold and—well, I am almost wild with care and anxiety for my family.

For over seven years I have had to wash to keep us alive, and I am so tired of it all and so discouraged. I do not believe anyone can know how hard it is, but Mr. Swift, do have mercy on us and help me with just this one boy. He is my boy, even if he is bad, and I love him and I know you are the one who can make him into the best kind of a man. Please find five cents to pay for the postage for an answer as soon as you can. From an Anxious Mother.'"

Louisa R. Vigeant did not write this letter, but I believe she could have provided many of the same words. Louisa was a laundress and perhaps this is how she met Mr. Haley, Franklin's father.

I searched for Mr. Haley in the 1900 Federal Census for Sault Ste. Marie and located a man named Thomas Haley who worked as a day laborer and roomed at a boarding house at 218 Water Street. Thomas was twenty-two and Louisa was nineteen and they lived only a couple of blocks away from one another. Thomas was born in Ontario, Canada.

Louisa renamed herself Euphemia when Franklin was born and this seems very curious. A euphemism represents an act of substituting a mild or vague term for one considered harsh or offensive. For a time I believed Louisa's change of names signified a euphemistic act, although this seemed a bit of a stretch for a young washer woman. Then one day I happened to read an advertisement for a Louis Pesha postcard. Pesha, like Edward Beebe, was a famous early 20th century Michigan postcard photographer. The advertisement noted that Pesha's Ontario home was in Euphemia. Digging through old Canadian census data, I discovered that Thomas Haley, the Sault Ste. Marie laborer, came from Euphemia, Ontario, Canada. Louisa was poor, but also clever. I don't believe that she ever married Thomas Haley, but she took his last name and then took his hometown as her first name, so that one day we might identify Franklin's father.

In the late summer or early fall of 1909, Franklin Haley arrived at the Beulah Home. Franklin must have been a tough little boy. The *Boyne Citizen* reported that he had been involved in many "scrapes" with the law in the Soo. These occurred before Franklin had reached the age of ten. It may well be that probate court or school officials encouraged or forced Euphemia to send Franklin to the Home.

My guess is that Franklin led Frank Hall on the candy theft adventure. Frank appears at the beginning of the *Boyne Citizen* report of the adventure, but then disappears and the remainder of the story deals only with Franklin. We learn that he ran away after the trial at the Home and that Deputy Sheriff Meeker captured him some seven miles away in the town of Boyne Falls. Franklin most certainly did not walk to Boyne Falls. He hopped the train.

The Beulah Home boys referred to it as "hoppin' the train" or just plain "hoppin'." Hoppin' required a boy to sneak on a train, paying no fare, as the train sat at or slowly pulled away from a depot or a crossing. The act was dangerous and all the Beulah Home boys had heard stories of those who had lost legs or lives while hoppin'. But this did not discourage the boys, particularly those who had grown up in railroad centers like Grand Rapids or the Soo.

The B.C.G.&A. owned one hundred seventy eight freight cars and only four passenger coaches. Franklin did not ride coach. He leaped into a boxcar or onto a flat logging car in Boyne City and held on tightly as the train gathered speed on its seven-mile route to Boyne Falls. Only one track ran out of Boyne City and all trains leaving town made their first stop in Boyne Falls. Most boys who were hoppin' did not know for sure where the train was going. When Franklin hopped off the train in Boyne Falls he probably did not know where he was. He still was a month shy of his tenth birthday when Deputy Sheriff Meeker captured him and returned him to Boyne City.

Back at the Home a "whiffletree chain" was locked to Franklin's right ankle to prevent him from again running away. A man named William Sutton who died in Massachusetts in 1680 invented the whiffletree, a pivoting horizontal crossbar that is attached to the traces running from a draft animal. Whiffletree chains are used to attach the whiffletree to the vehicle or implement that the animal is pulling. They are heavy objects. While the whiffletree chain did not defeat

Franklin, it did slow him down. Early on a morning in September 1909, he arose. He probably carried that heavy chain as he carefully escaped the Beulah Home, crossed the grassy area over to Charlevoix Street and slowly made his way down the hill toward the lake. At the bottom of the hill he turned east on Michigan Avenue heading toward Boyne City and the depot. He passed several houses and then he could go no further. It still was dark when he knocked at the door of the home at 102 West Michigan Street. Mrs. Thomas Burdick answered the knock and ushered in the small boy dragging the whiffletree chain.

Mary Burdick's husband Thomas and her older son both already had left to get to their jobs at the Iron Works. Her youngest daughter Ruth was eleven and she curiously examined the visitor who dragged the heavy chain. Mary prodded Ruth from the room as she heard the words that rushed from the mouth of the boy as he explained his predicament. He said that he had been badly abused at the Beulah Home and that he must escape and return to his mother in the Soo. Mrs. Burdick calmed the boy and seated him in a wooden chair at the dining room table. She asked the boy what he might like for breakfast. She turned and walked to the kitchen. And as she prepared breakfast, she dialed the number at the police station. At the other end of the phone line, a large man, Police Chief Richard Beach, listened with concern and excitement to the whispered story told by Mrs. Burdick.

Police Chief Beach walked quickly to the Burdick home. He removed the whiffletree chain from Franklin Haley's ankle. Perhaps this was at the request of Mrs. Burdick, yet the removal of the chain also must show some sympathy for the plight of the boy on the part of Beach.

Beach next took the boy to City Attorney Arthur Urquhart's office. Here Franklin repeated the "pitiful story of alleged cruelty" that he had told both Mrs. Burdick and Police Chief Beach. Urquhart did not believe the story and called Herman Swift asking him to retrieve the boy and return him to the Home. Later Urquhart would regret this decision. Richard Beach immediately would regret his decision to remove the whiffletree chain for, as the *Boyne Citizen* reported, Franklin once more escaped, running out of Urquhart's office and down an alley while Herman Swift was engaged in other business, probably with Arthur Urquhart.

At the time of publication of the *Boyne Citizen* article on the candy theft, Franklin Haley had not been recaptured although, interestingly, "two Beulah Home boys were sent after him." It may be that Franklin escaped, but I imagine that he was recaptured and returned to the Home. I know that he did not remain there for long. When the Boyne City Affair arose, Euphemia Haley convinced the authorities in Sault Ste. Marie to return Franklin to her.

In the summer of 1910, Franklin Haley lived with his mother in a boarding house at 409 Portage Avenue West in the Soo. Euphemia worked as a laundress. I do not know what later became of Franklin Haley, but believe that he set the stage and played the lead role in the first act of the Boyne City Affair, the Time of Troubles.

The second act of the affair took place between September and the end of November of 1909. Herman Swift had escaped Franklin Haley's accusations. The *Boyne Citizen* had argued that the boys at the Home, particularly those of "vicious habits and temperaments," get "home-sick and lonesome and imagine they are in prison." This argument inferred a basis for boys running away as well as for boys making up accusations of abuse in order to escape the Home. In spite of this, a number of Boyne City citizens were concerned by Franklin Haley's claims. In response, Herman Swift took the offensive and on October 5th, 1909 the *Boyne Citizen* published a front-page article written by Herman Swift. The article summarized Swift's offensive, the second act of the affair. The title of the article is: "The Beulah Home" and the subtitle is: "Interesting Article Printed in The Youth's (Outlook.)" The article reads:

"The work of the Beulah Land Farm speaks for itself. The results have already been accomplished and my seventeen-year's efforts in saving the homeless and friendless lads prove what can be done for them. All over the state and in other states are found the most excellent young men who have been given a helping hand at this home. It is too late for the ignorant 'croaker' or evil-minded 'knocker' to affect to any extent the minds of intelligent people or the true friends of the Home. During the summer excursion season we have often had as many as two or three hundred visitors at the Home in a single day from various cities of the state, and this great crowd of people are returning to their homes to tell what they know personally of what is being accomplished in Beulah Land and the true spirit in which the work is being done.

The various probate judges of the state, the humane societies, missionary organizations, churches, superintendents of the public schools, are all pleading for us to take scores of homeless lads we have no room for or means to feed and clothe. Perhaps five hundred appeals have been refused this year. This would indicate to us that we surely have the confidence of the best of people, and their belief that this is just the proper place for a homeless lad. Among the entire two hundred received this past year it is true that five have not made good and have run away. They preferred tobacco, drink, cheap theatres and absolute freedom, and it may be were defectives or to a certain extent degenerate. They should have our pity, and the remaining one hundred and ninety-five should not be condemned on account of those five, and the entire work of Beulah Farm pronounced a failure because five boys could not be retained long enough to absorb the spirit of the Home.

I know of a minister of the gospel who had five children. Four of them were the most excellent to be found but one was a black sheep. He had received the same love and care, and in fact had brought more sorrow to the father and mother than all the other children put together, but it seemed that nothing could reach him. No one seemed to think the father was a failure because one in five had not been brought to the right life, and not for a moment did the people of the place cast any suspicion on the other four children because the one brother determined to be an outcast.

Last Sunday afternoon two Boyne City Sunday school boys were visiting the Home, and were up in the big gymnasium. A gentleman and a party of ladies were being conducted through the Home by one of the Beulah boys. Just as they reached the gymnasium one of those two boys let fall a swear word, and instantly the gentleman turned to one of the ladies and said, 'Do you see the kind of training they have here?' The Beulah boy overhead the remark and at once informed the man that the boys were neither one of them members of the Beulah Home, but were from two of the best families in Boyne City. This seemed to make the matter all right and perfectly proper. Why people should demand a higher standard for poor little waifs taken from boxes and barrels and hallways and from the slums of our large cities, boys who have never known a mother's care or love or training; than they do for boys raised with the greatest of care from babyhood is something beyond me to understand. There have been visitors who have remained at the Home several weeks, and in all their stay have never heard an oath from a boy of the Home. There is no claim that these little unfortunate lads are perfect for their whole life has been in the wrong direction before coming to Beulah Land, but I am sure if each one of the eighty odd lads in our care made as much trouble as the ordinary boy from the best kind of a home that we would have our hands full.

No good work in the world but what is criticized and censured in some way or another, and during all the years *The Youth's Outlook* has been printed I have never made any reply to the fault findings of anyone. I am not here to please the people, but to save boys to a useful manhood and cannot spend my time following up little false reports or unkind statements that may come from unreliable sources. I trust that this may be the first and last time that I may spend my effort whatever to assure people, even when they read reports in a newspaper, that often it must be taken with a grain of salt. I have been receiving requests from different parts of the state from friends who have seen a false statement in a daily published in a certain city of the state, and asking me to explain the matter fully and make it right. For this reason I will take up the space and time and trust that in future if anyone is in any doubt or do not understand fully anything regarding the work of the Home or any unpleasantness that may arise, that instead of taking the statement of a reliable paper which gives unreliable information that they will write to the Home at once and ascertain the real facts.

The press of the state have shown this work every kindness and consideration, and I feel confident that the little article slipped in without their giving it any thought or realizing what result might be in harming a good work. The reporter from the city from which the report was sent (not Boyne City by any means) should not make statements which he does not know to be true, and should not just from one "lying wag" as he says condemn this great work being carried on, on the shores of Pine Lake. For the sake of the daily and also the reporter making the report, I do not think for a moment that the reporter had any idea of doing this work harm, and as he probably did not know much about it, simply desired some interesting news to send in."

This is a very important article. Herman Swift wrote it to defend himself and the Home against the effects of two recent negative pieces of publicity. The first of these was a local Boyne City matter, the theft of the candy and the subsequent run-away episodes of Franklin Haley. The second was a statewide matter represented by the publication of a critical article in one of the state's "daily" papers. In 1909, almost all the papers in northern Michigan printed on a weekly basis. Given this and the fact that friends of Swift's from different parts of the state inquired about the critical article, it appears it was printed in one of Michigan's major city papers, perhaps in Detroit or Grand Rapids. The fact that the critical charge in the article was not mentioned in Swift's response suggests that the charge may have been a claim of abuse at the Home and the "lying wag" may have been an employee at the Home. Whether or not this is true, Herman Swift used his written response to address two attacks with two major themes.

That first theme is that there are indeed boys who behave badly. In the first half of Herman Swift's response, he writes that the Home served two hundred boys in 1909 and only five of them ran away. My research suggests that Herman over-estimated the number of boys served and under-estimated the number who ran away, but regardless of that, Herman assured the citizens of Boyne

City that the bad boys ran away and the good boys remained at the Home. In fact, Herman advised that the eighty boys at the Home were on average better behaved than the boys from the "best kind of home," and inferred they were better behaved than the "Sunday School boys" from Boyne City.

In the second half of his response, Swift addresses the reporter's critical article. No good deed goes unpunished suggests Swift. He writes that no good work goes without criticism or censure. He implores the reader to keep in mind the mission of the Home when confronted with "little false reports or unkind statements." Finally, he requests that questions about the work of the Home or any "unpleasantness" be referred in writing to him "at once" in order to "ascertain the real facts." Herman Swift avoided use of the word "accusation" in his response, but the second theme in his writing was that one should take accusations against a man of good works with a "grain of salt."

Perhaps the most interesting piece of Swift's response falls toward the middle, the story of the "minister of the gospel who had five children." All of the children received the same attention, the same gifts. Yet four of them were good and one was bad. He was the "black sheep" and determined to be "an outcast." The story suggests that even in good families there are boys who are degenerate and unable to achieve goodness. I don't believe that Herman Swift subscribed to that suggestion or belief. In fact, in his response article he takes the position that he even could have saved the five bad run-away boys if they could have been "retained long enough to absorb the spirit of the Home." Herman did not believe that there were innately bad and vicious boys, but as he entered the Time of Troubles he would allow others to make that argument and he would build upon his own themes that boys could be bad and that men of good works often suffered unfair accusations.

On October 4th, 1909, the day before the printing of the *Boyne Citizen* article, Herman offered up another public relations favor to Boyne City. That day the Boyne City Council met and the meeting minutes reflect the mayor reported that: "Mr. Swift of the Beulah Home has offered the city two eagles for the City Park, and that there is also offered the city a bear for the park, and (the mayor) said the city ought to take them and after some discussion motion was made by Stanford, supported by Tainter, that the matter be suggested to the Board of Public Works to make arrangements for the bear and eagles in the park."

The "arrangements" were left to Police Chief and Street Commissioner Richard Beach who vigorously pursued the assignment. He visited the Beulah Home and also traveled to Petoskey to evaluate the cages and care for the animals in the Petoskey City Park. City of Petoskey officials talked Beach into purchasing two of their park deer for what the November 15th, 1909 Boyne City Council minutes reflect was a "cheap price." While some Boyne City Council members questioned the generosity of the Petoskey officials, the two eagles, the bear, and the two deer became the staples in what would prove to be a popular zoo in the park in the middle of Boyne City. The bear and the deer appear in many old Boyne City postcards. The only photo I have seen of the eagles is shown in Fig.25, a photo of an eagle named "Old Abe" posed with Herman Swift and a Beulah boy on the grounds of the Beulah Home in the winter of 1908/1909. I assume that Herman named the other eagle "Lincoln."

Old Abe (Fig.25)

VII

~

The Arrest

erman Swift woke up at 5:30 A.M. the morning of Wednesday, December 1st, 1909. He awoke at this time every day of the week other than Sunday when he slept until 6:30 A.M. The Beulah Home staff was busy waking and organizing the boys. Herman's days started when they woke up the boys. December 1st started out in a routine way as Swift dealt with minor issues at the Home and wrote summary notes of his recent two-week missionary trip downstate with the Boys Quartette. He had returned home from that trip the evening of November 24th, 1909, the day before Thanksgiving. Mid-morning December 1st the tone of the day changed dramatically when someone alerted Herman that Simon Mack had run away and was down at the Justice of the Peace office leveling serious accusations of abuse directly at Swift. Herman grew very worried and flew into action. He instructed the teachers, Mabel Hardy and Leonora Ferris, to assemble the boys in the classroom.

All the Beulah Home boys aside from Simon Mack were present when Herman Swift addressed them the morning of December 1st. Most of the boys were aware that Simon had run away and many were aware of Simon's mission to bring claims of abuse to the ears of the authorities in Boyne City. Herman preached softly about the objectives and accomplishments of his Beulah Home. He addressed in broad terms what he would term the false and harmful accusations of abuse by Simon Mack. Then he posed a question to all the boys. He stressed that they should answer truthfully without fear of punishment. Mabel Hardy who taught the big boys at the Beulah Home would later testify that Swift asked the boys to respond by raising their hands if: "they had ever been ill-treated or ill-used in any way while at the Beulah Home." Mabel testified that none of the boys raised their hands.

Merrill Griffin is the boy who plays the most significant role in this story. Merrill was nine years old when he sat in the classroom and listened to Herman Swift preach on the morning of December 1st. Merrill later would testify that Swift had asked the boys to raise their hands if: "Mr. Swift had treated them right at all times." Merrill would testify that he and several other boys, including George Gates, did not raise their hands in response to the question.

Following the December 1st morning meeting with the boys, Herman Swift returned upstairs to his office. Herman had concerns. Perhaps Merrill Griffin correctly remembered the

Merrill Griffin's Letter (Fig.26)

important question posed by Swift at the morning meeting in the classroom. Perhaps Swift had taken careful note of the boys who had not raised their hands. Herman sat at his typewriter. He may have typed several letters. It is certain that he typed at least one. The letter was written on Beulah Home stationary. A photo of the Home appeared at the upper left hand corner of the single page. A bold heading, "Beulah Land Farm for Boys," crossed the top. Beneath the heading ran a smaller subtitle, "For the Rescue and Care of Homeless and Neglected Boys, Boyne City, Michigan." The letter was dated December 1st, 1909. It reads:

"My Dear Mr. Griffin,

I have been told so many times that your boy is a lad who should not be here as he needs no correction and I must prove to our Board of Managers that he is a boy who needs the special care and help we can give him.

I know when he came that he needed lots of attention and needed to be taught to be honest and truthful. I would be glad to have you write me a few lines by return mail to submit to our Board telling just the condition of the boy while in Grand Rapids and how unreliable he proved and how very much he needed the very training which we strive to give. Hoping to hear from you at once I remain:

Yours most sincerely, Hermon L. Swift, Manager"

The afternoon of December 1st, Grace Swift mailed the letter to Edward Griffin in Grand Rapids. Edward was Merrill Griffin's father.

As Herman Swift typed in his office, Leonora Ferris stood in the classroom and softly addressed the group of little boys. She asked which of the boys had mothers or fathers. Then, nervously, she asked those boys to construct letters describing truthfully, in their own words, the conditions at the Beulah Home. She assured them that she would mail the letters to their parents and that they would not get into trouble. She told them not to say anything about this to Mr. or Mrs. Swift. She stood guard at the door and watched the little boys search for words and scratch on small pages of lined, second-rate, notebook paper. I don't know how many little letters were handed to Miss Ferris that day, but I do know that she received at least one. It is a letter written by Merrill Griffin to his father. In the upper right hand corner of the first page Merrill wrote "Boyne City, Dec. 1, 1909." The letter reads: "Dear Father, I have something to tell you and wish you would take me home. If you write and tell me some-thing about going home address it to Mrs. Ferris, Beulah Home. For it is some thing very inportent. Mr. Swift is trying to make pretty near all the boys... (Author's note: here Merrill describes the abuse and claims it has happened to him.)

The lady that I want you to address the next letter to will send this letter. Almost all the boys are mad at Mr. Swift. I will be very glad if you take me home. The police say that the words of the boys under twelve years old will count more than the big boys over twelve. Over half of the boys stick up for the right side. He has a whole list of names on a piece of paper. He has mine and my playmates and a whole lots of others. All most all of the boy did not like it here after they herd what Mr. Swift is making the boys do. We are trying to get him in prison. Three years ago this same thing was found out. She asked all of the boys this morning if they had a father and mother. Celistana says that if they do not stick up for Mr. Swift they will go to the Detenchion Hospital. I think if you were a little boy and was here you would not like it either. Tel mamma and see what she say's. Do not let anybody know about it. All of the three women are quite mad about it two. Mrs. Ferris asked me to stay and she asked me if I would write a letter to you in plain words. I thought this was a nice place at first but I do not think much of it know. I do not know any more to write so good by. From Merrel Griffin.

Kisses for you and mamma."

Fig.26 is the last page of Merrill's letter. Leonora Ferris did not send the letter to Edward Griffin. She gave it to either Arthur Urquhart or Police Chief Beach the morning of December 2nd. The letter suggests that Miss Ferris had discussed claims of abuse at the Home well before December 1st. "Celistana" refers to a boy named Celestino Paradies. Celestino came from Cuba and the Beulah boys called him "Cuba." He was sixteen years old in 1909. Going from the left side of the Fig.14 photograph of the boys with hockey sticks, Celestino is the second boy wearing a white shirt. He was a big boy and served as an "inspector," helping to maintain the rules of the Home. The boys liked Cuba, but some feared him.

Police Chief Beach knocked hard on the Beulah Home door the afternoon of December 1st. Attorney Arthur Urquhart and another police officer, probably Timothy Heaton, accompanied Beach. Grace Swift met them at the door. She graciously led them to the basement classroom and then she left. The boys were seated in the classroom. Herman Swift greeted the three city officials. Leonora Ferris was the only other adult in the classroom. She stood in a corner and she was crying.

Beach and Urquhart escorted Swift upstairs and into his office on the first floor. Beach said, "I suppose you know what we are here for." Swift responded that he had no idea of the matter until noon that day.

Simon Mack had provided Beach and Urquhart with names of boys he claimed would tell the same story of abuse that he had told. Urquhart asked Swift if he could question those boys. Swift was very courteous and one by one he called in several boys. Urquhart later would recall that all were big boys and: "each one denied that Swift had taken liberties with them and insisted that they liked Mr. Swift and that he was a good man." Urquhart also recalled that each boy used the same words. In spite of this, he was about to conclude that Simon Mack's charges were baseless and ready to close the investigation when there was a rap at the door of the office. Leonora Ferris stood at the door. She still was crying when she handed Urquhart a note containing the names of several of the boys. "I would like to have you talk with these boys before you go away," Miss Ferris whispered. She trembled.

Urquhart escorted Leonora Ferris to another room. Officer Timothy Heaton went down to the classroom, assembled the boys on Miss Ferris' list, and brought them upstairs to meet with Urquhart, Ferris, and Beach. What I will term the "Miss Ferris group" included the following boys: Edwy Crane, Elliot Fay, George Gates, Merrill Griffin, John Hosner, James Leys, and Earnest Wardell.

All seven of the boys initially took the position that Mr. Swift had always been good to them. Urquhart figured that Miss Ferris would not have given him the list and would not have been so distraught if the boys had not provided her with information of abuse at the Home. He engaged the boys in conversation for over a half hour without mentioning Herman Swift. Then he asked the boys if they liked Miss Ferris. Each enthusiastically said that they did. Then he asked if they ever lied to Miss Ferris. Each insisted that they would never lie to her. Then he asked if they had lied when they told Miss Ferris about Herman Swift's acts of abuse against them. At that point, all the boys said that they had not lied and that Herman Swift was guilty.

The afternoon of December 1st, Urquhart pulled out his notebook and completed individual interviews with the boys. Urquhart, Beach and Heaton then departed the Beulah Home. They returned to the city building and discussed their findings in a telephone conversation with County Prosecutor Nicholas. Herman Swift experienced a short period of relief. The Ferris group of boys must have spent a fitful night. Some of them hid in secret places either in the Home or the barn. The following morning the three city officials returned.

When they returned to the Beulah Home on Thursday, December 2nd, 1909, Urquhart ordered Beach to arrest Herman Swift. Herman was shocked. He asked permission to call an attorney and Urquhart allowed him to make that call. Swift dialed a number and probably spoke to either John Harris or Leonard Knowles, attorneys who represented the Beulah Home and its Board of Directors. Then Beach, officer Heaton, Swift, Urquhart, and six boys walked down the steps from the first floor to the basement of the Beulah Home. As the others walked out the lower level lakeside door of the Home and headed down the Charlevoix Street hill, Urquhart paused to speak with three women who stood in the hallway to the classroom. One of them was Leonora Ferris. She handed Urquhart several letters. All three women were crying. Urquhart later wrote that one of them asked if Swift would be allowed to return. He recalled another of the three women crying: "Don't let him come back. There is nothing that man wouldn't do to gain his own ends."

Police Chief Beach had taken custody of six of the seven Ferris Group boys. Arthur Urquhart had made the decision not to take James Leys into custody. James and Earnest Wardell were the only two big boys in the Ferris Group, probably bigger than Herman Swift. Additionally, in his interview, James claimed he only had experienced one attempted act of abuse by Swift. That act was interrupted by the appearance of a Mr. Brown who was doing repair work at the Home. When Brown appeared, Swift departed. So James was big and in Urquhart's opinion he hadn't experienced what legally might be considered a chargeable offense. Urquhart elected to leave James behind at the Beulah Home and later he would regret that decision.

The three city officials, Herman Swift, and the six boys walked through the December snow and the afternoon darkness, down Michigan Avenue, right down Lake Street, into town, and to the office of Justice of the Peace, Elisha Shepherd. Shepherd sternly advised Swift to be patient. He first had to deal with the boys.

Shepherd and Urquhart initially discussed placing the boys temporarily in one of the hotels in Boyne City. They recognized, however, the great likelihood of the boys roaming the streets of town and sharing their stories with passing citizens. Neither one of them chose to risk that situation. Shepherd placed a call to a hotel in Petoskey. A woman answered the phone and cheerfully agreed to board the six boys. Officer Heaton herded the boys out of Shepherd's office and marshaled them to the Boyne City railroad depot. There they boarded the train to Boyne Falls. The boys were thrilled to ride coach. After a brief stop in Boyne Falls, officer Heaton and his charges boarded the G.R.&I. train that traveled north to Petoskey. They arrived at the fine depot in Petoskey early in the evening of December 2nd. Heaton was pleased that he still had them all in custody. He walked the boys along the tracks, through the pretty city park, across Mitchell Street to the entrance to the Clifton House Hotel.

The boys were excited to be in Petoskey. On prior occasions a number of them had hopped trains and enjoyed the sights of the town before being apprehended and returned to the Home. Petoskey today remains one of the principal towns in northern Michigan. In 1909, it was a busy place, a prosperous place full of enterprising people and a major attraction for summer tourists and resorters. The town was home to a number of fine hotels, but Elisha Shepherd selected the Clifton to house the Beulah boys because he knew the rate would be reasonable, the other guests would less likely object to the boys, and because he knew the owners of the hotel, John and Mary Rowan. Mary taught the first writing school and served as the first music teacher in Petoskey. She had successfully raised four children. She was very well equipped to manage six boys. She placed the boys two to a bed and made it her mission to keep them busy and happy. From the first day on, the Beulah boys never said they were staying at the Clifton. They said they were staying at "Rowan's."

Early into the boys' stay at Rowan's Earnest Wardell ran away. Earnest felt uncomfortable as the only big boy in the group. His older brother boarded in a house just down the street from the Beulah Home and worked as a logger. Later some would blame Arthur Urquhart for spiriting Earnest away. Urquhart denied this, but whatever the case, Earnest ran away from Rowan's and probably worked in a logging camp with his brother. At some point in the first half of 1910, he apparently returned to the Beulah Home. Earnest Wardell, age 15, is among the Beulah Home inmates recorded in the April 18th, 1910 Federal Census.

When Earnest Wardell ran away from Rowan's he left behind five little Beulah boys: Edwy

Crane, Elliot Fay, George Gates, John Hosner, and Merrill Griffin. Urquhart had interviewed all five of these boys and felt each had a valid claim against Herman Swift. Urquhart knew, however, that prosecution of this type of claim is very difficult. The case turns on the words of a child versus the words of an adult. Success would depend greatly upon the child's stamina and ability to withstand the pressures exerted by skilled defense attorneys during examinations and possibly a trial of the case. Urquhart carefully had to evaluate each of the five boys and their claims. Additionally, he would have to gain the support of a parent or guardian to bring forward a case. Based upon these and perhaps other factors, Urquhart elected to pursue claims for Elliot Fay, John Hosner, and Merrill Griffin, but not to pursue claims for either George Gates or Edwy Crane.

George Gates probably left Rowan's during the month of December of 1909 or January of 1910. At that time, probably with Arvilla Gardner's assistance, George was placed with a family in Newburg Township in southern Michigan.

Edwy Crane

Edwy Crane is a mystery boy. He appears as a boy named Edwy Crane in Attorney Urquhart's notes and several times in depositions and trial transcripts related to the Herman Swift cases, but I have found no historical record of Edwy Crane. He may be one of three boys: (1) an eleven year old Illinois boy named Edward Cramer who is listed among the Beulah Home inmates in the April 1910 Federal Census, (2) a boy named Dewey Crain who was born to a couple identified as Rebekha and Friend Crain in Ora, Illinois in December of 1898, or (3) a boy named Laverne Crane who was born in Battle Creek in October 1896.

Sometime during December 1910 Charlevoix County officials placed Merrill Griffin into his father's custody. In January 1910, they removed the remaining two boys, Elliot Fay and John Hosner, from Rowan's and placed them in the Charlevoix County Poor Farm. The farm was established in 1895. Residents stayed in a colonial style brick building. The farm was a thirty-five acre working farm. Residents had to work to eat. The Poor Farm was located in a rather remote location on Peninsula Road outside of East Jordan and this was a key factor in the placement of the two Beulah boys.

Santa Claus arrived in Petoskey on the 1:40 P.M. train on December 24th, 1909. The day was cloudy with occasional light snow. All the children meeting Santa at the depot were escorted to the Fred Glass Drug Store and there each received a present. I imagine Mary Rowan happily shepherded the Beulah boys to the depot and to the Fred Glass Store.

Herman Swift waited impatiently in Elisha Shepherd's office the afternoon of December 2nd, 1909. His attorney arrived. Beulah Board members William H. White and Samuel C. Smith arrived a bit later. The attorney waived Swift aside and explained what he knew of the situation to White and Smith. Then the three men met privately with Swift who explained in confidant terms his defenses against the abuse charges. Swift had been in this situation before.

Justice of the Peace Shepherd conducted the arraignment hearing, reading the arrest warrant to those gathered: Swift, Urquhart, Swift's attorney, White and Smith. Shepherd asked Swift if he understood the complaint. Swift said he totally denied the accusation and the complaint, but indicated that he did understand it. Shepherd told the group he would hold an examination hearing the following Tuesday, December 7th, 1909. He fixed bail for Swift at fifteen hundred dollars. William H. White and Samuel Smith signed the bail. They were the two senior officers of Boyne City's First National Bank and were well aware of the substantial amount of money that the Beulah Home had on deposit at their bank. I imagine that Herman Swift traveled back to the Home gathering his thoughts as he prepared to face Grace.

William H. White and Samuel Smith stood on the sidewalk outside Elisha Shepherd's office. They expressed deep concern as they discussed the situation with their attorney. At this time they doubted that Herman Swift was guilty of the charges, but they knew very shortly they would be faced with scandalous publicity.

On Friday, December 4th, 1909, the *Boyne Citizen* printed an article right at the top and in the middle of the front page of that day's edition. The headline reads in large, bold letters: "SENSATIONAL ARREST." In somewhat smaller, bold letters, the sub-headline reads: "Herman L. Swift of the Beulah Home Must Face an Awful Charge." The article in part reads:

"Herman L. Swift, Superintendent of the Beulah Home for Boys was arrested Wednesday night on complaint of Richard W. Beach, on information furnished by Elliot Fay an inmate of the Home, 9 years of age, who came here from Ypsilanti, Mich. The charge made against Mr. Swift is taking indecent liberties with Boys...Prosecuting Attorney Nicholas will have the case for the people, and L.M. Knowles and J.M. Harris have been retained by the board of trustees of the Home to make a thorough examination of the charges and see that justice is done if the defendant is innocent, and that he is punished if found guilty.

Owing to the position held by Mr. Swift and the nature of the charges against him, the *Citizen* refrains from comment on the case at this time."

Articles concerning the Boyne City Affair quickly appeared in newspapers across the State of Michigan. Some highlighted the arrest and the charges, but in the early days of the affair many articles communicated a more balanced view. The Rowans had a daughter named Ethyl Farqulle who worked as a newspaper reporter, perhaps for the *Petoskey Evening News*. Ethyl had been aware of the Boyne City Affair, including many of its more sensational details, since December 2nd. She lived at the Clifton House. But the *Evening News* held off coverage of the story until Monday, December 6th, when it printed the following third page article headlined: "The Attitude of the Evening News in Regard to Boyne City Affair." The article reads:

"Some people have been curious to know why the *Evening News* has refrained from printing an account of the unfortunate affair which is alleged to have occurred at the Beulah Home at Boyne City.

There are several reasons why the *News* has kept silence, all of which it considers valid and reasonable, besides being humane. To begin with: the News has no positive evidence that the tales are true, and it is the policy of this paper to verify all important news stories before printing them.

Again, the *News* could see no good end that could be advanced by giving any further publicity to a disagreeable matter, neither to the public nor the parties most deeply concerned. Then, the man who is under suspicion, whether right or wrong, has a hard enough battle to fight, without this paper adding unnecessarily to his already heavy burdens.

There will be a hearing of the matter Tuesday and it will doubtless get a thorough airing, and the whole truth be known as it ought to be and until such time the *News* will give the accused the benefit of the doubt and hope that he will have no difficulty in not only completely clearing his own name, but that of the school which has been the pride of northern Michigan."

The *Charlevoix Sentinel* carried a front-page story on December 9th, 1909. The headline was: "Swift in Trouble" and the sub-headline: "The Beulah Home Manager Arrested on Charges of Taking Indecent Liberties." The article reads:

"The shocking news is being published in the state papers that Herman L. Swift, manager of the Beulah Home for Boys at Boyne City, was arrested Thursday on complaint of Elliott Fay, a thirteen year old inmate of the Home, on the charge of taking improper liberties with him and several other boys.

Swift was arraigned the same day and furnished bail in the sum of fifteen hundred dollars, W.H. White and S.C. Smith signing the bonds. Swift claims it is a conspiracy among a few boys who want to leave the Home. He protests his innocence, and is confident that the conspiracy will be exposed.

The Beulah Home has, under the management of Mr. Swift, gained an enviable reputation all over Michigan as a model of its kind, and has received much financial aid from many Michigan cities. Mr. Swift has exhibited qualities that peculiarly fit him for the work, and has always had a wonderful hold on the boys of his institution—ruling with kindness and rare judgment. We shall not believe these charges until they are proven beyond the shadow of a doubt. In a colony of boys of the nature of those at the Beulah Home it is not strange if there are some bad ones, capable of combining against the controlling power of the institution, however benevolently that power is exercised. In fact, while some of them are there solely because they are homeless, a large majority are waifs, and many others of an unruly and vicious nature who are sent there by parents.

We shall believe Mr. Swift innocent until the evidence is overwhelming that he is guilty."

The *Sentinel* writer included at least one error of fact: Elliott was nine and not thirteen. But the most important thing to be taken from this article is the paper's trust and support for Herman Swift.

VIII

~

The Justice Court Examinations

rthur Urquhart reluctantly handed over his notes and his file on the Swift matter to Alfred B. Nicholas. Nicholas had started up a law practice in the town of East Jordan in 1895. By 1909, he was practicing in partnership with his son A. Burton Nicholas. Nicholas and his wife Anna lived with two daughters in a home at 234 Garfield Street in the north side of East Jordan. The home must have been rather substantial. Fred Boosinger, the leading merchant in town, and William Malpass, the leading industrialist, owned homes right across the street. Malpass owned the East Jordan Iron Works, East Jordan's major employer in 1909 and today.

Alfred Nicholas had been voted into the position of Prosecuting Attorney for Charlevoix County in the November election of 1909. In this position, he succeeded Elisha Clink. Clink also practiced law in East Jordan and lived on Second Street right around the corner from Nicholas. Clink had won the Republican primary for the prosecuting attorney's position in 1908 and this led to his certain victory in the general county election in November 1908. Clink served as prosecuting attorney for one year and then returned to a private practice that was more lucrative. This opened up the 1909 Republican primary to Nicholas and he won that primary and of course won the general election. I assume that they were friends, but Elisha Clink was older and more experienced than A.B. Nicholas. Clink soon would become the principal attorney defending Herman Swift.

The hearing on the case against Herman Swift was called to order in Justice of the Peace Shepherd's court at nine o'clock the morning of Tuesday, December 7th, 1909. The *Boyne Citizen* reported that: "Owing to the prosecuting attorney (A.B. Nicholas) being busy in court at Charlevoix the case was adjourned until Tuesday, December 14th, at 9 o'clock. The bonds were continued."

Perhaps Nicholas was "busy," but perhaps Urquhart was buying time. He had read Merrill Griffin's December 1st letter to his father and had corresponded with Mr. Griffin. Perhaps Urquhart had asked Shepherd to provide Mr. Griffin the opportunity to travel to Boyne City.

The objective of the hearing on December 14th was to allow Justice Shepherd to examine the State's evidence in order to determine whether it was sufficient to bind Herman Swift over for trial in the County's Circuit Court. In this case, the evidence consisted entirely of the statements of three little boys, boys the *Charlevoix Citizen* editor undoubtedly would consider to be "waifs."

Elisha Shepherd's court was called to order at promptly nine o'clock on Tuesday, December

14th. Shepherd read the charges against Herman Swift. A.B. Nicholas was present to represent the people of the county. John Harris and L.F. Knowles were present representing the Board of Trustees of the Beulah Home. It seems at this time that Herman Swift had not engaged an attorney and chose to depend on Harris and Knowles to represent his interests.

Nicholas promptly requested a recess until four o'clock. The *Boyne Citizen* reported that this was: "to allow Nicholas to interview the boys and see what evidence the people had." This suggests that Nicholas had not interviewed the boys prior to the hearing. He totally was depending on Urquhart. But perhaps Nicholas was stalling to better prepare the boys for what would be unfamiliar, difficult and grueling experiences on the witness stand. Perhaps he was stalling to accomplish something else.

When court returned to session at four o'clock, Nicholas discharged Swift on the original warrant and then re-arrested him on another warrant. The warrant was based upon information provided by John Hosner.

Johnnie Hosner

The press frequently misspelled John's last name as Housner, but it was Hosner. John was born in Ypsilanti, Michigan on April 15th, 1899. In 1900, he lived with his father, mother, and six siblings in a rented home at 950 Huron Street in Ypsilanti. His father David was fifty years old and worked as a day laborer. His mother Lydia was thirty-eight. Lydia and David had ten children, but one of them had died in childbirth. The oldest child, a girl named Anna, was born in 1878 when Lydia was only sixteen. In 1897, Anna married a man named Nat McCauley. In the early 1900's, David Hosner moved his family to Ann Arbor where he worked in a restaurant. In 1907, David died. In 1908, Lydia was admitted to a hospital in Ann Arbor. John moved into Anna and Nat McCauley's home in Ypsilanti. In the winter of 1908, Anna placed John into the Beulah Home. John was only nine.

John Hosner was sworn in and took the witness stand in Justice Shepherd's court at four o'clock the afternoon of December 14th, 1909. Following is a summary of notes of John's testimony. Evidence indicates that Justice Shepherd took these notes. I have provided my own version of some of the questions John was asked, as these were not provided in the notes. I have omitted specific references to the abuses charged against Herman Swift:

PROSECUTOR: "John, tell me how old you are and where you have lived."

JOHN: "I am ten years old. I came from Ann Arbor to Ypsilanti, from there to Boyne City."

PROSECUTOR: "Who are you acquainted with at the Beulah Home?"

JOHN: "I am acquainted with Mr. Swift and some of the boys. Known Swift since coming to the home. Been attending school there. Slept on the third floor of Mr. Swift's house."

PROSECUTOR: "Tell me of the times you have been alone with Mr. Swift."

JOHN: "Mr. Swift took me to shows more than once. I have been alone with Swift in the guest room, also to his own room, also to the wash room, to the lower woodshed, went to the woodshed one night when we came from a show about a month and a half ago."

At this point Nicholas took John through a series of questions describing the acts of abuse. Of note is John's description of going to Swift's room to receive a gift of postcards. John described the first incidence of abuse in the guest room and the second in Swift's room. At this point, John Harris began his cross-examination.

HARRIS: "John, tell me your mother and father's names."

JOHN: "My mother's name was Liddie. Father's is David. He is dead. About three years. He worked in a restaurant in Ann Arbor."

HARRIS: "Tell me what kind of work you do at the Home."

JOHN: "I came there in winter. In spring I cut wood, worked on the farm, planted potatoes. This fall I sawed wood and worked on the new building."

HARRIS: "Before this all came up, did you ever tell anyone about being abused at the home?"

JOHN: "I told Jud Holly of Ypsilanti. He told me not to tell. He wouldn't. He told me not to snitch. He wouldn't."

HARRIS: "Tell me about the postcards."

JOHN: "I got them in Swift's room. He got three postcards for me."

At this point, the court session was adjourned until eight thirty the following morning. At that time attorney Knowles continued the cross-examination.

KNOWLES: "How old were you when you left Ann Arbor?"

JOHN: "Nine years old. Went from there to Ypsilanti, from there to Boyne City.

KNOWLES: "Who brought you here?"

JOHN: "Nobody. My mother went to the hospital and I had to come."

KNOWLES: "Who at the Beulah Home did you tell that Mr. Swift treated you poorly?"

JOHN: "I told Jimmy Fair of it. I told Jim not long ago about Swift making me do it. I told it to the cop and people in the room."

KNOWLES: "How did you know he was a cop?"

JOHN: "He had a badge on him."

KNOWLES: "John, are you afraid of cops?"

JOHN: "Sometimes I am."

KNOWLES: "Did the cop ask you about your problems with Mr. Swift or did you tell him?"

JOHN: "I told him."

KNOWLES: "Who else was there when you told the cop your story?"

JOHN: "Mr. Jones was in the room and Mr. Urquhart and Mr. Beach and some of the boys."

KNOWLES: "Were you afraid of Mr. Swift?"

JOHN: "Yes, sir."

KNOWLES: "Did any of the men in the room tell you that you must change your story?"

JOHN: "Mr. Urquhart said I had to tell the truth."

KNOWLES: "Did Mr. Jones put you up to making up a story and telling it to Miss Ferris?"

JOHN: "Mr. Jones did not put me up to tell Miss Ferris."

KNOWLES: "Tell me about Miss Ferris. Who told her the story first?"

JOHN: "She's a teacher in the Beulah Home. I think Elliot Fay told her. She has left there now."

KNOWLES: "When Miss Ferris talked to you did she take you on her lap?"

JOHN: "No, sir."

KNOWLES: "John, where are you staying?"

JOHN: "Have been staying at Mrs. Rowan's for some time now."

KNOWLES: "Has anyone visited you to discuss this story?"

JOHN: "Mr. Urquhart came up to see me. Yes, sir. Told me to stick to the truth."

KNOWLES: "Did you discuss the story with the other boys at Rowan's? What did Earnest Wardell have to say?"

JOHN: "Did not talk it over among ourselves and only Ernie Wardell told me that it was a lie that he had said. Don't know where Ernie is. He was over to Mr. Heaton's, but was with us at Rowan's. Ernie was taken away from Rowan's."

KNOWLES: "What do you think of Simon Mack?"

JOHN: "Don't like Simon Mack very good. I like Mr. Swift."

KNOWLES: "Did Simon Mack tell you and other boys he wanted you to stick by him?"

JOHN: "No, sir. Don't know what he told other boys."

KNOWLES: "Have you told any boys you wanted to get away from the Beulah Home?"

JOHN: "Yes, sir. Told George Wilmot."

KNOWLES: "Did you tell any boys you would like to see Swift behind prison bars?"

JOHN: "No, sir."

KNOWLES: "Did you ever tell any boy you would be willing to go to Jackson if you could see Swift behind bars?" (Author's note: there is a large state prison in Jackson, Michigan.)

JOHN: "No, sir."

KNOWLES: "What do you think of liars?"

JOHN: "I know it is wrong to tell lies."

KNOWLES: "Do you ever tell lies?"

JOHN: "If I do I am sorry for it afterwards."

KNOWLES: "Have you ever told Mr. Swift you were sorry for lying?"

JOHN: "Don't go to Swift and tell him I am sorry when I tell lies."

KNOWLES: "Did the cop or any men over there say if you did not tell on Mr. Swift they would do something to you?"

JOHN: "Forget what they said. They did not scare me into anything."

KNOWLES: "When you are afraid do you always tell the truth?"

JOHN: "No, sir. But afterwards I do when I get over being afraid."

KNOWLES: "Have you ever lied about the other boys?"

JOHN: "I have lied about the other boys sometimes. When talking to them I do not lie as much as tell the truth. Other boys have lied to me about things."

KNOWLES: "Did Jones ever tell you he wanted to own the farm?"

JOHN: "No, sir."

KNOWLES: "Have you ever lied about Mr. Swift?"

JOHN: "Never told anything about Swift I was sorry for. I would care if I lied about Swift some."

KNOWLES: "Did Simon Mack talk to you about this at all at Rowan's?"

JOHN: "No, sir."

KNOWLES: "Tell me which boys you told about your troubles with Mr. Swift."

JOHN: "The boys did not ask me. When I get mad at another boy and want to say anything mean about Swift I don't tell the boys anything."

KNOWLES: "Which boys discussed problems with Mr. Swift with you?"

JOHN: "Jim Fair and Merrill Griffin talked about it a little while before coming to Rowan's. I did not tell these boys this was not so."

KNOWLES: "Do any of you boys ever do or say anything to get even with Swift when you get mad at him?"

JOHN: "No, sir."

KNOWLES: "How long were you in the guest room with Mr. Swift that day?"

JOHN: "About twenty minutes."

KNOWLES: "Who told you to say twenty minutes?"

JOHN: "Nobody."

KNOWLES: "Mr. Beach, Urquhart and Jones had been over to talk it over with you boys. Did you boys talk it over after they left?"

JOHN: "Yes, sir."

KNOWLES: "Why did you not tell on Swift before?"

JOHN: "Don't know."

KNOWLES: "What did Jones say to you?"

JOHN: "Mr. Jones told me I must stick to the truth."

KNOWLES: "What did George Snell say to you?"

JOHN: "Don't know George Snell."

KNOWLES: "Did you work on the new building?"

JOHN: "I did work on the new building."

KNOWLES: "Did you work with Ernest Wardell?"

JOHN: "Ernie Wardell was my boss on the building."

KNOWLES: "Did you say anything about problems with Mr. Swift while working on the new building?"

JOHN: "I did not tell anyone about this while there."

KNOWLES: "Did Jones ask you anything about it while working there?"

JOHN: "No, sir."

KNOWLES: "When you told the story to Cop and Urquhart and Jones did you write it down?"

JOHN: "I think they did."

KNOWLES: "Did Urquhart tell you you must not change it afterwards?"

JOHN: "I believe Urquhart. Mr. Urquhart was good to me. I like him."

KNOWLES: "Did he tell you that you would not have to live at the home?"

JOHN: "No, sir. Not as I can remember."

KNOWLES: "What do you think of Mr. Jones?"

JOHN: "I like Mr. Jones. He is good to me."

KNOWLES: "Did he ever give you any candy?"

JOHN: "No, sir. The gum I was chewing here he gave to me."

KNOWLES: "Did Mr. Jones visit you at Rowan's?"

JOHN: "Mr. Jones was not up to Rowan's to see me."

KNOWLES: "What did they tell you about changing your story?"

JOHN: "After they put your answer down at the form I could not change, would have to stick to same answer."

KNOWLES: "Did you boys all agree to stick to same answers?"

JOHN: "Yes, sir."

KNOWLES: "Have you been crying this morning?"

JOHN: "Have not been crying."

KNOWLES: "Would you change your story if you could?"

JOHN: "No, sir."

KNOWLES: "Has Mr. Swift ever punished you?"

JOHN: "Mr. Swift whipped me once when I ran away this summer. I was gone one day when I ran away. Went to Petoskey. George Wilmot went with me. Went on train in summertime. When I went, the cop brought me back. Swift whipped both of us for it with a rubber slipper."

KNOWLES: "Had you ever been whipped before?"

JOHN: "I was whipped by my mother before coming to the Beulah Home."

KNOWLES: "Who did you stay with at the Beulah Home?"

JOHN: "I slept with Edward Crane."

KNOWLES: "Tell me about what you do at night at the Beulah Home?"

JOHN: "The bell rings, you go to chapel, have prayers, and go to bed."

KNOWLES: "How many boys are at Rowan's?"

JOHN: "Five boys stay at Rowan's."

KNOWLES: "Did Jim Leys tell you what Elliot Fay and Merrill Griffin told him about Mr. Swift before the cop came?"

JOHN: "Yes, sir."

KNOWLES: "What did you do when you left court last night?"

JOHN: "I stayed at Rowan's. We all sleep there. I sleep alone. Two sleep in another bed, two in another bed. Mr. Beach went there with me last night after we had supper."

KNOWLES: "Did you tell the other boys what happened in court yesterday?"

JOHN: "I went to bed. I talked with the other boys. I did not tell what they did down here."

John Harris and L.F. Knowles used the examination of John Hosner to build their case in defense of Herman Swift and the Beulah Home. The case was built on two legs. The first of these was that the boys accusing Swift of indecent liberties were little, lying waifs. The second was that Swift was the victim of a conspiracy. The leaders of the conspiracy were the farm manager, Sidney Jones, and Simon Mack. Jones had engaged Simon to enlist a number of the Beulah boys to falsely claim that Swift had abused them. Jones' motive was to gain control of Herman Swift's farm. The boys' motive was to leave the Home and return to their homes.

On December 17th, 1909, the *Boyne Citizen* published a front-page article covering the hearing in Justice Shepherd's court. The article reads:

"No arrest in this city in years has caused so much talk about the city, and at the examination, which has taken the most of three days before Justice Shepherd, standing room has been at a premium and many were turned away in an effort to hear the disgusting details as told under oath by three former inmates of the home."

Harris and Knowles did not take an aggressive approach in their questioning of John Hosner. They did not press him to gain more information on his claims of abuse. They chose not to increase public exposure to the "disgusting details."

John Hosner signed the transcript of notes taken during his testimony on December 14th and December 15th of 1909. In those notes, Justice Shepherd highlighted only one small item: "Jud Holly of Ypsilanti." In 1900, Judson Holly, his wife Ida, and their eight children lived in a home at 916 Railroad Street in Ypsilanti, right around the corner from the home of David and Lydia Hosner and their seven children. The Holly's and the Hosners must have been close friends. By 1909, Judson Holly was a fifty-seven year old widower. He worked as a foreman at a paper company. He still lived in the same home and that home was less than a mile away from the home of Nat McCauley and his wife Anna, John Hosner's older sister and caretaker. Holly knew Anna McCauley and he kept an eye out for the children of his deceased friend David Hosner. It seems that sometime in 1909 Holly traveled to Boyne City in order to check on John Hosner at the Beulah Home. On that trip, Holly probably told John of the death of his mother, Lydia or Liddie. John claimed he had told "Jud Holly of Ypsilanti" of suffering abuse at the Home, but it seems that neither the prosecution nor the defense pursued this matter.

The boys at the Beulah Home called John Hosner, "Johnnie." Johnnie Hosner was a fragile little boy. He probably had been crying before his appearance in court the morning of December 14th. Nicholas and Urquhart noted that in his testimony Johnnie made a few mistakes, including saying that: "he liked Mr. Swift." But for the most part they were very proud of his performance. He had used the words they coached him to use in describing the acts of abuse. Wherever possible, he had answered simply with the words "No, sir" or "Yes, sir." He had said he had not discussed the case with the other boys at Rowan's the evening of December 14th. Finally, he had maintained his composure as he sat in the large wooden chair in the scary courtroom and faced the attorneys, the Justice of the Peace, the crowd, and Herman Swift and answered questions for seven hours.

At the end of the seven-hour examination of John Hosner, Prosecuting Attorney Nicholas moved that Herman Swift be bound over to the County Circuit Court session scheduled for February 1910 in the city of Charlevoix. Justice Shepherd accepted that motion and fixed bail for Herman Swift in this case at four thousand dollars. Nicholas then re-arrested Swift on a complaint based on information provided by Elliot Fay. Shepherd immediately called Fay to the stand and a second examination began around mid-day Wednesday, December 15th, 1909.

Elliot Fay

Elliot Fay was ten years old the day he took the stand in justice court in Boyne City. His mother Maud lived in Jackson, Michigan. His father had worked as a streetcar driver. He was driving the streetcar when he was killed in an accident in Ypsilanti in 1908. He left Maud with nine children. The eldest was twelve. Maud was forced to send three of her sons to the Beulah Home.

Prosecuting Attorney Nicholas began the examination of Elliot Fay:

PROSECUTOR: "Tell me how long you have lived at the Beulah Home."

ELLIOT: "I have lived in Beulah Home a year and four months. Since in April before. After coming to Boyne City I have been at Beulah Home."

PROSECUTOR: "Are you acquainted with Mr. Swift?"

ELLIOT: "I am acquainted with Mr. and Mrs. Swift. Have known Swift a year and four months."

PROSECUTOR: "Where do you live at the Home?"

ELLIOT: "I have a room at the Home in first hall. George Gates slept with me. Hasn't slept with me all the time. Slept with Merrill Griffin and Eddy Fay part of time."

PROSECUTOR: "Tell me about your life at the Beulah Home."

ELLIOT: "We had plenty to eat at the Home. Did some work at the Home. Scrub and sweep, things like that."

PROSECUTOR: "Who brought you to the Home?"

ELLIOT: "My mother came here with me from Ypsi."

PROSECUTOR: "Did Mr. Swift ever take you to shows?"

ELLIOT: "Go to shows occasionally with Swift and the boys. When he left the Home went with boys and ladies. Ladies did not always go to shows."

Prosecutor Nicholas then led Elliot Fay through a description of acts of abuse by Swift. The examination continued:

PROSECUTOR: "Where is Willis Robert's room?"

ELLIOT: "Roberts room is in second hall. In going there turn left."

PROSECUTOR: "Where is Mr. Swift's room?"

ELLIOT: "Swift's room is in first hall."

PROSECUTOR: "Where is the schoolroom?"

ELLIOT: "Just down stairs. There are barrels, books, and magazines and coats there."

At this point, Prosecutor Nicholas turned over the examination to either John Harris or L.F. Knowles who apparently first asked Elliot what he did the day of December 2nd, 1909. Elliot said that he hid down in the classroom for half a day and then Tim Heaton, a Boyne City deputy police officer, took him with a number of other boys to Rowan's. Some of those boys had been hiding in the barn. Elliot also said that he had spent time at Arthur Urquhart's house.

KNOWLES: "Elliot, tell me about your family."

ELLIOT: "My father is dead. My brothers are home with mother. I think at Jackson. I have two brothers at the Beulah Home."

KNOWLES: "What did you tell your brothers about your problems with Mr. Swift?"

ELLIOT: "I never talked to them about it."

KNOWLES: "Which of the boys did you tell about your problems?"

ELLIOT: "I told Jim Fair and George Gates about it. George Gates and I was after cows when I told him. I told Jim Fair at night and George Gates also later him."

KNOWLES: "When did you tell George Gates?"

ELLIOT: "Merrill (Merrill Griffin) said Peter Majeski was up in the corn. George and I told Tiffany (the boys referred to Herman Swift as "Tiffany") the cows were out."

KNOWLES: "How long after this did you tell Jim Fair?"

ELLIOT: "About a week and George Gates told Fair also and Chester Kent also."

KNOWLES: "Did you tell any of the other boys about this?"

ELLIOT: "I talked with Edwy Crane and James Leys. Edwy Crane told me and James Leys he wanted to tell me something, that Tiffany was going to jail. It was one night while after cows. Don't know how long ago."

KNOWLES: "Did Mr. Swift ever punish you for running away?"

ELLIOT: "I never ran away. Swift punished me. He took a rubber slipper and spanked me."

KNOWLES: "When did this happen?"

ELLIOT: "Never but once. Don't know when. Long time ago down in the schoolroom. I went up to the dining room."

KNOWLES: "Have you ever been in this court before?"

ELLIOT: "With Urquhart. I was in this room a few days ago."

KNOWLES: "What questions did Mr. Urquhart ask you?"

ELLIOT: "Nobody asked me any questions here, but at the Beulah Home."

KNOWLES: "What did Mr. Urquhart do when he asked you questions?"

ELLIOT: "They marked it on paper. Was told I could not change it."

KNOWLES: "Did you believe you could never change it?"

ELLIOT: "I believed them. I could not change it if I told the truth. I know what lying is. If I told a lie and it was marked down I could not change it. Would be lying."

KNOWLES: "What do you think of Simon Mack?"

ELLIOT: "I know Simon Mack. I like him."

KNOWLES: "Did you tell Simon Mack that you would stick by him with this story?"

ELLIOT: "I did not tell him I would stick by him in this story. Never told any body I would stick by them."

KNOWLES: "Did Simon Mack and you talk about this at Rowan's?"

ELLIOT: "No, sir. I would not tell a lie about it. Could not change it and tell the truth."

KNOWLES: "If they would let you would you change it?"

ELLIOT: "Do not know. They told me to tell the truth. They told me to stick by it."

KNOWLES: "Did you tell any lies to the other boys?"

ELLIOT: "I don't think I ever told any of the boys over there any lies."

KNOWLES: "Would you tell a lie if a lot of men wanted you to?"

ELLIOT: "I would tell a lie if a lot of men wanted me to. If Urquhart wanted me to I would."

KNOWLES: "Did anyone want you to lie about Mr. Swift?"

ELLIOT: "I don't think any one ever wanted me to lie about Swift. I have told little lies about boys some times and thought it fun. If I had lied about Swift I would know it."

KNOWLES: "Would you like to live with Mr. Urquhart?"

ELLIOT: "I might like to live with Mr. Urquhart. If I could have my choice I would rather go away from the Home."

KNOWLES: "Would you tell a lie on Mr. Swift to get away from the Home?"

ELLIOT: "I would not tell a lie on Swift to get away. No one told me to tell on Swift. I told on him because I wanted to get it over."

KNOWLES: "Did you tell Mr. Harris any lies today?"

ELLIOT: "I don't think I told Harris any lies today. Mr. Swift knew I was in his room. I think Swift knows all about this."

KNOWLES: "Are you trying to get Mr. Swift in trouble?"

ELLIOT: "I'm not trying to get Swift into trouble."

KNOWLES: "Where was Mrs. Swift when you say you were in Mr. Swift's room?"

ELLIOT: "I think Mrs. Swift was down in the kitchen."

KNOWLES: "Did Mr. Jones ever give you candy?"

ELLIOT: "Mr. Jones gave me candy."

KNOWLES: "Why did Mr. Jones give you candy?"

ELLIOT: "I guess Jones told me I was a good boy."

KNOWLES: "Did Beach, Urquhart, and others tell you that Swift had done these things?"

ELLIOT: "No, I told them."

KNOWLES: "Did they tell you they would get you out of the Beulah Home?"

ELLIOT: "Don't know whether I will go back to the Beulah Home."

At this time, Knowles altered the approach he had taken in the examination of John Hosner. Knowles asked Elliot Fay direct questions about the alleged abuse. His questions suggested that Elliot might not know the meanings of some of the words he had used to describe the abuse. They also suggested that Elliot had been coached on how to describe abuse that had not occurred. Elliot closed this section of his testimony saying:

ELLIOT: "Swift made me do it. That's all I know about it."

KNOWLES: "What did Mr. Jones tell you about this story?"

ELLIOT: "Jones told me to stick to it. That's all. He told me to stick to it. That's all."

KNOWLES: "If you told a lie once would you tell it again?"

ELLIOT: "Sure."

KNOWLES: "Why would you stick to it?"

ELLIOT: "I have told a lie and stuck to it. About some apples. Said I did not take the apples. When my hand was bleeding I did it to."

KNOWLES: "Would you say things to hurt Mr. Swift?"

ELLIOT: "Don't know as I would tell anything to hurt Swift. Have told the truth about everything to you."

KNOWLES: "What did you tell Miss Ferris?"

ELLIOT: "I told Miss a Ferris that Swift done it to me. She asked me about it. I did not know what she was saying about it."

KNOWLES: "When Beach and Urquhart came over to the farm did you try to fool them?"

ELLIOT: "I did not try to fool them about this."

KNOWLES: "Are you afraid of Beach and Urquhart?"

ELLIOT: "I am not afraid of these men now."

KNOWLES: "If you could change your story would you?"

ELLIOT: "Don't know whether I could change my story or not. If they would let me I might."

KNOWLES: "Then what would you say?"

ELLIOT: "Would say it was not true. I might change my story."

KNOWLES: "Would you change it back again?"

ELLIOT: "Don't know. Don't know why I would."

KNOWLES: "If they wanted you to change your story, would you?" asked Knowles, pointing at Nicholas and Urquhart.

ELLIOT: "Yes."

KNOWLES: "What if I wanted you to change your story and Police Chief Beach told you not to?"

ELLIOT: "I don't know."

KNOWLES: "If you told me the truth and Mr. Urquhart a lie, I would stand by you if you told me the truth. Why don't you stand by Mr. Swift?"

ELLIOT: "Because he did these things to me."

KNOWLES: "Did you tell the prosecutor, Mr. Nicholas, about this?"

ELLIOT: "Talked with Nicholas about this man, yes, at Urquhart's office."

KNOWLES: "Are you sorry you told this about Mr. Swift?"

ELLIOT: "Don't know."

KNOWLES: "Did Miss Ferris take you on her lap when she talked to you about this?"

ELLIOT: "Miss Ferris took me on her knee when she talked with me about this."

KNOWLES: "What did Miss Ferris tell you?"

ELLIOT: "She asked me about it but I did not understand her. I told her I did not know. I knew when I got down stairs cause I saw George Gates. George Gates told me what Mr. Swift was doing to the boys and I went up and told Miss Ferris. Swift told me not to tell a lot of times."

HARRIS: "Did Miss Ferris tell you that you would not have to stay at the Home if you told these stories?"

ELLIOT: "Miss Ferris did not tell me that."

KNOWLES: "Have you told me any lies?"

ELLIOT: "I would be sorry if I told you any lies."

KNOWLES: "Did you tell the boys at the Home that you would tell on Mr. Swift if they would?"

ELLIOT: "No."

KNOWLES: "Would you rather have Mr. Jones run the farm?"

ELLIOT: "I would just as soon Swift would go away and have Jones run the farm. Think I would have a better time. Would like to have you get Swift away from there."

KNOWLES: "Would you lie to get Mr. Swift away from the Home?"

ELLIOT: "Don't know as I would lie to have Swift taken away from here."

KNOWLES: "Would you tell lies on Mr. Swift so Jones could get the job?"

ELLIOT: "I just as soon. Don't know that I ever told any lies on Swift so Jones could get the farm."

KNOWLES: "Would you say Mr. Swift did things to you so officers would come and get him?"

ELLIOT: "I might."

KNOWLES: "If Mr. Swift whipped you would you tell it so they would come and get him?"

ELLIOT: "Yes, sir."

KNOWLES: "If Mr. Swift whipped you would you tell a lie on him?"

ELLIOT: "I guess so. I would get even with him by doing so. Would keep on telling lies about him until I did get even."

KNOWLES: "What boys asked you if this story was a lie?"

ELLIOT: "Jimmie Fair."

KNOWLES: "Any other boys?"

ELLIOT: "Don't know if I did tell anybody or not. Just told Fair."

KNOWLES: "Do you know the difference between boys and boy?"

ELLIOT: "Yes, sir."

KNOWLES: "Do you want to change your story?"

ELLIOT: "I don't want to change my story."

KNOWLES: "Do you want Jones to run the farm?"

ELLIOT: "I want Jones to take care of the farm if he can. I like Mr. Jones."

KNOWLES: "Would you lie to help Mr. Jones?"

ELLIOT: "Just as soon lie to help Mr. Jones."

KNOWLES: "Just as soon tell Mr. Jones that Mr. Swift had done bad things to you. Then Mr. Jones would be mad wouldn't he?"

ELLIOT: "Don't know."

KNOWLES: "If you wanted to get Mr. Jones away would you tell Mr. Urquhart a story just to get rid of him?"

ELLIOT: "I would tell it."

KNOWLES: "If you wanted to get rid of anybody you would tell a bad story about them wouldn't you?"

ELLIOT: "Don't know that I would tell it on anybody. When I want to get even with any one I tell it, sometimes it is and sometimes it isn't so when I tell it."

KNOWLES: "Were you trying to fool me when you told me what Mr. Swift had done to you?"

ELLIOT: "No."

KNOWLES: "Did Mr. Jones put you up to this story?"

ELLIOT: "Jones never made me do it."

KNOWLES: "Did Simon Mack put you up to this story?"

ELLIOT: "Not any of the boys over there ever did."

KNOWLES: "Are you telling this story because Mr. Urquhart wants you to tell it?"

ELLIOT: "I'm not telling on Swift because Urquhart wants me to. He does not want me to."

KNOWLES: "Is it easy for you to lie about things?"

ELLIOT: "It is sometimes easy for me to lie about things."

KNOWLES: "If you went back to live at the Beulah Home would you change your story?"

ELLIOT: "If I went back to live with Swift don't know if I would change my story. Don't think I would. He might make me...again. This is the Swift that made me do it! This is all."

Elliot Fay's testimony ended in the early evening of December 15th. The strongest part of the testimony came at the conclusion when Elliot pointed directly at Herman Swift and said: "This is the Swift that made me do it!" Justice Shepherd highlighted this statement in his notes.

Knowles attacked Elliot much more aggressively than he and Harris had attacked John Hosner. Elliot talked too much on the witness stand. His testimony was inconsistent. Most importantly, he repeatedly admitted that he lied when he believed it was in his interest to do so.

The contemporaneous notes taken at the Elliot Fay hearing still reside in the file of the Elliot Fay case against Herman Swift. Justice Shepherd wrote these notes. At the conclusion of Elliot's testimony on December 15th, Shepherd wrote: "Subscribed and sworn to by Elliott Fay after having all of his testimony carefully read over to him by myself this 15th day of December A.D. 1909, Elisha J. Shepherd, Justice of the Peace." Elliot signed "Elliott Fay" at a place on the small notepad where Shepherd had written "Signed by."

Prosecuting Attorney Nicholas and City Attorney Urquhart were not pleased with the Elliot Fay hearing. They recognized this case was weaker than the Hosner case. In spite of this, at the conclusion of the hearing Justice Shepherd once more bound over Herman Swift to the February session of the Charlevoix Circuit Court. And Shepherd again fixed bail at four thousand dollars.

When the court session of December 15th ended, Herman Swift faced a bail bond requirement of eight thousand dollars. No one stepped forward to provide that bond. Herman had over eight thousand dollars on account as Trustee of the Beulah Land Farm for Boys at the First National Bank of Boyne City, but something prevented him from accessing that money. Deputy police officer Heaton escorted Swift to the office of Probate Judge John M. Harris. Timothy Heaton had operated a saloon in Boyne City prior to being appointed a deputy police officer. Swift later would testify that Heaton had assured him he could spend the night at either the Beulah Home or the New Boyne Hotel. Instead, Heaton left Swift outside Harris' office door. Heaton entered the office, closed the door and conferred with Harris. When he returned he advised Swift that he would have to put him in the lock-up and keep him there over night. They called the city lock-up the "two by four cell." Herman Swift would testify that it was a "place where drunks are kept, a dirty, filthy hole with no ventilation." Herman spent the night in that place. He never would forget his first night in a Charlevoix County jail.

The morning of December 16th, officer Heaton escorted Swift from the lock-up to Judge Harris' office where Herman met his wife Grace. John Harris had prepared a deed for conveyance of the Beulah Land Farm property from Herman and Grace Swift to the trustees of the Beulah Home. Later Swift would testify that Harris told him if he and Grace executed the deed transfer then the trustees would help him. Swift claimed that Harris told him: "We (the trustees) are your best friends and if you trust us we will take care of you and Mr. White agrees to meet all of your court expenses and we will see you through it and there will be no question of the outcome if you leave it to us." Herman refused to sign the deed. After this, other trustees, including William H. White, Samuel C. Smith, Godfrey Von Platen, and Peter McIntire, arrived at different individual times and attempted to persuade Grace to talk Herman into signing the deed. Herman continued to refuse the offer and Officer Heaton escorted him to Justice Shepherd's court where examinations of his accusers would continue that morning.

Merrill Griffin

Wallis Merrill Griffin was born in Grand Rapids on November 3, 1898. His mother's name was Florence and his father's name was Edward. Florence died of pulmonary tuberculosis on March 3rd, 1903. In 1905, Edward married a young woman named Nellie Proos. Nellie's mother's maiden name was Leys. The Proos' and the Leys were among the many Dutch families that arrived in Grand Rapids in the late 1800's. Nellie was eighteen when she married Edward Griffin. By 1909, Edward and Nellie had three daughters: Isabella Marie, age five; Edna May, age three; and Florence, age six months. They lived with the three girls and Merrill in a rented upstairs flat at 93 Pleasant Avenue in Grand Rapids.

Merrill got into trouble a number of times in Grand Rapids. He went before a probate court judge on at least two occasions, but Merrill's father would testify that the judge had not ordered Merrill to be sent away. On August 6th, 1909, Edward Griffin voluntarily took his son by train from Grand Rapids and placed him in the Beulah Home in Boyne City. Edward returned to Boyne City to attend the examination of his son in Justice Shepherd's court the morning of December 16th, 1909. Prosecutor Nicholas was not in court that day. Perhaps he felt satisfied with what he had accomplished the prior two days. City Attorney Arthur Urquhart substituted for Nicholas and began the examination of Merrill Griffin:

URQUHART: "Merrill, tell me how old you are and where you have lived."

MERRILL: "I am eleven years old. My home is in Grand Rapids. Four months since I left there. Came to the Beulah Home."

URQUHART: "Who brought you to the Beulah Home?"

MERRILL: "My father brought me."

URQUHART: "Are you acquainted with Mr. and Mrs. Swift?"

MERRILL: "I knew Swift, also Mrs. Swift."

Urquhart then asked Merrill questions about his claims of abuse by Herman Swift. Merrill testified that he had been abused on three occasions: in the guest room, in Willis Robert's room, and in Mr. Swift's own room. The last instance of abuse had occurred: "a week before I went to Rowan's." Merrill described details about Swift locking the door to his room and the furnishings in the room. Urquhart closed:

URQUHART: "Are you telling the whole truth?"

MERRILL: "Yes, sir."

Leonard F. Knowles then took up the cross-examination of Merrill Griffin:

KNOWLES: "Tell me when Mr. Swift first abused you. Was it a year ago?"

MERRILL: "Don't know when the first time was. Was not a year ago. It was last August because I was here in August. A little while after I came here."

KNOWLES: "Do you know why you were sent to the Beulah Home?"

MERRILL: "I know why I was sent to the Home. For being a bad boy. I stole and lied and ran away from home. I went with bad boys."

KNOWLES: "Have you told your father that you lie?"

MERRILL: "I have told my father I had lied to him."

KNOWLES: "If you tell a lie will you stick to it?"

MERRILL: "I would not stick to a lie now. If I told it, I would change it and tell the truth."

KNOWLES: "Do you know Cornelius Proos?"

MERRILL: "I know Cornelius Proos. He is my uncle. He lived at our home.

KNOWLES: "Did you ever sleep with Cornelius Proos?"

MERRILL: "I slept with him all the time he was there."

KNOWLES: "Did you ever tell lies to the other boys?"

MERRILL: "Never told many lies to the boys. They told me too."

KNOWLES: "Did you ever lie to Mr. Swift?"

MERRILL: "I never lied to Mr. Swift."

KNOWLES: "Do you know Mr. Jones? "

MERRILL: "I know Mr. Jones."

KNOWLES: "What do you think of Mr. Jones."

MERRILL: "I like Mr. Jones."

KNOWLES: "Would you rather have Jones run the Home or Swift?"

MERRILL: "I would rather have Jones for the boys than Swift."

KNOWLES: "Did Mr. Jones ever give you candy?"

MERRILL: "Jones did not give me candy."

KNOWLES: "What do you think of Mr. Swift?"

MERRILL: "I don't like Mr. Swift!" (Author's note: Justice Shepherd added an exclamation point to this response and noted in his transcript: "shook his head no!")

KNOWLES: "Would you lie to get even with Mr. Swift?"

MERRILL: "I would not lie to get even with Swift."

KNOWLES: "Where was Mrs. Swift when you claim that Mr. Swift took you to his room?"

MERRILL: "Mrs. Swift was down in the office. She was writing on a typewriter."

KNOWLES: "Now tell me the three places where Mr. Swift abused you."

MERRILL: "I said the first was in the office, the second in the toilet, and the third in the wash room."

KNOWLES: "Is this how you want it to appear in the records of the court?"

MERRILL: "That is."

KNOWLES: "What do you think of Simon Mack?"

MERRILL: "I know Simon Mack. I like him."

KNOWLES: "Did you tell Simon Mack about this?"

MERRILL: "I did not tell Simon Mack."

KNOWLES: "Did you tell Miss Ferris about this?"

Merrill: "I did not tell Miss Ferris. I wrote a letter and Miss Ferris gave it to the officer."

KNOWLES: "Who told you to write the letter?"

MERRILL: "Miss Ferris told me to write the letter. She told me to write it in my own words and I did."

KNOWLES: "Did you write the letter to get even with Mr. Swift?"

MERRILL: "I did not do it to get even with Swift."

KNOWLES: "Who do you sleep with at the home?"

MERRILL: "I slept with James Leys first. Now I sleep with Elliott Fay."

KNOWLES: "Did you tell Elliott Fay about this?"

MERRILL: "I did not tell Elliott Fay. I told James Leys and he told me Swift had done it to him too. This was down in the basement he told. He told me first then asked me if he ever done it to me. I told him yes."

KNOWLES: "When was the last time you claim Mr. Swift mistreated you?"

MERRILL: "The last time was November 23rd. It was after that I told Leys."

KNOWLES: "Are you sure about this? Do you know how long ago it was November 23rd?"

MERRILL: "The week before I came over here was the 23rd of November."

KNOWLES: "Are you lying about this?"

MERRILL: "Have not lied about it. Probably got a little mixed up."

KNOWLES: "Do you know when you wrote the letter for Miss Ferris?"

MERRILL: "I think it was the 23rd of November. I know because it was the day before we came to Rowan's house. I wrote the letter quite awhile before going to Rowan's. It was about two weeks before going to Rowan's."

KNOWLES: "Are you trying to send Mr. Swift to jail?"

MERRILL: "Don't know as I am trying to send Swift to jail. I don't know, but I know that is true what I have said."

KNOWLES: "Did you boys agree to tell the same story about Mr. Swift?"

MERRILL: "We boys did not agree to. They told me to tell the truth and that is what I am doing."

KNOWLES: "Are you telling this story so that Jones can run the farm?"

MERRILL: "No, sir."

KNOWLES: "Tell me about the first time you claim Mr. Swift mistreated you."

MERRILL: "The first time I was in the office. It was in August. Mr. Swift told me not to tell about it."

KNOWLES: "Tell me about the second time you claim Mr. Swift mistreated you."

MERRILL: "The second time I was in the toilet when Swift found me. It was four o'clock. I just heard town clock strike four. We heard it strike all along. When we go by one of the doors we can hear the clock plain."

KNOWLES: "Tell me about the third time you claim Mr. Swift mistreated you."

MERRILL: "Mr. Swift asked me to come up to Robert's room."

KNOWLES: "Do you remember Mr. Swift being away about the 23rd or 24th?"

MERRILL: "I do not remember Mr. Swift being away. No, sir."

KNOWLES: "Do you know what day Thanksgiving is?"

Merrill: "Do know. Thanksgiving comes on 24th of November."

KNOWLES: "Don't you remember Mr. Swift being away a long time before Thanksgiving?"

MERRILL: "Don't remember Swift being away a long time."

KNOWLES: "Do you remember what you did on Thanksgiving day?"

MERRILL: "Don't remember what I did. We have a big time every Thanksgiving. One thing I remember we did was to go to a show Thanksgiving."

KNOWLES: "Tell me again when was the last time you claim Mr. Swift mistreated you."

MERRILL: "I think last time was before Thanksgiving. I have no idea when it was."

Attorney Urquhart then called Merrill's father Edward Griffin to the witness stand. Griffin was sworn in. Urquhart asked him only two questions:

URQUHART: "Is Cornelius Proos a married man?"

GRIFFIN: "Yes, sir."

URQUHART: "Did Cornelius Proos ever sleep with your son?"

GRIFFIN: "No, sir."

Attorney Knowles then took the opportunity to cross-examine Edward Griffin:

KNOWLES: "Tell me why you are here."

GRIFFIN: "I am the father of Merrill Griffin."

KNOWLES: "When did Merrill leave your home?"

GRIFFIN: "Boy has not lived with me since August 6th this year."

KNOWLES: "Why was your boy placed in the Home?"

GRIFFIN: "Principally for running away."

KNOWLES: "What other troubles did you have with the boy?"

GRIFFIN: "He ran away and took money. He'd talk stories and afterwards correct them. Would lie and then own up to it."

KNOWLES: "Could you place any confidence in what he said?"

GRIFFIN: "Yes, sir."

KNOWLES: "Would he steal from other people?"

GRIFFIN: "Don't know."

KNOWLES: "Have you ever whipped your boy?"

GRIFFIN: "Have whipped him for lying to me."

KNOWLES: "Did that remedy the difficulty?"

GRIFFIN: "To a certain extent."

KNOWLES: "Did you ever write to Mr. Swift the boy was such a liar you could not do anything with him?"

GRIFFIN: "No, sir. Did not express it in them words. Never wrote Swift the boy was so bad I had no control over him whatever."

KNOWLES: "Isn't it a fact the principle reason for sending Merrill to the home was that he lied about everything and stole anything he could carry away and did immoral things?"

GRIFFIN: "No, sir!" (Author's note: in his transcript Shepherd added an exclamation point to this statement and the comment: "Emphatically no!")

KNOWLES: "Was the boy ever before Judge Jewel of Grand Rapids?"

GRIFFIN: "Twice before he went to the Beulah Home. The judge recommended him to be sent to the Home."

KNOWLES: "Where do you live?"

GRIFFIN: "In Grand Rapids."

KNOWLES: "Does Merrill have a cousin who frequently spent time with him in Grand Rapids?"

GRIFFIN: "The boy has no cousin in Grand Rapids. No cousin ever visited him frequently in Grand Rapids."

KNOWLES: "Do you know Cornelius Proos?"

GRIFFIN: "I know Cornelius Proos. He is Merrill's stepmother's brother."

KNOWLES: "Did Cornelius Proos ever stay at your home?"

GRIFFIN: "He stayed at my home several weeks. The boy never slept with him while there."

KNOWLES: "Is Cornelius Proos a married man?"

GRIFFIN: "Yes, sir."

KNOWLES: "Was he married when he lived with you?"

GRIFFIN: "No, sir."

KNOWLES: "Would Merrill confess to lying if he lied?"

GRIFFIN: "Most certainly."

KNOWLES: "Did he confess all the lies he has told so far as you know?"

GRIFFIN: "Yes, sir."

In his examination Merrill Griffin showed more confidence than either John Hosner or Elliott Fay. Merrill provided vivid detail of the claimed abuses. He stuck to the claim that he had been treated indecently three times, but when questioned about the dates and places of abuse his testimony was inconsistent and confused. Most importantly, Merrill had testified several times that the date of the last abuse was November 23rd, 1909. Herman Swift easily could prove that he was in southern Michigan on that date. At the end of Knowles' examinations, City Attorney Urquhart briefly re-examined Merrill:

URQUHART: "Merrill, I want to get something straight on the record. Was the first time Mr. Swift mistreated you in the guest room?"

MERRILL: "Yes, sir."

URQUHART: "Was the second time in Willis Robert's room?"

MERRILL: "Yes, sir."

URQUHART: "Was the third time in Mr. Swift's own room?"

MERRILL: "Yes, sir."

URQUHART: "Are you telling the whole truth and nothing but the truth?"

MERRILL: "Yes, sir."

Attorney Knowles certainly objected to this as leading the witness, but Justice Shepherd included it in the record of the examination.

I imagine that Merrill spent the night with his father in a hotel in Boyne City. Perhaps they spent the night at Arthur Urquhart's home. It had been a difficult day for Edward Griffin. He was a machinist, probably a tough guy, and certainly stubborn. But it must have been difficult to sit there and watch and listen to his little boy's testimony. Furthermore, he had been confronted with a new and distasteful issue.

James Leys

James Leys was twelve years old. He was from Grand Rapids and the son of Peter and Gertie Leys. Peter was a cousin of Edward Griffin's wife Nellie. James was not Merrill Griffin's cousin by birth, but he was a cousin by marriage. He also probably was one of the "bad boys" who hung out with Merrill in Grand Rapids. James Leys still was living as an inmate at the Beulah Home. He had been one of the seven boys in the Ferris Group, but Arthur Urquhart had elected to leave him behind when the other six boys were removed from the Beulah Home and taken to Rowan's on December 2nd, 1909. On that very day or shortly thereafter, James told Herman Swift that Cornelius Proos not only had slept with Merrill, but also had abused him. Edward Griffin did not believe this accusation, but now it was out in public and Cornelius certainly would be mad about this. More importantly, Edward's wife Nellie, Cornelius' sister, also would be mad. And this would have reinforced Nellie's belief that rather than fight the ugly public battle with Herman Swift, the better course would be to simply forget the matter and bring Merrill home. Edward Griffin strongly disagreed with this. He felt responsible for sending Merrill to the Beulah Home and now he was determined to get even with Herman Swift.

Following completion of the examination of Merrill Griffin, Justice of the Peace Shepherd once more bound Herman Swift over to the February session of the Charlevoix County Circuit Court. He again fixed bail at four thousand dollars. Swift now faced bail totaling twelve thousand dollars.

On December 16th, 1909, Herman spent his second night in the city lock-up, the two-by-four cell. The morning of December 17th, he again was escorted to the office of Judge John Harris. Harris again requested that Swift sign over the deed to the Beulah Land Farm property. He also probably asked Swift to sign over to the Board the custody of the Beulah Home funds on deposit with the First National Bank of Boyne City. Herman Swift later would testify that at this time Judge Harris told him:

"If he would sign over the deed the purported Board of Trustees would all stand by him and make him a free man without any doubt whatever, but if he refused to sign over the deed he would be a doomed man and there would be no hope for him. Then John Harris drew his chair a little closer and said in a low tone of voice: 'You know that I am in politics and that I am in with Judge Mayne and that I can swing things my way in this county. It is now for you to be the judge, it is within your power to save yourself and what is more to save that beautiful wife of yours. She won't be able to bear this long, you can save yourself and her. You can see what effect it will have on your wife. It will crush both you and her. You had better use your common sense and take the advice of your best friends who are right here to advise you what is best for your own good—to sign this deed.'"

Herman Swift would testify that as his conversation with Judge Harris continued, Harris suggested that he could give up title to the property for a time until the legal matters were settled. Herman asked what he might do if he were to give up the property. Harris said: "The world is wide and you and your wife could begin life elsewhere." Evidence suggests that Samuel C. Smith was present during this conversation between Swift and Harris. I believe Smith presented Herman with papers to transfer the funds at the bank to the Board of Trustees.

Herman Swift had faced this situation before in Buffalo and Leoni. On both those occasions he had elected quietly to depart and move on to a new location. For some reason on December 17th, 1909, sitting there with Samuel Smith and Judge Harris, Swift made the decision to fight to stay with the Beulah Home in Boyne City. It may have been that he now was married and did not want to disappoint Grace. Perhaps it was the fact that now for the first time he owned a significant property, one hundred and sixty acres. But certainly one of the reasons he elected to fight was that he thought he could beat the charges against him.

The morning of December 17th, a police officer escorted Herman Swift from Judge Harris' office to a boat in the Boyne City harbor. They sailed on that boat up the length of Pine Lake to the City of Charlevoix where Herman Swift was confined in the County jail. He would remain there until December 24th, the day before Christmas.

On December 17th, 1909, the *Boyne Citizen* ran a front-page article titled: "Bound Over to Circuit Court." Two subtitles read: "Hermon L. Swift is Taken to Charlevoix to Await his Trial" and "He was Unable to Furnish the Bonds in the Sum of $12,000." The article begins:

"The sad spectacle of a man who but a few short weeks ago was held in high esteem by the people of Boyne City, but now locked up as a prisoner is the result of the arrest and examination of Hermon L. Swift, superintendent of the Beulah Home, on a charge of taking indecent liberties with boys. No arrest in this city in years has caused so much talk about the city, and at the examination, which has taken the most of three days before Justice Shepherd, standing-room has been at a premium."

The same article ends:

"Last evening Mr. Swift was interviewed in jail by the *Citizen* and asked if he had anything to say to the public at this time. He claims the charges are instigated by boys of the Home out of revenge. He complained that the bail was excessive and said if he got bail now that more charges would be brought against him and more bail piled up.

The Beulah Home is being taken charge of by Mrs. Swift who is fully competent to take care of the Home. In fact, most of the care of the Home has been on her shoulders most of the time on account of the absence of Mr. Swift much of the time the past summer.

Work on the new addition has been suspended for the present."

As Herman Swift traveled to jail in Charlevoix, John Harris and his law partner, Ervan Ruegsegger traveled south to Traverse City. Harris was worried. He and the other Beulah Home board members had assumed the Home was incorporated. Michigan State law required incorporation of institutions such as the Beulah Home and Herman Swift was well aware of this based on his experiences in Leoni. Swift had suggested to the Board that the Home was incorporated and the incorporation was noted in several issues of *The Youth's Outlook*. But the Home was not incorporated. It had no legal existence and therefore Herman Swift personally owned the Beulah Land Farm property, both the real estate and the personal property, and he owned the money on deposit at the First National Bank. Herman had attempted to use this property as collateral to post bail and avoid going to jail in Charlevoix, but Harris had bluffed him out of this plan. Harris believed there might be some basis for bringing a charge of fraud against Swift based upon the premise that he had talked hundreds of people into donating money and goods to the "Beulah Home" when in effect they were donating directly to Swift. But this would be a lengthy and messy affair and would make the Board members appear stupid and incompetent. Most of all, Harris feared that he and the other Board members themselves might take on liability as a result of their negligence. This is why he took his law partner along on the trip to Traverse City. As the train curved around the eastern shore of Grand Traverse Bay and approached Traverse City, attorneys Harris and Ruegsegger discussed the predicament. They agreed that Harris already had pursued the best course, but had failed when Herman Swift refused to resign his position as superintendent and sign over the assets of the Home to the Board.

In Traverse City, attorneys Harris and Ruegsegger appeared before Judge Frederick Mayne who was holding court in that city. They requested and received a temporary injunction preventing Swift from accessing his funds on deposit at the First National Bank and from borrowing money against the Beulah Home property.

On Wednesday, December 22nd, 1909, the *Charlevoix Courier* printed a front-page article with four subtitles. The last of these reads: "Restraining Order Granted by Judge Mayne, Against Swift Using Funds of Beulah Home for his Defense." The article ends:

"The restraining order was granted because Mr. Swift maintained that he had a right to use the funds to secure his bondsmen so that he could have his liberty pending his hearing at the next term of court. The board of trustees composed of some of the most prominent residents of Boyne City, maintain that while they want to give Swift a square deal in every way, still they cannot endanger the home's money or property. The board wants the superintendent to step out pending the proceedings and then if he is found innocent, he will be given back his place. This Mr. Swift refuses to do, but a successor will be appointed to have charge while he is in jail. Mrs. Swift is still at the home and there are about 70 boys.

The matter of the control of the Beulah Home funds and affairs raises an interesting question. It has been represented by Mr. Swift, it is stated, that Beulah Home was a corporation...It is possible the Beulah Home has no legal status whatever.

Mr. Swift of course has not been proven guilty. In his position, he comes in contact with some of the worst boys in the world, boys who know every form of human depravity. It is within their power, if they chafe at the restraint imposed upon them, to fabricate stories that will ruin a man for life and this must be taken into consideration in viewing the matter.

Similar charges have been made against Mr. Swift in the past in different cities as well as in this community and the general opinion is that the matter should be thoroughly tried out at this time, in justice to the people as well as to Mr. Swift, who maintains that he is entirely innocent of the charges brought against him."

On Tuesday, December 21st, 1909, the *Boyne Citizen* carried a front-page article titled: "Swift Enjoined by the Court" and subtitled: "It is Doubtful if the Home has Any Legal Corporate Existence." The article ends:

"It has been the means of advertising Boyne City as no other industry in the city has and until the recent cloud has been cast about it, it has been known as an institution for uplifting homeless as well as wayward boys.

Relatives of Mr. Swift arrived in the city Saturday."

Herman Swift's older sister Hattie and his younger sister Blenn undoubtedly were the Swift relatives who arrived in Boyne City on Saturday, December 18th, 1909. Grace Swift would have graciously hosted their stay at the Beulah Home. The Home contained a guest room in the basement. One of Herman's sisters had stayed there for a number of weeks a few years earlier and this is probably where the sisters stayed during their visit to Boyne City.

On December 21st, 1909, Herman Swift sat in the county jail in Charlevoix. The Beulah Home Board members sat in their offices or in their fine homes in Boyne City and they stewed about the events of the past week. A few of the Board members, including Godfrey Von Platen and Peter McIntire, had contributed considerable time in service to the Beulah Home. Most of the members, however, had served in order to provide the power of their reputations to the Home. Now this had backfired on them. With the arrest and examination of Herman Swift, the Beulah Home had gone from being the best "means for advertising Boyne City" to being the worst. Papers around the state of Michigan referred to Swift's troubles as the "Boyne City Affair." Whatever the individual Board members felt about Swift's guilt or innocence in the matter, they all were concerned about their reputations and their association with the Beulah Home and with the Boyne City Affair.

The Board members had met to discuss the Beulah Home situation and had elected to pursue a strategy of gaining Swift's resignation and his agreement to sign over the Beulah Home property and money in exchange for their financial support in his defense against the criminal charges. Beyond that, they pursued an even more attractive strategy. This would involve gaining Swift's agreement to their demands and then making the criminal cases disappear through negotiations either with the county authorities or with the parents or guardians of the three boys who had brought the charges. If this strategy proved successful, a prolonged courtroom circus would be avoided, Herman Swift would leave town, and the negative publicity would soon disappear. The *Boyne Citizen* article of December 21st included the following sentence:

"The *Citizen* learns that it is the intention of the trustees to incorporate the institution and put it on a legal basis and put someone in charge of the same to continue in the good work for which it was founded."

Unfortunately for the Board members, Herman Swift would not agree to their demands. Over the coming months, Swift himself would pursue the strategy of negotiating with parents and guardians. Board member Peter McIntire would assist him. Swift and McIntire would achieve some success in these efforts, but not with Edward Griffin.

IX

~

The John Hosner Trial

On Friday, December 24th, 1909, A.B. Klise arrived in Boyne City. Klise was a very successful lumber baron who lived in Petoskey. He was a religious man and a strong supporter of Herman Swift and the Beulah Home. Herman had two accounts at the First National Bank of Boyne City. One was an operating account that contained two thousand dollars and the other was a construction fund for the new building that contained six thousand dollars. A.B. Klise had donated one thousand dollars to the construction fund. Klise told the *Charlevoix Citizen* that he had given the money to Swift: "with no string tied to it, for whatever use he (Swift) thought best to expend it. He finds Swift in jail with not a penny with which to defend himself—all funds, including his $1,000 gift, being tied up by injunction. Mr. Klise says that if Swift is guilty he should be punished; if innocent he should be vindicated. But while that question is unsettled Swift should have a square deal and he is determined that he shall have it."

Klise claimed that he met with Beulah Home board members W.H. White and Peter McIntire. Klise argued that the two men should post bond for Herman Swift. He might have based the argument on his friendship with fellow lumber baron White. He might have argued that Swift was not a flight risk and that the Home had plenty of assets to support the bail, in spite of the Board's negligence in not incorporating and thus putting at risk the money from all the donors, including his $1,000. He certainly would have argued that it was humane to free Swift before Christmas day. Whatever Klise argued, he was successful. W.H. White, Peter McIntire, and Samuel Smith signed a bond for Herman Swift and he was released from the Charlevoix County jail on December 24th, the day Klise arrived in Boyne City.

On January 3rd, 1910, the *Petoskey Evening News* reprinted an article taken from the *Traverse City Record Eagle*. The article was titled: "A Real Friend" and subtitled: "Herman L. Swift Found Him in A.B. Klise." The article reads:

"There has been much said concerning the action of A.B. Klise of Petoskey in his defense of Herman L. Swift, superintendent of the Beulah Home in the case which will soon be tried out in the court founded on charges of immoral behavior. That these sayings have been by persons who are not acquainted with Mr. Klise is very evident, for those who know him realize that he has been prompted in his steps by a desire to see justice to an accused man. He has not taken this stand because he would shield a criminal, but for the purpose of giving the man a fair shake, and such is a characteristic in Mr. Klise, who has large lumbering interests in Emmet and adjoining counties...

It certainly looks black for Mr. Swift and it is a dispensation of Providence that there is a Mr. Klise to come to his rescue."

The arrival of perhaps another "dispensation of Providence" was first advertised in a front-page article in the *Petoskey Evening News* on Friday, December 24th, 1909, the day that Herman Swift was released from the county jail. The article announced the upcoming visit to Petoskey of Reverend Rueben Torrey, the famous evangelist and leader of the Moody Church and Moody Bible School. The article was headlined: "Evangelist Torrey Is A Logical Preacher Void of Sensation." This posed a curious but perhaps coincidental contrast to the ongoing sensation of the Boyne City Affair. The article reads:

"Rev. R.A. Torrey, the world renowned evangelist, who will conduct the great revival campaign in this city in the near future, is not of the shouting, sensational type of revivalist, but of the plain gospel preaching order, with sound principles which he advances with clear and concise logic, obtained from a wealth of knowledge and observation masterly in its completeness. He is just the kind of man that conservative, undemonstrative people needs and wants. He advances nothing but cold, hard facts, couched in simple but effective terms, and he lifts his hearers from the depths of ignorance and procrastination to heights of light and knowledge and then compels them by his eloquence and sound reasoning to perceive their danger and grasp the opportunity of profiting by the knowledge newly gained.

The first meeting in the campaign will be held at 10:30 a.m. Sunday, Jan. 2nd. Rev. Torrey will be assisted in his work by the Rev. J. Jacoby, Charles Butler, Mrs. Butler, and Miss Anderson."

The first week of January 1910, the *Petoskey Evening News* provided no coverage of the Boyne City Affair, as it provided extensive coverage of the Reuben Torrey revival campaign. On January 3rd, in a lengthy article the *Evening News* quoted from one of Torrey's sermons the prior day:

"Have you ever thought of the tremendous power that there is in personal hand-to-hand work? I want to talk to you about the advantages of personal work.

The first advantage is that anybody can do it. You cannot all preach. I am glad you can't. What an institution this world would be if we were all preachers! You cannot all sing like Butler and Young. I am glad you can't, for if you could they would be no attraction and you would not come out to hear them sing and give me a chance to preach to you. There is not a child of God that cannot do personal work. A mother with a large family knows she can do personal work better that anybody else. An invalid can do personal work..."

Reverend Reuben Torrey left the bedside of his dying sister in Chicago on New Year's Day of 1910. Over the past ten years Torrey had preached to huge crowds in major cities in England, Germany, France, Japan, China and India. He held large and famous revival campaigns in New York City, Philadelphia, and Chicago. But this New Year's Day he was traveling by train to Petoskey, a small town in northern Michigan.

While in Petoskey, Rev. Torrey may have met with Herman Swift and provided him counsel on his troubles. Perhaps he had thought of Swift as he prepared some of the sermons for the

Petoskey campaign and even as he preached some of those sermons. Almost certainly, Rev. Torrey was concerned that Swift and the Boyne City Affair might become associated with the Moody Church and perhaps he felt some sense of responsibility or guilt. Rev. Torrey preached of people making "stupid mistakes" and said they should "go at it again." He preached of forgiveness and giving people second chances, but possibly he had given Herman Swift one too many. First, he had allowed Swift to return to Chicago and open boys' homes in that city and in Leoni Township, after the troubles Swift had encountered in Buffalo. Then Herman had encountered troubles in both Chicago and Leoni.

It seems that Rev. Torrey either was unaware of Swift's establishment of the Beulah Home in Boyne City or chose to keep quiet about Swift's prior troubles and not warn the citizens of that city. Now Herman once more was in trouble and Rev. Torrey undoubtedly was concerned. The Petoskey Revival Campaign certainly had lofty goals, but one goal may have been to distance the Moody Church from Herman Swift.

A.B. Klise gained Swift's bail and his release from the county jail. Klise also hired and paid for a defense attorney for Swift. That attorney was a man named Lisle Shanahan. Shanahan was admitted to the practice of law in June 1899 in Washtenaw County, Michigan. He moved to Charlevoix County later that year. Shanahan was thirty-five, one of the younger attorneys practicing in the County, and he had supported the liquor interests' side of the prohibition debate. Outweighing this, however, were the facts that Shanahan lived in the City of Charlevoix and was the most noted defense attorney in that city. A December 30th, 1909 *Charlevoix Sentinel* article reporting that Shanahan had been retained to defend Swift closed with the following comment: "Whether or not it (Shanahan's hiring) is as associate counsel with Judge J.M. Harris, we have not learned."

Judge Harris' position soon became clear when it appeared in a *Boyne Citizen* article reprinted in the *Charlevoix Sentinel* on January 13th, 1910. Harris advised the *Boyne Citizen* reporter that a week earlier he had stopped participating in the legal defense of Herman Swift. The article continues:

"That it seemed to him (Harris) that because of persistent misrepresentations made by some of Mr. Swift's friends, if not by Mr. Swift, himself, as to the attitude of the (Beulah Home) Board of Control, that some expression of the Board's position in the matter might be given and that this position was this: The Board felt from the first that Mr. Swift should have every opportunity to defend himself from the charges that were made against him and also that it was the duty of the Board to see that the interests of the Home were protected, and it soon appeared that Mr. Swift's idea as to what should be done was radically different from that of the Board. The Board, in carrying out its idea, asked Mr. Swift to temporarily surrender his Trusteeship and control to the Board pending the investigation and the trial in order that the public, who were contributing toward the support of the home, might feel that their contributions and the work was being protected and Mr. Swift contended that it was against his interest to do that and there was nothing to turn over in the way of a trust for the reason that it belonged to him personally. Mr. Swift suggested that he would use the money to secure any one providing his bail, and offered to turn it over to the members of the Board for that purpose. The Board were advised that if it were a trust fund for a particular purpose that such an assignment would be illegal and moneys nor properties could be used for that purpose and in order to further secure these interests and because of the (Swift's) inclination to make an assignment of it, the Board applied for and secured an injunction temporarily restraining any such disposition of the property and at that time didn't furnish bail for Mr. Swift for reasons that appeared to them as sufficient, and furthermore that it was in the interest of Mr. Swift not to give bail at that time. Later the bail required was given and bonds signed by individual members of the Board and Mr. Swift was released. The claim has been made that Mr. Swift was prevented by the Board from giving bond sooner. This is erroneous and quite unfair to members of the Board. After bail was given an article appeared in the *Charlevoix Sentinel* based upon information furnished by Mr. Klise of Petoskey, that the Board through his influence had furnished bail, and this is also a mistake because the Board didn't know Mr. Klise in connection with Mr. Swift's interests in any way at that time, and more than that the matter of the giving of bail at the time it was given was in pursuance of a policy adopted by the Board at the time that Mr. Swift was bound over.

So far as the injunction is concerned, the Board has felt that anyone who had made contributions to what is known as the building fund, and wanted to change that and give it to Mr. Swift or to withdraw it altogether, that the Board would have no objection to that. As a further indication of the Board's desire that Mr. Swift should be treated fairly in all matters, it might be proper to say that several members of the Board offered to contribute, personally, sufficient funds to secure to Mr. Swift a thorough trial. That, of course, upon condition that Mr. Swift would so arrange the property rights that the trust would be protected for the purpose for which it was established.

When asked if he expected to defend Mr. Swift in the criminal case brought against him, Mr. Harris said further, no, he didn't expect to. That he was, along with Mr. Knowles, designated and employed by the Board, with the knowledge of Mr. Swift, to look after his preliminary hearing from the criminal charges and that after that hearing the matter of Mr. Swift's defense had been suggested to him a number of times and that he never felt in a position to make the defense and finally told Mr. Swift that it would be impossible for him to do so, last that he still represented the Board in the matter of property interests and that Mr. Knowles, who was associated with him in the criminal hearings, is also consulting with him and the Board in reference to the property rights, but that neither of them are interested in the defense of the criminal charges."

When John Harris told the *Boyne Citizen* that the Board considered it "would not be in Herman Swift's interest to gain bail at that time" he was inferring that some Board members feared the public might lynch Swift if he were released from jail.

Herman Swift resided in the county jail in Charlevoix from December 17th to December 24th, 1909. He was not allowed to see or telephone his wife Grace. He was allowed to call an attorney. By this point Swift realized that Harris and Knowles would not defend him unless he gave into the demands to resign his position and sign the Beulah Home property and monies over to the Board. Swift placed a call to attorney Elisha Clink in East Jordan and Clink agreed to defend him. Clink would work with Lisle Shanahan who had been retained by Klise.

Clink and Shanahan quickly achieved results. On December 24th, the two attorneys representing Herman Swift persuaded the County Circuit Court to reduce each of Swift's three bonds from four thousand to one thousand dollars. It seems that John Harris spoke the truth when he said the Beulah Home Board members never met with A.B. Klise. But Klise had hired Shanahan. Shanahan had negotiated a reduction in the bonds. Then Board members, including White, Smith, and McIntire signed the bonds on behalf of Swift. So Klise could claim credit for that last fact even though he might never have met personally with the Board.

The bonds required Herman Swift to appear personally before the next term of the Charlevoix County Circuit on February 7th, 1910 in order to face the charges against him. Sometime later in January 1910, the Board members told Swift that they were dropping off their bonds and surrendering him back to the court, which meant back to jail unless he could post new bonds.

Herman Swift appeared before Judge Mayne in Circuit Court on February 3rd, 1910. Harry Nichols and Robert Paddock, both from the City of Charlevoix, appeared with Swift and provided bonds. The Board members were relieved and discharged from any further obligations on the bonds for Swift. Nichols and Paddock: "acknowledged themselves to be indebted to the People of the State of Michigan in the sum of three thousand dollars to be levied on their goods and chattels, lands and tenements to the use of the said people if the said Hermon L. Swift shall default in the conditions following." Herman Swift had not taken the time to make many friends in Boyne City, let alone in Charlevoix. Nichols and Paddock undoubtedly were Shanahan's friends and Shanahan had persuaded them to post the bonds for Swift.

The case of The People versus Herman Swift was the first case heard before Judge Mayne in the Charlevoix County Circuit the morning of February 7th, 1910. Swift waived his right to a reading of the charges against him and pleaded not guilty. Then one of the attorneys, probably one of the defense attorneys, either Shanahan or Clink, asked for a postponement. Judge Mayne continued the case to March 29th, 1910.

One week later, on February 14th, the *Boyne Citizen* printed a front-page article under the headline: "Two Boys Taken From Beulah Home. Chief Beach and City Attorney Urquhart Make Demand For Them" and a sub-headline: "Both Are Brothers Of One Of The Complainants in Criminal Case." The article reads:

"City Attorney Urquhart and Chief of Police Beach each yesterday went to the Beulah Home, armed with the proper authority and took from the home Arthur Fay, aged 3 years and Eddie Fay, aged 11 years. These boys are brothers of Elliott Fay, one of the complainants in one of the cases against H.L. Swift.

When the officials arrived at the Home and stated their errand, they were told that Mr. Swift was not at home and they would have to see him, that Mr. Swift was in East Jordan conferring with his attorney. The officers were told the boys were in their rooms. Mr. Swift was called up at East Jordan and told of the errand of the officials. Attorney Clink was called to the phone at the East Jordan end of the line and told City Attorney Urquhart that he had better not take the boys, as he might get his fingers burned, but in reply the City Attorney told him that he has already had his fingers burned several times and that they were becoming somewhat calloused. Then followed a long conversation with Mr. Swift, but the result was that while the telephoning was going on Chief Beach went on a still hunt through the home for the boys, a little boy was out in the hall and asked if he knew where the Fay boys room was, and was told that they were not there, but they were in Grandma's room, which is located in the basement of the home. To the basement went the chief and there he found both boys alone.

They were told to pack up their clothes and all their belongings and to come with the officers, which they did. The boys are now located in private homes in the city and will probably be sent to their mother in Jackson, if a more suitable home is not found for them.

Mrs. Fay writes that she has written repeatedly to have her boys taken from the home, but that nothing has been done and that no attention has been paid to her letters.

Mrs. Fay is a widow woman, her husband being a motorman on an electric car, and he was killed in a collision near Ypsilanti last spring. She sent her three children to the home, promising to pay for their board, but owing to circumstances has fallen behind in her payments to the home, and since the recent disclosures at the home has been anxious to get them from the place, but it is alleged has been unable to do so hence, she sent the City Attorney power of attorney in the matter.

There are now forty boys quartered in the home. The first case that will be tried against Swift is that of John Hosner."

Between December of 1909 and February of 1910, some thirty boys were removed from the Beulah Home. The three Fay brothers were among them. Through the course of this story and in Appendix I, I will discuss some of the other boys that I know were removed from the Beulah Home during this three-month period. By April 1910, the number of inmates at the Home had fallen from seventy to thirty-one (Appendix I).

Shanahan and Clink were buying time to prepare their case in defense of Herman Swift, but as days passed, publicity in Charlevoix County turned decidedly against Herman. On February 23rd, 1910, the *Boyne Citizen* printed the following front-page article under the headline: "Judge Willis Brown May Be Selected As Manager For The Beulah Home." The article reads: "It is authoritatively stated that Judge Willis Brown, of Boy City fame, is a candidate for the position of manager of the Beulah Home, at Boyne City, with the probability that he will be selected.

This is on the assumption that Mr. Swift is eliminated from propositions, which is also among the probabilities. Swift claims property interests and that fact may involve complications but those interested in the enterprise say that they are sure of their ground in deposing Mr. Swift.

Whatever the outcome of the pending criminal action against Mr. Swift, it is certain that his usefulness at the Beulah Home is a thing of the past. Swift may be a scoundrel or he may be a martyr. Whichever he is there is a strong crystallization of public sentiment against him which even an acquittal could not remove. Hence he should abdicate or be removed.

No better selection than that of Judge Brown could be made. His soul is thoroughly saturated with the modern boy movement and he has had very much experience in the work. If Judge Brown lands the job we may expect to see the Home and the Boy City amalgamated to some extent, although their aim and purposes are along different lines."

Attorneys Clink and Shanahan understood very well the irony in this article about Boy City. Judge Brown had founded the Boy City Institution in the city of Charlevoix. Boy City operated summer camps that offered various forms of recreation, but principally operated to teach boys the elements of good citizenship. The boys ran the camp as if it were their own city. They elected officials from amongst themselves and established their own laws and rules. Boy City camps ran in a similar fashion to the way that Herman Swift said his Boys' Commonwealth ran. But Boy City camps tended to attract boys from well-to-do families, boys like those who resorted in Charlevoix during the summer, not like the boys who lived year-long in Charlevoix, Boyne City, and East Jordan, and certainly not like the boys who resided as inmates at the Beulah Home. Not surprisingly, shortly after the *Boyne Citizen* article was published Judge Brown publicly discouraged any discussion of his replacing Herman Swift and managing the Beulah Home.

More than irony, attorneys Clink and Shanahan saw opportunity in the February 23rd *Boyne Citizen* article. They felt the article created prejudice among potential jurors in Charlevoix County and later they would use it and other negative articles printed in the county to support a motion for a change of venue of the cases against Herman Swift.

Judge Mayne, as scheduled, on the morning of March 29th, 1910, once more opened court with a hearing of the case of The People versus Herman Swift. Attorney Clink moved that the hearing be delayed. Judge Mayne accepted that motion and continued the case until the next term of the Charlevoix County Circuit Court on May 9th, 1910.

One day in late April of 1910, attorney Clink boarded a train in East Jordan and traveled southeast to the City of Ypsilanti. There he met with Anna McCauley, John Hosner's eldest sister. Clink told Anna that Charlevoix County authorities had committed John to the County Poor Farm. John had not attended school for five months. Clink advised Anna that he personally had investigated John's charges against Herman Swift and he believed that John had been put up to making those charges. Clink said he did not believe that the charges were true. Clink would state in a deposition in the case that he had visited Ypsilanti: "For the purpose of seeing Mrs. Nat McCauley, an elder sister and married woman who had acted as mother to the said John Hosner, for the purpose of getting her to make a personal investigation of the facts in the case of her brother and after such investigation by her if she believed the charges concerning her brother to be true to induce him to tell the truth and the whole truth concerning the matter on the stand upon the trial of said cause.

This deponent further says that the said Mrs. McCauley informed this deponent that she was poor and that both she and her husband worked for a living but that if she had the money with which to pay her expenses she would go from Ypsilanti to the County of Charlevoix and investigate the case of the People vs. Hermon L. Swift in which he was accused of having misused and ill-treated her brother.

This deponent further says that he then and there informed the said Mrs. McCauley that his client, Mr. Swift, would pay her expenses to and from the County of Charlevoix for the purpose aforesaid and this deponent did not at that time nor afterwards, agree that the respondent should pay the said Mrs. McCauley anything for her time over and above her actual expenses.

This deponent further says that the said Mrs. McCauley during the time of this conversation, all of which took place in the presence of another lady, said after she investigated the case if she believes the respondent guilty she would insist upon the case being prosecuted but that if she believed Mr. Swift to be innocent she would want the case stopped.

This deponent further says that the said Mrs. Nat McCauley did visit the Beulah Home and afterwards did visit her brother who was then being kept by the officers at the County Poor Farm and that from what she learned by talking with the inmates of the Home and other persons engaged there it appeared to her that the respondent was innocent and that the prosecution was unjust but that she had made up her mind that she would not be fully convinced of this until after she talked with her brother, the said John Hosner, and that within a few minutes after she saw her brother he laid his head in her lap and began to cry telling her that it was all a lie about Mr. Swift and that he was put up by others to tell it."

Some three years later, in February of 1913, a letter from Anna McCauley appeared in an issue of Herman Swift's *The Youths' Outlook*. The letter largely parallels the deposition of Attorney Clink, but adds several interesting details about Anna's investigation of her brother's case against Herman Swift. Anna wrote that she had escorted Johnnie away from the Poor Farm building and out on the grass in order to speak with him. Johnnie began to cry and admitted to his lies in no more than a matter of three minutes. He said a larger boy had put him up to lying, but he did not blame that boy as much as "he blamed Mr. Jones, the hired man, for setting him up."

Anna McCauley signed and swore to the truthfulness of her letter before a notary public. She closed the letter with the following statement: "There can be no doubt but that Mr. Swift has been a terribly wronged man and as own sister of the lad who brought the charges, I stand ready to do all in my power to make right the harm that has been done."

Anna McCauley had been staying at the Beulah Home for two weeks, but did not meet her brother John at the County Poor Farm until the afternoon of Sunday, May 8th, 1910. It was the day before John's scheduled appearance in the courtroom in Charlevoix. If Anna persuaded John to change his story, Clink did not want to give the prosecution any time to get John to change it again. My guess is that Clink and Shanahan had prepared legal documents providing Anna with guardianship over John. This had enabled Anna to meet with John at the Poor Farm, even though Nicholas had instructed Poor Farm officials not to allow anyone to speak to the boy.

Urquhart and Nicholas knew that Anna McCauley was staying at the Beulah Home. They were worried about Swift's influence over Anna and her influence over her brother John. They knew that John was fragile and had attempted to shelter him from Swift and his defenders by placing him at the Poor Farm. Now Anna had spoiled that plan. Urquhart responded by meeting with John at the Poor Farm on the evening of May 8th. John cried and told Urquhart that he had been pressured into changing his story.

Judge Mayne called the Circuit Court to order the morning of May 9th, 1910. The three cases against Herman Swift were the first cases on the Court's agenda. Public interest in the Swift cases was great and officers turned away many people who lined up to be spectators to the trial. Prosecutor Nicholas knew that Johnnie Hosner had recanted his story, but in spite of this Nicholas called up the Hosner Case as the first case to appear before Judge Mayne that morning. Johnnie Hosner was crying when he was called up to the witness stand and sworn in. He scanned the courtroom and took comfort from looking at his sister Anna. Anna sat with Grace Swift, right behind the defendant, Herman Swift.

John Hosner started off by stating that his claims against Herman Swift were all lies and that he had sworn falsely against Swift because he had a grudge against him. Nicholas tried in a number of ways to get John to change his mind. He felt comfortable that he could bring the boy back to his original story, the story that Urquhart and Nicholas firmly believed was true. Nicholas was unsuccessful, however, and Judge Mayne did not even attempt to seat a jury to consider the case. Defense Attorney Clink moved that the case be thrown out, but Nicholas objected and Judge Mayne called a recess and consulted with the prosecutor and the defense attorneys. Mayne ultimately ruled that the Hosner Case and the other two cases against Swift all would be held over to the Court's next session in August.

Herman Swift was a happy man the afternoon of May 9th, 1910 as he boarded a ship in Charlevoix joined by his wife, his defense attorneys, Anna McCauley, and Anna's brother John. The group traveled back to Boyne City where they celebrated their victory with a dinner at the Beulah Home that evening. Swift would claim that Johnnie Hosner's testimony that morning had exonerated him from all the untrue charges. His celebration was short-lived.

X

The Simon Mack Case

The Merrill Griffin, John Hosner, and Elliott Fay cases against Herman Swift were Charlevoix County Circuit Court criminal cases numbered 218, 219, and 220, respectively. All three of these cases were filed on December 14th, 1909. Between December 14th, 1909 and June 17th, 1910 criminal cases 221 through 225 were filed in Charlevoix County. These involved charges ranging from assault to the theft of fishing rods. One involved prosecution of a man for selling five glasses full of intoxicating cider for five cents apiece. Case number 226 filed on June 17th was another case of the People vs. Herman Swift. The case was brought on a claim of indecent liberties. The claimant was Simon Mack.

When Herman Swift first was arrested in December of 1909, Boyne City officials were careful to keep Simon Mack separated from the group of boys placed at Rowan's. Arthur Urquhart had placed Simon in a private home in Boyne City and then had arranged for him to be placed with a family in Lakeview, a Michigan town located one hundred fifty miles south of Boyne City. Urquhart and Nicholas had resisted the temptation to bring a Simon Mack case against Swift for fear that it would open up an opportunity for the defense to strengthen their Sidney Jones/Simon Mack conspiracy theory. Now that the Hosner case had cratered, Urquhart and Nicholas decided to face that risk and bring another case. On May 10th, 1910, the day right after the Hosner debacle, Urquhart filed a complaint based on charges of indecent liberties taken by Swift against Simon Mack. He filed the complaint with Justice of the Peace William H. Collins of the City of Charlevoix. Collins issued an arrest warrant the very same day and at one o'clock that afternoon Boyne City deputy police officer Timothy Heaton brought Swift by ship back from Boyne City to Charlevoix where he appeared in court before Justice of the Peace Collins. At the conclusion of the May 10th hearing, Herman Swift requested an examination on the charges before Justice Collins. Swift also requested a postponement of that examination. Collins released Swift on an additional bond of fifteen hundred dollars and established the date of June 15th, 1910 for an examination of the charges by Simon Mack. Charlevoix County newspapers printed news of Swift's arrest in the Simon Mack case right along with their coverage of his court victory in the Hosner case. On May 19th, 1910, the *Charlevoix Sentinel* printed a front-page article titled: "The Mistakes of Swift." The article reads: "In the matter of this odiferous Swift case the *SENTINEL* started out with the proposition that the accused was innocent until proven guilty, and viewed with some disapprobation what appeared to be a prejudgement. And we would not now express an opinion as to his guilt or innocence. But we do not hesitate to express the opinion that Hermon L. Swift is an ass, if not a criminal; and he may be both.

Three cases, all identical, appeared in the circuit court calendar for the May term. When the first of the three cases was called last Monday it was found that the young complaining witness had recanted and acknowledged that he had lied…Swift was almost immediately thereafter re-arrested on another count for the same offense, and the accused stands just where he stood before the bailiff's gavel fell last Monday.

Yet there appeared in the *Grand Rapids Herald* of last Tuesday morning (the morning right after the Hosner trial) a special news dispatch from Charlevoix, unquestionably written or dictated by Swift, that the defendant in this cause celibre had been vindicated and discharged from custody. Mr. Swift knew that two cases remained on the calendar even had not the first one been renewed by a new complaint. He knew that he was under $7,000 bail bonds to appear in August. With Mr. Swift silence is golden, but he does not appear to appreciate the fact. Lying to the public will not help him any, and either he or some fool friend, with his knowledge, lied in that Grand Rapids special."

If Herman Swift was responsible for the *Grand Rapids Herald* article, it probably represented a message from him to Edward Griffin's friends and family in Grand Rapids. Edward Griffin's wife Nellie would have taken particular interest in the article.

The Federal Census taken in April of 1910 lists thirty-one boys as inmates at the Beulah Home in Boyne City. Appendix I includes brief biographies of most of those boys. At the time of the 1910 census, Elliott Fay had returned to Jackson and lived with his mother Maud. Merrill Griffin had returned to Grand Rapids and lived with his father Edward and his stepmother Nellie. The 1910 census lists twenty inmates at the Charlevoix County Infirmary in South Arm Township. Nineteen of these inmates ranged in age from fifty-eight to ninety-two. The twentieth inmate was a ten-year old boy. His name was John Hosner.

The 1910 census lists Simon Mack as a "foster son" of Holly and Clara Blanding of Lakeview in Montcalm County, Michigan. Holly managed a furniture factory. Simon was thirteen years old. In the census, he indicated that the birthplaces of his mother and father were "unknown" and that he was born in "Wyoming." This seems to me to tell us a little bit about Simon.

On June 15th, 1910, Simon Mack traveled to Charlevoix where he appeared as a claimant in an examination held before Justice of the Peace Collins. Defense attorneys Shanahan and Clink and Prosecuting Attorney Nicholas agreed to postpone the examination until ten o'clock the following morning. Simon Mack was called to the witness stand at precisely ten o'clock the morning of June 16th, 1910. Herman Swift was present during this examination. Arthur Urquhart began the examination:

URQUHART: "State your name."

SIMON: "My name is Simon Mack."

URQUHART: "Tell us where you have lived."

SIMON: "My home is at Lakeview, Michigan. Before living at Lakeview my home was in

Charlevoix County and I lived at Boyne City a little over four years. I came there in August 1905 (Simon had just turned nine years old) and left Boyne City about December 24th, 1909. While living in Boyne City I made my home at what is known as the Beulah Home."

URQUHART: "Are you acquainted with Hermon L. Swift?"

SIMON: "I am acquainted with Swift, also known as Ifeny (Author's note: Tiffany) who is manager at the Beulah Home."

URQUHART: "Where did you stay at the Home?"

SIMON: "While I lived there during about the last three months I had a room to myself. During two or three occasions while living at the Beulah Home I had a room to myself. The first time I had the room to myself about a week. The second time about six months. During the last three months I had a room at the Beulah Home Mr. Swift came to my room a number of times, one or two in the day time and the rest in the night. The last time he visited my room was about the 24th of November of 1909.

I fix on this date because it was when they were having court in Charlevoix, but I went to Mr. Urquhart's office and it was about six days before that time."

Urquhart continued the examination, questioning Simon about his claims of indecent liberties taken by Swift against him. Simon claimed the abuse had occurred "about forty times." Urquhart's examination closed:

URQUHART: "These acts that you have testified to regarding Mr. Swift's conduct toward you did they all occur in Charlevoix County?"

SIMON: "Yes, sir."

Attorney Clink then took up the cross examination of Simon Mack:

CLINK: "Are you acquainted with Mr. Urquhart?"

SIMON: "Yes, sir."

CLINK: "How long have you known him?"

SIMON: "About seven months."

CLINK: "Are you living at a home now that Mr. Urquhart secured for you?"

SIMON: "I was staying at a boarding house in Boyne City where he put me, and there was a lady there and she got me a home down at Lakeview and I am staying there at the present time."

CLINK: "Mr. Urquhart made the complaint in this case, did he not?"

URQUHART: "Objected to as immaterial and irrelevant."

SIMON: "I do not know what you mean."

CLINK: "Did you go with Mr. Urquhart before Mr. Collins in this case on the 10th of May last?"

SIMON: "Yes, sir."

CLINK: "Mr. Urquhart was present?"

SIMON: "Yes, sir."

CLINK: "Were you sworn on that date?"

SIMON: "Yes, sir."

CLINK: "Mr. Urquhart was sworn?"

SIMON: "Yes, sir."

CLINK: "Now it says in the complaint that on or about the 29th of November, 1909, at the City of Boyne City—that on or about that date Mr. Swift took indecent liberties with you. Is that it?"

SIMON: "Yes, sir."

CLINK: "How do you know that it was that date?"

SIMON: "I do not know that it was that date."

CLINK: "How near to that time do you know it was?"

SIMON: "I could not say."

CLINK: "Was it within a week of that date?"

SIMON: "About."

CLINK: "It would be a week before that date?"

SIMON: "I do know that it was that date."

CLINK: "It would be about a week before that?"

SIMON: "Yes, sir."

CLINK: "It was not a day before that, was it?"

SIMON: "I do not know."

CLINK: "Do you know whether it occurred a day before the court or not?"

SIMON: "Yes, sir."

CLINK: "Did it?"

SIMON: "The day I came down here on the 29th of November?"

CLINK: "Do you know whether it was on the 28th of November or not?"

SIMON: "No, sir."

CLINK: "Do you know whether it occurred on the 29th of November or not?"

SIMON: "No, sir."

CLINK: "Do you know whether it happened on the 27th of November or not?"

SIMON: "No, sir."

CLINK: "Or whether it was any other date in November do you?"

SIMON: "I do not know any certain date."

CLINK: "Now, how many times did Mr. Swift have anything to do with you in November, that is, taking indecent liberties with you?"

SIMON: "About five times."

CLINK: "How many?"

SIMON: "About five times."

CLINK: "Where did the first of those five times occur—that is taking indecent liberties with you?"

SIMON: "I do not remember where he did it first, but as near as I can remember it was in my room."

CLINK: "Where was your room?"

SIMON: "The last one in the hall, toward the middle of the building, right hand side of the hall."

CLINK: "Every time that he had anything to do with you was in this room?"

SIMON: "No."

CLINK: "Where else?"

SIMON: "In the office, in the attic, in the woodshed, in the furnace room, and in his room."

CLINK: "Well, when did he take indecent liberties with you in his office?"

SIMON: "I do not remember the exact date, but lots of times."

CLINK: "Tell us one time."

SIMON: "I cannot tell one time."

CLINK: "Is it possible for you to tell any particular time when he treated you wrongly?"

SIMON: "Yes, sir."

CLINK: "When?"

SIMON: "I do not remember the date. A boy seen me."

CLINK: "What boy?"

SIMON: "Harold Lane."

CLINK: "Who else saw you excepting Harold Lane?"

SIMON: "Homer Lane."

CLINK: "Who else saw you except Homer?"

SIMON: "Harold Lane, Homer saw me in my room."

CLINK: "The other Lane boy saw you in Mr. Swift's room?"

SIMON: "Yes, sir."

CLINK: "Anybody else see you at any time?"

SIMON: "Not that I know of."

CLINK: "The last two times that Mr. Swift took indecent liberties with you, where were they?"

SIMON: "In my room."

CLINK: "What room are you talking about?"

SIMON: "The room I slept in..."

CLINK: "You said something about fixing the date of these two times by the time court was in Charlevoix, was that the way you remembered the date?"

SIMON: "When he called on Mr. Nicholas, it was just a little while before."

CLINK: "Who?"

SIMON: "Mr. Urquhart."

CLINK: "Just a day or two before?"

SIMON: "About five days before."

CLINK: "Are you sure about that?"

SIMON: "Yes, sir, about."

CLINK: "And then it would be six or seven days before that that the other time occurred?"

SIMON: "It was about two days."

CLINK: "You said it was five days and now you say two days prior."

SIMON: "I don't understand."

PROSECUTOR NICHOLAS: "Take all the time you want."

CLINK: "You said it was about five days before Mr. Urquhart telephoned here. Mr. Swift was arrested the same day he telephoned here on the other charge."

SIMON: "I think so."

CLINK: "Now, it was about five days before his first arrest in this case, was it?"

SIMON: "Yes, sir."

CLINK: "And this other occurrence, the next to last, was either the night before or two nights before the last, was it?"

SIMON: "I do not understand."

CLINK: "On your direct examination you stated that the last time Mr. Swift had anything to do with you, that is, taking indecent liberties with you, was in your room."

SIMON: "Yes, sir."

CLINK: "And now you say it was about five days before his arrest in these other cases. You know of the other cases, the Fay case, you know about Mr. Swift being arrested in the Fay case don't you?"

SIMON: "I do not know that he was arrested. I do not know when he was."

CLINK: "You knew that he was arrested?"

SIMON: "No, I did not."

CLINK: "Did you know that he had been arrested in any other case?"

SIMON: "Yes, I think the Hoffman case."

I believe the "Hoffman case" refers to an indictment for indecent liberties brought against Herman Swift in Boyne City at a date prior to 1909. Swift had avoided trial on that charge, but Clink was not happy that Simon Mack had brought up the matter. Clink quickly changed subjects in his examination caring not to hear anymore about the "Hoffman case." Nicholas and Urquhart were well aware of the Hoffman indictment, but Judge Mayne had advised them to steer clear of reference to any past charges against Herman Swift.

Attorney Clink then asked Simon a series of questions about boys he had roomed with at the Beulah Home and a series of questions about any other times that Simon claimed Herman Swift had abused him. Simon indicated that initially he slept with his older brother who only stayed at the Home for a period of three months. Then Simon roomed with a boy named Archie Fryfield. After that he roomed with Harry Perline, a boy who left the Beulah Home in the spring of 1909. Clink did not concern himself too much with Simon's other claims of abuse. The defense attorney was pleased because he felt he had boxed Simon into claiming the last two events of abuse had occurred in a time frame when Herman Swift had a solid alibi of being away from the Home. The cross-examination continued:

CLINK: "Did Mr. Swift have to punish you while at the Home?"

SIMON: "Yes, sir."

CLINK: "About the same as the other boys?"

SIMON: "He punished me like he did the other boys."

CLINK: "You ate at the same table as the others?"

SIMON: "Yes, sir."

CLINK: "Slept in a room like the others...?"

SIMON: "Yes, sir."

CLINK: "And was treated just the same as the other boys?"

SIMON: "Yes, sir."

CLINK: "On your direct examination you said that Mr. Swift came to your room once or twice in the day time and the rest of the times he came at night, is that right?"

SIMON: "Yes, sir."

CLINK: "That the last time was November 24th."

SIMON: "I do not know the exact date."

CLINK: "Within a day or two of November 24th?"

SIMON: "Some time along there."

PROSECUTOR NICHOLAS: "I submit that has been answered twenty times. He said he did not quite remember that it was on the 24th."

THE JUSTICE: "He said about the 24th."

CLINK: "The 24th was the third week of the month. You are sure it wasn't as far back in the month as the 7th?"

PROSECUTOR NICHOLAS: "I submit that the question has been asked and answered a dozen times, and I insist that the question be not asked anymore."

CLINK: "If that is true it won't hurt the boy to say so."

THE JUSTICE: "We are not trying the case here in this court."

CLINK: "We have the right to know as definitely as possible what we are charged with."

THE JUSTICE: "The boy says he doesn't know. Give it as near as you can remember."

SIMON: "It was the 20th, along about that date, I could not remember."

Clink then asked Simon more detailed questions about his claims of abuse. At one point Clink asked: "Who told you to say 'I don't remember' in answer to my questions."

Clink's cross-examination continued:

CLINK: "What time did you go to bed at the Home?"

SIMON: "About eight o'clock, or half past eight, and sometimes nine o'clock and sometimes later than that."

CLINK: "Did the boys all go to bed at the same time at the Home?"

SIMON: "I do not know as they go exactly the same time."

CLINK: "They go to their rooms at the same time?"

SIMON: "Yes, sir."

CLINK: "Was there a bell that rang at night for them to go to bed?"

SIMON: "The bell rang for prayers and then they went to bed."

CLINK: "Did you all go to bed?"

SIMON: "Yes, all that was there."

CLINK: "All the boys that are at the Home attend prayer?"

SIMON: "No, sir. Sometimes boys are in the kitchen."

CLINK: "When not at work they are at prayer?"

SIMON: "I know I always went in."

CLINK: "Boys were not at work outside except driving team?"

SIMON: "Sometimes."

CLINK: "Would they be working on the farm at eight or nine o'clock?"

SIMON: "No."

CLINK: "When not driving team were they away from the Home?"

SIMON: "Not always."

CLINK: "Where were they?"

SIMON: "Downtown."

CLINK: "At what time did the boys get through work in the kitchen and go to bed?"

SIMON: "Just as soon as they got through work."

CLINK: "And if prayers are over do they go to bed as soon as they are through work?"

SIMON: "Most generally."

CLINK: "Is it a rule that every boy goes to bed at a certain time?"

SIMON: "Not every boy."

CLINK: "What boy has the right to stay up after the time for going to bed arrives? Did you ever stay up after prayers?"

SIMON: "Yes, sir."

CLINK: "On what occasion?"

SIMON: "When Mr. Swift was coming home."

CLINK: "When Mr. Swift was at home did you have the right to stay up after prayers?"

SIMON: "No, sir."

Clink then returned to questioning Simon about the acts, dates, and times of day of the instances of abuse. Simon indicated that initially he did not know that acts of gross indecency are wrong. He claimed he finally realized this because some of the other boys teased him about it. He testified that boys, including Homer Lane, Harold Lane, Hershel Moffatt and Celestino Paradies, had teased him. Clink closed by asking Simon if he would claim that he had ever been abused by anyone other than Mr. Swift. Simon answered: "No, sir."

The examination of Simon Mack in the Charlevoix Court of Justice of the Peace Collins ran much longer than any of the three examinations in Justice Shepherd's courtroom in Boyne City. The reason for this is rather obvious. In the examinations before Justice Shepherd, Herman Swift was defended by attorneys Harris and Knowles who represented the interests of the Beulah Home and its Board and not Swift's. In the Simon Mack examination before Justice Collins, attorney Clink represented Herman Swift and Clink's sole interest was defending Swift. Clink knew that at trial it was very important for an attorney only to ask questions when he knew the answers he would receive. In a hearing or examination, however, it made good sense for an attorney to raise any questions, no matter how damaging the answers might be, in order to best prepare a proper defense at trial.

Simon Mack was on the witness stand in Justice Collins' court from ten o'clock in the morning until noon, when Collins called a one and one-half hour recess for lunch. The examination then continued well into the afternoon. When it was completed, Collins again called a recess until eight o'clock that evening. This would allow time for the court stenographer to complete the transcript of the hearing and time for Collins to review that transcript and write his findings. At eight o'clock, Collins court again was called to order. Collins read the complete transcript of his deposition to Simon Mack. Simon agreed the transcript was correct and he signed it in large cursive letters. Justice Collins scribed his findings in curious, officious fashion and he read those findings to the parties to the hearing:

"It was made to appear to me the said Justice of the Peace that said offense was committed as charged in said complaint and warrant and that there was probable cause to believe said Hermon L. Swift to have been guilty thereof. I the said Justice of the Peace thereupon on the said 16th day of June 1910 require and order the said Hermon L. Swift to enter into a recognizance in the sum of two thousand dollars conditioned for the appearance of the said Hermon L. Swift at the next term of the Circuit Court in and for the County of Charlevoix to answer to such information as might be filed against the said Hermon L. Swift for said offense and in default thereof to be committed to the County Jail of said County of Charlevoix until the next term of said Court to answer to such information. That the said Hermon L Swift did enter into such recognizance as required by me as above set forth, I the said Justice of the Peace did thereupon discharge the said Hermon L. Swift from further custody."

Clink was not surprised that Collins had bound the Simon Mack case over for trial. Collins scheduled the case to be tried in Charlevoix County Circuit Court on August 15th, 1910. The other three cases against Herman Swift were among the criminal cases scheduled for that same day. While Clink was unhappy with Collins' ruling on the hearing, he was pleased with the results he had achieved in his examination of Simon Mack. Most importantly, he had placed boundaries around the dates Simon had claimed that the last two instances of abuse had occurred. Simon had testified they occurred between November 7th and November 24th of 1909. In fact, he testified that the last act occurred on November 20th. Clink could prove that his client, Herman Swift, was not in Boyne City on those dates. Between November 7th and November 24th, Swift was on the road with the Beulah Home Boys Quartette entertaining and raising money in southern Michigan.

XI

～

The Merrill Griffin Trial and the Boys Quartette

O n May 12th, 1910, the *Charlevoix Sentinel* reported on the John Hosner trial in an article subtitled: "Prosecution Falls Down on One of the Three Swift Cases."

Surprisingly, Judge Mayne had allowed the prosecution a continuance in the Hosner case. Prosecutor Nicholas and City Attorney Urquhart elected to continue the case for two reasons. First, it placed an added burden on Herman Swift in terms of required bail bond money. Second, and more importantly, Nicholas and Urquhart believed that dropping the Hosner case would provide some vindication for Swift and would reduce their prospects for success in the other cases.

As the August 15th, 1910 trial date approached, the prosecution faced the question of which case to bring first. Clearly, it would not be the Hosner case. Nicholas and Urquhart viewed Elliot Fay as a fragile witness and they did not wish to repeat their experience with Johnnie Hosner. Simon Mack was the oldest of the four boys by a period of almost three years. He also by a long stretch was the most confident. But if Simon was not a liar, at a minimum he showed a propensity to exaggerate. Furthermore, pursuing the Simon Mack case would open up the opportunity for the defense to probe and promote its theory of conspiracy among Sidney Jones, Simon, and the other three boys: John Hosner, Elliott Fay, and Merrill Griffin.

Merrill Griffin arrived in Boyne City with his father Edward on the evening of August 14th. Merrill's stepmother Nellie's fears were met when the prosecution decided to lead with Merrill's case. It is likely that Nellie had grown very angry when Edward agreed to bring Merrill to Boyne City to sit as the key witness in his case against Herman Swift. Nicholas and Urquhart spent the evening of August 14th preparing Merrill for the trial.

The morning of August 15th, Judge Mayne, presiding in the Charlevoix County Circuit in Charlevoix, called up his first case, Criminal Case number 218, the People versus Herman Swift. The press would refer to this as the Griffin case.

In the Griffin case, Prosecutor Nicholas, assisted by City Attorney Urquhart, represented the People. Elisha Clink represented Herman Swift. Court records show that an attorney from Cadillac, Michigan, "Mayor Gaffney," assisted Clink. Lisle Shanahan, the attorney who practiced in the City of Charlevoix, apparently was dealing with other matters and did not represent Herman Swift at this trial. Gaffney was a man named Francis or Frank O. Gaffney, a well-known defense attorney in Cadillac, a large town by northern Michigan standards that lies fifty miles south of Boyne City. In August 1910, Gaffney reputedly was positioned to soon take office as Michigan's 28th Circuit Court Judge. He had been elected to the office of Mayor of Cadillac on April 4th, 1910.

Jury selection represented Judge Mayne's first order of business in the Griffin case trial. A regular jury pool had been organized for the August session of court, but the *Boyne City Evening Journal* reported that in regard to the Griffin case: "It was impossible to secure a jury from the regulars for the reason that most of them were found to be incompetent on account of having formed opinions or for other causes." Court officers called in additional juror candidates. The judge worked with the prosecutor and the defense attorneys for a day and a half and finally at noon on August 16th, 1910, he was able to summon and swear in a jury.

The *Charlevoix Sentinel* in a front-page article on Wednesday, August 17th, 1910, noted: "Both sides announced Tuesday noon their satisfaction with the following jurors: William Wood, Thomas Shapton, George Olney, Charles Rounds, Mat Allen, Nat Burns, George Saunders, Ralph Dye, Frank Nelson, George Ager, William Seymore, and Thomas Cunningham."

The trial of Herman Swift as defendant in the Griffin case would occupy the time of Judge Mayne, his court and the twelve jurors for a full week, from August 15th to August 21st of 1910. Early Saturday morning on August 20th, two boys clung to a capsized canoe in Pine Lake just south of the City of Charlevoix. A passing ship's captain saved the boys just as they were about to drown. The rescue garnered newspaper coverage across the State of Michigan. The most complete coverage appeared in an article published in the *Charlevoix Sentinel* on August 24th, 1910. The article was titled: "SAVED FROM DROWNING" and subtitled: "Captain Weaver Picks Up Two Boys Saturday Morning" and "Were Sailing from Beulah Home to Charlevoix When Canoe Capsized." The article reads:

"For the second time this season Capt. Weaver, of the steamer Cummings, has been instrumental in saving lives. Saturday morning on the down trip (from Charlevoix to Boyne City) he picked up two boys who were clinging to an overturned canoe in Pine Lake. An object was seen in the water a mile or so off Ironton (a village located at the entrance of the South Arm into the main body of Pine Lake) by one of the crew, who thought it might be a flock of wild geese and he called the attention of the captain, who, with the aid of his glass, soon made out a boy's head bobbing up and down with the waves and a hand wildly waving. The boat was headed for, a mile or two away, and under a full head of steam soon came up to them and pulled aboard two very wet and very tired lads, who were nearly exhausted. They were Floyd Bishop and Evan Dunn, two boys from the Beulah Home. They said that they could not have stood it much longer for they had been in the water for more that three hours.

The boys left the Beulah Home at 3 o'clock in the morning in a small and frail canoe and with a homemade sail rigged up. All went well until far down the lake, and when abreast of the entrance to the South Arm, when a gust of wind upset the craft and plunged the lads into the water. They both succeeded in securing a hold on the capsized boat and hung on with desperation and with alternating hope and fear, until the Cummings was sighted when they did their utmost to attract attention. For a time they felt that they were doomed to continue the struggle but finally the boat was headed their way and their joy knew no bounds. They were on their way

Quartette of Boy Speakers and Singers (Fig.27)

to Charlevoix and Capt. Weaver left them here but took the canoe to Boyne City."

On Sunday, August 21st, 1910, the *Grand Rapids Herald* published an article about the rescue of the two boys on Pine Lake. This article was much shorter than the *Sentinel* article, but the *Herald* article concluded with the following interesting note: "Bishop is known as the boy orator of Beulah Home."

Floyd Bishop by a large degree was the most famous of the Beulah Home boy entertainers. The whole group of Beulah boys entertained visitors at the Home and entertained crowds at churches and halls in the Boyne City area. But when Herman Swift traveled to southern Michigan to entertain, promote, and raise money, he took along only four of the Beulah Home boys, the "Boys Quartette."

Fig.27 is a photograph of the: "Quartette of Boy Speakers and Singers from the Beulah Land Farm for Boys, Boyne City, Mich." Perhaps Edward Beebe took the photograph in a room at the Beulah Home. I believe the photograph was taken sometime in 1908. It then was utilized to produce a printed postcard in Germany, probably in a production run of over two thousand copies. Herman Swift sold the postcard at places where he and the Boys Quartette performed.

I believe that the boy on the far right in the photograph is Ora Crampton; the boy second from the right is a boy that Herman and Grace Swift called "Blackeyes"; the boy second from the left is Evan Dunn; and the boy to the far left is Floyd Bishop.

Ora Crampton

Ora Crampton was sixteen in August 1910 and he still resided as an inmate at the Beulah Home.

He was born in Saginaw, Michigan on March 23rd, 1894. His mother Susan May was married in 1892. She was fifteen years old. Susan May Crampton gave birth to a boy she named Cleo in 1893. In 1894, she gave birth to Ora. Susan May had just given birth to a third, and as yet unnamed, child when the Federal Census was taken in the summer of 1900. She lived with that baby, Ora, and Cleo in a home in Mecosta County, Michigan. The home was owned by Susan May's brother. Her husband did not live there. At some point, Ora, and probably his brother Cleo, were placed in the Beulah Home. Later, Cleo, his wife Edna and their children lived in Charlevoix County. Ora Crampton's World War I draft registration indicates that he was a short and slender boy.

Evan Dunn

Evan Dunn was born in Indiana on April 9, 1892. His mother's maiden name was Lizzie Hollis. Lizzie died sometime before 1900. In 1900, Evan lived with his father Alonzo and his grandmother Clara Hollis in a home in Marion County, Indiana. Evan's father worked as a foreman at a wheel works. I believe that Herman Swift recruited Evan to the Beulah Home because he recognized the boy was an excellent speaker and singer. Evan was eighteen and no longer resided at the Beulah Home the night when he and Floyd Bishop stole a canoe and almost drowned in Pine Lake.

Floyd Bishop

I believe that Floyd Bishop was born in North Dakota and was fourteen years old in 1910. Floyd was one of nine children. He had two living parents. His father ran a livery stable. The members of the family were Baptists. It seems that Herman Swift recruited Floyd to the Beulah Home, just as he had recruited Evan Dunn, because Floyd was an exceptional singer and speaker.

Floyd Bishop sent a letter from his new home in Osler, Saskatchewan, Canada to Herman Swift at the Beulah Home on October 17th, 1910. The letter was published in the January 1911 issue of *The Youth's Outlook*. In an abridged version, it reads:

"My Dear Mr. Swift: By this time you are doubtless wondering how I like my new Prairie home and seeing our minister has 'hit the trail for more schoolin',' I will write you and tell you all about it.

We were dropped off the train at a small place called Osler and were informed by the postman that we should strike the trail out past that little bluff, 'Yes, that's it, take the straight one,' he said, 'and stick to it, it's nigh on to four miles,' and then he was gone. Then we were in a fine pickle. I searched the prairie for miles around, but could see nothing that I thought looked like a bluff and only small clumps of trees here and there, so I struck out for the trees he had pointed out and found the 'trail' and arrived at my new home a little after dark. Everyone seemed glad to see me, but of course they did not know what day I would arrive and so did not meet us...

I suppose, like any other farmer you will want to know what the land is like. The surface is a black clay loam, sounds funny but it is really fine land. It does not look a bit clayey to me, but it is, I am told. It goes to a depth of about eighteen inches and is fully as rich as any I have ever seen in Michigan. Oats have yielded as high as a hundred bushels to the acre, and this year, although it was a very poor year, wheat yielded as high as forty-seven bushels to the acre, and all this on land that has never been fertilized and has been worked for ten or a dozen years...

The thing that impressed me most at first was the wonderful clear atmosphere (Author's note: Quite a contrast to the atmosphere in Boyne City in 1910)...I have often looked across the dead level toward Osler four miles away, and it seemed that the buildings were raised high up on some hill...At night the sight is equally wonderful, as we can see the lights of Hague, six miles away to the north, then follow down the line and see all stations by their lights until you are stopped at Saskatoon 24 miles away. I am told the elevators at Roster, twenty-two miles away, can be counted some mornings.

I remember the good old days at Beulah Home and how someone would start and then everyone would begin to talking about the wonderful sunsets. Well, I always thought they were fine, but out here with no hills to obstruct the view they are something different...

Well, how is everyone at the Home? How I would like to be back for a few hours or days and visit with all the 'kids' and give you the camp bear hug for all you have done for me. I bet you sometimes think I don't care a 'whoop' for what you and Beulah Home has done for me, and I probably show it too, but just wait until I get my homestead, summer after next, and get started there, and maybe I can show you I do care in a far more practical way than by words.

Well, it is getting late and I must close before I get to going again about my Prairie Home and the great Northwest, or there will be no sleep for me. Remember and drink about ten gallons of the cocoa cereal the first chance you have for me, and eat my usual number of seventeen pancakes, because I miss the Beulah Home cooking and Beulah Home in general.

Always with best love and wishes, Your Boy, Floyd Bishop"

Floyd proved in his letter that aside from being an excellent singer and speaker he also was a fine writer. Herman Swift added the following note to the conclusion of Floyd's letter: "Many thousands of people all over Michigan will remember Floyd Bishop as the champion speaker of the Beulah Boys Quartette. His fine impersonations and Negro dialect selections were seldom equaled. Those who have heard him give: 'Why Don't You Laugh?' or 'Angelina Johnson' or 'The One Legged Goose,' will never forget him. Floyd is certainly making good in the most excellent far western home in which he has been placed, and he is another living proof that it certainly pays to 'Give the Boy a Chance.'"

In February 1909, the Boys Quartette included Floyd Bishop, Ora Crampton, "Blackeyes," and a boy Herman and Grace called "Sunbeam" (Fig.24, p.65). Sunbeam had replaced Evan Dunn. Later in 1909, Earnest Wardell joined the Quartette replacing Sunbeam. The members of the Quartette epitomized the fact that positive life outcomes were possible for boys who had lived as inmates at Herman Swift's Beulah Home.

In 1930, Earnest Wardell lived in Royal Oak, Michigan with his wife Francis and five children. The eldest of the children was a girl named Ernestine. Earnest worked as a construction foreman.

In 1930, Ora Crampton lived in Lansing, Michigan with his wife Hazel. He worked as a barber. Ora's mother Susan May had remarried. She lived in Lansing with her husband and her oldest son Cleo.

In 1930, Evan Dunn lived in New Haven, Connecticut with his wife Grace and their daughter Patricia. Evan worked as a sales engineer for an electronics manufacturer.

Floyd Bishop enlisted in the Canadian Army on May 22nd, 1918. He was five feet six inches tall with blue eyes and brown hair. He indicated that he was single, a Baptist, and a farmer. Floyd had homesteaded a farm and eventually he acquired 160 acres, just like Herman Swift had done.

At three o'clock in the morning of Saturday, August 20th, 1910, Evan Dunn and Floyd Bishop stole a canoe and attempted to sail the length of Pine Lake from the Beulah Home in Boyne City all the way to Charlevoix. They almost drowned as a result of this endeavor. Many Michigan newspapers reported on the rescue of the two boys, but none of them mentioned why they were willing to risk their lives to get to Charlevoix. Evan and Floyd certainly were going there to support Herman Swift as he faced his accusers, the Judge, and the jury in the Circuit Court in that city. I imagine the two boys, wet clothes and all, headed to the courthouse when the captain of the *Cummings* set them on land in Charlevoix. They either attended or attempted to attend the trial of the Griffin case against Herman Swift. The case went to the jury the afternoon of August 20th. I imagine that Herman Swift arranged passage for Evan and Floyd on a ship that traveled from Charlevoix back to Boyne City that same day. They probably stayed at the Beulah Home that evening, but within a short time of this date, both boys would leave Boyne City and never return.

The jury in the Griffin case worked from one o'clock in the afternoon until eleven o'clock the evening of Saturday, August 20th. They returned Sunday morning to continue deliberating the case. On Wednesday, August 24th, the *Charlevoix Courier* reported the results of their deliberations: "The jury continued in continuous session until Sunday afternoon when they were discharged, being unable to agree. They were nearly evenly divided, the poll at the close, standing at seven to five (seven of the jurors favored acquittal and five favored a finding of guilty).

The case was very hotly contested, Prosecutor Nicholas ably looking after the interests of the people and making out a strong case, while the defendant's attorneys, Messrs. Clink and Gaffney, put up a strong conspiracy defense. The outcome of the case is very unsatisfactory to everybody as it was hoped that the matter might have been decided both in justice to Mr. Swift and the people."

Herman Swift returned to the Beulah Home the evening of Sunday, August 21st, 1910 and probably celebrated with Evan Dunn, Floyd Bishop, and the other boys at the Home. But Herman was far from totally satisfied. Judge Mayne hadn't dismissed the case against him. Instead, Mayne carried over the Griffin case as well as the three other cases against Swift to a court session in December. This decision seemed to favor the prosecution, giving them more time to prepare and perhaps to develop additional cases against Herman Swift. But Mayne may simply have been reacting to the fact that the Swift case had tied up his court for a week. He had other cases and though they were much less sensational than the Swift case; he had to deal with them. Possibly he thought that given enough time the prosecutor and the defense attorneys could negotiate some sort of deal on the charges against Swift. This would suggest, however, that he underestimated the tenacity of Nicholas and Urquhart and the stubborn character of Edward Griffin.

On Thursday, August 25th, 1910, the *Charlevoix Sentinel* printed an article titled: "Swift and the Beulah Mess." The article reads: "It does not require any extraordinary powers of discernment to recognize the fact that Swift and Beulah Home must be divorced if Beulah Home is to live and serve the philanthropic purpose for which it was established. Guilty or innocent, Swift should go. If he is innocent, fate seems to be pursuing him with relentless hatred, as the evidence disclosed the fact he has elsewhere been twice indicted for the same offence, and once before charged with it here.

Mr. Swift holds the title in the Beulah Home's property, and he cannot be disposed. He has eight thousand dollars in the Boyne City bank that was collected for Beulah Home purposes. He is possessed of all the sinews of war and will unquestionably fight to the end. But the fight is costing the people of Charlevoix County a good bit of money.

Swift's usefulness is ended in this-neck-of-the-woods. Five-twelfths or better of the people believe him guilty, and he cannot shake that conviction. Moreover, the people are beginning to hold their noses; they cannot much longer endure the stench. Guilty or innocent, Herman L. Swift has developed into a nuisance and a mighty expensive one. The philanthropist, like Caesar's wife, should be above suspicion."

Back on December 30th, 1909, a newspaper in Jackson, Michigan, reporting on the mid-December arrest of Herman Swift in Boyne City on charges of abuse of boys at the Beulah Home, had included the following comment: "(Swift) conducted a similar establishment in Jackson County some ten years ago and it came to an end because of exactly similar accusations. Swift obtained possession of an abandoned building and fifteen or twenty acres of land on the outskirts of Leoni Village and filled the house with waifs from Detroit, Chicago and other large cities. Some of the boys charged Mr. Swift with incomprehensible misconduct."

Reports of other past charges against Herman Swift had appeared widely in newspapers across Michigan, but prior to the August 25th, 1910 *Charlevoix Sentinel* article they received little coverage in Charlevoix County papers. It was true that rumors of past charges had circulated throughout the county, but the county newspapers had refused to print mere rumors. The past charges against Swift passed beyond the rumor stage as a result of the trial of the Griffin case.

In the Griffin case trial, Swift's attorneys elected to place him on the witness stand in his own defense. The result of the trial, the seven to five dead lock, suggests this tactic proved successful. On the other hand, by placing Swift on the stand defense attorneys Clink and Gaffney had provided Prosecutor Nicholas the opportunity to ask the defendant about similar charges or indictments he had faced in past years. During the trial, Nicholas suggested to Swift that he had in his possession copies of three indictments filed against Swift in the City of Chicago. He asked Swift about those indictments and Swift said he did not remember them. Swift responded that he had not been in Chicago for a long time when Nicholas asked him when he had last been in that city. Nicholas thus publicly raised the possibility that these indictments might still lie open and that that fact kept Herman Swift away from Chicago. Revelation of the past charges did not sway all of the jurors in the Griffin case trial, but as these revelations were published in Charlevoix County newspapers the public's opinion of Swift grew even more negative.

The August 25th, 1910 *Charlevoix Sentinel* article also inferred that Judge Mayne had ruled in Herman Swift's favor in the civil or chancery suit brought against him by the Beulah Home Board of Directors. In that suit the Board was attempting to take ownership and control of the Beulah Home property and monies away from Swift. The *Sentinel*'s reference to the decision in the civil case was untrue as the case remained unsettled, but the published claim that Swift held title to the money and property and could not "be disposed" would hold some sway with jurors in a subsequent trial and prove harmful to Herman Swift.

XII

The Motion for Change of Venue

On November 21st, 1910, attorneys Lisle Shanahan and Elisha Clink sent Prosecutor A.B. Nicholas a notice that they had filed a Motion for Change of Venue of the criminal cases against Herman Swift. Judge Mayne presiding in the Charlevoix County Court House would consider the motion on November 28th. Shanahan and Clink annexed a copy of the motion to the notice:

"And, now comes the said defendant, by his attorneys, Lisle Shanahan and Elisha N. Clink, and moves the said Court for an order and rule changing the venue of the above entitled cause to another County, which Motion is based upon the following grounds, to-wit:-

First. That the defendant is unable to procure a fair and impartial trial within the County of Charlevoix, on account of the prejudice against him of the people within the said County who would otherwise be competent to act as jurors on the trial of said cause.

Second. For the reason that there is a civil suit now pending in the Chancery Division of this Court, by the purported Board of Trustees, for the Beulah Land Farm for Boys, against the defendant, concerning title to the land and all the personal property of the said Home, and that the purported Board of Trustees, or a majority of them, have expressed themselves to so many people, at diverse times and places, derogatory of the good character and high standing of the defendant...

Third. That each and every paper within the said County of Charlevoix, have published what purported to be the People's side of this and the other causes now pending against the respondent, and each and every article have contained many false and libelous statements, ... Copies of which articles are hereto attached and made part of this Motion.

Fourth. That each and every paper within the said County of Charlevoix have published articles concerning the civil suit..., which said articles contained false and libelous statements derogatory of the good character and high standing of the defendant...

Fifth. That the Prosecuting Attorney, Sheriff and his appointees are prejudiced against the respondent...

This Motion is based upon the record and files in this cause and upon the affidavits of Hermon L. Swift, Elisha N. Clink, Lisle Shanahan, Robert W. Paddock, John S. Baker, Archie Swinton, Harry Nicholls, Peter F. McIntire, William Deadman, William Lewis, Samuel Richardson, Fred

E. Boosinger, W.R. Niegarth and additional affidavits to be filed and served later."

Aside from Herman Swift, his two defense lawyers, and Board member Peter McIntire, nine other men not directly involved in the case filed affidavits in support of the change of venue motion. All nine men stated that they had seen negative newspaper treatment of Herman Swift and had heard widespread public condemnation of Swift and that these facts would prevent him from receiving a fair trial in Charlevoix County. Only two of these nine men were farmers. Among the other seven: John S. Baker managed one of the upscale resort hotels in the City of Charlevoix. Archie Swinton was a popular merchant and Harry Nicholls owned a gristmill in that same city. William Deadman was a veterinary surgeon in Boyne City and probably cared for animals at the Beulah Land Farm. Finally, Fred E. Boosinger owned the largest clothing store in East Jordan. His name appeared in large letters on the face of that store and in advertisements run in local papers. Boosinger was one of the most well known men in Charlevoix County.

Hermon Swift began his affidavit stating that: "He has been a resident of the City of Boyne City for about eight years last past and that during all the time he so resided in this County he has managed and controlled 'The Beulah Land Farm for Boys" the same being a home for waifs and homeless boys ranging in age from Eight years upward.

The Home usually contains from Thirty to Eighty boys and he supports said Home by his own labor and that of the boys and by public contributions of interested friends of the Beulah Home, who reside in this and other states.

Most of the boys at the Home are boys who have no home of their own and have been taken from the streets and slums of the City and the others are boys of an incorrigible nature and disposition and cannot be controlled by their own parents and have committed crimes, and many of them have been arrested and nearly all of them have been addicted to the use of intoxicating liquors of one form or another and also to the use of cigarettes.

Many of the boys when they come to the Home are ragged and dirty and are addicted to stealing and use of profane and obscene language and it requires a great deal of time and attention to get the bad element of the boys under control so that they can be managed by myself and my employees. It requires considerable money to procure food, clothing, schoolbooks, school teachers, and other necessaries for the Home and boys and considerable time is taken up in giving entertainments to the public in different parts of the State for the purpose of obtaining funds with which to conduct the Home as aforesaid...

On account of time being taken up with work in caring for the Home and the boys he has not had the time to go visiting and to form acquaintances and make personal friends throughout the county, but on account of the work he is doing he is well and generally known by reputation within the County.

The Beulah Land Farm for Boys consists of a large building and some smaller ones and about One Hundred Sixty Acres of land which he purchased and owns and has owned ever since he came to the City of Boyne City and he paid for it with his own money and the purported Board of Trustees, or any member thereof, never paid One Dollar of their own money or of any money collected through the public from donations by any person toward the purchase price of said property known as "The Beulah Land Farm for Boys" or in any manner whatsoever."

Swift's affidavit then described his shabby treatment at the hands of public officials in Boyne City and Charlevoix. It detailed the efforts by the Board of Trustees to take the Beulah Home properties and money from him, adding:

"During his last trial...Mr. Nicholas brought into the case the question of ownership of the property and argued to the jury to the effect that if he (Swift) was not guilty of the offenses charged that he was guilty of trying to cheat and defraud the public by getting title or keeping title to the property known as the Beulah Land Farm for Boys."

The closing of Swift's affidavit included the following:

"He has been informed and believes said information to be true and therefore charges the facts to be that every county office connected with the trial have each and every time and on every occasion when the question arose concerning the charges he expects to be tried on, have expressed themselves in an emphatic manner that they believed he was guilty of each and every offense and of similar offenses that occurred at Leoni...

He is fully satisfied and believes that many persons, who would otherwise be competent jurors, have been prejudiced against him to such an extent that they would not now constitute a fair and impartial jury or a part thereof on account of the civil proceedings herein before referred to and the actions of the complainants of said cause."

Elisha Clink filed and swore to a twelve-page affidavit that accompanied the motion for a change of venue. Clink's affidavit included the following:

"That this deponent (Clink) has been informed that Elisha H. Shepherd just prior to the opening of his court for the examinations (the examinations of Elliott Fay, Merrill Griffin, and John Hosner shortly after the initial arrest of Herman Swift) expressed himself to the effect that prior to this time similar complaints had been made against the respondent in Boyne City and that they had been white washed over but that this case would not be white washed and the respondent would have to stand trial in the Circuit for the County of Charlevoix, thereby passing judgment upon the probable guilt or innocence of the respondent without first having heard any sworn testimony in the case. He (Shepherd) placed his recognizance in each case at the outrageous amount of $4,000."

Clink's affidavit claimed that potential jurors were prejudiced by (1) Prosecutor Alfred B. Nicholas' comments to people throughout the county, (2) by the behavior of attorneys Alfred Nicholas, Burton Nicholas, A.G. Urquhart, and Hon. John M. Harris who in the first Griffin trial would: "congregate in a bunch where the jury could see them" and (3) by the coverage of the Swift case in the county newspapers.

Clink's affidavit concluded: "This deponent further says that he has carefully investigated the causes of action and the evidence on the part of the defendant and believes that the arrest and charges are the out-come of a conspiracy, by others than the boys, and of a desire for revenge on the part of the boys who have alleged that the offenses have been committed because they were not permitted by the respondent to have their own way and do as they desired but on the contrary were compelled to obey the rules of the home..."

Lisle Shanahan's affidavit paralleled Clink's.

Peter McIntire's affidavit filed in support of the change of venue motion reads as follows: "Peter F. McIntire, being duly sworn, deposes and says, that he is a resident of the City of Boyne City, Charlevoix County, Michigan, and has been for a great many years last past and is well acquainted in said City.

Deponent further says that he is a member of the purported Board of Trustees for the Beulah Land Farm for Boys and at the time he became a member of said Board it was with the distinct understanding that he assumed no liability and further that the duty of the Board would consist of counseling and advising with Hermon L. Swift the owner and manager of said Home and of auditing the accounts of said Home.

Deponent further says that he never understood and never claimed, and does not now, that the Board owned the real property known as the Beulah Land Farm for Boys or had any real or equitable interest in it...

This deponent further says that he has visited the Home personally since the charges now pending against the said Swift were made and before and that at all times he has found the Home in good condition and the work of Mr. Swift well done.

Deponent further says that he has investigated the charges personally and believes each and every of them to be false and untrue in whole and in part.

Deponent further says that he is opposed to the Injunction Proceedings now pending in the Chancery Division of the Circuit Court ... so far as the injunction relates to any property other than the funds known as the New Building Fund and now on deposit in the First National Bank of Boyne City.

Deponent further says that he is opposed to the Injunction being continued against the Home and is opposed to the action now pending in the said Court for the removal of Mr. Swift and his wife from the said Home...

Deponent further says that he does not believe that the said Hermon L. Swift, if tried for any of the offenses of which he now stands charged, can have a fair and impartial jury and a fair and impartial trial within the said County of Charlevoix."

All of the original Beulah Home Board members must have given some thought to the risk of personally being sued as a result of the criminal and civil charges against Herman Swift. Most of those Board members had too much money, and several had too little money, to worry about being sued. Peter McIntire seemed to fall in the middle of these two groups and had just enough money to worry about personal financial exposure to the Swift legal problems. More importantly, a number of the Board members may have felt that Swift was innocent, but McIntire was the only one of those who provided support to Herman, including his support on the motion for change of venue.

Judge Mayne compressed the five grounds cited in the defense's motion for a change of venue into three grounds that he cited in his decision: the publication of certain articles in the County, the conduct of certain prosecution officials in the last trial, and the opinion or affidavits filed by certain county citizens to the effect that public sentiment would deny Herman Swift the opportunity for a fair trial.

On the matter of newspaper articles, Judge Mayne in his decision wrote: "I have noticed the articles in the papers referred to (in the motion for change of venue) very carefully and I do not recall—except in the article just last referred to (the *Charlevoix Sentinel* article of August 25th, 1910) any reflection upon the character of this respondent in any of the other articles. A statement of the case has been made but I do not recall that the writers expressed any opinion as to the guilt of the respondent in any of those articles. In fact, in the *Sentinel* article it is left an open question whether the acts were committed or not. He does there express an opinion that the conduct of Mr. Swift was not wise and I think that it was unfortunate that that article was written—from the standpoint of the Court; but I don't know that, if a juror had read each of those articles that the natural result would be a conclusion of guilt—or of innocence, from the articles themselves.

If I thought for one moment that the opinion of the writer of that one article—that five men of every twelve had formed an opinion I certainly should grant a change of venue or a new trial if a conviction were had. I, myself, am not, from observation, of the opinion that newspaper articles have the weight in prejudicing a jury that many people believe, even where they express an opinion. They understand that newspapers employ news agents and reporters and that it is their business to fill space and to report incidents and they also understand that many of those things reported as true today are corrected the next day, thereby filling two columns of space instead of one. So I don't think that the influence of the newspaper article upon the average juror is so great as many people believe."

The second claim in the motion for a change of venue, the complaint related to the prejudice and the behavior of the prosecuting officials during the August trial, Judge Mayne took as personal criticism of the way he ran his court. In his decision on the motion Judge Mayne wrote: "I do not recall except in the case of an application for leave to see one witness, that any question was raised concerning the conduct of any of the officers on the last trial and in relation to the prejudice which the officers entertained or that they now entertain towards the respondent, if such be true, I notice that there isn't a single affidavit to the point that any one of those officers has expressed any opinion to any person in this County upon this question so that, if they do entertain or have any prejudice as to those who have sworn they do not, they have at least not been guilty of—according to the affidavits—of attempting to influence the public thereby.

I observed carefully the conduct of the jury in the former trial and in relation to the conduct of the trial—if the matter were material in this case, which I question, but during every intermission during that trial the jury were either sent out by the back door, the audience not allowed to rise or pass out and during those intermissions when there was liable to be discussions, if discussions were had they were not in the presence of the jury—that is not in the courtroom and what took place in general could not be observed by the jury—of course, they had to mingle more or less, and I observed very carefully indeed because the nature of this case is such and the position of the parties that there was more than the ordinary tendency to have discussion of the case and I am satisfied that nothing was done to prejudice the jury."

With regard to the third ground for changing the venue of the case, the affidavits filed with the motion, Judge Mayne, wrote the following: "With an acquaintance in this County extending over nearly a third of a century and all of us being neighbors, and more or less intimately acquainted with each other's business, I was impressed with this fact: that a big majority—that is not a big majority, but more than half, were either parties interested—Mr. Swift, himself, or his counsel, and a majority of the others were those who are known as the warm personal friends—not only clients and business acquaintances but the warm personal friends of counsel in the case. Now that, of course, doesn't mean that they were influenced by improper motives, but I am of the opinion that, by reason of their friendship and their close relationship, their opinions may have been influenced and formed to a greater or less extent by this acquaintanceship and friendly interest in counsel as is but natural. I am not referring to anything outside of what we all experience."

Judge Mayne denied the motion for a change of venue. He read his opinion in court and when he concluded, attorney Clink politely asked him to grant the defense the benefit of an exception. This represented a formal objection to the judge's denial of the change of venue motion and would create the opportunity for the defense to again present this motion at a later date. Judge Mayne granted that exception.

The hearing on the change of venue motion concluded on November 28th, 1910. Early the next month the *Boyne City Journal* carried an interesting article reporting about robberies at the Beulah Home. Over the next few weeks a number of newspapers in Charlevoix and Emmet Counties reprinted the article. On December 12th, 1910 the *Petoskey Evening News* reprinted it under the headline: "BEULAH HOME ROBBED" and the sub-headline: "Manager Swift Says Evidence in his Case Was Stolen:"

"Mysterious burglaries which are said to have occurred at the Beulah Home may have their effect in delaying the trial of the case which is now set for December 27th. Nothing was taken except files of testimony to be used in the cases against Swift, he states.

Mr. Swift was reluctant to discuss the robberies when asked about them Friday morning, but finally told the story. He says that on three occasions, each of them occurring when he was out of the city, the home has been entered, at one time three men being seen in the halls.

On another occasion one of the boys at the home is said to have grappled with a man in the hall on the third floor. Breaking away the fellow, who was in his stocking feet according to the lad, ran to the porch and slid down the three stories to the ground, running away in the direction of the lake. The last entrance occurred the night before Halloween. The two dogs were heard barking and in the morning the pigeon holes in Mr. Swift's desk and that of his wife as well were found rifled.

Oddly enough, so Mr. Swift states, nothing was missing except the files in the cases against him. He has been in correspondence with persons all over the state whose testimony might be favorable to him and all of this mass of matter was taken.

'Copies of some of it are in my lawyers' hands, and I think by the 27th I shall be able to get hold of most of the rest by writing to the people again,' said Mr. Swift Friday morning. 'It strikes me as a mighty mean and low down trick to play.'

Swift does not accuse anyone of entering the house but intimates that it is odd nothing is missing but matter of this kind, valuables seemingly having been passed deliberately by. This fact, it is plain to see, makes him suspect that the entrances have to do with the case against him.

Claiming that their client, Herman L. Swift of this city, could not get an unprejudiced jury in the county, his attorneys Lisle Shanahan of Charlevoix and E.N. Clink of East Jordan asked Judge Mayne some time ago for a change of venue to another county.

Judge Mayne denied the application whereupon the attorneys applied to the Supreme Court (of Michigan) for a writ of mandamus to force Judge Mayne to show cause why the change of venue should not be granted. This application was denied and now the trial of the case has been set for December 27 in the Charlevoix County Circuit Court—*Boyne City Journal*."

A Petoskey jeweler had donated sets of flatware eating utensils for each of the Beulah Home boys. The boys ate from wooden bowls and plain ceramic plates, as did Herman and Grace Swift when they ate with the boys. When entertaining, however, the Swift's and their guests enjoyed delicious meals, using fine silver and eating from bone china. Afterwards, as the boys cleaned up they remembered Mr. Swift's admonition to care for the china and keep good track of the silver. They had never seen the word "Tiffany" before, but they read it on the silver, and they referred to Mr. Swift as "Tiffany." The robbers did not steal the china and did not steal the silver, but they were accused of stealing testimony in defense of Herman Swift from people across the state of Michigan. None of this testimony would appear in the trial of December 27th, 1910.

XIII

~

The Second Trial of The Griffin Case

Christmas of 1910 fell on a Sunday. Edward Griffin, his wife Nellie, and their four children attended church in Grand Rapids that morning. I imagine Nellie praying that Edward would change his mind. Now she and Edward had three daughters: Maria was five years old, Edna was three, and baby Florence was one. Nellie's stepson Wallis or Wallace had turned twelve the prior month on November 3rd, 1910. Wallace Merrill Griffin had left the Beulah Home in Boyne City and returned to his home a year earlier and they had taken to calling him Wallace and no longer called him Merrill. Wallace was progressing well in school and had stayed out of trouble since returning to Grand Rapids.

Nellie Griffin prayed in church and then the family went home. They lived on a tight budget, but that day Nellie served a wonderful Christmas dinner and then they opened presents. The three girls laughed in delight, ignorant of the gloom and apprehension falling over their parents. And when the children went to bed that night, I imagine Nellie beseeching Edward not to take their son Wallace Merrill back to Boyne City the following day. Merrill had already gone through one Swift trial the previous August. He and the family had endured the pressure and the humiliating disclosures. Nellie's relatives, the Leys and the Proos, had been dragged through the affair. I believe Nellie felt it was time for another boy to take the heat and all the negative publicity.

But Edward Griffin was tough and he was stubborn. He had promised Prosecutor Nicholas and City Attorney Urquhart that he would bring Merrill to Boyne City. He felt guilty for having allowed Merrill to be sent up to the Beulah Home and he was determined to seek justice and to punish Herman Swift. The morning of December 26th, 1910, Edward and Wallace Merrill Griffin boarded a train in Grand Rapids and traveled to Boyne City. That evening they spent a good deal of time with Nicholas and Urquhart. Using the same logic that compelled them back in August, the two attorneys had once more decided to place the Griffin case first in their line-up of cases against Herman Swift. The case was scheduled for trial the following morning.

The case of The People vs. Herman L. Swift, the Griffin case, was called before Judge Mayne in the Charlevoix County Circuit Court the morning of Tuesday, December 27th, 1910. The judge worked with the attorneys for the prosecution and the defense and after one and one half days finally seated a jury. The prosecutor or defense attorneys use what are termed preemptory challenges to eliminate a potential juror without any cause or basis. Both sides in a case are allowed a maximum number of these challenges. Swift's attorneys exhausted all their preemptory challenges in the seating of the jury in the Griffin case.

The Herman Swift criminal case might have been tried against standards established in at least two State of Michigan criminal statutes. The first of these was an 1897 debauchery statute that criminalized any act of indecent liberties taken by a male fifteen years of age or older against a male fourteen years of age or younger. The second was a gross indecency statute established in Act 198 of the Michigan Public Acts of 1903. Act 198 was passed on June 10th, 1903 and made it illegal in the State of Michigan for any male to engage in acts of indecency with another male. Act 198 established the punishment for such act as a term of confinement in a state prison for a period of up to five years or a fine of up to five thousand dollars or both. These two statutes were similar, but it seems the standards of proof were not as stringent in Act 198 and the prosecution charged Herman Swift against the standards of that Act. When the Swift jury was seated, the defense attorneys immediately moved to halt the trial on the basis that Act 198 was unconstitutional. Judge Mayne swiftly over-ruled that motion, but did recognize the objection or exception filed as a motion by the defense. The judge then swore in the jury.

Following the swearing in of the jury, defense attorney Clink again requested the judge to approve a motion for a change of venue. To support the motion, Clink had attached an affidavit containing copies of a number of articles that recently had appeared in Charlevoix County newspapers. He introduced this affidavit as Exhibit "A" in the trial proceedings. One of the articles in the affidavit was printed in the *Boyne City Evening Journal* on December 23rd, 1910. The article reads:

"This paper does not wish to do Mr. Swift an injustice. It does not wish to prejudice his case nor to prejudice him. It is confident he will get a fair trial. We have seen some signs, however, that various means were being used to create public sentiment favorable to him; trying to create the impression that he was a martyr. Frankly we think Mr. Swift has been guilty of trying to 'work' the 'paper.'"

The other newspaper articles introduced in Exhibit "A" all focused on a claim that Judge Mayne had ruled in favor of Herman Swift in the civil case. One of those articles appeared in the *Charlevoix County Herald* under the headline: "Judge Mayne Holds that Swift is Sole Owner of Home and Benefactions Worth $10,000." This published claim was untrue, but it would influence a number of the jurors.

Judge Mayne again rejected the change of venue motion and attorney Clink promptly objected to that decision. Judge Mayne noted the objection and turned to Prosecutor Nicholas. Nicholas called Merrill Griffin as his first witness. Merrill took the witness stand early the afternoon of December 28th, 1910. Nicholas began his examination.

In answering Nicholas' initial questions, Merrill responded that he had lived at the Beulah Home at Boyne City, Charlevoix County. He went there in August of 1909. He left: "because Mr. Swift was making me to do everything." He knew Mr. Beach. He had met with him a day or two or three before he left the Beulah Home. Mr. Urquhart was with him when he left with Beach. Nicholas' examination continued:

Nicholas: "Were you alone with Mr. Beach and Mr. Urquhart at this time?"

MERRILL: "There was a whole lot of other boys that went with us."

NICHOLAS: "Did you talk with Mr. Swift?"

MERRILL: "I had no talk with Mr. Swift after Mr. Beach and Mr. Urquhart left the Home. I did have a talk a day or two before Mr. Beach was there with Mr. Swift. Mr. Swift called me into the wash room and asked me if I would stick up for his side and if I did he said he would write home and tell my father that I was a good boy and he would think that I would be all right at home again."

NICHOLAS: "Where did you live at the Beulah Home?"

MERRILL: "I had a room on the third floor of the Beulah Home at first, then on the second floor. I was never in any of those rooms alone with Mr. Swift."

Merrill next testified that Mr. Swift had first abused him in the "guest room." He gave detailed responses to Nicholas' questions including mention of a book he had taken time to leaf through while in the room. The examination continued:

NICHOLAS: "Now where was the next time?"

MERRILL: "In Willis Roberts' room."

CLINK: "I, at this time object to the introduction of the commission of any other alleged offense, the prosecutor having elected this particular offense by introducing evidence of it first."

JUDGE MAYNE: "That has been held in some cases, but I think there is a case later than that that holds that the prosecution is not bound by the testimony of the first act presented."

CLINK: "Note an exception."

NICHOLAS: "Where is Willis Roberts' room?"

MERRILL: "On the second floor. I was there."

CLINK: "This is all under my objection incompetent, immaterial, and irrelevant and wholly inadmissible and as tending to prejudice the jury against this defendant."

Judge Mayne: "Yes, proceed, it is taken under your objection and exception."

Merrill then described the abuse that he claimed occurred in Willis Roberts' room and finally described the third instance of abuse that he claimed occurred in Swift's own room. Merrill claimed the first act of abuse occurred in September and the last two occurred in November of 1909.

Attorney Clink's cross-examination of Merrill Griffin began the morning of December 29th. The cross-examination included the following:

CLINK: "Did you ever sleep with your Uncle Cornelius?"

MERRILL: "I don't know who I slept with..."

CLINK: "Yesterday to Mr. Nicholas you said the second time happened in November also. Was that right?"

MERRILL: "Yes, sir."

CLINK: "And the first time in September and each of the other two times was..."

MERRILL: "In November."

CLINK: "Now in Justice Court (Author's note: Justice of the Peace Shepherd's court in Boyne City) you said the first time happened in August. Was you telling the truth then?"

MERRILL: "September."

CLINK: "Did you ever drink beer behind the lumber piles in Grand Rapids?"

MERRILL: "Not that I remember of. I used to drink beer before I came to the Home. But do not remember of drinking beer behind the lumber piles in Grand Rapids. I drank the beer at home. Never drank any away from home."

CLINK: "Before coming to the Beulah Home did you use tobacco?"

MERRILL: "I did not use tobacco that I remember of."

CLINK: "Before coming to the Beulah Home were you in the habit of lying?"

MERRILL: "I was in the habit of lying to my father before going to the Home. I would not stick to it."

CLINK: "In Justice Court you said: 'When I lied I would stick to it.' Was that true?"

MERRILL: "I would sometimes but not all the time. I don't tell any more lies. I have not told any more since I left the Home."

CLINK: "Did Mr. Swift or any of the teachers at the Beulah Home talk to you about your lying?"

MERRILL: "Mr. Swift never talked to me about telling lies. Nor any of the teachers that I remember."

CLINK: "Do you remember meeting with Mr. Swift a few days before he was arrested?"

MERRILL: "I remember a few days before Mr. Swift was arrested of all the children going in one room. I was one of them."

CLINK: "At that meeting was the question asked of you: 'Have you always been treated right by Mr. Swift and as kindly as your own father would treat you?'"

MERRILL: "I don't remember."

CLINK: "Do you remember any question of that kind being asked?"

MERRILL: "I remember one question being asked. If I would stick up for his side, and if I would write home and tell my father that I was a good boy and would write home and tell him that I would be a good boy at home. That was in the school room."

CLINK: "You never forgot that question did you?"

MERRILL: "No, sir."

CLINK: "Now was that in the school room the time the boys were together?"

MERRILL: "No, sir not that question."

CLINK: "Do you remember holding up your hand in answer to the question that Mr. Swift had treated you right at all times?"

MERRILL: "No, sir."

CLINK: "Do you know whether that kind of question was asked at that time?"

MERRILL: "No, sir."

CLINK: "Well, did you see any of the boys in the school room holding up their hands in answer to the question at that time?"

MERRILL: "Yes, sir. I saw them holding up their hands."

CLINK: "How many of them held up their hand?"

MERRILL: "Very nearly all of them. George Gates didn't hold up his hand. I don't remember whether he was the only boy, but he was one of them."

CLINK: "Did you see any others that didn't hold up his hands besides Gates?"

MERRILL: "Yes, sir, one was me."

CLINK: "You weren't to hold up your hand if Mr. Swift had done anything wrong to you. Is that right?"

MERRILL: "Yes, sir."

Defense attorney Clink at this point once more probed the issue of whether Uncle Cornelius had abused Merrill. Merrill said he hadn't. Clink then turned to questions related to the December 1st, 1909 letter that Merrill had written to his father.

CLINK: "How long was that letter written before you went to Mr. Rowan's?"

MERRILL: "I don't know. It was written after Thanksgivings Day."

CLINK: "What happened to that letter?"

MERRILL: "Well, Miss Ferris gave it to Mr. Beach. And Mr. Beach took it on Thanksgivings Day."

At this point, Judge Mayne asked for the letter. Police Chief Beach handed the letter to Mayne and Mayne handed the letter to attorney Clink who showed the letter to Merrill.

CLINK: "You wrote that?"

MERRILL: "Yes, sir."

Clink then moved to place the letter into evidence in the trial. Nicholas objected, but perhaps after conferring with Urquhart, he changed his mind.

NICHOLAS: "No, we withdraw the objection."

On December 29th, 1910, Merrill Griffin's December 1st, 1909 letter was entered into evidence in the trial as "Exhibit 1."

CLINK: "Now why did you write to your father that Mr. Swift had abused you two times and now you say it happened three times?"

MERRILL: "I don't know. I didn't know that they were having papers."

CLINK: "Why then did you write in this letter that you was trying to send Mr. Swift to prison?"

MERRILL: "All the rest of the boys were—were writing those letters. The other boys that were with me were all trying to send Mr. Swift to prison. I don't know whether they were trying to send Mr. Swift to prison or not but they was writing letters to their parents."

CLINK: "Did you see them writing letters?"

MERRILL: "I saw one boy give Miss Ferris a letter. That was Roy Fenton. I don't know what was in the letter. I was trying to get him in prison when I was telling Mr. Beach these things what I claimed he had done to me."

CLINK: "Which official said the word of a boy under twelve years would be taken before the words of older boys?"

MERRILL: "I don't remember. I think it was Mr. Beach or otherwise Mr. Urquhart."

CLINK: "Was Mr. Jones helping you boys get Mr. Swift into prison?"

NICHOLAS: "Objected to as calling for a conclusion of the witness."

JUDGE MAYNE: "Objection sustained."

CLINK: "Exception taken. I ask that because we expect to show a conspiracy."

JUDGE MAYNE: "When the time comes you may show that. But I don't think this is a proper question to ask this boy considering his age."

CLINK: "We expect to be able to show that this boy is one of the tools of Mr. Jones."

JUDGE MAYNE: "When the time comes you may show that. I don't think that this question at this time to this boy is proper."

CLINK: "Exception."

JUDGE MAYNE: "You have the right to ask the boy anything that Mr. Jones said or did to him, but not for his conclusions."

CLINK: "What did Mr. Jones say to you if anything about making this complaint?"

MERRILL: "Nothing that I remember."

CLINK: "What did officer Beach say to you bout making this complaint?"

MERRILL: "I did not complain to Mr. Beach. He asked me questions and I answered them about Mr. Swift. Mr. Beach came and asked me questions."

CLINK: "How did Mr. Beach get hold of your letter?"

MERRILL: "Miss Ferris told me that she gave it to Mr. Beach. She said she would send it away to my father and then she said that she read it. And she thought she would give it to Mr. Beach."

CLINK: (Pointing at Merrill's letter): "What do you mean by saying here that three years ago this same thing was found out?"

MERRILL: "Miss Ferris told the boys that—that was before we went into the big boys school room."

At this point in the trial, Nicholas interrupted the proceedings.

NICHOLAS: "I think I will ask permission of the court to make a further opening statement of the position of the people."

CLINK: "If Mr. Nicholas is going to make a further statement, let it be done in the absence of the jury from the room."

JUDGE MAYNE: "Perhaps his statement is a further statement to the jury."

NICHOLAS: "Yes, sir, as to the matter of this case as to what the people expect to be able to prove."

CLINK: "I object at this time to his making any further statement of the case."

JUDGE MAYNE: "Is this something that the defense have had notice of, so they would know?"

NICHOLAS: "Yes, sir—this was noticed in the last term of court."

JUDGE MAYNE: "And now you wish to make an additional statement of something you expect to prove, that you didn't cover in your opening?"

NICHOLAS: "Yes, sir."

JUDGE MAYNE: "You may proceed and do it."

CLINK: "Note an exception."

JUDGE MAYNE: "Note an exception. If the subject matter was objectionable at that time it is objectionable now. And if objectionable now, it would have been then. You may proceed."

NICHOLAS: "Gentleman of the jury, we further expect to be able to show in this case that the defendant, Herman L. Swift, is a hypnotist and that he—"

CLINK: "We wish an exception to that statement of the prosecutor."

JUDGE MAYNE: "Yes, sir, you may have an exception to all that is said."

CLINK: "We want an exception to all of it—with leave to specify the grounds later. At this time we say that it is immaterial, irrelevant, incompetent, and improper."

JUDGE MAYNE: "Yes, the stenographer has your objection and the grounds. Proceed."

NICHOLAS: "Now when you get through Mr. Clink."

CLINK: "And not alleged in the information and that the defendant has had no notice of it—no notice of these further allegations."

JUDGE MAYNE: "The prosecution may make their further statement."

CLINK: "Note an exception. Also that it is done and made at this time, for the sole and only purpose of prejudicing this jury against the respondent."

JUDGE MAYNE: "Proceed Mr. Nicholas."

NICHOLAS: "And that he practices hypnotism and that the witness Merrill Griffin is the subject of hypnotic suggestion exercised upon or over him by this defendant. We will show that he is capable of exercising this influence and practices it on occasion not only over this child but over others."

Nicholas' curious claim that Herman Swift practiced hypnotism effectively became a part of his opening statement to the jury, even though he introduced the claim later in the trial. Nicholas later would state that he intended to raise the hypnotism charge in his opening statement, but had omitted it as an oversight. Case files do indicate that at the first Merrill Griffin trial in August 1910 the prosecution had an expert witness who was prepared to testify in support of the hypnotism charge. The witness was a Boyne City physician, Dr. Judson Bennett. The *Boyne Citizen* referred to Bennett as the: "dean of the local medical profession, both in respect to age and length of residence in Boyne City." Bennett was a very serious looking old man with a long gray beard. The prosecution stated that he had traveled to attend to a boy at the Beulah Home. At the Home, Bennett observed Herman Swift hypnotize the boy. This enabled the doctor to perform a minor surgery without the aid of anesthetics. Bennett claimed Swift had boasted of his powers to hypnotize others. It seems that Bennett did not testify in the first Griffin trial and he certainly did not testify in the second. By making the hypnotism charge in the second trial Nicholas took on responsibility for proving the charge to the jury. Dr. Bennett was subpoenaed as a witness in the second trial, but never was called to the stand. Nicholas provided no evidence to support the hypnotism charge and thus never proved it.

On the surface, the prosecutor's case was very simple and consisted of only one witness, a little boy who testified of indecent liberties taken on him by Herman Swift. Around this straightforward and simple charge, however, there floated inferences of past acts of abuse by Swift, the civil case against Swift, and the charge of hypnotism. The jury could not avoid some consideration of these inferences.

Clink continued his cross-examination of Merrill Griffin:

CLINK: "At a time did Simon Mack say to you 'Will you stick to this against Swift?' and did you reply: 'No, I don't want to for it isn't true' or words to that effect?"

MERRILL: "No, sir."

CLINK: "Did Simon Mack say to you: 'If you will lie about Mr. Swift your father will believe you first and if we succeed we can both go back to Grand Rapids and have fun with the girls' or words to that effect."

MERRILL: "No, sir."

CLINK: "At that time and during the latter part of your conservation with Simon Mack, did you finally say to him that 'You would stick and try to bust up the home so that you wouldn't have to come back' or words to that effect?"

MERRILL: "No, sir."

CLINK: "I asked this morning the same questions about Robert Sparks."

Judge Mayne: "Now wouldn't these be matters of direct proof so it wouldn't be necessary to ask all these questions?"

CLINK: "If we offered them as direct proof, the question would arise, what was the object?"

Judge Mayne: "Wouldn't it be rather to show a conspiracy and admissible under that head?"

CLINK: "Yes, your honor, certainly."

Judge Mayne: "Well, if in the opinion of the Court it becomes necessary, you may recall him (Merrill Griffin). It may be admissible upon other grounds, but if I should consider it necessary for impeaching purposes, I will permit you to recall him."

Prosecutor Nicholas then took the floor in the courtroom and proceeded with a re-direct examination of Merrill Griffin.

NICHOLAS: "When was your first examination in this case?"

MERRILL: "That examination was held in Boyne City. Mr. Shepherd, Justice Shepherd, wrote down my answers. Mr. Urquhart and Mr. Harris asked me questions."

NICHOLAS: "Was Mr. Knowles there?"

MERRILL: "I don't remember if Mr. Knowles was there."

NICHOLAS: "Were you again a witness in this case?"

MERRILL: "I was a witness when this case was tried before. You and Mr. Clink asked me the questions."

NICHOLAS: "How old were you when this case commenced?"

MERRILL: "I am twelve years old now. I was eleven I think when the case was commenced."

NICHOLAS: "How much money did you steal when you were in Grand Rapids before you came to the Beulah Home?"

MERRILL: "I took some money from my father when I ran away at Grand Rapids. One time I went to my aunt's and one time to Ottawa Beach. I took about three or four dollars."

NICHOLAS: "Mr. Clink asked you if you were over to the court, what court was that?"

MERRILL: "The Juvenile Court in the Probate Office."

NICHOLAS: "How many times were you in that court?"

MERRILL: "I don't know how many times. My father and mother went with me. That was for running away from home and taking the money. It was about a month before I went to the Beulah Home."

NICHOLAS: "Now you said that you sometimes drank beer at home."

MERRILL: "When they had beer to drink at home they gave me some."

NICHOLAS: "Now at the time you were at the Beulah Home, Mr. Clink has stated, that the boys were called into a room. Were you asked to say how Mr. Swift treated you?"

MERRILL: "Yes, sir."

NICHOLAS: "Did he want the boys at that time to sign different papers, did he ask you to sign a paper?"

MERRILL: "No, sir. I don't know whether he had any papers for the boys to sign."

NICHOLAS: "Were boys allowed up in the sleeping halls during the day?"

MERRILL: "They had a rule at the Home that no boy was allowed upstairs before he had done up the work except as they were allowed permission. If they were caught upstairs they were fined."

Nicholas: "Did you see any other boys at the times that Mr. Swift took indecent liberties with you?"

MERRILL: "I saw no boys in those particular rooms at the time I went to the guest room, nor in the hall when I went to Willis Robert's room nor when I went to Mr. Swift's room."

NICHOLAS: "Tell me when the last act of indecency occurred."

MERRILL: "The last act of indecency occurred just before he went away and that was in November. When I went up to his room the last time he gave me one-half dozen postcards. He gave me those postcards before he went away, and had a whole lot of them packed in his suitcase. The suitcase was open at the time I saw it. He was gone about a week or so. He had been home from his trip about two days before Thanksgivings night."

Attorney Clink then took the floor of the courtroom and proceeded with a re-cross-examination of Merrill Griffin.

CLINK: "Where were you when the police arrested you in Grand Rapids?"

MERRILL: "I was down at the inter-urban station."

CLINK: "Did you ever use tobacco?"

MERRILL: "I never used tobacco. I did swear and use bad language in Grand Rapids and told bad stories and things of that kind."

CLINK: "Did you always do just what Mr. Swift told you?"

MERRILL: "Yes, sir."

This ended the testimony of Merrill Griffin and concluded the prosecutor's case. Prosecutor Nicholas representing the People had called only one witness and presented a simple case. Defense attorneys Clink and Shanahan would call many witnesses and present a rather complex case. Representing Herman Swift, the two attorneys waged their defense on three fronts. First, they would attempt to prove to the jury that Merrill Griffin was a bad boy, a boy who swore, drank, smoked, stole, was abused by his uncle Cornelius Proos and, most importantly, was a liar. Second, they would prove that Merrill's story was inconsistent and, importantly, that Herman Swift had an alibi. They would prove that Swift was out of town the day Merrill claimed he was abused for the third and last time. Third, they would prove that Merrill was part of a conspiracy. The Beulah Home farm manager, Sidney Jones, was the leader of the conspiracy. Jones had convinced Simon Mack to gather a group of boys and develop a common story of abuses against them by Swift. Jones' motive was to gain control of the Beulah Home farm and the boys' motive was to leave the Home and return to their homes.

Defense Attorney Clink first called Police Chief Beach to the witness stand. Before questioning Beach, Clink introduced into evidence as Exhibit "A" the complaint signed by Beach when Herman Swift was first arrested. The complaint had been amended within a few days of its filing and it is not clear if Exhibit "A" was the first or second form of the complaint. Beach's testimony was confused and rambling. Clink's key objective was to gain Beach's confirmation that the complaint stated that Herman Swift abused Merrill Griffin on November 23rd, 1909 and Beach had no choice but to confirm that fact. Later in the trial, the prosecution recalled Beach to the witness stand.

NICHOLAS: "Do you wish to make any correction in your statement that you made yesterday in regard to the time of complaint being made?"

BEACH: "I think I became somewhat confused in regard to the two complaints and, in my testimony in regard to the second complaint. I had the first complaint in mind at the time—till after I left the stand. I was aware I had made a mistake in the time and circumstances of issuing the complaint."

CLINK: "What difference do you mean? What time? What are you driving at? I don't understand the correction you are making."

BEACH: "Well, I don't exactly remember the exact question you asked me relative to the issuing this complaint and the investigation that was made, but when I was answering some of your questions, I had the investigation that was made prior to the issuing of the first complaint when the investigation was made at the home when I investigated this story of Merrill Griffin's and my answers were not in connection with the issuing of the second complaint. As a matter of fact, the boy was not there at all at the time of issuing the second complaint—or at the time the second complaint was made, nor he wasn't there present at the time the first complaint was made out. The talk with Griffin was in the afternoon and toward evening and the complaint was made out that evening—that was the first complaint. That complaint was made before he went to Rowan's. It was within a few days after the arrest was made that he was taken to Rowan's. I had nothing to do with him being taken to Rowan's. We used the same date as to the time the offense occurred in the second complaint that was in the first and that it was obtained from Merrill Griffin prior to the first complaint and that was the only knowledge that I had at the time."

Nicholas (On Redirect): "As a matter of fact did you have anything to do with fixing that particular date in the second complaint?"

BEACH: "I think you prepared that complaint which you presented to me for my signature. I don't know the exact date Merrill fixed in connection with some event. He said it was some time before Thanksgiving day because they remembered Thanksgiving day as a special date. They were taken in a body to a picture show. He also said that at the time of the commission of this act he was given some postal cards by Mr. Swift."

CLINK (On Re-cross): "Did the boy tell you he received the cards after Mr. Swift returned from a trip?"

BEACH: "I don't think he said at that time to me that Mr. Swift had been away from home and had returned. I don't think he said those postal cards were prepared for any special trip. He said they were cards gotten ready to be taken away by Mr. Swift on some trip to dispose of them or sell them in some way."

CLINK: "They were prepared for use in all trips, were they not?"

BEACH: "I didn't so understand it. I didn't understand how they were prepared. I simply understood from him that those postal cards were gotten ready to be taken on this trip that he was taking. That was the only thing he spoke in relation to this trip."

It seems that in the second trial the prosecution encouraged Merrill to note some items that were in the rooms where he claimed to be abused at the particular time of the abuse. In the case of the third instance of abuse in Swift's room, Merrill cited the postcards. Curiously, in the case of the second abuse, Merrill cited the presence of Swift's small black dog. The jury in the second trial would pay attention to the postcards and the small black dog and the defense would object strenuously to the fact that neither the postcards nor the dog were raised in testimony in the first trial.

Clink called James Leys as his second witness for the defense. James' birth name was Bastian and he was born in Grand Rapids on February 1st, 1898. Both his parents, Peter and Gertie, were born in Holland. Significantly, James' father Peter was a cousin of Merrill Griffin's stepmother Nellie. James resided as an inmate at the Beulah Home for three years, but had left the Home and returned to his family in Grand Rapids sometime between the spring of 1910 and the time of the second Griffin trial in December. I imagine that Peter Leys brought his son from Grand Rapids to appear as a witness in defense of Herman Swift at the trial in Charlevoix. The tension between Peter Leys and Edward Griffin must have reached a very high level. Clink began his examination of James Leys:

CLINK: "Do you know whether or not Merrill used to drink beer away from home?"

JAMES: "Yes, sir."

NICHOLAS: "We object to that."

JUDGE MAYNE: "I don't see how that can be material. The answer may be stricken out."

CLINK: "Give us an exception."

Clink focused his questions to James Leys on the matter of the conspiracy against Herman Swift.

Clink: "Did you know Merrill Griffin at the Beulah Home?"

JAMES: "Merrill Griffin was at the Beulah Home for about six months while I was there and roomed with me."

CLINK: "Did you ever hear Merrill Griffin talk with Simon Mack about getting Mr. Swift?"

James: "While I was at Beulah Home I heard Merrill Griffin and Simon Mack talking about Mr. Swift, or about this particular trouble. I think it was the day the officers came or else the day before. I heard Simon say 'will you stick against Swift?' Merrill said: 'No, my father sent me here not to lie or steal but to be a good boy.' Then Simon said: 'your father will believe you first.' Then Simon kept on talking to him in a lower tone. I don't know exactly what he was saying. Then Merrill said 'yes.' Simon said you tell the officers when they come that Swift abused you in the guest's chamber and in one or two other rooms. I don't know exactly. I was right above them on this porch when I heard them."

Attorney Clink then called Earnest Wardell to the witness stand. Clink attempted to use Wardell's testimony to prove Sidney Jones' role in the conspiracy. Judge Mayne took the position that at that point no evidence had connected Jones with the case and therefore the relationship between Wardell and Jones was unimportant. Clink proceeded to ask Wardell a series of questions. Each of these was followed by an objection by Nicholas, sustaining of the objection by Judge Mayne, and an exception by Clink.

CLINK: "Do you know Mr. Jones?"

EARNEST: "I know Mr. Jones. He did the farm work and other work that Mr. Swift asked him to do. He was the overseer of the new building and also the overseer of the farm."

CLINK: "State what you heard Mr. Jones say against Mr. Swift."

EARNEST: "He told me that Swift had found it out and for me to say yes to everything the officers told me and that it would be all right."

CLINK: "What was said about that—about what was found out—that Swift had found out, if you know, what had Swift found out that Mr. Jones referred to?"

Earnest's testimony as to what "Swift found out" almost certainly referred to the alleged conspiracy, but it was stricken from the record. His testimony continued:

EARNEST: "I talked with the officers at Beulah Home and Mr. Jones was present. When the officers came to the Beulah Home they asked me questions. They asked me if Mr. Swift had abused me and I said no. Then Mr. Jones raised his finger and said what did you tell me and then I said yes. I was taken to Mr. Rowans. I stayed there about a day and a night."

Attorney Clink then asked Earnest a series of questions: While at Rowan's did Earnest notify the officers that he had lied about Mr. Swift abusing him? Was he frightened when Mr. Jones pointed his finger at him? Why did he tell the officers that Mr. Swift had abused him? Did Mr. Jones in Earnest's presence try to get Simon Mack to induce Earnest and other boys to make accusations of abuse against Mr. Swift? All of Earnest Wardell's answers to these questions were stricken from the record, but it probably is safe to assume that he consistently answered: "Yes."

Some portions of the testimony in the second Griffin trial were stricken from the record. Over the years other portions either were lost or removed from the case file. It appears to me that most, if not all of these, had no bearing on the ultimate disposition of the case. In any event, Prosecutor Nicholas' initial cross-examination of Earnest Wardell is missing from the case file. Earnest later would reappear as a trial witness.

Attorney Clink called Mabel Hardy as the third witness for the defense. Mabel was sixty-eight years old. She had worked as a public school teacher in a number of Michigan cities and had performed deaconess work in the City of Detroit. Her home was in Brown City, Michigan, but in December 1910 she resided at the Beulah Home. She had been the teacher for the older boys at the Home for the past two years. Mabel testified:

"I know Merrill Griffin. I believe he was in my room in company with my scholars and in the presence of Mr. and Mrs. Swift and another teacher, Miss Ferris. On the day of the arrest, the boys were assembled in my room and Miss Ferris's pupils were brought in the room. All the boys were present excepting Simon Mack who was downtown. This was before the arrest. The arrest I believe was made the 1st day of December. This question was put to the boys: 'How many of the boys have never been ill treated or ill used in any way while in the Beulah Home and the boys responded. All the boys (Author's note: words stricken) as far as I could see voted (Author's note: words stricken) then the question was put if any of the boys have been ill used and no hands were raised. Merrill Griffin was present at the time. Before the question was put Mr. Swift assured the boys that no punishment would be administered whatever.

Mr. Swift was not at home on the 23rd day of November 1909. He was away on a trip with the quartette at that time. He left the home about ten or twelve days before that and did not return until late in the afternoon or evening of the 24th, the day before Thanksgiving on the late train. The boys of the home attended a show in the afternoon of Thanksgiving Day. I went to the show with them."

Nicholas (On Cross-examination): "Did Mr. Swift make you a nice Christmas present about $25.00 or something like that the last Christmas a year ago."

CLINK: "Objected to."

JUDGE MAYNE: "Sustained."

NICHOLAS: "By what other name was Merrill Griffin known?"

MABEL: "I think he had the name in the Home of Sunbeam."

NICHOLAS: "Do you know of the boys signing statements which had been prepared by Mr. Swift for each of them to sign in which they were asked to exonerate him from any charge of this kind?"

MABEL: "I can't recall that I do."

NICHOLAS: "Did you ever see any of those statements?"

MABEL: "I saw some that were not made by Mr. Swift."

NICHOLAS: "Were all the boys in your room asked to sign such a statement as that?"

MABEL: "They were."

Mabel Hardy left the Beulah Home shortly after the conclusion of the second Merrill Griffin trial. She took a teaching position at Ypsilanti State Normal. Over the next few years she would continue to write letters in support of Herman Swift. Leonora Ferris, the teacher of the Beulah Home's little boys, left the Home shortly after Herman Swift's arrest in December of 1909. She taught school in Greenville, Michigan in Montcalm County and did not testify in any of the Swift trials.

Robert Sparks

Attorney Clink called as his fourth defense witness a boy named Robert Sparks. Robert was twelve years old. He still resided as an inmate at the Beulah Home. He had been there for three years. Robert may have come from Eaton County. He testified:

"Merrill and I were punished together by being seated on the front stairs. I saw Merrill on the day the policemen came to the home and had a talk with him about the trouble. He said he didn't have much faith in the story that Mr. Swift done those things but that he was going to stick up for Simon Mack and that I was a fool if I didn't too."

CLINK: "Are you acquainted with Simon Mack?"

ROBERT: "I am acquainted with Simon Mack."

CLINK: "Did you ever hear him wrongfully try to act up any of the boys against Mr. Swift?"

JUDGE MAYNE: "You need not answer that question witness. The Court rules it out."

CLINK: "Note an exception."

JUDGE MAYNE: "Counsel, I think quite well knows that that is an improper question without ever the Court passing upon it."

ROBERT: "I heard Simon Mack talk with Elliott Fay."

CLINK: "If that question was in relation to him going against Mr. Swift, state it."

NICHOLAS: "The People object as asking for a conclusion."

JUDGE MAYNE: "Objection sustained."

NICHOLAS (On Cross-examination): "Witness, did you ever testify at the former trial of this case?"

ROBERT: "No, sir."

JUDGE MAYNE: "I will say Mr. Clink that there were some questions excluded yesterday that I think might be material, considering testimony that was later introduced connecting Mr. Jones and the other party. I did state then, that if later Mr. Jones was sufficiently connected with the transaction, that I would let the statement be considered, so you may cover that point, if you wish—that is present them, and I will pass upon them again."

Robert Sparks then responded to questions from attorney Clink and provided evidence that related to the Sidney Jones conspiracy against Swift. This testimony is stricken from the record, but the record does retain Prosecutor Nicholas' cross-examination of Robert.

NICHOLAS: "When was the first time you told this story?"

ROBERT: "The first time I told this story, which I repeated in Court, was about a year ago. I told it to Mr. Swift and Miss Hardy, they wrote it down. I was in the office at the time."

NICHOLAS: "Have you referred to the paper or memorized the story?"

ROBERT: "I did not memorize it or refer to the paper, but I have thought it over so I could remember the testimony."

NICHOLAS: "Did you ask Mr. Swift to see the paper?"

ROBERT: "I asked him twice to see the paper. The second time just before coming down here."

NICHOLAS: "Is your testimony the same as what's on the paper?"

ROBERT: 'I don't know that my testimony here in court is exactly the same as that on the paper, but it is just as near as I can remember."

CLINK (On Re-exam): "Did Mr. Swift come to you and ask you to make a statement in this case?"

ROBERT: "Mr. Swift did not come to me and ask me to make a statement, until I told him that I knew some things. The paper that was written—is in my own words."

CLINK: "Did Mr. Swift ever ask you to change your evidence in any way?"

ROBERT: "No, sir."

CLINK: "Has anyone in behalf of Mr. Swift ever asked you to change your evidence?"

ROBERT: "No, sir."

NICHOLAS (Further Cross-exam): "Haven't you ever seen this paper more that just the twice—your testimony."

ROBERT: "Yes, sir."

NICHOLAS: "Yes, I thought so, more times than twice, haven't you?"

ROBERT: "Just once or twice each time when I would want to remember it."

NICHOLAS: "Yes, now who would let you have the paper when you wanted to look it over?"

ROBERT: "Mr. Clink had the real copy."

NICHOLAS: "No, no, who would let you have the paper when you wanted to look it over?"

ROBERT: "Mr. Swift."

NICHOLAS: "Yes, Mr. Swift let you have it each time, did he?"

ROBERT: "Yes, sir."

Samuel Valentine

Attorney Clink called a boy named Samuel Valentine as his next witness for the defense. I believe that Samuel was born in Troy, Ohio in April of 1896. His mother Emma had eleven children, but three had died at an early age. His father Samuel worked as a laborer in an umbrella factory. He died sometime before 1910, probably in 1907 when young Samuel was sent to the Beulah Home. Young Samuel still resided as an inmate at the Beulah Home in December of 1910. He testified that he had been living at the Home for a period of two years and five months. Samuel must have been counting the months. He testified:

"I heard Simon Mack express himself at the Home against Mr. Swift. He said he did not intend to stay in the G.D.S. of a B. and he would make it mighty tight for Swift if he did. I know Mr. Jones. He worked at the farm and on the new building and I worked under him. I heard Mr. Jones say that the reason he went against Mr. Swift was because he worked the boys too hard and made slaves of the boys."

CLINK: "How did Mr. Jones say the words that he was against Mr. Swift?"

SAMUEL: "Yes, sir. Mr. Jones said that he would like to get hold of the Home because he could run it better than Mr. Swift did."

NICHOLAS (On Cross-exam): "When did you first know about this testimony?"

SAMUEL: "The first I knew anything about it was 1909 when it first came up."

NICHOLAS: "Tell me about what you did right at first."

SAMUEL: "I wrote on a piece of paper for Mr. Clink what I had to tell about Jones. I first wrote it in my own hand and then Mr. Swift copied it on a typewriter and sent it to Mr. Clink. I was present the time it was written. He sent one copy to Mr. Clink and kept one. I afterwards saw the typewritten paper with that testimony on it. I saw it when Mr. Swift wanted to know if it was all right. The last time I saw it was about a week or half week ago. I saw it whenever I asked Mr. Swift to see it."

CLINK (On Re-exam): "Now Samuel was I present at the school room at the time you wrote this down, your statement?"

SAMUEL: "No, sir."

CLINK: "Did you write it at my request?"

SAMUEL: "Yes, sir."

JUDGE MAYNE: "Mr. Clink, in order that the ruling may be correct, do you claim that you made the request of this boy personally, if so, he has a right to testify to it, if not, it would be hearsay."

CLINK: "I don't know your Honor, some of them I did, I know."

NICHOLAS: "The boy says Mr. Clink was not there."

JUDGE MAYNE: "Very well, if Mr. Clink was not there, it remains stricken out."

Donald Thomas

The judge ruled that Samuel Valentine's statement be stricken from the record, but that did not happen. Attorney Clink then called to the stand a boy named Donald Thomas. I believe Donald had come to the Beulah Home from Albion, Michigan. He was thirteen years old. He had lived at the Beulah Home for two years, but I believe he no longer lived there at the time he testified regarding comments against Herman Swift by both Simon Mack and Sidney Jones. That testimony was stricken from the record. In response to Prosecutor Nicholas' cross-exam, Donald testified: "I was seated in the play room with the rest of the boys. I didn't tell in the presence of all the boys. I wrote it down and handed it to Mr. Swift. He gave it to Mr. Clink. I think Mr. Swift made a typewritten copy of it, but I didn't see him. I saw the paper after it was made. The last time was two or three days before we came over here. I saw in that paper what I was to testify to here in Court; I don't know whether I saw the paper the time of the last trial or not.

NICHOLAS: "Well, now wasn't you up in the Ferguson House one night?" (Author's note: probably the home of widow Laura Ferguson at 324 Cedar Street in Boyne City.)

DONALD: "Yes, sir."

NICHOLAS: "And didn't Mr. Swift then have in his grip all what the boys were to testify to and read it over to the boys?"

CLINK: "We object to that. There is no evidence now of it."

JUDGE MAYNE: "Answer. Note an exception."

DONALD: "He never read anything to me. It may have been a day or so after I wrote it down what I was to testify to before it was in typewriting. Mr. Swift handed it to me to see if it was the same and I said it was. It was read all over. I read it again just before we came over here. Mr. Clink kept one of the papers. I got the one I read over from Mr. Swift."

Celestino Paradies

Attorney Clink then called Celestino Paradies as the next witness for the defense. Celestino was sixteen years old. He was from Cardenas, Cuba. He had lived as an inmate at the Beulah Home for four or five years. The boys called him "Cuba."

CLINK: "Did you know Simon Mack?"

CELESTINO: "Yes, sir."

CLINK: "Did you hear Simon Mack say anything about getting even with Mr. Swift."

CELESTINO: "Yes, sir."

CLINK: "What was it?"

CELESTINO: "He said he worked for his board and ten times over at one time and he has got mad at Mr. Swift because Mr. Swift put him out of his room and charged him a dollar for going into another boy's room. That is a rule of the Home."

JUDGE MAYNE: "No, just tell what he said."

CELESTINO: "He said he was going to get even with him."

CLINK: "Were you acquainted with Mr. Jones?"

CELESTINO: "Yes, sir. Mr. Jones said Mr. Swift was a S. of a B. At another time he said he could run the Home better than Mr. Swift and would give the boys more time to play. He said I could get two dollars a day anywhere else and not to work there for Mr. Swift."

NICHOLAS (On Cross-exam): "Didn't you act as a policeman in 1909?"

CELESTINO: "I don't know."

NICHOLAS: "Oh, you know—can't you remember that long?"

CELESTINO: "No, sir."

NICHOLAS: "You can't remember back as far as November, 1909?"

CELESTINO: "No, sir."

NICHOLAS: "Can you remember back as far as August, 1910?"

CLINK: "We object to that as unfair to the witness."

JUDGE MAYNE: "Answer. Note an exception…"

NICHOLAS: "Did you ever talk over with Mr. Swift what you were going to swear to here in Court?"

CELESTINO: "I don't think I did."

NICHOLAS: "Now, witness, do you want this jury to understand that you don't know whether you ever talked over what you would swear to with Mr. Swift?"

CELESTINO: "I had it wrote down but I told it myself."

NICHOLAS: "Yes, who wrote it down?"

CELESTINO: "Miss Hardy, our school teacher, I think I told her what I knew and she wrote it down."

NICHOLAS: "Then did they have that copied on the typewriter?"

CELESTINO: "Yes, sir."

NICHOLAS: "Yes, then you read it over to see if that was what you were going to tell when you got down here to Court didn't you?"

CELESTINO: "I read it to see if it was right what I said."

NICHOLAS: "Yes, and it was down on that paper what you was going to swear to?"

CELESTINO: "I guess so."

NICHOLAS: "Who had that paper when you read it over?"

CELESTIINO: "I did when I read it over, but Mr. Swift handed it to me."

NICHOLAS: "Did you ask him for it?"

CELESTINO: "Yes, sir."

NICHOLAS: "What did you want of it?"

CELESTINO: "So I could remember."

Frank Gustin

Attorney Clink called as the next witness for the defense a boy named Frank Gustin. Frank was from Flint, Michigan. He was fifteen years old. His father had died in 1907 and Frank was sent to the Beulah Home in 1908. In the summer of 1910, Frank's mother Edith worked as a housekeeper and lived in the home of a farmer named Samuel Bacon. The farm was located in Flushing Township, just outside Flint. At the inception of the Boyne City Affair, Edith had retrieved Frank. Frank continued to live with his mother when he testified in the second Merrill Griffin trial in December 1910:

FRANK: "I heard Simon Mack talk to Roy (Roy Fenton) and he told Roy that he was a fool if he didn't go against Mr. Swift, because he could go back to Onaway and smoke and have a lot of fun. Right after he got through talking with Roy he came over and talked to me. Yes, sir two or three days before Mr. Swift was arrested, he wanted me to say that the boys had to work too hard and that they was not treated well…

CLINK: "Well, was it true that you had to work too hard?"

NICHOLAS: "Objected to as irrelevant and incompetent."

JUDGE MAYNE: "Objection sustained. Exception taken."

CLINK: "How many hours a day did you work?"

NICHOLAS: "The People make the same objection."

JUDGE MAYNE: "Objection sustained. Exception taken."

FRANK: "Simon Mack said to me I don't care whether you do or not Gustin but you are a fool if you don't. I heard Mr. Jones say that Mr. Swift was a damn fool for going around and telling the boys about the boat so that they would all go down the lake with him. He said if he had control of the Home and he would run it right and the boys wouldn't have to work so hard and he was all the time telling how much better he could do than Mr. Swift—"

JUDGE MAYNE: "No, no, just tell what he told you, the last part of the answer is stricken out."

NICHOLAS (On Cross-exam): "I think you testified at the last trial, that you went to Flint, didn't you?"

FRANK: "Yes, sir."

NICHOLAS: "Did you write down on a piece of paper while in Flint what you were going to testify to when you came to Court?"

FRANK: "Yes, sir."

NICHOLAS: "Did you not testify at the last trial that you read that over, the evidence that you were going to testify to a number of times and then tore it up the paper and threw it away?"

CLINK: "Just wait a moment please, till I get an opportunity to make an objection."

JUDGE MAYNE: "Your objection is made and over-ruled."

CLINK: "How?"

JUDGE MAYNE: "Your objection may be considered as made and over-ruled."

CLINK: "Note and exception."

FRANK: "I simply wrote it down and threw it away. I didn't read it at all."

NICHOLAS: "How long was you writing it down?"

FRANK: "About five minutes."

NICHOLAS: "On that paper did you have written down all you were going to testify to up here?"

FRANK: "Yes, sir."

NICHOLAS: "Did you ever make a statement in writing and sign it as to what you would testify to?"

FRANK: "I never signed it."

NICHOLAS: "But you made a statement of it?"

FRANK: "I simply wrote it down at Mr. Swift's request, at the Home, what I knew about the case."

NICHOLAS: "Before you left the Home?"

FRANK: "Yes, sir."

NICHOLAS: "Why did you write it down on paper?"

FRANK: "Just because I felt like it."

NICHOLAS: "Had you had that same feeling come over you before?"

CLINK: "Objected to as immaterial."

JUDGE MAYNE: "Objection sustained."

Two other Beulah boys, Ora Crampton and Emery Weaver, testified for the defense in the second Merrill Griffin trial, but their testimony was not saved within the trial records. Ora Crampton certainly testified that he was a member of the boys' quartette and that for a period of two weeks prior to November 25th, 1909 he had traveled with Mr. Swift to various sites in southern Michigan.

Emery Weaver

Emery Weaver provided testimony related to Sidney Jones' conspiracy against Swift. Emery was born on October 13th, 1895 in the town of Sunfield in Eaton County. He was of medium height, thin, with blue eyes and light brown hair. He had a crooked leg and walked with a limp as the result of a mistreated break. Emery grew up on a farm in Gladwin, Michigan. He was the youngest of six children. The oldest, a sister named Alice was eighteen years older than Emery. Emery probably had been sent to the Beulah Home as a result of the death of one or both of his parents. Beulah Home boys frequently were the youngest children in their families. When Emery testified at the second Merrill trial, he no longer lived at the Beulah Home. Earlier in 1910, he had been placed with a young couple, Delbert and Clio Townsend, who lived on a farm located just west of Boyne City. Emery worked with Delbert who was a beekeeper, a trade that seems at least in one way unsuited for a boy with a bad leg.

Earnest Wardell then was recalled as a witness for the defense.

CLINK: "What was said in your presence at that time, by Mr. Jones and others in regard to getting rid of Mr. Swift?"

NICHOLAS: "Objected to as immaterial, irrelevant, and calling for a conclusion of this witness."

EARNEST: "Mr. Jones said he was going to get him out of here with the help of the boys, ain't we boys. Simon Mack replied: 'I guess so.'"

CLINK: "Now what did Mr. Allison (Author's note: Allison claimed to have worked as a laborer on the new building project. He would testify later in the trial.) say if anything before Mr. Jones spoke?"

EARNEST: "He asked Mr. Jones what Mr. Swift shook that boy for the night before."

CLINK: "What did Mr. Jones say?"

NICHOLAS: "To which we object as immaterial, irrelevant, and incompetent."

JUDGE MAYNE: "The objection is sustained unless it was something further along the line of getting rid of him."

CLINK: "Yes, sir. It follows right up along that line."

JUDGE MAYNE: "Witness, you were to give all the conversation that Jones gave—say what Mr. Jones said."

EARNEST: "He said he was going to get rid of Mr. Swift with the help of the boys."

CLINK: "At that time were you working against Mr. Swift?"

NICHOLAS: "We make the same objection."

CLINK: "With Mr. Jones?"

NICHOLAS: "The same objection."

JUDGE MAYNE: "That would be a conclusion, let him state what he was doing, well, he may answer, yes or no."

EARNEST: "Yes, sir."

NICHOLAS (On Cross-exam): "Yes, sir, and when you told it to Mr. Snell wasn't Mr. Snell the man that said to go down and inform the authorities, isn't that the case?"

CLINK: "Mr. Nicholas—"

NICHOLAS: "Well, now that is all right, I am talking to this witness."

CLINK: "Well, don't go up so very near to the witness, stand back a little."

EARNEST: "I told Mr. Snell about accusing Mr. Swift of this offense because Mr. Jones told me that if I would tell Mr. Snell about it that it would help him out about getting the Home."

NICHOLAS: "Now was this the first time you talked to Mr. Jones about this?"

EARNEST: "We talked about the bank book. He was running down Mr. Swift. I don't remember the month it was. It was somewhere around fall. It was quite awhile before Mr. Swift was arrested. I did not tell the jury a moment ago that this was the first talk."

NICHOLAS: "Now witness—just look at me when you are answering those questions."

CLINK: "He has the right to look where he pleases, he should look at the jury."

NICHOLAS: "Now I want to ask you again when did you have your first talk with Mr. Jones and was you alone on this occasion?"

EARNEST: "I don't know exactly—I don't know whether I was alone or not now."

NICHOLAS: "You haven't very much of a recollection in regard to the first talk is that right?"

EARNEST: "Yes, sir."

CLINK: "We object to it and take exception to the remark of counsel as prejudicial and unfair to the witness."

Attorney Clink then called Grace Swift to the witness stand. Grace testified that she and Herman had been married for about five years and that during that time she had resided at the Beulah Home. Then she testified that she did indeed remember the period prior to Thanksgiving Day in 1909. Herman had been away from the Home for two weeks. He had not returned to the Home at any time during that period. He did return on the five o'clock afternoon train on November 24th. Grace's testimony provided important support to Herman's alibi that he was not at the Beulah Home on November 23rd, the day the warrant for his arrest claimed he had abused Merrill Griffin. Grace's appearance on the witness stand, however, allowed Prosecutor Nicholas to enter into the evidence of the trial two letters that Grace had written to Edward Griffin.

The first of these letters was entered as exhibit "a." Grace mailed this letter to Mr. E.C. Griffin in Grand Rapids, Michigan on September 8th, 1909. The letter reads:

"Dear friend: Your letter received also the ten dollars for which you will find receipt enclosed. Your boy is well and is a good boy. We call him Sunbeam because he is sunny and somewhat resembles our Sunbeam of other days. Trust the change will be permanent and that he will become a fine young man.

Thanking you for the money, I remain,

Yours most sincerely, Mrs. Grace Swift."

Exhibit "b" was a letter that Grace sent to Mr. Ed Griffin on October 13th, 1909. The letter was offered and received into the evidence of the trial without objection. It reads: "Dear friend: Your letter received also the ten dollars which has been passed to your credit. Merrill is well and getting along nicely as usual. We have no very stormy weather at present. A very light fall of snow. The boys are all glad of it. We are always glad for it as it will soon mean coasting and skating.

With best wishes, I remain most sincerely, Mrs. Grace Swift."

CLINK (On Re-exam): "Mrs. Swift, this letter shows that on September 8th you received ten dollars from Mr. Griffin."

GRACE: "Yes, sir."

CLINK: "Do all the boys in the Home pay in that way?"

NICHOLAS: "Objected to as immaterial and irrelevant."

JUDGE MAYNE: "Objection sustained. Exception taken."

CLINK: "Were many of the boys—that were there at that time, in the Home supported by Mr. Swift without any aid from people or their parents?"

Grace Swift certainly answered yes to that last question, but her answer is stricken from the record.

Roy Fenton

Roy Fenton was the last of the Beulah boys who testified for the defense in the second Merrill Griffin trial. I believe that Roy was born in Sanilac County in southern Michigan in September of 1898. His mother Jerusha had six children, but only three survived early childhood. In 1900, Roy lived with his parents, an older sister Bertha, and an older brother Ray on a farm in Sanilac County. By 1910, the Fenton family had moved to Onaway, a small town in the far north of Michigan's Lower Peninsula and both Roy and his brother Ray were inmates at the Beulah Home. Roy testified:

ROY: "I know Mr. Jones and Merrill Griffin. I had a conversation with Merrill Griffin in regard to this trouble. He said Mr. Swift never did any such thing to him but his uncle in Grand Rapids used to lots of times. I am acquainted with Simon Mack. Simon Mack asked me who I was going to stick up for and I said I was certainly going to stick up for Mr. Swift. He said I was a fool to stick up for him, because he could go back to his sister in Grand Rapids and I could go back to Onaway. Simon Mack asked me to tell the officers of the law that Mr. Swift had done bad things to me and I said no. I heard Simon Mack tell Elliott Fay to say that Mr. Swift had done bad things to him and Elliott said he would. Simon Mack said he was going down after the officers. This was two or three days before Mr. Swift was arrested."

CLINK (On Re-exam): "Has any person paid anything to Mr. Swift for your board, clothing and education since you have been to the Beulah Home?"

NICHOLAS: "That is objected to as immaterial, irrelevant, and incompetent."

JUDGE MAYNE: "The objection is sustained."

CLINK: "Note an exception."

Someone took a pen and scratched through the portion of the trial transcript covering attorney Clink's question on re-exam, the objection, and the judge's response. The trial transcript includes none of the prosecutor's cross-exam of Roy Fenton, but we will find this in a later filing by The People in this case.

Attorney Clink next called William Allison to the witness stand. Allison was forty years old. He worked as a stonemason. He testified that he resided in Deerfield Township in Mecosta County and that he had lived there and in neighboring Montcalm County for the last thirty-five years. Allison did not testify why he had traveled a distance of some one hundred and fifty miles north to Boyne City, but did testify that in November of 1909 he traveled there seeking work at the Beulah Home.

CLINK: "Are you acquainted with Mr. Swift, Mr. Jones, Rueben Bacon, Ernest Wardell, and Simon Mack?"

ALLISON: "I am acquainted with Mr. Swift and Mr. Jones some and the boys known as Simon Mack, Earnest Wardell and also Rueben Bacon a little."

CLINK: "Did you seek work at the Beulah Home?"

ALLISON: "Yes, sir. I went to the Beulah Home for employment on the 23rd of November 1909. Mr. Swift wasn't at home. I saw him on Friday the 26th of November and began work for him at noon of that day. I am a mason and contractor and worked for Mr. Swift four and one-half days. I laid stone on Friday afternoon and Saturday. I heard Mr. Jones say on Monday the 29th that Mr. Swift was not fit to run Beulah Home and that he ought to be put out. On the 30th of November I heard a conversation between Mr. Jones and Simon Mack concerning Mr. Swift. The conversation was that he ought to be put out and asked the boys if they—He said won't we boys and Simon Mack answered 'yes, sir.'"

CLINK: "Where were you at the time of this conversation?"

ALLISON: "We were going to work. There was on the wagon Mr. Bacon, Simon Mack, Earnest Wardell, and Mr. Jones."

CLINK: "I wish you would give all the conversation concerning Mr. Swift on that wagon and in which Mr. Jones took part."

ALLISON: "I asked Earnest Wardell if he ever went out with Mr. Swift on a lecture and he said that he did, he almost always went. I said you must like that. No, he said, 'I would rather drive them gray horses.'"

JUDGE MAYNE: "That isn't an answer to the question that was asked."

CLINK: "Well the rest of it is what we want."

ALLISON: "Well, you will get it now. He said he didn't like to stand up in an audience and sing and talk and I asked him if he ever got any money and he said he did."

JUDGE MAYNE: "Did Jones participate in this conversation witness?"

ALLISON: "He was right there. I will tell you here it comes in pretty quick."

JUDGE MAYNE: "It is what Mr. Jones said we want. Not those others."

CLINK: "We have already shown that Earnest Wardell was working with Mr. Jones against Mr. Swift."

JUDGE MAYNE: "We'll take the answer."

ALLISON: "Well he said he did and I asked him how much was the most he ever got and he said six dollars."

JUDGE MAYNE: "Just tell us what was said witness."

ALLISON: "Well, I said that—it came in anyway with the conversation that Mr. Swift wasn't so bad. No, he said, he wasn't too bad, and then Mr. Jones looked at him and he said no and then Wardell dropped his head and he said 'no, he hain't any too good.' I asked him why he didn't get possession of the place and also if Mr. Swift was the head beetler. Mr. Jones said he wasn't, that there was a lot of monied men back of him (Author's note: Swift). Mr. Jones talked as though he was going to get possession of it."

The trial transcript retained in the case file does not include the record of Prosecutor Nicholas' cross-examination of William Allison. This is unfortunate because the questions probably were probing and Allison's answers certainly were fascinating. Curiously, Allison testified that he had traveled the long distance from his home to Boyne City seeking work. He arrived at the Beulah Home on November 23rd, finding Herman Swift away on a trip. Then he returned on November 26th, finding Swift had returned. These claims supported Swift's alibi defense.

More importantly, Allison was the only adult who testified in support of the conspiracy defense. Allison testified that he was acquainted with Mr. Swift, Earnest Wardell, and Simon Mack. He had undoubtedly talked a lot and listened a little to both Swift and Wardell. I'm not certain that he had met Simon Mack. He testified that he was "a little" acquainted with Reuben Bacon and that probably was true. Bacon was fifty-six years old. He lived with his wife and one son at 108 N. East Street in Boyne City. In the 1910 Federal Census, he listed his occupation as "laborer, work outside." Bacon probably worked on the new building construction at the Beulah Home. Neither side called him as a witness in the second Griffin trial. Allison testified that he was acquainted "some" with Sidney Jones. Jones later would testify that he might recognize Allison by sight, but that he did not recognize his name.

Attorney Clink called James Henderson as his last defense witness. Henderson was the stenographer for the Circuit Court of Charlevoix County. Clink questioned Henderson about inconsistencies between Merrill Griffin's testimony at the first trial in August of 1910 and his testimony at the second trial in December 1910. None of Henderson's testimony remains in the case file. Clink then rested his case.

Prosecutor Nicholas presented at least three witnesses for The People in Rebuttal. The first rebuttal witness was Edward Griffin. Nicholas took Griffin through the December 1st, 1909 letter that Griffin had received from Hermon Swift. Nicholas initially had objected to introduction of this letter as evidence in the case. Now, importantly he saw it as the only trial evidence available to support Merrill's testimony.

On cross-examination, Edward Griffin responded to attorney Clink:

GRIFFIN: "I was a witness in Justice Court on the examination and swore that my son had never slept with Cornelius Proos. That was true or I would not have sworn to it. My son has known Cornelius Proos in the neighborhood of seven years."

The prosecutor called Sidney Jones as his second rebuttal witness. In response to a series of questions from the prosecutor, Jones testified:

"I am acquainted with Mr. Swift and have known him since 1909. I went to work on the Beulah farm about the first of June that year. I done general farm work and worked on the new building there. I know Simon Mack, Earnest Wardell, and Mr. Snell. I may know Mr. Allison to see him, but I do not recollect him by his name. I recall the arrest of Mr. Swift in December of 1909. I have heard what the complaint was against him. The first talk or charge that I heard against Mr. Swift was about the 29th of November. I heard it from Simon Mack and Earnest Wardell. They were simply talking amongst themselves, not to me then. This first talk was about three and one-half miles from the Home. It was when we was drawing stone from—up towards

Horton Bay. There were only two boys and myself present at that time. It was about eight thirty or nine in the morning of the 29th. I am not sure but what it was the 30th of November 1909.

I saw Mr. Snell at noon that same day. I told Mr. Snell about it at noon. When the boys came to work after dinner (this refers to work at the site of the new building) what I heard them talking about and told them to come over to where Mr. Snell was and told them if they was lying to own up because it was an awful thing but if they were not, to tell Mr. Snell all about it. Then in my presence they told Mr. Snell what they had reported to me in the morning. I didn't take any steps at all to have the boys report it to the officers. I asked Mr. Snell what we would do and he said report it to the Chief of Police. I never had any talk with Merrill Griffin in regard to this matter. At this time Earnest Wardell and Simon Mack were the only boys that I ever heard make a report of this character.

I took no further steps to cause the arrest of Mr. Swift, nothing at all. I made no effort to secure the management of Beulah Home. I never had any conversation when Mr. Allison was present. I don't know who Mr. Allison is. I never talked with Mr. Allison at all. I know he is a stonemason. I never tried to bring about a conspiracy to oust Mr. Swift from the Home or from its management. The first talk that ever arose as far as I know personally about the alleged acts of misconduct of Mr. Swift was about the 29th of November. I quit work there the 1st of December.

I saw Mr. Beach and Mr. Urquhart at the Home. I was not present when they made the complaint examination. I never made any effort to have Earnest Wardell make a statement as to his conduct with him. I never sought to influence him in any way to make any statements against Mr. Swift. I never made an effort to have Simon Mack report what he alleged occurred between he and Mr. Swift. I did not make any statement after this report was current in which I said Mr. Swift was not fit to run the Home. I do not know a man by the name of Bacon. I may at sight. I do not know of any strangers that was with me, Simon Mack, and Earnest Wardell at the gravel pit. I don't ever recall going to the gravel pit with the wagon when those boys were along. We drove to the stone quarry. That was three and a half miles away. I do not recall a time when besides myself, Wardell, and Mack a stranger was along, but I do remember driving out with Mack and Wardell were with me and a boy by the name of Kent who drove the team.

We did not have any conversation while on the wagon going to the quarry in relation to this matter, but after we got out to the quarry that is where the boys told me about it. About noon right near the new building I had the boys relate this story to Mr. Snell and there was no one else present at the time. I never had any conversation in which I berated Mr. Swift's conduct in the management of the Home and I never had any trouble with Mr. Swift while working there. I resigned my position.

I never stated to Donald Thomas that Mr. Swift was a damn fool and made slaves of the boys. While I was at the Home there was no favoritism shown among the boys in the interest of their work. I had no interest in favoring one over the other. I never in the presence of Samuel Valentine said that I would like to get hold of the Home and that I could run it better than Mr. Swift. I never made that remark to anybody. I never made a remark in the presence of the boy known as 'Cuba' in substance that he was a fool to work for Swift when he could get two dollars a day."

On cross-examination by attorney Clink, Sidney Jones testified:

"I was at the Home about six months. I worked with the boys most of the time and had some of the boys around me all the time and Mr. Swift was around part of the time. He laid out the work and I had the boys do it.

I never used any profane language or told any vulgar stories in the presence of the boys when Mr. Swift wasn't present. I never heard anything from the boys against Mr. Swift until the 29th of November if I remember right and during all that time I had charge of the boys.

On many occasions I would have an opportunity to talk with one boy if I so desired and they would have a great many opportunities to talk with me. I did not go to Mr. Swift and tell him that the boys had reported bad things to me about him, but did go and tell Mr. Snell. I never saw Mr. Swift do anything out of the way while there. Mr. Swift did not request me to resign. I was hired for the year there. I told him that I did not think we could get along under the circumstances and he said to me that if I wasn't tied up in the spring and they went ahead with the farm work he would like to get me back."

Prosecutor Nicholas called George Snell as his third and last rebuttal witness. Snell was the construction manager for the new building project. He testified:

"I have resided in Boyne City for about eight years. I am a contractor and builder and was living there in November of 1909 and in that month was employed at the Beulah Home. I am acquainted with Sidney Jones.

I reported that indecent behavior was taking place between Mr. Swift and some of the boys in the institution. I first learned of that about the last of November 1909. The first knowledge that I got was from Mr. Jones but he didn't tell me exactly what they were. The facts themselves I got from the boys. When Jones first talked to me there was no one else present but he and I. There were other boys close by but not within hearing. Then I interviewed those other boys later and questioned them quite closely. They were admonished to tell nothing but the absolute truth. After this talk with the boys we continued our work until evening and then made complaint to the officers of the City.

Mr. Jones and I went to the officers. I did most of the talking. At this interview no effort was made by Mr. Jones to have Earnest Wardell and Simon Mack color their statements. I never had any conversation with Merrill Griffin and his case was not known to me at the time. When we went to the Justice or Magistrate's office we went with the police."

The case file contains no records of attorney Clink's cross-examination of George Snell.

The prosecution rested its case the evening of Friday, December 30th, 1910. Herman Swift did not testify in his own defense in the second Merrill Griffin trial. Perhaps the defense attorneys chose not to provide the jury further exposure to details related either to the previous charges against Herman Swift or the civil case brought by the Board against Swift.

On the morning of December 31st, 1910, the trial opened with Prosecutor Nicholas' closing statement or argument. That argument included the following:

NICHOLAS: "You all know gentlemen (of the jury), that acts such as these are classed under the general name of pederasty. You all know perhaps that such acts are very common—common in large cities while they may be comparatively unknown in rural communities. You all admitted to me upon your examination that you believed that these acts are committed—low and degrading as they are, we must admit that they do take place."

CLINK: "Note an exception to that."

NICHOLAS: "Let's see about Herman L. Swift, whether he committed this act low and dastardly as it may be, besotted as it may be—it matters not how many times the act may be committed unless, perchance someone happened to be by, you gentlemen all know that those degrading low, filthy, disgusting acts are committed in the utmost privacy."

CLINK: "Note an exception to that."

NICHOLAS: "And the men that perpetrate that act can say it is my word against yours—my word against the word of my victim—well, you might say why don't you bring in those other boys if there was an act performed against them."

CLINK: "Note an exception."

NICHOLAS: "But gentlemen each of these acts is an offense in itself and you can only confront the defendant with the particular witness in each particular act."

CLINK: "Note an exception."

NICHOLAS: "Gentlemen of the jury, Mr. Clink asks this boy why didn't you testify to that before on the examination or on the last trial. Well, those postal cards are little things, of course, but that is the kind of evidence that convinces me and should satisfy your minds of the guilt of the respondent."

CLINK: "Note an exception."

NICHOLAS: "So far as that wife is concerned, I have every sympathy with her, I pity her from the bottom of my heart. The man who will do these things charged in this information, he is not merely a common criminal, he is a dangerous criminal, he is a scourge in the community, he is a vampire, he is a man that puts childhood under his feet for the sake of gratifying his lust. I presume you know that a man who—if he commits this offense charged here—you undoubtedly know that he has no use for a wife, the man who indulges in these vile practices cares nothing for the private society of his wife."

CLINK: "We object to that as extremely prejudicial to the respondent."

NICHOLAS: "No one has denied that that act took place."

CLINK: "We except to that. It is contradicted by everybody"

NICHOLAS: "Not a soul, not a witness has come here and contradicted that boy that this act did not take place, not a soul has contradicted it"

CLINK: "We take an exception to that."

NICHOLAS: "The very fact that it is a child makes it easier for this transducer to perform the act then laugh him to scorn and his efforts to bring him to justice. The very fact that he stands high in society makes his dirty, low efforts and acts the easier to accomplish because he says when confronted with the accusation and when apprehended he at once says: Why—W-H-Y-Y-Y—what little urchin is he to be believed against ME? Didn't I pick him up out of the streets—out of the gutter?

Prosecutor Nicholas then took up the letter that Merrill had written to his father on December 1st, 1909. The letter had been introduced as Exhibit "A" and Nicholas read it to the jury.

CLINK: "Your honor might I say but one word in regard to this letter, Exhibit "A" that Mr. Nicholas read to the jury and commented on?"

JUDGE MAYNE: "Well, the letter has been read several times to the jury. But you may say a word if you think it necessary."

CLINK (Reading a sentence from the letter): "I thought this was a nice place at first but I don't like it now." Clink continued: "The evidence shows that it (Merrill's first claimed act of abuse) was in August the first time and in September—not later the second."

Elisha Clink then presented his closing argument to the jury. When the trial transcript was consolidated, the person responsible removed a portion of Prosecutor Nicholas' closing argument. Perhaps reflecting a form of individual bias, he removed all of attorney Clink's argument for the defense. From the numbered pages in the transcript, we can determine that the delivery of Clink's argument took up roughly twice the time that Nicholas had taken. I imagine that Clink's argument was comprehensive and well organized and that it was delivered with spirit, if not with emotion.

Judge Mayne's charge to the jury was saved in the case file. That charge includes the judge's summation of attorney Clink's argument. Clink concurred with that summation and thus we have some sense of the content of Clink's closing argument. Unfortunately, we lack the ability to sense the spirit and emotion of Elisha Clink's delivery.

Judge Mayne on his own motion charged and instructed the jury as follows:

"Gentlemen of the jury:

The information in this case charges an offense under Act No. 198 of the Public Acts of the State of Michigan for the year 1903. I will now read as much of it as is necessary, in my opinion, to have you understand what that law is:

Sec. 1. "Any male person who, in public or private commits, or is a party to the commission of, or procures or attempts to procure the commission by any male person of any act of gross indecency with another male person, shall be deemed guilty of a felony and upon conviction thereof shall be punished."

The charge in this case is that Hermon L. Swift, a male person committed an act of Gross Indecency with another male person, namely Merrill Griffin, in the County of Charlevoix and State of Michigan, in the month of November 1909, the date alleged being the 23rd of November, 1909. I will charge you in relation to this date later in my charge.

The People allege that this act of indecency occurred between two persons on three separate occasions: first, in the guest's room, then in the room of one Willis Roberts and finally in the room of Mr. Swift, in what is known as Beulah Home in this county.

The defendant, Mr. Swift, asserts his innocence. He alleges that he is not guilty of these offenses. He denies each and every statement made by Merrill Griffin as to this transaction. He does this by his plea of not guilty. Under the law, he is presumed to be innocent of this offense. He alleges that at the time and place when it is alleged by Merrill Griffin that he committed this offense, he was not there at the Home at all, but elsewhere—in other words he pleads what is called an alibi. He also alleges a conspiracy; that among the boys at Beulah Home who for reasons of revenge concocted this scheme; that they started these stories and brought about this prosecution for the purpose of injuring Mr. Swift. And further that one Jones who was connected with the farm, wishing to profit thereby, aided and abetted the boys—made use of them for the purpose of removing Mr. Swift from the superintendency or management of the farm that he himself might profit thereby and obtain that position.

Have I stated the position of the People Mr. Nicholas?"

NICHOLAS: "Yes, sir."

JUDGE MAYNE: "Yours, Mr. Clink."

CLINK: "I think so your Honor."

JUDGE MAYNE: "The purpose, gentlemen of the jury in calling your attention to these facts—that is, the claims of the People and the assertions of the defendant is that you may understand and apply the law that I may give you—that you may make a correct application of the legal principles which I shall lay down in my charge.

In this as in every criminal case questions of law and of fact arise. It is for the Court—I mean by that myself as trial judge to instruct you—a part of this Court—to determine the facts in the case. My duty is to aid you in coming to a correct determination of these facts, not to influence you at all, but to leave it to you to determine and find from the evidence in the case what the facts are—it is my duty to give you the law and your duty to determine the facts in connection with the law as I give it to you—you may not like the law that I give you but you are to accept it as the law and whether I like the facts as you may determine them is entirely immaterial. It would be highly improper for me to try to influence you and improper for you to be influenced if you should think that I was trying to influence you in anything I might say in relation to these questions of fact. Jurors are independent of the Court and must decide the facts in accordance with the evidence given in open Court.

Now, to determine those questions of fact, witnesses have been sworn and have given their testimony. You have seen them and heard them and it is your right to believe or to disbelieve the testimony of any witness and to disbelieve the other parts of his testimony if you do not consider it worthy of belief. It is for you to determine the credibility of each and every witness, to weigh his testimony and having weighed it to give it just such importance as you think it should receive in arriving at your verdict. In so doing you have a right to consider the appearance of the witness upon the stand, to consider his age, his experience. You have a right to consider the opportunities he had for knowing the facts concerning which he testified as well as the actual knowledge he had, particularly you have a right to, and should consider any bias or interest which any witness may have shown if you find any witness had any bias or showed any interest in the result of this case.

Now in this, as in every criminal case, the respondent is presumed to be innocent until he is proven guilty by evidence which satisfies the minds of the jurors of his guilt beyond all reasonable doubt and I would say here now, gentlemen, that the verdict of a jury is the verdict of twelve men and each and every juror stands upon an equality with his fellow jurors in responsibility in arriving at that determination, in arriving at a verdict the duty is equally upon each one of you, so that when rendered, the verdict will represent the opinion of each individual juror—I will say more upon that point later.

Now, I have used the term reasonable doubt and you have heard it several times in the trial of this cause and I will now tell you what is meant by a reasonable doubt:

A reasonable doubt is a fair doubt, growing out of the testimony in the case. It is not a mere imaginary, capricious or possible doubt but a fair doubt, based upon reason and common sense. It is such a doubt as may leave your minds, after a careful consideration of all the testimony in this case, in that condition that you cannot say you have an abiding conviction, to a moral certainty of the truth of the charge here made against the respondent. A reasonable doubt must, at all times, gentlemen be such a doubt as appeals to your reason and be based upon the evidence in the case. This reasonable doubt extends to each and every essential element of the offense with which the respondent in this case is charged.

Now, during the trial of this cause the Prosecuting Attorney asked leave to amend his opening statement. He asked to be permitted to include the question of hypnotism or mesmerism. Nothing has been said or done, no evidence has been introduced up to this time of any hypnotic power—if such a thing exists, and I don't say whether it does or not and it is quite immaterial in this case whether it does or does not on the part of the respondent. So you will not consider this phase of the case at all. The Prosecution in opening their case must present all the matters upon which they expect to rely and Mr. Nicholas, the Prosecuting Attorney, included this, but during the trial of the cause he has not entered upon that phase of the case and it is withdrawn from your consideration.

Now, gentlemen, you observed, possibly, in the statute that I read to you that the term "Gross Indecency" is used. I don't know that our Supreme Court has ever defined what constitutes that Act of offense. The Legislature, in this Act I read, did not specify what particular Acts constitute gross indecency. They seem to assume—and I charge you, that gross indecency means such acts as the common sense of society would regard as grossly indecent, as extremely indecent. And particularly, I charge you in this case that—the act(s) charged in this case is an act of gross indecency and as such is punishable under our laws.

Now, as to the time of committing this offense in the manner of stating it, as adopted by the Prosecuting Attorney in this Information, I will say it is not necessary for the People to allege the identical day of the month upon which the offense was committed. It is charged as being upon the 23rd day of November. If you find that this act took place as claimed by the People but that it was not on the 23rd but on some other date prior thereto, during the month of November, that is sufficient upon which to render a verdict of Guilty.

The People for the purpose of proving the time—because that is one of the things they must prove, presented the evidence of Merrill Griffin. He was unable to specify the date, as he claimed of the month by the particular date as the 23rd of November, but he did try to cover that date by telling what he was doing. Now, from all the testimony in the case, it is for you to determine, whether at some date, prior to the 23rd of November—or on the 23rd, this thing occurred that Merrill Griffin says did occur. If you find from the evidence with that degree of certainty with which I shall charge you later, and have already charged you, that this thing took place but it was at a date prior to the 23rd of November, then the fact that it did not occur on the 23rd would not justify you in returning a verdict of Not Guilty.

The defendant in this case asserts an alibi. Now, an alibi means that this defendant was not there at the particular time and place testified to by Merrill Griffin, that he was somewhere else, in the southern part of the State. Now an alibi is as legitimate a defense as any other, in fact, it is a perfect and conclusive defense. Mr. Swift could not commit this offense if he was in the southern part of the State; he must have been at Beulah Home and in that room of the Home with Merrill Griffin when he committed it.

Now some testimony has been admitted as to a trip that Mr. Swift made. This offense if committed at all must have been committed prior to his making that trip; it could not have occurred during his absence—of course you need no law to tell you that, gentlemen. The question is did it occur as claimed by the boy and it must have occurred before taking that trip if it did occur at all.

As to a conspiracy: In general, gentlemen, I say that it would be immaterial in this case as to what kind of a man Mr. Jones was or what of a boy Simon Mack was, whether they were good or bad, virtuous or vicious or what their motives may have been, provided you find that Mr. Swift did do this thing that the witness Merrill Griffin says he did do. This evidence of a conspiracy is introduced for the purpose of enabling you to determine as to the motives of Merrill Griffin— to show you that this thing did not take place, in explanation of his acts, that he was doing this, that he was instigated thereto by someone else, or by some improper motive of his own—that of getting even and, as such, you will give it weight. No matter how deep the conspiracy was of those other parties, no matter how much they intended to hurt him, or how vicious or depraved they may have been, if you find that the respondent, Hermon L. Swift, did those acts to Merrill Griffin, he is equally guilty as though no conspiracy had existed; but you must consider this in connection with his testimony for the purpose of determining whether Mr. Swift did or did not do these acts of which complaint is made. That is the purpose of this testimony and you must give it weight in accordance as you believe it to be true or not true in the matter of deciding whether this act took place that the witness Griffin says did take place.

Now, in relation to other offenses, either civil or criminal, to which reference has been made; these cases are not on trial here. The prosecution could not introduce evidence that Mr. Swift had committed crimes upon other persons, nor could they introduce any evidence bearing upon the civil case. That would be casting too much of a burden upon the People, or, possibly give them too much power. The respondent could not be asked to come in and defend against other cases either civil or criminal, in this case. Under our laws only one case can be tried at a time and we are now trying the case of the People against Hermon L. Swift in which it is alleged that he committed these acts of gross indecency with Merrill Griffin. We are not trying any other case and—except as I instruct you as to previous acts, in relation to Merrill Griffin, you will not give other alleged offenses any consideration.

Now, in relation to those previous acts: they claim that the respondent, Mr. Swift, had twice before committed this offense. Now you might find that to be true gentlemen, and yet if he did not commit this third act you could not bring in a verdict of guilty against Mr. Swift. Why? Because he is on trial for this third offense, this last offense, the one in his own room, as the People claim, at a time prior to his leaving Beulah Home on a trip, that is the time he is on trial for. Now what is the purpose of introducing evidence of those other two offenses? Simply this: to show the relationship that existed between the respondent and Merrill Griffin, so that you could see the relationship between the two, the position which they sustained the one to the other and in that way to assist you in determining whether this offense was committed or not. That is the purpose of that—merely to aid you in determining whether he committed the offense charged against him and not for the purpose of convicting him of those two other offenses. So you will determine, in this case, the guilt of the respondent solely with relation to the offense charged—the third offense, although you need not find, to bring in a verdict of guilty that it took place on the 23rd of November; as I have said, you should consider the other two cases as showing the relationship of the parties and as an aid in determining whether this particular offense was committed—from all the testimony in the case, because all the testimony in the case must be considered together and you will consider those other two offenses alleged in connection with all the other evidence in the case as bearing upon this one question; that is as the act that is said to have taken place on the 23rd day of November.

Now, in this connection you have heard considerable testimony introduced as impeaching testimony and the cross-examination of witnesses for the purpose of showing contradictory or conflicting testimony. The purpose of this class of testimony, gentlemen, is to enable you to determine the truthfulness of the witnesses so you may know what weight to give their testimony, to determine their credibility in this particular case. If the witness makes contradictory statements, to the extent that you deem him unreliable that is one of the things you should consider in the case; you will take all the testimony of all the witnesses and determine the issues which I submit to you from the testimony which you believe.

Now, in this case the respondent did not see fit to take the stand and testify in his own behalf. The law presumes him innocent and, under our law, he has the right to go upon the witness stand. In former times he did not have that right, and, in some countries he doesn't have it yet, but in this State he has that right. If he does not elect to take the stand and testify in his own behalf, the burden of the People is not lessened at all. They still have to prove him guilty beyond a reasonable doubt and you are not, in this particular case, to draw any inference of guilt against this respondent because he did not go upon the stand. You cannot infer that he is guilty because he did not. You are to take the testimony that is in the case in determining the issues. So you will not consider it an admission of guilt on the part of Mr. Swift that he did not go upon the stand, nor will you give it any weight in your determination of the case.

Now, it is your duty to consider the testimony of all those witnesses. There are twelve of you jurors, each one of you having an individual responsibility equal to that of each and every juror in the case. You are to take this testimony and harmonize it, it is your duty to harmonize it if possible with the innocence of the accused, because under our law it is the duty of the jurors in every criminal case to enter upon the trial of the case with the presumption of innocence and harmonize all the testimony in the case in accordance with the presumption that he is innocent.

Now taking all the testimony in this case it is your duty—basing your verdict thereon—to harmonize all the testimony, if, from this testimony, you find that the respondent is guilty then it is your duty to return a verdict of guilty. If on the other hand you find the respondent not guilty—that is, that he did not do this act, it is equally your duty to return a verdict of Not Guilty. You are not here to convict Mr. Swift; you are not here to exonerate him, you are here to determine the facts of the case in accordance with the law. If you find from the evidence that he did this act with which he is charged, then it is your duty to bring in a verdict of guilty. If you find that he did not, then it is your duty to return a verdict of not guilty. Or if you should find that—after taking all the testimony in the case under consideration there exists a reasonable doubt—as I have defined it—as to the guilt of the respondent, then it is equally your duty to bring a verdict of Not Guilty.

In arriving at your conclusions, the prosecuting attorney made one statement that he did not intend to make—that he had no right to make and that you have no right to consider. It is difficult after a strong argument made in behalf of the respondent and the prosecutor in answering it, possibly, not to take a strong position, in any event, the prosecutor said to you: "This is the kind of evidence that convinces me and it should satisfy your minds..."

NICHOLAS: "Just a moment your Honor, I have authority for that very language, identical..."

JUDGE MAYNE: "All right, I will see it."

Prosecutor Nicholas then approached the bench and handed a book to the judge.

JUDGE MAYNE: "I don't know gentlemen if it makes much difference if he was within his authority. It is not his opinion that is to govern. It is yours. The Supreme Court may have said that that is not an error, but what I want to impress upon your mind, even if it was within the law is, that is not his opinion nor my opinion, not whether his mind is satisfied, but whether your mind is satisfied.

Now, if your mind is satisfied as to the guilt of this respondent, then return a verdict of guilty. If it is not, then you should not do so. You may retire with the officer.

One thing, gentlemen, I will state. I think possibly—you all know this. All witnesses in this case—or in any other—stand on an equality before the Court. There is no law that says that the testimony of a woman has any greater weight than that of a man. The testimony of a woman should be weighted the same as you would weigh the testimony of any witness. You have the perfect right to believe the testimony of a woman in preference to that of a man, or the testimony of a man in preference to that of a woman, but you don't believe a woman just because she is a woman. It is because the facts and circumstances are such as to cause you to believe her testimony in preference to that of a man, if you do so believe her. And it is the same with the testimony of a child as that of a woman. All witnesses stand upon an equality before the Court, as I have already instructed you.

The Prosecuting Attorney has just handed me a citation that, he says, justifies him in the language he used in his argument. But if that is true, as I have said, it is not upon his opinion that you are to go but upon your own opinion based upon the evidence in the case, so in this case when you render your verdict it is to be based upon your own interpretation of the testimony and the application of the law as I have given it to you."

At noon on December 31st, 1910, Judge Mayne placed the jurors: "under the charge of Frank McWain and William J. Weilel, officers of the court, duly sworn for that purpose, to consider of their verdict to be given" in the case of the People vs. Herman L. Swift.

The twelve jurors all were residents of Charlevoix County. In terms of age, two were in their thirties, six in their forties, and four in their fifties. They all were married and in total had forty-seven children. Eleven of the jurors were farmers. Juror number twelve, William F. Johnson, owned an ice cream manufacturing company. Johnson at thirty-five was the youngest of the jurors and in his modern city suit he cut a different figure from the others in their country Sunday going to church outfits. He probably looked more like the attorneys in court than like his fellow jurors. He and his wife Neta lived in a fine house at 154 Antrim Street, just up from the lake and right around the corner from the courthouse in the City of Charlevoix. My guess is that William Johnson served as jury foreman and played the major role in jury deliberations. In ensuing years he would continue to be the juror who played the major role in the case against Herman Swift.

Curiously, toward the end of his instructions to the jury, Judge Mayne told the jurors to weigh equally the testimony of men and women. His comments infer a belief that the jurors might very well weigh the testimony of a woman over that of a man. This would have favored the defense in the case, as they were the only side to call women to the witness stand. All twelve of the jurors were men. In 1910, women were not allowed to sit on juries in the State of Michigan.

In an unintended way, attorney Clink was happy that the judge had instructed the jury not to give more weight to the testimony of a woman. And he also was happy that the judge had instructed the jury to pay no attention to the fact that the prosecution had not called to the witness stand the other boys who had made charges against Swift. In a similar unintended way, Prosecutor Nicholas was happy that the judge's instructions had emphasized that the jury should pay no attention to four matters: (1) the claim of hypnotism, (2) the fact that Swift had not testified in his own behalf, (3) Nicholas' courtroom statement that "this is the kind of evidence that convinces me and should satisfy your minds," and (4) the other charges against Swift, including the civil case.

The jurors deliberated through the afternoon of December 31st. At one time they returned to the courtroom and requested instructions from the judge on several points. The judge refused the request, commenting that the court stenographer was not present. At midnight the jury returned to the courtroom with a verdict. They had unanimously found Herman L. Swift guilty of the charge brought against him by the People.

The jurors were very tired, but they had not taken much time arriving at this decision. One of them later would claim the decision was reached on only the second ballot. He also would claim that in the first balloting the vote was eight to four in favor of Swift, but by the second ballot the minority of four had convinced the other eight to change their positions to arrive at a unanimous verdict of guilty. Whether this is true or not, Herman Swift was swiftly found guilty, but the case would drag on for years, and the secret deliberations of the jury on that last day of 1910 would become very public.

Hermon Lee Swift was applicant number 422 when he was accepted into the Moody Bible Institute on March 19th, 1892. His Bible Institute personal file includes a record of events in his career through the next to last entry made on December 3rd, 1900. The last entry in large, bold, cursive letters reads: "Dropped, about 1901—immoral conduct charges proved." The entry is initialed "J.H.H." It is not dated.

XIV

~

The Appeal

Early the first week of January 1911, papers across the State of Michigan reported Herman Swift's conviction in articles under bold front page headlines: "Beulah Home Supt. Is Found Guilty" (*Detroit News*), "H.L. Swift is Found Guilty" (*Detroit Free Press*) and "Beulah Home Manager Guilty" (*Grand Rapids Herald*).

During that same week, a scandalous rumor began to circulate in Charlevoix County. People whispered that they heard the jury in the Swift trial unfairly hastened its verdict for several reasons. First, simply was the fact that jurors were tired and wanted to get home to celebrate New Years Day. Second, within their deliberations several jurors supposedly argued that if they didn't find Swift guilty the prosecutor would just bring along another case against him and the County would be forced to spend more money on the matter. Third, people said several jurors argued that Swift had ten thousand dollars on deposit at the bank, more than enough to mount an appeal in a higher court.

In spite of these rumors, most people in Charlevoix County were pleased that the jury had convicted Herman Swift. County newspapers did not gloat, but rather reported the conviction in a matter-of-fact way. All these articles reported that Swift would appeal his conviction.

Apparently feeling some pressure, Judge Mayne publicly reported that he had not reached a decision in the civil case against Herman Swift. The *Charlevoix Sentinel* carried the following article on January 5th, 1911: "'An absolute falsehood,' said Judge Mayne of the report that he had decided the civil suit against Herman L. Swift by the trustees of the Beulah Home to determine the ownership of the Home and of the donations that have been made by charitable people all over the state of support. 'I have made no determination whatever of that case and do not expect to make any until after the trial of the criminal cases now pending,' continued the Judge. 'I have purposely refrained from handing down any decision in this matter, not wishing it to have any effect one way or the other in the trial of the criminal case.'"

Immediately following the announcement of the jury's verdict at midnight on December 31st, Prosecutor Nicholas had moved that sentencing of Herman Swift take place on January 6th, 1911. Judge Mayne approved that motion. Elisha Clink had other matters to attend to, but as early as January 2nd he began to work on an appeal of the verdict in the Swift case.

The morning of Friday, January 6th, 1911, Herman Swift traveled to Charlevoix and appeared for sentencing before Judge Mayne in Circuit Court. The hearing was brief. Attorney Clink requested time to prepare either a motion for a new trial in Circuit Court or a motion to remove the case to the Michigan Supreme Court. Judge Mayne approved Clink's request for additional time. He also approved a reduction in the bond in the Hosner Case from four thousand to one thousand dollars. Mayne set Swift's total bond at four thousand dollars. He demanded two sureties on the bond and demanded Swift's appearance in Court for sentencing on January 25th, 1911.

In early 1911, faced with the devastating judgment of the jury, the negative publicity, the condemnation in the community and the prospect of again returning to jail, Herman Swift grew both anxious and fearful. But he diligently worked to support his attorneys as they sought to gain either a new trial in Circuit Court or an appeal before the Michigan Supreme Court. When not involved in this work and when he could take his mind off his problems, Swift focused on three key tasks: rebuilding his board of directors, boosting the enrollment of inmates at the Home, and promoting his good works at the Home in order to raise money.

When Herman Swift arrived in Boyne City and established the Beulah Home, he assembled a Board of Directors consisting entirely of very successful men who maintained leading reputations in the city. Given the conviction of Swift and all the attendant negative publicity it is not surprising that all those original board members had resigned.

Starting in the late summer of 1910, Herman Swift assembled a new Beulah Home Board consisting of five members: William H. Hill, Albert B. Klise, John M. Hall, Morley E. Osborn, and Reverend C.A. Glass. Two things can be said of all five of these men. First, they all were convinced that the charges against Swift were untrue. Second, they all understood that the Beulah Home properties and money belonged personally to Herman Swift and that the Board had no claim against these assets.

William H. Hill was president of the Hill, Cascara Company in Detroit and Albert Klise was a wealthy lumber baron from Petoskey. Both men were major supporters of Swift and the Beulah Home. Each had contributed at least one thousand dollars to Swift and his mission to save homeless and troubled boys. Hill served as President of the new Beulah Home Board and Klise served as Treasurer.

William Hill, like Herman Swift, was an exceptional salesman. In 1885, Hill founded the W.H. Hill Company in Detroit. The company became one of the country's largest manufacturers and sellers of patent medicines, products Hill termed proprietary preparations. Its most famous product was Hill's Cascara Bromide Quinine. People referred to the company as Hill's Cascara Company. The product was sold in tablet form, priced at ten cents for a small box containing ten tablets. William Hill's serious, bearded face stared out from advertisements appearing in hundreds of United States newspapers. He became as recognizable as his hero Theodore Roosevelt. "Kill that cold with Hill's Cascara Quinine Bromide. Neglected colds are dangerous. Safe and most dependable family remedy for colds, headaches, and LaGrippe. All druggists sell it. Demand the red box bearing Mr. Hill's portrait and signature," read the advertisements.

John M. Hall was the man who served as superintendent of the Bay View Assembly from 1886 to 1898. He had been recruited back to that position in 1908 following a difficult financial period at the Bay View Association. Hall edited, published, and owned a prestigious literary publication, the monthly *Bay View Magazine*. His wife Mary's father David Fox was one of the owners of the Flint Wagon Works. David Fox died in 1901 and his company was merged with Buick Car Company to become the Buick Motor Division of General Motors. In 1903, John and Mary Hall used the profits from the magazine and their share of the proceeds of the sale of Flint Wagon Works to construct a beautiful mansion at 165 East Boston Boulevard in Detroit. They built on a lot they acquired in a new subdivision just off Woodward Avenue. There were only thirteen lots on East Boston Boulevard and it was the most prestigious address in the city.

The February 1903 edition of *The Bay View Magazine* included an article written by Edmund Kirke and titled "Rambles in Detroit." When a young judge named Augustus Woodward designed the city of Detroit in the early 1800s, he prophetically laid out the streets using a hub-and-spokes approach patterned after Pierre Charles L'Enfants design of Washington D.C. Wide avenues run out in different directions from Campus Martius Park near the Detroit River. Woodward Avenue, named after the judge, has been the most famous and most beautiful of those spokes. Edmund Kirke described the: "long vista of Woodward Avenue, rows of private palaces overhung with great trees and seated amid beautiful grounds that are parks in miniature." A number of the figures in this story: Lemuel Bowen, D.M. Ferry, Captain Stevens, William H. Hill, Joseph L. Hudson, and Franz Kuhn, lived in palaces on Woodward Avenue or adjoining streets. John and Mary Hall's neighbors on East Boston Boulevard included Joseph L. Hudson. Hall and Hudson's friendship probably dated back at least to the time when Herman Swift acquired the Boyne City Beulah Home property. John M. Hall possibly took over the publishing of Herman Swift's *Youth's Outlook*. More importantly, his willingness to serve as vice-president of the new Beulah Home Board provided an important boost to Swift's reputation and to his prospects for gaining support, particularly among the influential elites in Detroit.

Charles A. Glass referred to himself as an "Evangelical Clergyman." He served as a pastor in one of Boyne City's churches when he joined Herman Swift's Board. Pastor Glass must have considered Swift either to be innocent or a man who had repented and thus deserved forgiveness. Glass's membership on the Board at least to some degree countered the negative publicity that Swift received in Charlevoix County.

The fifth Board member Morley E. Osborn served as Board Secretary. Osborn was thirty-six years old and worked as the superintendent of public schools in Hastings, a town in Barry County in southern Michigan. Hubert Bell, the superintendent of the Boyne City schools, served on the original Beulah Home Board. Bell left Boyne City and moved to Ann Arbor in 1910. For obvious reasons, Bell's successor as Boyne City school superintendent did not serve on the Beulah Home Board. Morley Osborn did. Osborn may have become acquainted with Swift at one of his entertainment and fund raising revival meetings in southern Michigan. I suspect that Osborn assisted Swift in raising enrollment of inmates at the Home. Many guardians, probate courts, and youth prison authorities no longer would refer boys to the Beulah Home following the arrest and trials of Herman Swift in late 1909 and 1910. In spite of this, he slowly began to rebuild enrollment and by 1912 over fifty boys once more resided as inmates at the Home.

Even against the backdrop of his conviction, Herman Swift actively resumed his fund raising efforts. He had lost his two principal performers, Floyd Bishop and Evan Dunn, but he developed other boy singers and speakers and they traveled to raise money, focusing on places friendly to Swift like Detroit and Eaton Rapids

Herman Swift and defense attorney Lisle Shanahan appeared at the January 25th, 1911 sentencing hearing at the Circuit Court in the City of Charlevoix. Elisha Clink for some reason did not appear. As a result of Clink's absence, Shanahan requested a further deferral of sentencing. Judge Mayne approved that request and ordered Swift to report to the Court for sentencing at ten o'clock A.M. on January 31st. On that date, attorney Clink appeared and again requested a delay in sentencing in order to gain more time to prepare his appeal. Judge Mayne approved this request and deferred the sentencing until "the first day of the next term of this Court," February 6th, 1911.

On February 6th, Herman Swift and Lisle Shanahan appeared in Circuit Court as the judge had ordered. Elisha Clink again did not appear. Shanahan advised the judge that Clink was ill and Shanahan again moved that sentencing be deferred. Judge Mayne approved this motion and ordered Swift to report for sentencing "the first day of the next term of this Court."

During this period in early February, Elisha Clink publicly announced his candidacy for the Republican nomination for the position of 13th Circuit Court Judge, the position held by Judge Mayne. Clink was well aware that a victory in the Republican primary ensured him of gaining that position. On February 11th, 1911, Judge Mayne publicly announced that he would seek re-election. The *Charlevoix Herald* supported Clink, writing: "Attorney Clink is so well known, not alone in his home town here (East Jordan) but throughout the district, that anything the *Herald* might say would seem superfluous. The *Charlevoix Sentinel* endorsed Clink writing: "His opponents will realize that they must go some. His legal ability is recognized all over the circuit and his friends are legion. Mr. Clink has always been a progressive in his political ideas."

In spite of these endorsements for Clink, on March 4th, 1911, the *Herald* reported that Judge Mayne won the primary contest by a margin of over one thousand votes. This effectively meant that he would serve another six-year term as 13th Circuit Court Judge. The Swift case certainly did not boost attorney Clink's chances in this election. Herman Swift must have been disappointed by the result. Judge Mayne was happy and the matter did not serve to build his friendship with attorney Clink.

On May 8th, 1911, Judge Mayne opened Court and heard arguments on attorney Clink's motion for a new trial. Clink presented the argument for the defense. D.H. Fitch represented the People as Prosecuting Attorney for Charlevoix County. A.B. Nicholas, "assistant prosecuting attorney," assisted Fitch.

The 1911 business directory for the town of East Jordan listed three practicing attorneys: Elisha N. Clink, Alfred B. Nicholas, and Dwight H. Fitch. Dwight Fitch won the Republican primary for the position of Charlevoix County Prosecuting Attorney and then in November of 1910 won the general election by an overwhelming margin. Fitch was forty-three and lived with his wife Jennie in a Garfield Street home located next door to East Jordan Iron Works owner William Malpass, a few blocks from Elisha Clink, and right across the street from Alfred Nicholas. Nicholas, like Clink the year before, had decided not to run for another term as prosecuting attorney. Nicholas returned to the more lucrative private practice of law. He also may have wearied of the Swift case. In any event, Nicholas served as an assistant to Prosecuting Attorney Fitch at the May 8th hearing before Judge Mayne. He would continue to assist Fitch's prosecution of the Swift case for another two years.

Judge Mayne listened to the arguments for and against the motion for a new trial and at the conclusion of the May 8th hearing he took the matter under advisement. The parties returned to Circuit Court on May 19th, 1911 to hear the judge's decision. Judge Mayne over-ruled the motion for a new trial and ordered Herman Swift to appear in court for sentencing on June 6th, 1911.

The morning of June 6th the parties appeared in Judge Mayne's courtroom. Court records show that attorneys for the defense now included Elisha Clink and "Bundy and Travis." The law firm of Bundy and Travis was located in Grand Rapids. It was one of the pre-eminent law firms in the State of Michigan. McGeorge Bundy served as President of the Grand Rapids Bar Association for the year 1906 and Phillip Travis served as President for the year 1909. Both Bundy and Travis were qualified and experienced in arguing cases before the Michigan Supreme Court. Furthermore, their former law partner, Robert Montgomery, had just recently retired from the Michigan Supreme Court. Montgomery continued to live on Townsend Street in downtown Lansing, within walking distance of the Supreme Court, and he still had strong connections at that Court. Elisha Clink felt that engaging Bundy and Travis gave him the best chance to gain an appeal hearing of the Swift case by the Michigan Supreme Court.

At the hearing in Judge Mayne's courtroom on the morning of June 6th, 1911, Elisha Clink introduced Phillip Travis to the judge. The judge grimaced a bit. He did not know Travis personally, but he knew the man by reputation. And he realized the chances for Herman Swift to gain an appeal hearing at the Supreme Court had just risen dramatically. The defense again moved for a deferral of sentencing. Judge Mayne approved the motion in order to give the defense and prosecution time to settle a Bill of Exceptions, a proposed defense motion to appeal to Michigan's Supreme Court. The judge ordered Herman Swift to reappear for sentencing the morning of June 17th, 1911.

The morning of June 17th the parties once more appeared in court. And once more Elisha Clink was sick and did not appear. As a result, Judge Mayne ordered a further deferral until the morning of June 26th. His order included the statement that the defendant would not be required to appear for sentencing on June 26th, if the parties had agreed on a Bill of Exceptions prior to that date. This meant that if the parties agreed upon the terms of an appeal to the Supreme Court then Judge Mayne's Circuit Court would lose the authority to sentence Herman Swift until either the appeal was rejected or the Supreme Court heard and ruled on the case.

Neither Herman Swift nor his attorneys appeared at the June 26th sentencing hearing. Judge Mayne sent out an order that they must appear on June 28th. On June 28th, they did appear and Clink argued for more time to complete his appeal to the Supreme Court. Judge Mayne took the matter under advisement and Herman Swift would not appear in Court again until August 21st, 1911.

On August 21st, Elisha Clink changed his course in the case. Appearing before Judge Mayne, Clink filed his second motion for a new trial in Charlevoix County Circuit Court, placing on hold his appeal to the Supreme Court. Clink supplemented this motion with four affidavits signed by men who had served as jurors in the second Merrill Griffin trial. The first of these was a lengthy affidavit signed by Conrad Schneider on July 26th, 1911. Schneider owned and operated a Bay Township farm located near the Beulah Home property. A copy of his affidavit later was published in the January/February 1913 edition of Herman Swift's *The Youth's Outlook*:

"Conrad Schneider, being duly sworn, deposes and says that he was one of the twelve jurors who sat in the case of The People vs. Hermon L. Swift, which said trial began on or about the 27th day of December, 1910, and ended on the 31st day of said month.

Deponent further says that the verdict of guilty was rendered which was against the weight of evidence offered on the trial of said cause in the opinion of this juror, and which was his opinion at the time of the rendition of said verdict.

Deponent further says that he understood on the trial of the case, from what the court said and from the argument of Mr. Nicholas, who was at that time prosecuting attorney for the county, that the jury was only to consider the evidence of Merrill Griffin, the complaining witness, and that they were not to consider the evidence of the twelve or thirteen witnesses offered on the part of the respondent, Hermon L. Swift, and that if he had so understood that they were to weigh all the evidence offered on the trial of said cause, that he never would have joined in the rendition of the verdict of guilty.

Deponent further says that it is his opinion that the weight of evidence was all on the part of the respondent, Hermon L. Swift.

Deponent further says that some of the jurors said that if there was a disagreement there would be another trial anyway and a still greater expense to the county and to the taxpayers, and that if it was not right, that Mr. Swift would take his case to the Supreme Court.

Deponent further says that he is fully convinced in his own mind that at least two of the jurors were determined to convict Swift, even before the trial, as they were prejudiced against him to such an extent that it would not have made any difference to them what the testimony was.

Deponent further says that things were said in the jury room which were not offered in evidence and which would prejudice, and in the mind of this deponent did prejudice the jury against the respondent.

Deponent further says that among the things which were said, that Swift had eight or ten thousand dollars in the bank which he could use to get him out of the trouble in the Supreme Court if he wanted to, and in my mind this helped to influence the jury against Swift.

Deponent further says that another juror said that it would do no good to disagree for that before three suns went down that Swift would be arrested all over again.

Deponent further says that he said in the jury room that he had one of the Beulah Home boys working for him and that he used such bad language before himself and his boy that he was obliged to return him to the Home.

Deponent further says that he believes this had its effect to help influence the jury and should not have been mentioned.

Deponent further says that just after the jury was dismissed he told Mr. McClellan, one of the jurors, that it was a dirty shame to convict an innocent man; that the next morning following this deponent told Edward Davis, his neighbor, that he believed right had not been done, and told his wife and children, that he would be glad if he could take the matter back and make it right.

Deponent further says that on Tuesday, January 12th, 1911, he told Reverend Holliday of East Jordan, Michigan, who was visiting his home, that he knew that the evidence was in favor of the respondent, and that he was never so surprised in his life as at the verdict.

Deponent further says that on January 18th, 1911, he saw for the first time, after the trial, the respondent, Mr. Swift, and said to him the same things that he had to Reverend Holliday and to his neighbors.

Deponent further says that he does not now, and never has believed the respondent, Mr. Swift, guilty of the charge or of any other crime.

Deponent further says that in his opinion justice and right demand that Mr. Swift be granted a new trial in the case in which he was a juror.

And further the deponent sayeth not."

Conrad Schneider signed this affidavit before Sabin Hooper, a notary public in Charlevoix County. Attorney Clink approached a number of the other jurors to see if they had opinions similar to those of Conrad Schneider and to see if they might sign an affidavit in support of Herman Swift's motion for a new trial. On July 27th, 1911, three other jurors signed sworn affidavits before notary publics in Charlevoix County. The January/February 1913 edition of *The Youth's Outlook* also printed copies of those affidavits. They were much shorter than Schneider's. Jurors Walter Kahler, John McClellan, and Henry Kunkle signed the affidavits. Each of the three men expressed the opinion that Hermon L. Swift deserved a new trial. In their affidavits, Kahler and Kunkle referred to inappropriate discussion in the jury room of "issues not brought out in court," particularly Swift's financial position. The McClellan and Kunkle affidavits referred to "falsehoods" and "untruthful statements" told on the witness stand by Merrill Griffin.

On August 26th, 1911, the parties to the case again appeared before Judge Mayne.

In 1911, the State of Michigan criminal law codes included section Number 957 which stated: "Affidavits of jurors cannot be received to impeach a criminal verdict." Judge Mayne may well have cited this, among other things, when in Circuit Court on August 26th he denied attorney Clink's second motion for a new trial.

On September 5th, 1911, Elisha Clink filed a Bill of Exceptions in the Swift case, an appeal to the Michigan Supreme Court. The judges of the Supreme Court agreed to hear the case. Herman and Grace Swift, attorney Clink, attorneys Fitch and Nicholas, Judge Mayne, Edward Griffin and the people of Charlevoix County waited for the decision of the judges of the Michigan Supreme Court. It would not come until November 8th, 1912.

It is clear that back in December of 1909 the Beulah Home Board obtained an injunction preventing Herman Swift from using the Beulah Home property or the money he had on deposit with The First National Bank of Boyne City to assist in his efforts to gain bail or defend himself against criminal charges. It is not clear that the Board ever brought a formal lawsuit against Swift in this matter. Having investigated the situation, the Board's attorneys probably quickly concluded that they did not have much of a case. Furthermore, bringing the case and then losing would prove that the members of the Board had been negligent in allowing Swift to gain sole ownership of the property.

Circuit Court records suggest that Judge Mayne never issued a decree or ruling on a case filed by the Beulah Home Board against Herman Swift. It appears that sometime in the summer or early fall of 1911, any such case against Swift was dropped and the injunction against his use of the money and property was lifted. This was fortunate for Herman, as he needed collateral to finance his expensive appeal to the Supreme Court. On October 18th, 1911, Herman Swift through quit-claim deed transferred title in the Beulah Land Farm property to William H. Hill, president of both the Hill, Cascara Company and the Beulah Home Board. Perhaps this was a temporary transfer to gain Hill's financial support and to allow the two men to see the outcome of the Supreme Court appeal. Whatever the case, it was a sad day for Herman Swift.

XV

The Appeal Continues

Floyd Elliott Starr was born May 1, 1883 on a farm outside the small southern Michigan town of Decatur. Late in life, as he discussed his own biography with his son David, Floyd Starr recalled an incident when he was a small boy. His parents over the dinner table were talking about the possibility of adopting children. Floyd interjected: "Well, when I get big I'm going to buy a farm and adopt fifty children to live on it." In 1913, Floyd Starr founded the Starr Commonwealth for Boys on a forty acre farm near the railroad town of Albion, Michigan, some twenty miles from Decatur. In founding the Commonwealth, Floyd's principal core belief was that: "There is no such thing as a bad boy." Today the Starr Commonwealth is much larger, famous, successful, and holds the broader core belief that: "There is no such thing as a bad boy or girl."

Floyd Starr forsook a career of farming and instead pursued one that built upon his oratory skills and missionary drive. He worked for a number of years for the Loyal Temperance Union an offshoot of the Women's Christian Temperance Union. He developed a strong relationship with Dr. John Kellogg in Battle Creek and worked on establishing a Healthitorium in Chicago. Under Kellogg's care, Starr overcame a bout with tuberculosis and enrolled in Albion College. He graduated from Albion at the age of twenty-seven in June of 1910 and married Harriet Armstrong on Christmas Eve of 1910.

Starr's dream remained the establishment of a school for troubled boys, but he lacked the money and the experience required to accomplish that dream. He continued to ponder this when in 1912 Herman Swift offered him the position of assistant director for The Beulah Land Farm for Boys in Boyne City.

Floyd and Harriet Starr moved into the Beulah Home in the summer of 1912. Floyd and Herman Swift made an interesting and very compatible pair. Both were skilled at oratory and fund raising. Both had grown up on farms and had the ability to manage farms, but chose the care of troubled boys as their mission in life. Both were only five feet six inches tall. In the summer of 1912, Herman Swift was forty-one and Floyd Starr was twenty-nine. Swift would prove an excellent teacher for Starr. And Starr would provide strong support for Swift through the remainder of the Time of Troubles.

The January/February 1913 edition of *The Youth's Outlook* included a letter written by Floyd Starr in defense of Herman Swift. The letter reads in part:

"Several months ago I entered Beulah Home as assistant to Hermon L. Swift, the founder and manager of the institution. The position was one of my own seeking and that, too, with full knowledge of the accusations that had been made against the gentleman.

The charges that had been preferred against him influenced me not in the least, except to make me more eager to co-operate with Mr. Swift and to render every possible aid in my power to give. Eight years of close friendship had been entirely sufficient to convince me of his absolute purity, honesty, nobility of character and genuineness of perfect manhood. I had visited in the Home and met and talked with the boys under his care; by every possible method I endeavored to sound these little lads to their very depths in order to learn more of the life and spirit of their 'Daddy Swift.' I even talked with relatives of the lads whose false testimony was responsible for the sore persecution that has fallen to this friend of boys. I encouraged every youth to tell me all, thinking that I ought to know of an absolute certainty the true nature of this man, believing that even friendship should not blind me to truth, and that if he were guilty, which I certainly did not believe, I ought to know it and to raise my voice against him for the sake of the boys under his influence. Spurred on by this thought, my investigation went on.

Court records were placed in my hands; affidavits from jurors, stating that while they had taken oath to render a decision according to their best judgment, they had perjured themselves by failing to abide by their oaths, and had voted Mr. Swift guilty when they believed him innocent of the crime of which he was accused. They voted against him on general principles; voted against him because they had heard or read that he was trying to steal the Beulah Home from some committee, and thought he deserved punishment for that; voted against him because two jurors who evidently had made their decision before hearing the testimony were for conviction, and their disagreement would mean a new trial and Mr. Swift could better afford to carry the case to the Supreme Court than the county could afford to stand the expense of a new trial. These poor, ignorant perjurers did not know that the Supreme Court considers only technicalities and that they might be the means of sending a man, whom they themselves considered innocent, to the penitentiary...

Further, letters from the very boys who testified against Mr. Swift were placed in my hands—letters begging for pardon and for re-admission to Beulah Home—letters boldly declaring that every word of the testimony given by them was a LIE. Signed statements from every one of the three lads who appeared against him were also placed in my hands and these statements further emphasize the confessions in their personal letters as to the utter falsity of their testimony. I learned too that these boys confessed that they had been induced to lie on the witness stand by men who were in favor of the liquor interests which Mr. Swift had so valiantly and fearlessly fought.

For days I delved deep into the records; I talked with both friends and foes of the Home and of Mr. Swift, and after hearing both sides I drew my own conclusions, and cast my lot with Mr. and Mrs. Swift, to fight side by side with them—yes to die with them if need be, for it is the duty of every man to aid and protect the oppressed and persecuted, to uphold the righteous and to put down inequity...

Friends, the Bible being true, when it says, 'He that loveth is born of God and knoweth God,' then Mr. Swift of all men I have known is most certainly born of God and knows God, for who can be found who can ever love as he loves? He has the real spirit of the Christ in loving and saving the little ones whom no one else loves or cares for. How strange it is that when a man starts a saloon to ruin boys by the hundreds and the thousands that no one finds fault; but when someone starts a home to save the lads from lives of vice and crime, at once the cry goes out from those who are too infinitely selfish to help others, that there must be some selfish motive at stake and that no one could actually care for this class of boys and love them for their own sakes. Why is it? Is it because they who are so wickedly negligent regarding the helpless condition of their little brothers, seek to justify themselves by trying to condemn those who are sacrificing to help the least of these?

I would that all the people of Michigan could know the awful outrageousness and injustice of this whole matter, even as I do, and I am sure they would not rest until this wrong had been righted. They would demand a complete vindication of Mr. Swift—

First, because he is INNOCENT and that thousands of people who know him personally will never believe him otherwise.

Second, because of the work he had done in rescuing over two thousand boys from crime and deepest degradation and developing them into noble, useful men.

Third, because of the effect such gross injustice would have upon the two thousand boys whom Mr. Swift has lifted up and who know far better that anyone else what he has done for them.

Fourth, because of the thousands of boys Mr. Swift could still redeem to a noble manhood. Those who condemn him will not reach out a helping hand to rescue or save even one little lad, and yet they will cruelly deprive a man who has labored in this line of service for nearly a quarter of a century, of the privilege of saving thousands more of these little lads who belong to nobody—but God.

Now friends, you who believe in this boy-saving proposition, do you not feel it is your duty to stand loyal and true to the man who has spent many of the best years of his life doing for these little waifs what so few others could do, even if they were so inclined? Personally, I want every friend of Beulah Home to know, yes, every enemy too, that so long as God gives me breath I shall stand by Mr. Swift and by Beulah Home, and shall use my voice, my pen, my every power to secure justice for the one man in all Michigan who is best able to make Beulah Home the power for good that it should be.

Floyd E. Starr, Asst. Manager, Beulah Land Farm for Boys."

Floyd Starr's letter refers to letters and statements: "begging pardon and seeking re-admission to the Beulah Home," from three boys who had testified against Herman Swift: Elliott Fay, John Hosner, and Merrill Griffin. His statements in regard to this matter seem a bit exaggerated and probably are based on three items that were in Herman Swift's files. The first of the three was indeed a sworn statement of Elliott Fay. On October 8th, 1912, Elliott signed this statement before Christie A. Stearns, a notary public in Jackson County, Michigan:

"I, Elliott Fay, age thirteen years, being duly sworn, depose and say: My sworn statements in the Justice Court at Boyne City, Mich., about three years ago against Mr. Hermon L. Swift, are false and untrue. I was then only nine years of age and easily influenced and was homesick and lonesome and was promised that I could get back home and see my mother if I would only say things charged against Mr. Swift. All the time I have known Mr. Swift he has treated me kind and right in every way and I have no charges against him whatever, and I am now sorry that I was ever influenced to lie about him. Mr. Jones and Simon Mack are the ones who started me against Mr. Swift and I know they started all the trouble for they wanted to get Mr. Swift out of his place.

Elliott Fay"

Elliott's letter resided in a Herman Swift file along with a letter that Elliott's mother Maud Fay had written to "William H. Hill, President of the Beulah Home Board." Maud's letter was mailed from Jackson, Michigan on February 23rd, 1912. It reads:

"Dear Sir—My husband was killed in a street car accident four years ago, leaving me with nine children, the oldest one twelve years of age.

Mr. Swift came to my help and took three of my boys. In the time of trouble at the Home I sent for my boys. They have now been home over a year and four months and I am fully convinced that the influences for good over them of Mr. Swift and the Home have been the very best. They showed such good manners and training when they first returned. The boys have nothing but the best of words for Mr. Swift and I take no stock in the mean lies against him.

I believe so fully in Mr. Swift as a Christian man that I do not know of any place where I would rather have my boys when they need a home.

Yours Sincerely, Mrs. Maud Fay"

Second, Floyd Starr examined a letter from John Hosner. In that letter John wrote that he was sorry for lying about Mr. Swift and he asked Mr. Swift to forgive him. This letter resided in a Herman Swift file next to a letter from John's guardian and sister, Mrs. Nat McCauley. Mrs. McCauley's letter concluded:

"There can be no doubt that Mr. Swift has been a terribly wronged man and as own sister of the lad who brought the charges, I stand ready to do all in my power to make right the harm that has been done.

Mrs. Nat McCauley, 330 E. Forest Ave., Ypsilanti, Mich.

Subscribed and sworn to."

Anna McCauley's letter appeared in this form in the January/February edition of *The Youth's Outlook*. The notary public was not identified and the letter clearly was sent to someone other than Mr. Swift, probably William H. Hill.

Third, Floyd Starr examined a "letter or statement" from Merrill Griffin. This resided in the form of a postcard in Herman Swift's files. The claim was that James Leys, Merrill's cousin, had approached Merrill on a sidewalk in Grand Rapids. James asked Merrill to write a letter to Mr. Swift. James claimed he had given Merrill a postcard and that Merrill had written on that postcard as James stood some fifteen feet away. James included the postcard in a letter that he sent to Herman Swift. The envelope containing the letter and the postcard was stamped: "Grand Rapids, Mich., October 26th, 1911, 9 A.M." On the front of the postcard was written: "Mr. Swift, Bulah Home, Boyne City Mich." On the back was written: "I am sorry what I said about you and me. It is not true what I said about you. Simon Mack put me up to it in the front yard." The postcard was signed: "Merrill Griffin" and it would become a key piece of evidence in the Herman Swift case.

Floyd Starr's letter referred to three boys who were witnesses against Herman Swift, but there were four witnesses. The fourth was Simon Mack who had testified against Swift in Justice

Court in the city of Charlevoix. Starr could find no letters or statements from Simon Mack. That was in spite of the fact that Swift and his supporters had attempted to acquire such a letter. Those attempts did yield an indirect statement from Simon and that indirect statement was in Herman Swift's files, contained in a letter Swift had received from William J. Allison, the mystery man who had testified for the defense in the second Merrill Griffin trial in December 1910. Allison wrote the letter from his new residence in Flint, but for many years he had resided in Montcalm County, close to the home in Lakeview where Simon Mack had been placed when he left Boyne City on December 24th, 1909. Allison's letter reads as follows:

"When I came from Flint the last part of June or first of July (1910) I went to Lakeview, Mich., and got into a conversation with the city marshal, General Ward, and I asked him if he had plenty to do nowadays. He said he had been quite busy with a suit between a boy in the village and the school superintendent and the superintendent took a change of venue and took his case from Lakeview to Howard City, and one of the witnesses was a boy from Boyne City, and he had to take his evidence quick because there was an officer to take the boy to Boyne City as a witness in another case. I asked him the boy's name and asked him if he was a sandy haired boy and he replied he was. I then asked what his name was and he said he could not remember. I then asked if he could remember the name if I gave it and he said he could. I said, 'Was it Simon Mack?' He said, 'It was.' I then asked where he was. He said, 'Up this side of the cemetery in a little factory,' and I said I know the boy and I am interested in the matter and am going to see him. Then I asked the marshal to go with me, but he said he did not have time.

Then I went alone and on the way I stopped and talked with August Wilcox a short distance from the factory, and I asked him if he would go with me. He said he would. When we got to the house where the parties lived who run the factory, Wilcox and I stopped, and there were two ladies standing in front of the house. I asked the elderly lady if there was a boy there by the name of Simon Mack. She said, 'There is.' I asked, 'Where abouts is he?' and the answer was, 'There he goes toward the barn.' I started and called aloud, 'Simon.' He stopped and looked around. I walked up a short distance from him and then asked if he remembered me. He said he didn't. Then I asked, 'Don't you remember the mason who worked up at the Beulah Home?' He said, 'Oh, yes I do.' I asked him, 'Was you up on Swift's trial?' He said he was. I asked him if the case came off then and he replied, 'No.' Then I said, 'Your evidence and that of Earnest Wardell's does not seem to agree.' He replied, 'No.' He said, 'Earnest isn't in it.' I said, 'What?' Then he replied, 'He is not onto his job.' Simon then appeared to not want to talk anymore."

William Allison's letter sat in a Herman Swift file, but Elisha Clink knew that he could not use the letter as evidence in the Swift case and Floyd Starr did not refer to it in his letter in defense of Herman Swift.

During 1912, Herman Swift diligently worked on a public defense of his own. The most important outgrowth of this work took shape in the form of *The Victories of A Boy*, a book that Herman published and copyrighted in 1912. The book is: "Dedicated by the Author To Nobody's Boys—But God's." It is a book written in two parts. The second part is titled: "Beulah Land Farm For Boys" and represents a fifty page series of previously published articles: tributes to Herman

Swift, his works, and results at the Beulah Home. One of these articles is an extract from a Hermon Lee Swift lecture titled: "The Religion of Christ." This lecture includes the following observation: "You know the sparkling snows of Mt. Hermon and the chrystal waters of the Jordan River are constantly pouring their wealth into the sea, and yet the sea is Dead, and the reason it is Dead is because it is always receiving and never giving."

The first part of the book *The Victories of A Boy* is a one hundred thirty two page story of the same name. The story is attributed to Ethelyn Dyer and Ethelyn's last name appears on the binding of the book, but I believe the name represents a pen name for Herman Swift, who perhaps constructed it as a play on the name Emeline or Emma Dryer, an important early leader in Dwight Moody's Christian mission in Chicago.

Herman Swift began writing the *Victories of A Boy* shortly after the completion of the first Merrill Griffin trial in August of 1910. Individual chapters appeared in serial form in *The Youth's Outlook*, where the story was titled *The Camp Kid*. It is important to recognize that Herman Swift wrote the story, because it is allegorical. It represents Herman's *Pilgrim's Progress*.

Many of the references in the story *The Victories of A Boy* speak for themselves in the context of the life of Herman Swift. The leading character in the story, a boy named Doddsy, represents Herman's version of John Bunyan's "Christian" in *Pilgrim's Progress*. Doddsy heroically sweeps across life moving from a start as a rough lumber camp kid typical of the Beulah boys aided by Herman Swift to a finish as a man just like Herman. Doddsy's mentor, Arthur Hunter, is a sophisticated, rich young man from Detroit who has accepted a mission to serve less fortunate people, the "other half." Perhaps Arthur represents a composite of several of Herman's wealthy Detroit supporters combined with Herman's vision of an ideal boyhood. Arthur's father is never seen in the story. His mother is religious, serving, kind, sophisticated and wealthy. She seems Herman's vision of the ideal mother. Herman's mother Lucy was religious, but neither sophisticated nor wealthy. Perhaps she was more strict than kind, more like Mrs. Meade, the kitchen servant in the story, than like Mrs. Hunter. Doddsy's girlfriend Gretchen represents Grace Swift. Gretchen's father had the curious facility to drink in moderation in Germany but not in the United States. Perhaps this hints at something about Grace Swift's father. Gretchen dreamed of becoming a deaconess and this suggests that Grace once held a similar dream. Doddsy boldly lied in a situation where he was accused of stealing chewing tobacco and this might remind the reader of the Beulah boys who brought charges against Herman Swift. At a crescendo point in the story, Doddsy gets lost in a poor and desperate part of Detroit "near Woodward Avenue." Woodward Avenue plays an interesting symbolic role in *The Victories of A Boy* and in this book. Finally, as an adult, Doddsy establishes the "Shiloh Boy's Home," an orphanage which lies in a garden beside the banks of a "swiftly-moving river" and this is the way it should be because this is John Bunyan's "Beulah Land," a beautiful garden on the banks of the River of Death.

Supreme Court Briefs

The defense and the prosecution each provided lengthy briefs to the Supreme Court of the State of Michigan when that court agreed to take on appeal the Herman Swift criminal case. The case was given Michigan Supreme Court Case No. 24922. Interestingly, the defense titled their brief for respondent and appellant: "The People vs. Herman L. Swift" while the prosecution titled their brief for the people and the appellee: "The People vs. Hermon L. Swift." E.N. Clink, Attorney for the Respondent and Philip H. Travis, Of Counsel, filed the brief for the defense. Onderdonk, a printer in Travis' hometown of Grand Rapids, printed this brief. Franz C. Kuhn, Attorney General for the State of Michigan, Dwight H. Fitch, Prosecuting Attorney, and A.B. Nicholas, Assistant Prosecuting Attorney, filed the brief for the prosecution.

The brief for the defense runs the length of forty-seven pages. It begins with a "Statement of Case" which reads in part as follows:

"Prior to November 1909, the respondent, Herman L. Swift, had for some years managed and conducted at Boyne City a farm for wayward boys.

The character of those who were sent to and received there would somewhat resemble that of the inmates of a reform school. They came quite largely from cities, and many of them were of criminal tendencies, and accustomed to truancy, vice and petty crimes and offenses.

Mr. Swift stood high as a man and as a specialist in this line of work. He and the institution were widely and favorably known, its charitable work being supported in part by contributions from various parts of the state.

A day or so prior to December 1, 1909, the community and surrounding country were greatly surprised and shocked to learn that charges of a scandalous nature had been made against Mr. Swift by some boys who had been committed to the home. These charges were first brought to the attention of the authorities by Sidney Jones and a Mr. Snell, the former employed as an assistant and overseer on the farm, and the latter as a carpenter. Jones first told Snell, claiming to have heard about the charges from Simon Mack and Ernest Wardell, two of the older boys at the Home. Mr. Swift was hastily arrested on complaints of indecent acts between male persons made by John Hosner, 10 years old, and Elliott Fay and Merrill Griffin, two other young boys.

Wardell made similar charges, but the record does not disclose that any arrest was made thereon. Either then or later it transpired that Wardell's charges were false and incited by Mack and Jones, Wardell appearing and testifying for the defendant on the trial of the present case.

Examinations were held at Boyne City and Mr. Swift was bound over for trial on the complaints made by Hosner, Fay, and Griffin.

Hosner was removed from the Home and appears to have been kept in charge of the turnkey at the jail and at the County Home until shortly prior to the time when the case was to come on for trial in May 1910, the prosecutor evidently having selected that as the strongest case to be first brought to trial. Efforts were made by the authorities to keep anyone from seeing Hosner but shortly prior to the trial his sister went to the County Poor Farm, where he was then being kept, and saw him, and to her he confessed that the charges he had made against Mr. Swift were false. He was then taken before the prosecutor, before the case was actually called for trial, and stated to him that all that he had sworn to on the witness stand at the examination was a lie...

When this case was called for trial defendant's counsel insisted that either the case be tried or that he be discharged, but this the court declined to do, merely continuing the case.

The Griffin case was then selected by the Prosecutor for trial and came on in August 1910. On the first trial the jury disagreed, the newspaper accounts stating that they were about evenly divided.

This case was again brought to trial in December 1910 and January 1911. This time the jury finally agreed upon a verdict of guilty, which verdict was based upon the unsupported testimony of the boy Merrill Griffin. Since then at least four of the jurors have made affidavits that they did not believe Swift was guilty; that the jury were influenced by outside considerations, and that they thought he ought to be granted a new trial.

It is needless to say that all of these matters which transpired before the second trial were of great notoriety particularly in Charlevoix County where the Home was located and where the examinations and first trial were had. Owing to the position and standing of Mr. Swift and the nature of the charges made against him these matters were widely discussed in and out of the newspapers and there was great prejudice and excitement in connection therewith. Before the second trial was commenced respondent's counsel made a motion for a change of venue, basing the same upon affidavits made by sundry citizens of the county of high standing, showing the great publicity and discussion which had followed the charges, and that for these and various reasons it would be impossible for Mr. Swift to have a fair and impartial trial in that county. No counter affidavits were filed and the motion was disposed of upon those filed by the defendant. The denial of this motion is one of the things upon which error is alleged on this record.

On the trial Merrill Griffin was the sole witness on the main case of the People, and his testimony was not corroborated by any fact or circumstance, in any respect whatever. It appeared, by his own testimony, that before going to the Home he had lived in Grand Rapids; that he came to the Home because he was a bad boy; ran away...

On the part of the defendant the evidence was strong that there was a conspiracy backed by Jones and Mack to have these charges made against Mr. Swift in order that he might be deposed so that Jones would get the management of the Home and so that the boys would either get away from it or be subject to Jones' authority instead of Mr. Swift's...

The defendant was much hampered in making his defense by the rulings of the court on evidence, especially evidence tending to establish the alleged conspiracy. At first the court was not disposed to admit evidence on this theory at all. Later his position was somewhat modified but much of the evidence offered on this phase of the case was rejected and these rulings are assigned as error.

There were also sundry rulings on evidence pertaining to other phases of the case which are also claimed to have been erroneous and prejudicial and which are also assigned as error.

After the conviction a motion for a new trial was made and held under advisement by the court for a considerable period of time. Later, and shortly after the motion was denied and after affidavits had been made by several of the jurors showing that they did not believe in respondent's guilt and that the verdict had been affected by matters which ought not to have reached the jury, the motion was renewed being based in part upon the proposition that the verdict was against the weight of evidence and that respondent had not been proven guilty beyond reasonable doubt. The denial of this motion is also assigned in error.

Remarks made by the prosecuting attorney in argument are also assigned and relied upon as error; also certain instructions and ruling of the court in giving his charge and refusing certain requests preferred by defendant's counsel.

After the trial of the case had been commenced and the introduction of evidence had proceeded for a time, the prosecuting attorney asked permission of the court to make a further opening statement, to which defendant's counsel objected and excepted. Thereupon the prosecuting attorney was allowed to state that Mr. Swift was a hypnotist and practiced hypnotism...

The People introduced no evidence whatever to support this prejudicial statement...In the charge to the jury the court called attention to the fact that no evidence had been offered in support of this supplemental statement of the people's case and told the jury not to consider that phase of the matter. In view, however, of the nature of this case and the influence which such a statement might have on the jury even though no evidence was offered in support of it, it is apparent that the statement was highly prejudicial and error is now assigned thereon."

The Brief for the People runs forty-two pages in length. It begins in part as follows:

"Appellant's 'Statement of Case' is a resume of the testimony offered on the part of the respondent at the trial of the case and includes references and citations to newspaper comments as well as conclusions of counsel which are not facts and which form no part of this case. We do not admit that such 'Statement of Case' is a statement of facts according to rule and beg leave to submit the following as Appellee's Statement of the Facts: The Beulah Land Farm for Boys was, at time of the commencement of this suit, a private institution conducted by the respondent, Hermon L. Swift. At that time he had under his immediate charge and control some 25 or 30 boys from 8 to 15 years old. These boys came to the Home through the influence of respondent and were supported there by charitable donations received from various parts of the State and the financial assistance of the parents of many of them. Many were there as boarders on an arrangement made by Mr. Swift with their parents and guardians.

Something like a week or ten days prior to the first of December 1909, complaint was made to the Prosecuting Attorney of Charlevoix County that respondent had been guilty of scandalous conduct with several of the boys. The Prosecuting Attorney directed one of the Deputy Sheriffs of the County to remove these boys from the Home until an investigation could be made by him as to the truth or falsity of these charges, he at the time being engaged in the trial of criminal cases in the Circuit Court. After an investigation lasting several days a complaint was made by the Chief of Police of Boyne City, in said County and warrant issued on the fifteenth day of December 1909, and the respondent taken into custody. The complaint was based on Act No. 198 of the Public Acts of 1903 (the brief then recites the Complaint.)

The respondent demanded an examination, which was duly had and resulted in his being bound over to the Circuit Court for Charlevoix County for trial. In August 1910 a trial was had, the jury disagreeing. The case was again brought to trial in December 1910, the jury finding respondent guilty as charged in the information. From this verdict the respondent appeals to this Court.

Before the second trial respondent moved for a change of venue, basing his motion on the records and files, on numerous newspaper articles and the affidavits of several persons. This motion was denied. Respondent renewed this motion at the time of the second trial, after the jury had been examined on their voire dire. The newspaper clippings and affidavits have been included in the record and form about the first 70 pages thereof.

Following respondent's conviction in December 1910, several applications were made for a new trial, based on alleged errors of the second trial, and the affidavits of some of the jurors which had been procured by respondent's counsel. These applications for a new trial were all denied and the reasons for the denial of them were given in writing by the Court at the request of counsel for respondent. The errors assigned as a basis for this motion and the affidavits of the jurors are incorporated into the record and will be found on pages 189 to 211, inclusive."

Phillip H. Travis argued the case for the defense before the State of Michigan Supreme Court. He spent little time reciting the "Statement of the Case." That and the appellee's "Statement of Facts" each added color or nuance to the case. Neither would have been of much consequence to the Supreme Court judges, but it is interesting to note the prosecution's description of the Beulah Home as a "private institution."

The defense and the prosecution provided contrasting characterizations of the Beulah boys. Herman Swift frequently would comment that he had helped two thousand boys. Fitch and Nicholas wrote that there were "some 25 or 30 boys" at the Home. Clink and Travis described the boys as "wayward," coming from cities, of "criminal tendencies," and "somewhat resembling inmates of a reform school." Fitch and Nicholas wrote that the boys were at the Home "through the influence of respondent" and "many were there as boarders on an arrangement made by Mr. Swift with their parents and guardians." The truth lay somewhere between these two characterizations and one characterization suited some of the boys and the other suited the other boys at the Home. Now, one hundred years later, it is difficult to attach one or the other characterization to any individual Beulah boy. It is clear that most of the boys did not come from "cities" and almost all those that did came from the city of Grand Rapids.

Phillip Travis focused his arguments to the Court on the one hundred twenty seven items in the Bill of Exceptions that he and Clink had filed in their appeal. His goal was to obtain a change of venue and a new trial for Herman Swift. Travis organized his argument into seven parts. Later in this story we will examine the importance of the number seven to Herman Swift.

First, Travis argued there were errors in not granting a change of venue. He cited the newspaper articles and the citizen affidavits. He cited the fact that the prosecution offered no counter argument or any affidavits to support their opposition to a change of venue. He objected to Judge Mayne's comment in court that: "the affidavits in support of the motion were not entitled to full faith and credit."

Travis specifically cited the affidavits signed by the four jurors, stating: "We appreciate that under ordinary circumstance the affidavits of jurors are not admissible to impeach the verdict, but is seems to us that in a case like this it is competent to show, by affidavits of jurors, that extraneous matters did reach them and enter into their deliberations, not so much to impeach the verdict as to throw light upon the propriety or impropriety of granting this motion for change of venue.

We also appreciate that under ordinary circumstances and conditions the granting of a motion for a change of venue is discretionary with the trial court. Where, however, the showing is undisputed and the facts stand un-contradicted it is clearly the duty of the appellate court to review such ruling and if upon the prima facie case made by the affidavits the motion ought to have been granted, then reverse the case and so order."

Second, Travis argued that the trial court had not allowed the defense to fairly pursue their claim of a conspiracy. Attorney Clink had peppered this portion of the trial with objections and many of these were included in the Bill of Exceptions filed with the Supreme Court. Travis argued:

"The People did not put Simon Mack on the stand either in rebuttal or otherwise, nor did they swear the boy Elliott Fay either to contradict what Fenton (Beulah boy Roy Fenton) swore to about Mack's inciting him to make the charge or otherwise. Under these circumstances it was not only proper but highly important to the defendant's case that at least the ordinary latitude be permitted in the introduction of evidence to establish the conspiracy. This latitude should be increased rather than diminished by the fact that this was a criminal case involving the character and liberty of the defendant. An examination of the record and rulings on this subject will, however, disclose that defendant's counsel were much restricted along this line and were not allowed to introduce much evidence which had a direct bearing on the question of conspiracy and the rejection of which must necessarily have been prejudicial to the defendant." Importantly, several of Travis' arguments to the Supreme Court allow us to learn of testimony that was stricken from the trial court records:

"Miss Hardy, a teacher at the Home, was called for the defense and testified that a day or so before the arrest all the boys at the Home except Simon Mack, were gotten together in a room and the question was put to them if any of the boys had been ill treated, none of them responding. If her statement was correct that all of the boys except Simon Mack were there it would have included Griffin, Fay, Wardell, and Hosner and would have amounted to a material admission on their part that the charges which they subsequently publicly made against Mr. Swift were false. It was therefore important to the defense to show that all of the boys were present in the room, and on re-direct examination defendant's counsel asked her to tell the jury how she knew that all of the boys were in the room. Thereupon the court of its own motion ruled out the question saying she had covered it, that it was hearsay and immaterial anyway, to which defendant's counsel excepted (Assignments 59 and 60). (This indicates exceptions numbers 59 and 60 in the Bill of Exceptions.) It is true that the witness had covered that subject in a general way, but it was also proper to show upon what information she based her statement that all of the boys were in the room. It might have appeared that the roll was called or other measures taken so that it enabled her to testify positively and without likelihood of mistake that the boys were all there. It would not have been hearsay. Neither was it immaterial, but on the other hand highly material. This voluntary ruling of the court was not only erroneous but the statement which he made that the evidence was immaterial was also prejudicial...

Emery Weaver testified that he had heard Mr. Jones say he would like to kick Mr. Swift out of there, and that if he was there the boys would not have to work so hard, and that the boys were 'damn fools' for staying there. The witness was then asked how Mr. Jones treated Merrill Griffin in regard to work, and he answered that he babied him. The prosecuting attorney moved that this be stricken out as calling for a conclusion. Motion was granted and exception taken (Assignment 72). Defendant's counsel then asked him to state what work Mr. Jones had Merrill Griffin do, which was also objected to as immaterial, incompetent, ruled out and exception taken

(Assignment 73). It would seem that it was clearly proper to show not only the charges which Jones was making against defendant and the efforts he was making to incite prejudice, hatred, and false charges, but to show in addition that he favored the boys he was trying to influence, like Merrill Griffin, by babying him in the work, and if that statement was objected to as calling for a conclusion, to show what work Mr. Jones had Merrill Griffin do...

It will be seen from the foregoing that it was with great difficulty and under considerable adverse criticism from the court that defendant's counsel were able to get into the case any evidence of consequence with regard to the conspiracy matter. Yet notwithstanding all of this and by reason of the persistent effort made under adverse circumstances, sufficient evidence of that character was presented to convince any fair minded man that these charges against Mr. Swift were the result of a conspiracy and of outside influence being brought to bear upon these young boys. All of the matters discussed under this heading seem to have been pertinent to that subject and their rejection by the court exceedingly unfortunate and prejudicial. Not only the rulings but the attitude of the court tended to greatly hinder, embarrass, and discredit this branch of the defendant's case.

The charge of the court on this part of the case was also unfortunate and tended in the same direction. He gave the jury no instructions which recognized any possible merit in the claim of conspiracy, and on the other hand gave instructions well calculated to minimize the effect of the evidence on that subject (Assignment 108)...He told the jury in substance that it was immaterial what kind of a man Jones, or what kind of a boy Mack was, whether they were good or bad, virtuous or vicious, or what their motives may have been provided they found that Mr. Swift did what Griffin claimed...This was well nigh equivalent to saying to the jury that even if they found that a conspiracy did exist and that Hosner, Wardell, and Fay had been induced to make their charges by reason thereof, the same being false, still it was not a very material matter and that the jury could still find that what Griffin claimed was true, in which event the conspiracy would be immaterial."

Third, Travis presented an argument based upon the numerous trial court defense objections against the prosecutor's introduction of "Evidence of Previous Alleged Offenses" committed by Herman Swift on Merrill Griffin. Travis argued:

"Without at this time referring in detail to the other evidence along this line, it is sufficient to state that the prosecutor was permitted to put in evidence and place before the jury testimony of the complaining witness to the effect that the same offenses had been committed by Mr. Swift on two occasions prior to the one in question, and this was done against the objection and exception of defendant's counsel, who claimed that in a case of this character the evidence should be confined to the particular offense on which the conviction is sought (Assignments 5, 6, etc.)."

This was an important argument, particularly because the defense had a strong alibi defense against "the particular offense on which the conviction is sought." In support of this argument, Travis cited the case of People vs. Jenness, 5 Mich. 305. The opinion in that case reads in part:

"As a general rule, in criminal cases, the commission of other, though similar, offenses by the defendant cannot be proved for the purpose of showing that he was more likely to have committed the offense for which he is on trial, nor as corroborating the testimony relating to such principal offense...

But, in case of a crime consisting of illicit sexual intercourse, which can only be committed by the concurrent act of two persons of opposite sexes, evidence of previous familiarities and acts of intercourse is admissible, as tending, necessarily, to show concert and a common design of both parties to commit the act charged, and habitually to indulge their criminal desires as opportunity might offer. Such evidence proves a greater probability of the commission of the offense charged..."

The Jenness case provided strong supportive precedence to the defense in the Swift case, but only if the exception clause in the Jenness opinion was not relevant to the Swift case. Travis did not attack this exception clause on the basis of the obvious fact that Swift and Griffin were not of the opposite sex, but rather through the evidence introduced by the prosecutor in trial court that Merrill Griffin did not participate in "concert and a common design...in the act charged."

Travis closed this argument stating:

"For these reasons we insist that it was erroneous and highly prejudicial to allow the complaining witness, uncorroborated, to testify to these alleged previous offenses."

Fourth, Travis argued a series of objections to the prosecutor's "Statement to the Jury as to Hypnotism." He recognized that the trial judge had instructed the jury not to consider the comments on hypnotism in reaching its decision. But he added:

"Those remarks of the court were far from constituting a complete cure of the error...That the statement was calculated to be prejudicial we believe no one will question. That it was improper and must have been known to be improper under the circumstances is equally apparent."

Fifth, Travis argued that at trial court defense counsel had offered a number of "Requests to Charge" and that the trial judge had refused to include any of them in his charge to the jury. The defense had offered twenty-two requests to charge to Judge Mayne. These were requests that the judge include specific language on twenty-two points as he gave his closing instructions. While the judge in a general manner did cover many of those points in his instructions, he rejected defense counsel's specific language on all twenty-two requests. Defense counsel assigned error to all twenty-two of those rejections. They focused most strongly on the judge's refusal to accept their requests to charge related to their alibi defense. The most important of these included three assignments:

Assignment 10: "I charge you that if the evidence offered on the part of the defendant, to the effect that the said Hermon L. Swift was in the southern part of the state at the time the people claim the offense was committed, raises a reasonable doubt in your minds as to whether he was present at the Beulah Land Farm at Boyne City at the time the evidence of the people alleges the offense to have been committed, then you should not convict the respondent."

Assignment 12: "The defense of an alibi, as it is called, is as legitimate a defense as any other defense, and you are to give the same credit to witnesses who testified concerning it as to those who testified to anything else, and, if you believe it to have been established, then you are bound to acquit the defendant."

And, Assignment 18: "I further charge you that you must all be on one mind as to whether the defendant, Hermon L. Swift, was at home at the time the evidence in this case alleges the act to have been committed and you are not at liberty to convict the defendant, part of you believing that he was in the southern part of the state at that time and part of you believing that he was at home, and if you cannot all agree that the defendant, Swift, was at home at that time you should not convict the defendant."

Sixth, Travis attacked Prosecutor Nicholas' trial court closing argument. He objected to Nicholas' claim that: "such acts are very common, especially in large cities," pointing out that Nicholas had provided no proof of this. He objected to Nicholas' claim that: "the defendant could not ask why the prosecution did not bring in the other boys if there was an act against them, because, as he (Nicholas) stated, each of the acts is an offense in itself and the prosecution could only confront the defendant with the particular witness in each separate act." Travis argued that Nicholas could not make this statement without putting the other boys on the witness stand. The Clink and Travis Supreme Court brief acknowledged that placing those boys on the stand would have better allowed them to develop their conspiracy theory.

Travis objected to Nicholas' closing statement comments on the postal cards: "Why, gentleman of the jury, those postal cards are a little thing of course, but that is the kind of evidence that convinces me and should satisfy your minds of the guilt of the respondent" (Assignment 119). Travis argued:

"It is true that the court told the jury it was their opinion and not that of the prosecutor which was to control and if it were the only error in the case, it might be possible that it would not justify a reversal, but when taken in connection with all the other errors which occurred on this trial, it is a matter which cannot be properly overlooked."

Travis objected to Nicholas' statement to the jury that: "No one had denied that the act took place, that not a soul, not a witness had come and contradicted the boy that the act did not take place, that not a soul had contradicted it" (Assignments 121-122). Travis argued:

"These statements were both improper and untrue. They were improper because thereby it was sought to direct attention to and base an argument on the fact that upon this trial Mr. Swift had not taken the witness stand. They were untrue because the charges were denied by his plea of not guilty and also by the evidence of at least two or three witnesses to admissions made by Merrill Griffin that the charges were false and by a mass of other testimony tending in the same direction."

Finally, in this portion of his argument, Travis objected to Nicholas' inferring that the jury should favor the complaining witness because he was a child and because the defendant stood high in society. Nicholas had stated: "Is that little urchin to be believed against me? Didn't I pick him up out of the streets, out of the gutter?" Travis argued: "It seems to us that this was improper argument" (Assignment 123).

Travis closed his argument to the Supreme Court with his seventh and final major point. That was that the "weight of the evidence" called for a new trial. Travis noted that this argument had been offered in the second motion for a new trial that was presented to the trial court in August of 1911. He commented that his prior arguments supported this point and then he turned to an attack on Merrill Griffin's credibility. The heart of The People's Case in both Griffin trials rested upon that credibility. Travis began:

"As has been heretofore stated, the conviction was procured upon the uncorroborated testimony of Merrill Griffin, who had been sent to the Home because he was a boy, who at an early age, was a truant, a liar, and a thief, whose parents had lost control over him, who had been arrested by the police, been before the Juvenile Court two or three times and finally sent by that court to this Home. The only witness called by the People on rebuttal, of consequence, was Sidney Jones, the backer of the alleged conspiracy, who it developed on cross examination was a man who had left his wife, eloped with a young lady and gone to the State of Alabama, for which he was arrested and confined in the jail at Harbor Springs.

That Merrill Griffin, at the time these charges were made and this trial was had was still an unmitigated liar is so clearly shown by the record in this case that no one can fairly question it!"

Phillip Travis continued his argument with a discussion of Merrill's inconsistent and confused testimony concerning his relationship with his uncle, Cornelius Proos. He concluded with a discussion of Merrill's inconsistent and confused testimony concerning the dates when he alleged that Herman Swift had abused him:

"There can be no possible doubt on the record in this case that for about two weeks prior to Thanksgiving 1909, Mr. Swift was not at the Beulah Home, but was away on a trip in the southern part of the state. Nor can there be any doubt that at the time the complaint was made, within a very few days after the date of the alleged offense Merrill Griffin said that this date was November 23rd. He knew then that such a statement was absolutely false because impossible, and no conviction ought to be sustained simply because later he on some occasions changed his testimony so as to leave a loop hole for finding that it happened before Mr. Swift went away on this trip, two weeks earlier.

We have not the time and it is not necessary to go entirely through the testimony of this witness and show the many contradictions, inconsistencies and omissions existing therein. Sufficient to say we have only made a start on detailing them and that the record is full of such things. On separate occasions he would testify to the same thing in the same way, and in nearly every instance there would be some variation in the story."

Franz C. Kuhn, Attorney General of the State of Michigan, represented the People in arguing the case of the People vs. Herman Swift before the Michigan Supreme Court. Kuhn graduated from the Literary Department of the University of Michigan and received a degree from the Michigan Law School in 1894. He had served as County Prosecuting Attorney and as a probate judge in Macomb County in southeastern Michigan. He took the position of State Attorney General in 1910.

People described Franz Kuhn as affable. He also was articulate and tough. In the Swift matter, prosecuting attorney Alfred Nicholas had presented a simple case for the People in the trials at the Circuit Court in Charlevoix County. Now, facing a 127 count Bill of Exceptions, the case for the People had become complex.

The brief filed for the People began with the "Appellee's Statement of Facts" followed by a statement of "Errors in Respondent's Statement of the Case" that in part reads: "Respondent's so-called 'Statement of Case,' while not a statement of facts, contains so much of argument and so many irrelevant and erroneous statements that we cannot pass them unnoticed.

There is absolutely no basis for the statement that respondent was hastily arrested as stated in their brief on page 3. Neither is there anything in the record as to any complaint made by Wardell, and the conclusions made therefrom are unwarranted and unfair.

The references made to the Hosner case on pages 3 and 4 are wholly unwarranted and misleading. No efforts were made to keep anyone from seeing Hosner. He was simply removed from the evil influences of the Home and placed where he would be available as a witness. Even then he was spirited away and according to his own statements made later to the prosecutor was induced to change his story on a threat that he, too, would be prosecuted and sent to jail if he didn't. Hosner was not sworn upon this trial.

The record will show that the verdict of the jury was not based on the unsupported testimony of Merrill Griffin, as stated in respondent's brief on page 3. It is true there was no other testimony as to the overt act, and none could be had except from respondent himself, and it was not denied by him other than by his plea of not guilty. The verdict of the jury on this question should not be disturbed.

Judge Jewell of Grand Rapids did not send Merrill to the Home. He came there under the private arrangement made between Mr. Swift and Merrill's father, and the father paid most if not all the expenses.

Several references are made to the affidavits and newspaper articles to sustain contentions made. We insist that this is improper and that such affidavits and newspaper articles can only be used and considered, if at all, for the purpose of enabling this court to pass upon the correctness of the rulings of the court below in denying the motions for a change of venue and for a new trial."

Franz Kuhn's brief and his argument before the Supreme Court were organized to generally parallel the brief and the argument of Phillip Travis. Kuhn began his argument:

"The bill of exceptions sets forth 127 assignments of error, but counsel for respondent in their brief discuss more or less about 50 of them, the other 77 apparently having been abandoned. We, therefore, refrain from discussing those not relied upon. The bill of exceptions is needlessly prolix and does not comply with the rules and practice of this court, and were it not a criminal case we would ask that the appeal be dismissed. It is subject to all the criticisms made by this court in People vs. VanAlstyne, 157 Mich. 368."

In his brief, Kuhn grouped the 50 remaining assignments of error under seven headings. He made extensive reference to applicable Michigan State law and to prior court opinions. As he argued before the Supreme Court, Kuhn knew that he must deal successfully with all fifty remaining assignments of error, while Phillip Travis only had to prevail on one.

Under the heading "Change of Venue" Kuhn's citations included:

(1) Michigan Act No. 67, Public Acts of 1909: "The defendant in a criminal case has no absolute right to a change of venue. The conclusions of the court ought not to be disturbed except in case of a clear abuse of discretion."

(2) People vs. Burke, 157 Mich. 108: "The denial by the trial court of a motion for change of venue will not be reversed on error where the showing of local prejudice consisted of articles in a local newspaper connecting the respondent with the attempted robbery of a bank, and it does not appear that any difficulty was experienced in drawing an impartial jury."

Kuhn argued to the court: "Counsel for respondent concedes that the granting of a change of venue is discretionary with the trial court, and the only question open for argument is whether there has been an abuse of that discretion.

It is true that no counter affidavits were presented in opposition to the motion and none seemed necessary. Many matters alleged in favor of the motion were in the nature of complaints as to alleged occurrences at the previous trial, and implicated officers of the court and members of the bar of high standing, the falsity of which was peculiarly within the knowledge of the trial judge. The other affidavits were more in the nature of opinions of the affiants, who were friends of respondent or his attorneys. The newspaper articles were in the most fair and impartial...Some of the articles were known to have been published at the instance of respondent. The court was far from being satisfied that it was his duty to order a change of venue and in denying the motion he was most zealous in protecting the rights of respondent, and in order that no injustice might be done and that the respondent might have a fair trial by an impartial and unprejudiced jury, he informed counsel that the motion might be renewed at the time of trial of the case if any difficulty was experienced obtaining such a jury...

Counsel for respondent did renew the motion at the second trial, but no difficulty had been experienced in securing a fair, impartial, and unbiased jury. Only a little more than a day was taken in securing the jury, which seems remarkable in so important and serious a case. Counsel make no claim that such a jury was not obtained. The examination of the jury on their voire dire is not set forth in the record. It must, therefore, be conclusively presumed that such a jury was obtained and that they were not improperly influenced. And such was the fact. With the parties in court with their witnesses, a fair, impartial jury, unbiased and uninfluenced, ready to be sworn, it is difficult to see upon what reason or law the trial judge could order a change of venue or be charged with an abuse of discretion if he did not."

Second, Kuhn addressed the "Statement of Prosecutor as to Hypnotism" In his argument he pointed out to the court that Dr. Judson Bennett, a "reputable" Boyne City physician, was sworn as a witness at the first Griffin trial and subpoenaed as a witness for the second trial. Kuhn completed his argument of this subject:

"The statement (on hypnotism) was made in the utmost good faith, and the fact that evidence was not introduced on this phase of the case, was most favorable to the respondent, and its omission at the opening statement of the case was due entirely to inadvertence. The judge in his charge eliminated this phase of the case from the consideration of the jury, and we submit no error was committed."

Third, Kuhn addressed the "Exceptions as to Admission of Evidence, Conspiracy." His brief cited a number of legal cases supportive of the trial court's handling of the introduction of evidence related to the conspiracy defense. Kuhn argued:

"Counsel for respondent states on page 25 of his brief that, 'notwithstanding all of this and by reason of the persistent effort made under adverse circumstances, sufficient evidence of that character was presented to convince any fair-minded man that these charges against Mr. Swift were the result of a conspiracy, and of outside influence being brought to bear on these young boys.' We entertain an entirely different view as to the weight to be given to the testimony of respondent's witnesses, and are of the opinion that any fair-minded man will look with astonishment and suspicion upon this testimony, when it is discovered that for months and months prior to the trial of the case these witnesses had been provided with typewritten statements by respondent which contained the testimony they were supposed to give when upon the witness stand, and when it is further discovered that these witnesses were reviewing these typewritten statements and memorizing their contents at frequent intervals, and up to within a few hours prior to their testifying...

Mr. Swift, the respondent, was the sole owner of the Home, and that he could be deposed by the methods suggested by counsel is ridiculous in the extreme...Mr. Jones was a hired man whose reputation was well known by Mr. Swift at the time that he was employed, and when he resigned his position it was with the distinct understanding that if Mr. Swift went ahead with the farm work in the spring he would again want Mr. Jones...

Mr. Snell testified that he was the person who reported the alleged misconduct of Mr. Swift with Earnest Wardell and Simon Mack, to the police at Boyne City...That the case of Merrill Griffin was unknown to him at the time. There is nothing in the record which discloses that Mr. Snell is charged with being a co-conspirator...

Certainly counsel does not contend that Swift should be acquitted if it were shown that the act complained of was actually committed, but the commission of it was brought about through a conspiracy."

Fourth, Kuhn addressed the: "Exceptions as to Admission of Evidence, Other Offenses." This referred to the appellant's exceptions to evidence entered at trial court on the other two alleged offenses by Herman Swift upon Merrill Griffin. Kuhn argued:

"We admit the general rule to be that on a prosecution for a particular crime evidence of other crimes committed by the respondent, wholly independent but of the same sort, is irrelevant and inadmissible. But to this rule there are many exceptions...One of the exceptions to the rule is found in prosecutions for offenses commonly designated sexual affairs or sexual offenses, and it is our contention that the evidence of the prior offenses committed was admissible under this latter exception."

Kuhn then referenced the case of People vs. Jenness, 5 Mich. 305, the same case Phillip Travis had cited on this matter. Kuhn argued:

"The offense with which Mr. Swift is charged, has but recently been created by statute and the particular offense described in the information is of so revolting a nature, and to the ordinary mind so improbable, that people generally cannot believe it possible. Taken alone, unexplained, it would seem highly improbable that the respondent would have taken young Griffin to his own room, in broad daylight, and when his wife, several teachers and several other little boys were in and about the same building, and there for the first time commit such an atrocious, and unnatural act without fear of an outcry by his victim, and without fear of detection. But when it is shown that it is only one of a series of like offenses, committed with the same party, it is apparent why, in this particular instance, he had no fear of discovery through outcry, or alarm from Griffin...

Counsel state that it was not contended that a habit of this kind had been established between the complaining witness and the respondent...We cannot see what difference it makes whether a habit had been formed between the respondent and witness Griffin. The rule as to the admission of evidence of former acts would equally apply. We are not prepared to say but that evidence might have been admitted showing like conduct between Mr. Swift and certain other boys for the purpose of proving that Mr. Swift did have such a habit. We fail to see where any prejudicial error was committed in the introduction of evidence of these former offenses."

Fifth, Kuhn addressed the "Remarks of Prosecutor in Argument to Jury." He argued to the court:

"We first invite the Court's attention to the language used by the prosecutor, covered by the first four assignments, 113, 114, 115, and 116. It will be observed that these remarks of the prosecutor are but fragments of his argument and do not fairly express what was said by him. In one or two instances it might appear that the language was addressed particularly toward the respondent, but such was not the case. When it is understood, as it clearly appears from this Record, that these remarks were not directed toward the respondent but were a discussion of the commission of this offense in general, we fail to see wherein these remarks were in any manner prejudicial to the respondent.

We are surprised that counsel should so far forget himself and the ethics of the profession as to deliberately charge the prosecutor with making certain prejudicial remarks which he did not make, and of which there is no record...

There was no mention made by the prosecutor in his address to the jury of Simon Mack, Elliott Fay or John Hosner, nor did he offer any excuse for not calling them, and we challenge counsel to show that such a thing was done, and had counsel for respondent desired the evidence of any of these boys, they were in Court and could have been sworn had they expressed such a wish. It appears as though counsel had deliberately attempted to misconstrue the remarks of the prosecutor that error might be predicated thereon.

Respondent's assignment of error 119 relates to an alleged error committed by the prosecuting attorney in his comment on certain testimony given by young Griffin. The prosecutor in the course of this testimony called attention as to what was said by Griffin which caused him to remember that the last alleged act of indecency was just prior to Mr. Swift making a trip to the southern part of the State. The prosecutor made use of this language: "That is the kind of evidence that convinces me and should satisfy your minds of the guilt of the respondent." We contend that there was no error in this remark; that he had a right to call the attention of the jury to such portions of the evidence as satisfied his mind as to the guilt of respondent, and to argue that it should convince the jury as to defendant's guilt. Almost the identical language used by the prosecutor in the case at bar was discussed by this Court in the case of People vs. Hess, 85 Mich. 129, and on page 134 this Court said that he had the right to "state to them (the jury) what evidence before them convinced him and should convince them of such guilt." Although the trial judge (Judge Mayne) told the jury they should not consider this statement by the prosecutor, we still maintain that the argument was proper...

We now discuss assignments 121 and 122, which are the last exceptions to the remarks of the prosecutor argued by appellant, and appear on page 39 of his brief. The exceptions are based on the statement made by the prosecutor in his argument that "no one had denied that the act took place." This remark by the prosecutor was directly in reply to Mr. Clink, one of defendant's council, who in his argument had assumed to repeat the testimony given by Mr. Swift upon the witness stand. And it is our contention that when defendant's counsel go so far in their remarks to the jury as to quote alleged testimony given by a witness who was not sworn in the case, that the prosecutor was justified in the use of the language which he employed in this instance, and that under such circumstances it cannot be said that such a course was prejudicial to the rights of respondent, and constituted reversible error."

Sixth, Kuhn addressed "Requests to Charge." In his brief he noted that all of these related to Herman Swift's alibi defense. He summarized the case that the defense cited in its brief, People vs. Hare, 57 Mich. 518:

"It appears in the case above cited that one Billington professed to have been present at the place and saw the act done, and knew the place where, and the time when it was done, and no other testimony appears as to the time and place. From the above it clearly appears that the particular, and we may add, the hour of the day when the killing was done was positively established by the witness Billington. And from this testimony McCrone could not have been killed at any other time. Under this evidence the Court says that the requests (to charge) should have been given.

In the case at bar the complaint alleged the offense was committed on November 23rd, 1909...

The prosecuting attorney found it impossible at the trial to fix the exact day and hour of its commission. Young Griffin could not fix the date, but at different times he stated, 'It was a little before Thanksgiving Day that the last act was committed, about a week or two before'... 'I have no means of remembering it except the post cards. I know he was away, but I don't know how long before the 24th'...' 'When I went up in his room the last time he gave me one-half dozen post cards. He gave me those post cards before he went away, and he had a whole lot of them packed in his suitcase. The suitcase was open at the time I saw it."

Finally, Kuhn addressed the "Motion for New Trial." Under this heading, attorneys Clink and Travis had concluded their brief and their argument before the Court with an attack on the testimony and character of Merrill Griffin. This formed a natural conclusion for Kuhn, as the People's case against Herman Swift rested almost solely on the testimony and character of Merrill Griffin. Kuhn argued:

"Respondent's counsel charge he had been sent to the Home because he was a truant, a liar, and a thief...

The basis for these charges is that the boy left his home upon two occasions, at one time going to his aunt's, and at another to Ottawa Beach, a few miles from the city.

He is charged as a thief because he took three or four dollars from his father.

We presume that there are few boys who have not done as much, and committed as great if not greater sins in their early youth, and yet are not branded as criminals, and it is cruel to make such accusations. The child had lost his mother and was living with a stepmother, and it is fair to presume from the boy's leaving home that the relationship between stepmother and stepson was not as congenial as it might have been. It is also fair to presume that this was one of the main reasons why the boy was placed at the Home, by his father, and not by Judge Jewell as claimed by respondent, for Judge Jewell had no authority to send him there. In fact, the father states upon his examination in Justice Court that his main reason for placing the boy at the Home was because he ran away...

We do not deny that there are some discrepancies in the testimony of Merrill Griffin, but when it is borne in mind that he was a young boy, subjected to a grilling cross-examination by criminal lawyers of long experience, and that months had elapsed between the time of the examination in Justice Court and the trial of the case, it is not to be wondered at that this difference in his testimony appears...

The jury had the advantage of seeing this boy and hearing his testimony, and measuring and comparing it with the other testimony given in the case, and we submit that their verdict should not be disturbed...

To our minds the cases of Hosner, Wardell, and Fay have no place in this case...Young Hosner through influences brought by Mr. Swift was threatened with imprisonment if he did not retract. This so called retracting did not come to the notice of the prosecutor until the Hosner case had been called for trial in the Circuit Court. After it was too late to bring the case to trial at that term of the Court, young Hosner admitted to the prosecutor, sheriff, and probate judge, with tears in his eyes, that the reason he changed his story was because his sister, who had been brought from the southern part of the State by Mr. Swift, told him if he did not they would put him in jail, and (Hosner) reasserted that what he had testified to in Justice Court was absolutely true. This has no part in this case and we would not mention it were it not for the fact that respondent's counsel are attempting to take unfair advantage of the circumstance."

Attorney General Kuhn closed his argument with the only evidence he had that corroborated the testimony and character of Merrill Griffin. Ironically, the evidence came from the pen of Herman Swift. In a November 10th, 1909 letter to Merrill's father, Herman wrote: "I am glad to report that he (Merrill) is doing fine in school in every way, and in fact, we have not been able to find any fault with him whatever. He is O.K."

Kuhn then read the letter Herman Swift wrote to Edward Griffin on December 1st, 1909. That letter begins: "I have been told so many times that your boy is a lad who should not be here as he needs no correction," and ends: "I would be glad if you would write me a few letters by return mail to submit to our Board, telling just the condition of the boy while in Grand Rapids, and how unreliable he proved, and how much he needed the training which we strive to give."

Kuhn continued: "These letters were written—one but a short time before and the other a few days after complaint was made to the Chief of Police of Boyne City—and we inquire who was better able at that time than respondent to judge of the character and truthfulness of this boy, and express an opinion of his general deportment. Inasmuch, therefore, as young Griffin bore such an excellent reputation, vouched for by Mr. Swift, we insist that the jury were fully warranted in accepting his testimony as true...

No stronger corroboration or endorsement of his character for truth and veracity, and hence no more cogent reason for the acceptance of his evidence by the jury, can be urged than the recommendation of respondent himself.

We have carefully examined each and every objection and reason assigned by respondents counsel for a reversal of the verdict, and are unable to discover any valid or legal reason therefore. The jury found the defendant guilty from the evidence presented for their consideration. No claim is made that a fair and impartial jury was not had. We therefore respectfully urge that the verdict should be affirmed and the defendant remanded for sentence."

XVI

~

The Michigan Supreme Court Decision

Today the Michigan Supreme Court includes seven justices and four of them are women. In 1912, the Court included eight justices and all of them were men. The defense had titled the case: "People vs. Herman Swift." The prosecution titled it: "People vs. Hermon Swift." The Supreme Court dealt with this ambiguity by titling the case: "People vs. Swift." Five justices sat on the Supreme Court bench and considered the arguments in the Swift trial. Joseph Steere was one of those justices.

Steere graduated from the Literary Department of the University of Michigan in 1876. His biography terms him a "scholar with incomparable diction and enviable literary style" and notes that he was a "slight man and a practicing Quaker."

Steere moved north to Sault Ste. Marie, Michigan in 1878. There he served several years as prosecuting attorney and then thirty years as a circuit court judge for northern Michigan's Chippewa County. Steere was appointed to the Supreme Court in 1911 and would serve until 1927. He was a man who would have had great empathy for Judge Mayne, circuit court judge in northern Michigan's Charlevoix County. Attorneys Elisha Clink and Phillip Travis probably became very concerned when they heard the rumor that Justice Steere had been selected to write the Court's opinion in the case of the People vs. Swift.

It seems that the Supreme Court heard the Swift case sometime during the summer of 1912. Justice Steere's opinion notes at its conclusion that: "Justice Blair, being ill, took no part in the decision." In the summer of 1912, Supreme Court Justice Charles A. Blair lay ill in bed at his home at 305 Seymour Street in Lansing. He died there on August 30th, 1912. It is likely that attorneys Elisha Clink and Phillip Travis again became very concerned when they learned that the Justices had appointed Attorney General Franz C. Kuhn to fill the vacancy on the Court created by Justice Blair's death.

Justice Steere's Opinion

Justice Steere's opinion in the Michigan Supreme Court case of People vs. Swift was published on November 8th, 1912. It reads in part:

"In December 1910, respondent was convicted by the verdict of a jury in the circuit court of Charlevoix County under an information charging him with having, on November 23, 1909, committed an act of gross indecency with a boy named Merrill Griffin in violation of Act No. 198 of the Public Acts of 1903...The offense is charged to have been committed at the 'Beulah Land Farm for Boys,' located near Boyne City in Charlevoix county, an institution promoted and conducted by respondent and of which said Merrill Griffin, a lad about 11 years of age, was an inmate. The place was commonly called the 'Beulah Home.' It was advertised and conducted as a farm home for the detention, care, and training of wayward boys. It was supported by contributions from charitably inclined persons in various parts of the state, payments made by parents and guardians of boys detained there, and the products of the farm upon which the boys were required to work. At the time of the alleged offense there were some 25 or 30 boys at the Home, whose ages ranged from 8 to 15 years.

It is sufficient, without going into the unsavory details, to say that the information clearly stated facts which constitute the offense charged under the statute, and the boy Griffin positively testified to such facts. The act complained of is claimed to have been committed secretly in respondent's room in the Beulah Home; there being no witnesses to such conduct but the two participants. Respondent's denial was by a plea of not guilty. The substantive case necessarily rested on the evidence of Merrill Griffin, the only direct witness who testified. The testimony introduced by the defense was an attack upon the credibility of the witness Griffin, and in support of a claim of alibi and a conspiracy against respondent to depose him from management and control of the Beulah Home.

The bill of exceptions presents for our consideration 127 allegations of error claimed to have been made by the circuit court during the trial of the cause. While they have all been examined and considered, many of them call for no comment beyond crediting defendant with saving all possible questions for review. It would be a remarkably versatile court which could freight with that many errors a case in which the controlling issue was a question of the veracity of one small boy.

After sorting over these allegations with a view to classifying them, they seem to condense into the questions of whether there was prejudicial error in the court denying defendant's motion for a change of venue; in a statement made by the prosecuting attorney in his opening as to hypnotic powers possessed by respondent, which was not later substantiated by testimony; in the admission and rejection of certain testimony, as to similar previous acts between the parties and an alleged conspiracy against respondent; in certain remarks made by the prosecutor in his argument to the jury; in the charge of the court; and in its refusal to grant a new trial. The case had been previously tried, resulting in a disagreement of the jury. When it was again called up for consideration, before the second trial began respondent moved for a change of venue, presenting lengthy affidavits by himself, his attorneys, bondsmen, and others, together with various newspaper clippings and other matters which occupy 66 pages of the printed record."

Justice Steere's opinion summarized the history of the case in regards to the allegations or exceptions claimed under the issue of Change of Venue. My citing of the opinion will omit this summary as well as the historical summaries that Justice Steere provided regarding all the questions he considered. His opinion continued:

"(1) Act No. 67 of the Public Acts of 1909 provides: 'Each of said courts, upon good cause shown, may change the venue in any case pending therein,' etc. It is only 'on good cause shown' that the court has any power to act, and then he may grant the change in his discretion. In the early case of Greely vs. Stilson, 27 Mich. 153, it was said: 'A motion for change of venue is, unless where otherwise provided by law, a matter which rests in discretion and is not a subject for review.' It is, however, now recognized that where rulings on such motions are a clear abuse of discretion, manifestly subversive of justice, they may be reviewed and corrected on writ of error.

(2) It is an elementary general rule that in criminal cases the respondent must be tried in the county where the crime is charged to have been committed; but the court may, in exceptional cases, where a special showing makes it plain that the ends of justice so demand, or where statutory provisions expressly so provide, change the venue to another county. Where there are no mandatory, statutory provisions, it is now settled beyond question that the court's action in ordering such a change or refusing it is discretionary, and not to be disturbed on review, unless there clearly appears a palpable abuse of discretion. 12 Cyc. 243, and cases cited.

A considerable portion of the newspaper clippings presented with the motion for a change of venue relates to the chancery suit over the Beulah Home. The result of that suit is stated in the clipping of December 24, 1909, from the *Charlevoix County Herald*, presented when the motion was renewed at the trial. (Author's note: the chancery suit was not settled until 1911.) By that clipping the public was advised that respondent had been vindicated and found to be in the right in his suit with the purported trustees of the Home, who he claimed had slandered him, and it would also appear in that connection that the judge who heard that suit, and who was presiding in the criminal case, could and would fairly and impartially dispose of matters coming before him in which respondent was interested. The clippings, taken as a whole seem to be such as are often found in local newspapers in relation to somewhat sensational events and criminal proceedings thought to be of general interest. They purport to report the charges against defendant and events as they took place in that connection, in court and out. With one possible exception, no positive opinion was offered as to the guilt or innocence of the respondent. On the whole, they are of that class of publications usually appearing in the public press when such matters arise and with which all newspaper readers are more or less familiar.

(3) 'Newspaper reports are ordinarily regarded as too unreliable to influence a fair-minded man when called upon to pass upon the merits of a case in the light of evidence given under oath, and it is now a well-settled rule that a juror, although he may have formed an opinion from reading such reports, is competent if he states that he is without prejudice and can try the case impartially according to the evidence, and the court is satisfied he will do so.' 24 Cyc. 298

(4) This offense is charged to have been committed in November 1909. The motion for a change of venue was passed upon over a year later, when the case was on the calendar for a second trial. The lapse of time which intervened was a matter proper for the court to take into consideration; it being well known that, even in cases where adverse public sentiment and prejudice are aroused at the time, public feeling and interest soon abate. This is so well recognized that counsel for defendants in criminal cases are prone to seek delay.

(5) It has been held that the court is not precluded from acting in part on personal knowledge possessed by it. Giese vs. Schultz, 60 Wis. 449, 19 N.W. 447. This is particularly applicable

to certain charges in the affidavit of counsel for respondent relative to prejudicial conduct of members of the bar and officers of the court in connection with the case. The warrant was issued in this case by complaint of the marshal of Boyne City after an investigation made by city and county officials. Some of the official misconduct complained of is charged to have occurred during the progress of the first trial, in and around the courtroom. Charlevoix County is large geographically, with a population in the neighborhood of 20,000. The judge had presided at the trial of this case once before in that county at a time less remote from the date when the offense was charged to have been committed, had officially acquired knowledge of the prevailing sentiment amongst those called as jurors at that time, and knew something of what would be encountered in passing upon jurors' qualifications at the second trial.

(6,7) It was proper and lawful for him to defer final determination of the motion until after the examination of the jurors in the case as to their qualifications, and if a fair and impartial jury could be obtained, as appears to have been the result, it is held that this may justify denying the motion, even though other facts apparently entitling the accused to its being granted may have been shown, for the actuality of the main fact 'demonstrates the possibility of its existence.' 12 Cyc. 249, and cases cited. It has even been held that a failure, or delay, or difficulty in obtaining impartial jurors is not conclusive in such a case. But that does not seem to have occurred here. The length of time spent in getting a jury, or the fact that respondent exhausted his peremptory challenge, is not of controlling significance. Under the dilatory system of examining and selecting jurors which often prevails, days, and sometimes weeks, are spent in such examinations in sensational cases, and, if that could be made a controlling ground for change of venue, it would offer special inducement for counsel to exhaust their peremptory challenges and delay the case to the limit when examining jurors. We are not advised how many jurors were excused in this case, or the nature of their preliminary examinations, except as the judge, who has been upon the bench for many years, states: 'In no important criminal case within my experience has the absence of prejudice in those summoned as jurors been more marked.' It is difficult, and often impossible, for appellate courts to see matters as they actually existed and appeared on the trial to the presiding judge, and that should not be overlooked in passing upon a question of the proper exercise of discretion. We are not prepared to say that there was an abuse of discretion in this instance."

Justice Steere then reviewed the history of the Hypnosis Question. His opinion continued:

"(8,9) We cannot assume that the statement was made in bad faith. It is asserted that it was not. 'It is true that counsel referred to some matters not established by the testimony. In the opening of a case some latitude must be allowed counsel in stating what they expect to prove. That on the trial they may not be able to show all that they claimed is not necessarily an indication that the statement was not made in good faith.' State vs. Grafton, 89 Iowa, 109, 56 N. W. 257. Failure to prove what it was stated to the jury the prosecution expected to be able to prove can well be urged as more disconcerting and, at least, as prejudicial to the prosecution as to the defense, and it would open the door to the defense for a caustic argument to the jury, which is not usually overlooked when such opportunities present themselves. The judge in his charge emphasized the failure of the prosecution in that particular and did what he could to eliminate the subject from the deliberation of the jury. 'A failure to prove all that the prosecuting attorney in his opening to the jury in good faith stated he expected to prove is not ground for reversal.' People vs. Ecarius, 124 Mich, 616, 83 N.W. 628."

Justice Steere then reviewed the history of the Similar Previous Acts Question. His opinion was followed by seven citations and concluded:

"(10)...The following language in an early case, by Judge Christiancy, in which the admission of such testimony was upheld, is particularly applicable here: 'In the order of nature, facts do not occur single and independent, isolated from all others, but each is connected with some antecedent fact, or combination of facts, from which the fact in question follows as an effect from a cause torn from this necessary connection, and exhibited alone, many real occurrences would appear under the guise of falsehood, and truth itself would be made to lie. To permit the evidence, therefore, of an isolated transaction, which could only be made to appear probable by exhibiting the antecedent facts which induced it, and yet to exclude from the investigation all such antecedent facts, would be to set at defiance the order of nature and the laws of truth which God has stamped upon the human mind.' The principles there laid down have more than once been cited with approval and followed.

(11) It was claimed by respondent that his prosecution was the result of a conspiracy, instigated by one of the older boys named Mack and a hired hand on the farm named Jones, in which some of the younger boys were induced to participate; the purpose being to depose respondent from control and secure his position for Jones, after which Mack and the other boys would have easier times and, with Jones' acquiescence, might ultimately escape from the farm. In the early stages of this inquiry, various questions propounded by counsel for the defense, relating particularly to Jones' words and acts, were objected to and sustained, but later in the trial the court said to defendant's counsel: 'I will say that there were some questions excluded yesterday that I think might be material, considering the testimony that was later introduced connecting Mr. Jones and the other party. I did state then that if later Mr. Jones was sufficiently connected with the transaction I would let the statement be considered. So you may cover that point if you wish—that is present them—and I will pass upon them again.' After this statement by the court, testimony including what Jones said and did, was introduced. That subject was quite fully gone into, and we think ample opportunity was given defendant to present all legitimate testimony offered.

(12) It is urged that the case should be reversed on account of certain unfair and prejudicial remarks of the prosecuting attorney in his argument to the jury...In his reasons for denying a motion for a new trial, the court said: 'These remarks, if prejudicial, which I do not so consider, were in direct answer to allegations of fact made by respondent's counsel in his argument that respondent personally and other witnesses had testified to certain facts. This statement by counsel was incorrect. If the prosecuting attorney were to deny these assertions of fact by counsel for the defense at all, he must use either the exact language which he employed or other language of the same import. He cannot, in justice to the people's cause, allow these statements to go unchallenged.' Respondent was not sworn, and of course did not personally testify.

We are unable to say from the record that these remarks were not justified by the arguments of opposing counsel or warranted by the evidence, or that the court did not properly exercise the discretionary control which we have held rested with him.

Numerous errors are assigned of refusal of the court to give defendant's requests to charge and on the charge as given. Twenty-two requests were presented. While none of them was given in the language of the request, and they were all marked 'refused,' the material substance of many was given and the subjects they presented covered beyond the possibility of being seriously questioned. Counsel particularly complain of failure to give seven enumerated requests related to the alibi feature of the defense...

(13) Time was not of the essence of this offense. It could be stated in the information as one time, and the proof might show another; evidence could be given of such an act within the jurisdiction of the court and the statute of limitations, and the act indicated by the evidence could thenceforth be deemed the act charged. The boy Griffin was unable to give the exact date, by month and number. The prosecution appears to have early recognized that he could not clearly do so. Counsel stated to the court that he relied on a specific act committed a week or two before the date set upon in the information, 'on or to wit, on or about that date, it might have been a week or two weeks before that.' Griffin testified to three distinct transactions—one in the summer, in August, in 'Willis Robert's room,' one before that in the 'guest room,' and the one on which the prosecution relied for conviction in respondent's room. 'A little before Thanksgiving Day the last act was committed—about a week or two before.' 'About a week before I went to Rowan's,' 'when I went up in his room the last time he gave me one-half dozen postal cards***He had a whole lot of them packed in his suitcase. The suitcase was open the time I saw it. This last act of indecency occurred before he went away and that was in November.' 'I have no means of remembering except the post cards.' In answer to suggestive questions as to dates, his testimony was inharmonious and unsatisfactory. His best knowledge of the time was manifestly by its relation to the season of the year and other events which would naturally interest a young boy. It appeared from other testimony that respondent was away from the Home on a trip of 10 or 12 days, returning on the evening of November 24th. Griffin testified to his going on that trip (Author's note: Justice Steere is incorrect on this point), though unable to give dates, and consistently maintained the act took place shortly before.

(14) So far as the principles involved in the requests quoted apply to the facts in issue in this case, we think the instructions given were sufficient. On that branch of the case the court said in part: 'Now as to the time of committing this offense,***I will say it is not necessary for the people to allege the identical day of the month upon which the offense was committed. It is charged as being on the 23rd day of November. If you find that this act took place as claimed by the people, but that it was not on the 23rd but on some other day prior thereto during the month of November, that is sufficient***Now an alibi is as legitimate a defense as any other; in fact, it is a perfect and conclusive defense...The question is, did it occur as claimed by the boy? And it must have occurred before taking that trip if it did occur at all.' On the question of reasonable doubt, and the jurors all being of one mind before they could convict, we think the court charged fully and correctly, in language as plain and easy for the jury to understand, as that contained in the request presented by counsel.

(15) We think the court also sufficiently instructed the jury as to the manner in which proof

of the previous offenses should be considered by them He stated to them that, even though they should believe such previous offenses had been committed, they could not find respondent guilty unless they were satisfied beyond reasonable doubt that he committed the third specific offense, on which the prosecution relied...

Without referring further to the exceptions taken to the charge of the court, we are satisfied that the case was fully and fairly submitted to the jury by a charge which covered all material issues involved, advising the jurors of the nature of the case and their duties in that connection. The issue of fact for them to decide was well defined and simple. The rules of law for them to follow in deciding the facts were elementary. If once clearly stated to them in plain language, technical elaboration in varying phraseology, with delicate distinctions over which counsel themselves might, and often do, disagree, would seldom aid and often bewilder.

After the verdict, respondent's counsel made a motion for a new trial, basing his application on the court's denial of a change of venue and various other errors alleged to have arisen in the case. This motion was denied and later renewed; counsel alleging that the verdict was against the weight of evidence and that certain jurors convicted respondent against their inclination, claiming to have misapprehended the charge of the court and to have been improperly influenced by the persuasions of other jurors. In support of the latter proposition the affidavits of certain jurors were presented.

(16) No question of extraneous influence was raised, and it is well settled that the affidavits of jurors cannot be received to impeach their verdict...

It is most strenuously urged in support of the motion for a new trial that the verdict is manifestly against the weight of evidence...To sustain this contention, the testimony and character of the witness Griffin are reviewed and vigorously attacked...

That there are contradictions in his testimony is apparent; that he was a mauvais sujet, a wayward boy, and entrusted to respondent's care for that reason is undisputed. All his shortcomings and the inconsistencies of his story were thoroughly sifted and emphasized before the jury. When he was on the witness stand, skilled counsel, equipped with the testimony he had twice previously given, before the justice and on the former trial, subjected him to a grueling cross-examination which laid bare all the shortcomings of his short life and disclosed from every angle the weak points in his testimony. He was a boy 11 years old, evidently of immature intellect, in no sense competent to hold his own in such an endurance run, or by cunning to either meet or evade the searching quiz of respondent's attorneys. He was before the eyes of the jury to be observed and studied; they saw and heard the worst. His story was undisputed, except by its alleged self-contradictions and the impeachment of his character and veracity. Apparently he was not altogether bad if respondent's measure of him is to be credited. About the time these troubles arose, in a letter to the boy's father dated November 10th, 1909, respondent wrote: 'I am glad to report that he is doing fine in school and everywhere, and in fact we have not been able to find any fault with him whatever; he is O.K.' We are asked to set aside this verdict, against the judgment of the jury and the trial judge, on the ground that the testimony was a malicious falsehood, instigated by Jones, the hired man, and some of the boys on the farm, in a conspiracy to compass respondent's ruin and get rid of him, to which the public officials were a party, either knowingly and maliciously or as ignorant and misled tools. Their conduct and motives are questioned and impugned.

In reviewing that proposition we can with propriety consider somewhat the nature and history of this case as disclosed, not only by the testimony taken at the trial, but the record as a whole. It is a criminal prosecution, instituted in the name of the people of this state, presumably in the public interest, for the suppression of crime and protection of society. While such is the presumption in all criminal proceedings, it is not always the fact. In this case matters were taken charge of by public officers; the complaint was made by the city marshal after an investigation of conditions at the institution had been made both by city and county officials. The matter was first called to their attention by one George Snell, a contractor and builder of many years residence in Boyne City, who happened to be working at the Beulah Home. He is not shown to have had any interest or motive beyond that of any other citizen, and testifies that he had not. He says that he first learned of such conditions from Jones, who told him something of certain talk among the boys; that he himself then interviewed the boys and got the facts from them, that in such interviews he particularly admonished them to tell nothing but the truth and, after talking with them, he later, accompanied by Jones, laid the matter before the officers. Jones, when called as a witness, frankly corroborates this; states that he overheard the boys talking among themselves; that he told Snell of it, who questioned the boys and said it should be reported to the officers. He emphatically denies that he had any thought of a conspiracy or any motive of personal interest, or made any attempt to influence the boys in any way. He denies that he ever even talked with the witness Griffin about the matter. To set aside this verdict is to find that this young boy, under the circumstances which the history of this case discloses, was able with a fabricated story to fool and deceive Snell, the city and county officials, the jury who heard the case, and the judge who denied the motion now under consideration, all of whom were on the ground, with opportunities to hear and see and judge the facts not available to one with only the printed record before him.

(17) It is to be borne in mind that in the trial of criminal cases the special prerogative of the jury is to judge the facts and in that connection pass upon the credibility of witnesses, to be confronted by whom, in the presence of the court, is the constitutional right of the accused when put upon trial—a provision of law which emphasizes the importance of those who are to judge hearing and seeing the witnesses—thus in effect making hearing and seeing part of the evidence. In reviewing the decision of the trial court denying a motion for a new trial, based upon the claim that the verdict was against the weight of evidence, the appellate court does not pass upon the facts in the case further than to determine whether or not there was manifest abuse of discretion. We are unable to conclude that this was the case here...

For the reasons heretofore stated, the conviction is affirmed."

XVII

~

The Appeal to the Governor

Herman Swift's defense attorneys received the verdict of the Supreme Court with deep disappointment, although they were not surprised. Swift himself must have been discouraged, despondent, and fearful of the prospect of becoming an inmate in a Michigan State prison. Prison time would be tough indeed for a small man charged with the crime for which he was convicted. He prayed. And with purpose and resolve he supported his attorney's work on an appeal for a pardon from the Governor of the State of Michigan.

In late October 1912, Herman Swift had presented Elisha Clink with a copy of the postcard that James Leys claimed to have received from Merrill Griffin as they stood on a sidewalk in Grand Rapids. Clink already had in his possession affidavits from four of the Griffin case jurors that denounced their verdict and called for a new trial. Now he took the Griffin postcard and individually approached the remaining jurors in an attempt to gain denunciations of the verdict from them. He began this effort in his hometown of East Jordan and on November 25th, 1912, he obtained the following signed statement from juror Samuel Persons:

"Hon. H.L. Swift, Dear Sir: I am now greatly in doubt in regard to your guilt. I was one of the jurors that decided your case. Since then I have learned things that caused me to change my mind in regards to your guilt. Respectively yours, Sam Persons."

Clink attached to the Persons statement a signed statement from juror Grant Hammond. That statement simply reads: "I have read the above and agree with Mr. Persons. Respectfully, Grant Hammond, juror."

On November 25th, Clink traveled to the town of Norwood on the shore of Lake Michigan. There he obtained the following statement from juror C.H. Moorehouse:

"Mr. H.L. Swift, Boyne City, Mich., Dear Sir: I was one of the twelve jurors that sat in the case of the People vs. yourself and rendered a verdict of guilty.

I am now satisfied that we were mistaken in regard to your guilt and am sorry that we rendered a verdict of guilty. Other matters were discussed in the jury room which were detrimental to you and not offered in evidence and in my opinion they had considerable weight in causing some of the jurors to decide against you. I make this statement freely so that the wrong done you, may be righted. Respectfully, C.H. Moorehouse."

Clink stayed overnight in Norwood. The following morning, on November 26th, he obtained the following statement from juror John D. Walker:

"Mr. H.L. Swift, My dear Sir: I was one of the jurors on your case. In the jury room the question of your having money that you got about eight thousand dollars they claimed dishonestly from people that you could use it in going to the Supreme Court and that would save our county taxes. I am now fully satisfied that Mr. Swift was innocent at the time we convicted him. Public sentiment at the time was strongly against Mr. Swift and it had its influence in convicting him. Respectfully yours, John D. Walker"

Clink made the short trip from Norwood north to the City of Charlevoix the evening of November 26th. On November 27th in Charlevoix he obtained two additional signed statements from jurors. The first came from George Meggison:

"Mr. Swift: When I was talking to Mr. Clink I told him that the jurors did not discuss any subject except the evidence given at the trial, but as I stated to Mr. Clink and yourself, there were other things spoken of, one being that you had ten thousand dollars in Boyne City that you could use if you took your case to the Supreme Court. That statement was corrected by another juror who said the money was in chancery. I believe my verdict as a juror would be different in the case of Mr. Swift if the card shown me by Mr. Clink had been in evidence at the time of the trial of Mr. Swift. Geo. Meggison"

The second statement signed in Charlevoix came from juror F.W. Smith:

"Mr. Hermon L. Swift: At the time of your trial I believed you to be guilty, but after seeing a card from Merrill Griffin saying his statement was false, I hope there will be fair play shown you. Yours truly, F.W. Smith, Juror."

By the end of the day on November 27th, attorney Clink had in his possession affidavits from four jurors and signed statements from six jurors. He now had verdict denunciations from ten of the twelve jurors who sat in judgment at the second Griffin trial. Clink undoubtedly approached the remaining two jurors, Rueben H. Walton and William F. Johnson, and reviewed the Merrill Griffin postcard with them. It seems, however, that he never gained denunciations of the verdict from these two men.

Elisha Clink felt great pressure to complete his appeal for pardon and deliver it to Governor Osborn in Lansing. November 27th was a Wednesday. Herman Swift remained free on bail, but the Supreme Court had remanded the case back to the Charlevoix County Circuit Court and Swift's sentencing in that Court was scheduled for the following Tuesday, December 3rd, 1912.

Michigan Governor Chase Salmon Osborn was a self-made man and a man of seeming political contradictions, a Republican Progressive. Osborn was born in a log cabin on a farm in Huntington County, Indiana on January 22, 1860. His parents named him after the famous abolitionist, Salmon Chase. After receiving a degree from Purdue University, Osborn worked for a short time at the *Chicago Tribune* and then moved to Northern Wisconsin where he engaged in iron mining activities in that state as well in the adjoining area in the Upper Peninsula of Michigan. He moved to Sault Ste. Marie, Michigan on the far eastern edge of the Upper Peninsula. There he purchased and managed a newspaper. He became postmaster in Sault Ste. Marie in 1889, was appointed the Michigan State Fish and Game Warden in 1895, and State Commissioner of Railroads in 1899. By this time Osborn was a wealthy man and lived in a very fine home at 718 Cedar Street in Sault Ste. Marie. He earlier had attempted unsuccessfully to obtain the nomination of the Republic Party for the position of Governor, but in 1910 he did gain that nomination and in November 1910 he became the only resident of the Upper Peninsula to win election as Governor of Michigan.

Chase Osborn took office as Governor in early January 1911 and addressed the State Legislature on January 5th. That address stressed bi-partisan cooperation, fiscal restraint and discipline, and socially progressive legislation. He outlined a goal of worker's compensation legislation based upon the principal that: "the working person does not alone work for his immediate employer, but indirectly labors for and is compensated by all of those who use the product of the labor involved." He outlined other goals including: laws controlling women and child labor, laws providing for more stringent inspections of mine safety conditions, and a law requiring a wood lot on every farm. He spoke at length of the popular and controversial topic of regulation of liquor traffic. Here Osborn struggled with the conflict between his progressive belief in the benefit of eliminating the evil influence of alcohol on the masses and his republican belief that people should be allowed access to alcohol if that is what they desired and if they had the money to pay. He balanced this conflict by supporting the local option and proposing that in places where alcohol was legal, the number of saloons must be limited to one per thousand citizens. In his inaugural address he added an observation that: "man must not drive man so hard. Conditions for the masses must be improved." In that address, Governor Osborn also proposed a law that would restrict the time a person served as Governor to one four-year term. This law was not passed, but Chase Osborn abided by his proposal and early in his first year in office he announced he would not seek re-election to a second two-year term.

By Monday, December 2nd, 1912, Governor Osborn had been overwhelmed with requests for him to pardon Herman Swift. Many of these came from social missionary and progressive individuals and organizations from the Detroit area. Additionally, Governor Osborn had received a package from Elisha Clink. Clink did not repeat the mistake he had made when he presented the Supreme Court with an overly complex and unfocused brief on behalf of his client, Herman Swift. Clink's package to Osborn included the four affidavits and the six statements signed by the jurors. He sent along the letters from Elliot Fay and John Hosner that recanted the charges they had brought against Herman Swift. And he sent the alleged Merrill Griffin postcard. Aside from this, Clink probably included a summary letter that described the basis for Herman Swift's innocence. He concluded by requesting a pardon for Swift or at least a hearing on the matter.

On Tuesday, December 3rd, 1912, Herman Swift appeared in Charlevoix County Circuit Court to receive his sentence from Judge Mayne. His behavior was subdued. Judge Mayne asked him if he had anything to say prior to sentencing. Swift had not testified in his own defense at the trial that took place almost two years earlier. Now he stood and quietly spoke. He made what the *Charlevoix Sentinel* termed an: "impassioned appeal to the Court, giving eight reasons why he should not be sentenced, the first of which was that he was innocent." It is very likely that Herman Swift actually said that he was innocent and then gave seven reasons why he should be believed. The *Charlevoix Sentinel* indicated that one of Swift's sisters was present at the sentencing and: "made a plea for the exercise of mercy on behalf of the accused." Blenn Swift probably made this plea.

On December 3rd, 1912, Judge Mayne sentenced Herman Swift to serve a sentence of from one to five years at the Michigan State Reformatory in Ionia. At the end of the sentencing, the judge placed him into the custody of Charlevoix County Sheriff F.P. Robbins.

Herman Swift spent the night of December 3rd in the Charlevoix County jail. Early the following morning, Sheriff Robbins released him from jail and then led him to the railroad depot in Charlevoix. There the two men boarded a Pere Marquette mainline train for the two hundred ten mile trip south to Grand Rapids. When they arrived in Grand Rapids they had to change trains, departing the north-south train and boarding the east bound Detroit, Grand Haven, and Milwaukee train. The D.G.H.&M. maintained a depot in Grand Rapids at mile marker 158. East at mile marker 126 the railroad maintained a depot at the Ionia State Prison.

At the Grand Rapids depot, a man carrying a telegram from Lansing approached Sheriff Robbins. The telegram was from Governor Osborn and advised Robbins to release Herman Swift because he, the Governor, had paroled Swift. Robbins was able to contact the Governor by telephone. A week later, the *Boyne Citizen* reported what happened next:

"Robbins courteously, but positively informed Governor Osborn that he was authorized to deliver Swift at Ionia, and he intended to do so, after which he would not be responsible and they could do as they liked with the man.

Naturally, this displeased the governor, but with Robbins to deal with he soon found nothing else would be tolerated, so the base of operations was changed to Ionia and shortly after Swift was landed there he was released on the governor's order. Charlevoix county people generally do not like the releasing of this man, but they certainly commend their sheriff for his 'stand pat' to duty attitude."

As far back as August 1910, during the first Merrill Griffin trial, Charlevoix County newspapers became aware that their coverage of the Swift matter had become an important issue in the case. They knew copies of county newspaper articles formed a significant portion of the legal record and that the defense leaned on these articles as a basis for their Change of Venue Motion. The prosecution had asked the newspaper editors to restrict or avoid further writings on the Swift case and they largely had complied with this request. Both the prosecution and the defense appear to have remained publicly silent regarding the Supreme Court decision and the opinion issued on November 8th, 1912. When the case returned to the jurisdiction of the Charlevoix County Circuit Court and the date of sentencing arrived, newspaper coverage reappeared in a dramatic way in Charlevoix County and across the State. Newspaper accounts in southern Michigan tended to support Herman Swift while those in the north were very critical of the man, the legal system, and the sentence.

The evening of Herman Swift's sentencing, the *Evening Journal*, the only daily newspaper published in Charlevoix County, printed a small article at the top center of the front page. The headlines covered more space than the article. The main headline utilized the newspapers largest available print and reads: "Herman L. Swift Gets Sentence to Ionia." The second headline, in only somewhat smaller print, reads: "Convicted of Improper Conduct With Boys at Beulah Home Received Sentence Today." The article reads as follows:

"Herman L. Swift, founder and for years manager of Beulah Home for boys, who has been in bad light and before the courts for a long time because of alleged misconduct with boys in the institution, on one count of which he was convicted and the lower court's decision recently affirmed by the supreme court of the state, appeared in the circuit court at Charlevoix today for sentence and received a term in the reformatory at Ionia for a period of not less than one year nor more than five years, with the court's recommendation of one year."

The following week, the *Evening Journal* printed a retraction, stating that it was in error when it reported that Judge Mayne had recommended a sentence of one year. The retraction concluded: "This correction is made without any request from the court, being prompted by our spirit of fairness to Judge Mayne, and hope that it may in a measure put an end to the comments on the part of the public."

The Friday, December 6th, 1912 edition of the *Boyne Citizen* reprinted the *Evening Journal* article using the same type and placing it in the same position on the front page. That edition of the *Citizen* also included an editorial titled: "Swift's Sentence." The editorial reads:

"It has been generally believed that as soon as Swift's case was ended by sentence the public would drop the matter as justice having been satisfied, and comment soon cease altogether. However, this is far from the real condition in and about Boyne City since the announcement of sentence came out in the 'Journal' Tuesday evening.

It is not our intention to criticize the courts, neither in the higher body's extended time in which to pass upon the merits of the case, nor our own circuit body for the sentence imposed, but it should be remembered that the crime of which Mr. Swift stands convicted was not only committed here, but upon inmates of an institution located here, the mission of which is and has been to make good men out of unfortunate boys, and that, too, by the founder and manager of the home.

Boyne City people have considered the unfavorable notoriety the place has been given through this crime to be detrimental, but have waited (sometimes not very patiently perhaps) for the courts to wipe out the stain. Scores of our people even refused to believe in the guilt of Mr. Swift until the preponderance of evidence against the man overwhelmed everything and but few there are who now lack confidence in the statements made by the witnesses at the trial.

To the ordinary individual it is not given to understand the full meaning of the law and the punishment for various offenses in the criminal calendar, therefore our judgment of making the 'punishment fit the crime' may be erroneous, but it would never be possible to convince the general public that Swift, after both the circuit and the supreme court pronounced him guilty of the fiendish crime, should get off with a sentence of probably only one year."

On Friday, December 6th, the *Boyne City Times* printed an article titled: "Will He Be Pardoned?" The article reads: "Herman L. Swift, manager of the Beulah Home, was sentenced Tuesday to one to five years in the state reformatory at Ionia. This case has now been in the courts for about two years and according to reports there will be strong efforts made for pardon, in fact it is stated that the same is being worked on at the present time and citizens of Boyne City are talking of circulating an anti-pardon petition among the people, the same to be presented to the governor. Many believe that Governor Osborn will issue the pardon and one county paper has said that such a thing would be a fitting end to the state's chief executive's administration."

That same day, the *Evening Journal* printed an editorial titled: "People Displeased." That article reads: "It would indeed be hard to print a word picture showing the indignation that prevails throughout this county because of the outcome or at least the present status of the Swift case; and it is particularly fortunate for the good name of our city and county, as well as for Mr. Swift himself, that he was not at home on Thursday evening. Many expressions were heard concerning drastic action against the convicted man and it seemed almost certain that had Swift been seen on the street the talk would have quickly been transformed into action.

The reason for this feeling was the announcement through the state dispatches that Governor Osborn had temporarily paroled Swift with permission to leave the state. At the time of the first arrest of Swift on the charges for which actions he was subsequently convicted, the people were justly indignant. Boyne City has always been proud of Beulah Home and the work among boys that it was endeavored to accomplish, but then they had sufficient faith in the laws of the state and courts to enforce same, so they took little if any mere interest in the case than in any cause of such magnitude of offense. But when Swift's trial brought out facts concerning which Swift was shown to have made misrepresentations, the long time between the conviction by the circuit court and the affirmation of that decision by the supreme court, the realization of the common people that the penalty for the charge under which Swift was convicted is so much smaller than they had anticipated, and, finally the action of Governor Osborn in paroling the convict before the officer had landed the prisoner at Ionia, and without investigation, forbearance ceased to be a virtue and by this time it cannot be denied that there is more than a little justification for the feeling that exists.

The offense for which Swift stands convicted (and there are other counts pending against him on the court docket for similar conduct) is so heinous that it is hard for decent people to believe in the guilt of a man who posed before the public as Swift did. Besides Swift is alleged to have continued his misstatements giving people to believe that he had proven his innocence and convinced the people who were most active against him that he was a sadly persecuted man. No doubt, these had something to do with the influence that was brought to bear on the governor to secure the parole, but it looks like short sightedness on the part of our chief executive to act as he has without first thoroughly investigating the case more than to take the statements of Swift and his personal friends.

Where are the men who were directors of Beulah Home when the crimes are alleged to have been committed? At first they refused to believe, but soon became convinced of Swift's guilt. They might be consulted.

What about the documentary proof concerning Swift and his standing in other communities? That is certainly available for the enlightenment of Governor Osborn and should be demanded by him.

What of the petitions signed by hundreds of people—including business and professional men whose standing in the community and whose word are both beyond contradiction? Surely the governor will not refuse to take them into consideration in finally—considering this matter.

It is announced that on the 12th (Thursday of next week) there is to be a hearing of this matter in Lansing in which Prosecutor Fitch and perhaps other attorneys will present many of the conditions surrounding the Swift case about which the governor may not be aware and it is hoped these facts may be given their due consideration."

Assistant Prosecuting Attorney Alfred B. Nicholas was not one of the attorneys who accompanied Prosecutor Fitch to the hearing with the Governor on December 12th, 1912. Shortly after receiving word of the Michigan Supreme Court's November 8th decision in the Swift case, Nicholas sold his home in East Jordan and announced that he and his wife Anna were moving to Meridian, Mississippi. His son and law partner A. Burton Nicholas, as well as his two daughters Madge and Clara, had already moved to Meridian. A December 7th, 1912 *Charlevoix County Herald* article described a farewell banquet that the Charlevoix County Bar Association held for attorney Nicholas one evening the prior week. Honorable John M. Nicholas served as: "'It' at the banquet, the flow of soul pointing to guests to make speeches...Mr. Nicholas, in response, referred briefly to his life and work in this county and the cases which compelled him to seek a home elsewhere." The *Herald* does not state this, but it seems clear that the Swift cases where among those that "compelled Nicholas to move." The Boyne City Affair had worn out Alfred B. Nicholas.

The same *Herald* issue of December 7th, 1912 carried an article titled: "Swift Sentenced, Probably Last Chapter Written in Well-Known Case." That article concluded: "This has been one of the hardest fought legal battles in the history of northern Michigan. A determined effort will be made to secure a pardon from Gov. Osborn by influential friends of Swift including W.H. Hill, the Bull Moose leader, of Detroit."

On December 4th, 1912, when Herman Swift was released at the Ionia Reformatory on the basis of the Governor's pardon he knew better than to return to Charlevoix County. I believe he traveled with a friend to his hometown of Eaton Rapids. The weekend of December 7th and 8th, 1912, he made appearances in a number of churches in the towns of Eaton Rapids and Charlotte. The *Charlotte Republican* reported: "Herman Swift was greeted at the Baptist Church here last Sunday by a very large audience. His pictures showed very well the work which he has taken up and for which he has made his name known all over the country. A collection was taken and about $100 was raised."

I believe that early the following week, perhaps Monday, December 9th, 1912, Herman Swift traveled to Chicago to be at the bedside of his wife Grace. Grace reportedly was extremely ill. She certainly was eight months pregnant. Some time earlier, Herman had moved Grace from the Beulah Home to the Chicago home of his sister Blenn and her husband John Basim. This was done to remove Grace from the swirling controversy in Charlevoix County and to place her close to the advanced medical facilities available in Chicago. Additionally, Swift was well aware of the rigors that winter brought to the Beulah Home building. Floyd Starr's biography notes that he and his wife Harriet spent the winter of 1912/1913 living in the Beulah Home. In the latter part of 1912, Harriet had advised Floyd that she was pregnant. Starr's biography, referring to that winter, continues: "Under the best of circumstances, living conditions at the one-time summer hotel would have been less than ideal for a mother to be. During a Michigan winter, survival in the drafty frame structure must have been a sheer test of endurance."

Herman Swift spent several days with Grace and then traveled to Lansing to prepare for his pardon hearing before Governor Chase Osborn. Charlevoix County newspapers assailed Swift and the pardon hearing. Depending upon their political leanings some attacked Governor Osborn, while others supported him as they kept their fingers crossed that he would not grant Herman Swift a pardon. On December 6th, the *East Jordan Enterprise* printed the following editorial under the title, "Osborn Again:"

"A week ago it was stated in these columns that Probably Governor Osborn would either pardon or parole H.L. Swift of Beulah Home malodorous fame. The guess was straight as ere the prison doors had closed on him, Osborn turned him loose for ten days, and Prosecuting Attorney Fitch must next week go to Lansing and 'show cause' to our 'Reform Progressive' governor why the law and its penalty for crime in this case should not be overridden and set at naught! This, however, is only a concrete example of the cardinal principle of Progressive doctrine, the recall of judicial decisions. In this case Swift, after a fair trial in which his interests were looked after by E.N. Clink—one of the ablest attorneys of the Michigan bar, was convicted of a revolting crime, more heinous because of the hypocritical pretensions of Swift, and on appeal the entire proceedings in the trial court were affirmed. This conviction represented great labor and expense by the people expended that through the punishment of the guilty, others would be deterred from crime. Now when the conviction is had and sentence is passed, comes 'his excellency' the governor to nullify it all. Under these conditions of what use are courts? You are all safe if you stand in with his administration."

Governor Osborn scheduled two days of public hearings on the request for a pardon of Herman Swift. Swift's attorneys presented their arguments on Wednesday, December 11th, 1912. Osborn had reviewed a great deal of background material related to the Swift case and he demanded that many witnesses appear at the hearings. The witnesses included the boys who had brought charges against Herman Swift, most notably Merrill Griffin.

The January/February 1913 issue of *The Youth's Outlook* was published by the Board of Directors of the Beulah Home as a final call for either a new trial or for a pardon for Herman Swift. It contained a thorough review, from the Swift side, of the Osborn hearings. That review is titled "Gov. Osborn Investigates" and reads in part as follows:

"...It is impossible to give a complete report of everything that was done by the Governor, but after an investigation, remarkably thorough, he became firmly convinced that Mr. Swift is innocent, although he frankly admitted that when he began the investigation, he was prejudiced against Mr. Swift. He had the post card which James Leys claimed he saw Merrill Griffin write and in which, said Griffin declared that the statements he had made in court were untrue. He had Merrill Griffin write this message from dictation and also obtained many other copies of Merrill Griffin's handwriting and he was absolutely convinced of the identity of the post card. He said at the hearing that there was absolutely no question in his mind but that the post card had been written by Merrill Griffin, and in fact, everyone who saw the post card at the hearing and compared it with the other message written by Merrill Griffin, was satisfied that the handwriting was the same...

Incidentally, Governor Osborn said that he had found from his investigation that charges similar to this one made against Mr. Swift, were very frequent in Homes dealing with the same class of boys. He found that this was the usual method by which vicious boys endeavored to 'GET EVEN' with those who attempted to enforce authority over them. Such boys know that this charge is the one charge that will give them a hearing. He found also that almost always the investigations proved the charges to be false, and that the boys who made the charges usually retracted the same when their desire for revenge had passed away.

The *Detroit News-Tribune* reports as follows. Dec. 13, 1912: 'Governor Osborn believes postal is genuine. He says, 'Personally I am convinced that the Griffin lad wrote the card...'

The *Hillsdale Daily*, Dec. 16, 1912, reports as follows: What Governor Osborn said: 'Governor Osborn said tonight that the boys had testified that they had given false testimony at the trial of Herman L. Swift, and that they had PERJURED THEMSELVES. This, he says, had been obtained from the boys in a written statement.'"

I believe that, while obviously slanted, the treatment of the Osborn parole hearings in *The Youth's Outlook* article was largely factual. Just a few days before the Swift hearing, on December 7th, 1912, Governor Osborn had pardoned a convicted murderer who had served sixteen years in prison. He had received a great deal of negative publicity over this, but putting the facts together, it seems that the Governor's natural course would have been to pardon Herman Swift. And perhaps this did not happen because another man intervened in the matter. I believe it is very likely that on the evening of December 11th, 1912, Governor Osborn sought the advice of Associate Justice Joseph Steere. Justice Steere's fellow justices had elected him to hold the position of Chief Justice for the 1913 term of the Supreme Court.

Osborn and Steere were two very different men. Steere was small and rather shy, while Osborn was large and socially outgoing. Osborn had worked in the mining and newspaper businesses, as well as holding a number of public offices. Steere's career had been dedicated to the law. Osborn had married at the age of twenty and he and his wife had five children. Steere had never married. Osborn was a Presbyterian and Steere a Quaker. Osborn lived in a mansion, while Steere probably never owned a home, preferring to board at the comfortable, old Wentworth Hotel when Court was in session.

Justice Steere worked in Lansing, but he never became a Lansing resident. In 1912, he was a resident boarder in a home at 314 Court Street in Sault Ste. Marie. The home was two blocks away from Governor Osborn's mansion and this is important. Governor Osborn was the first Michigan Governor from the Upper Peninsula and Justice Steere was the first Supreme Court Justice from the Upper Peninsula. Upper Peninsula residents have a great affinity for one another.

Governor Osborn almost certainly sought the counsel of Justice Steere the evening of December 11th, 1912. Steere would have listened to Osborn's observations and thoughts and carefully determined the course he figured the Governor might take. It seems the Governor asked him for advice and Steere suggested the best course might be to send the case, the Merrill Griffin post card and all, back to the Circuit Court in Charlevoix County. Steere probably thought to himself that once back there, Circuit Court Judge Mayne was unlikely to reverse the decision of the jury, his circuit court, and the Michigan Supreme Court.

The following day, December 12th, 1912, Charlevoix County Prosecuting Attorney Fitch stood before Governor Osborn at the Swift pardon hearing. Fitch suggested that Judge Mayne was willing to re-open the case and consider the Merrill Griffin post card evidence. Osborn quickly agreed with this suggestion. He ended the hearing by granting Herman Swift a new parole of sixty days. In December 1912, Chase Osborn was serving as a lame duck governor. His successor, Woodridge Nathan Ferris, had been elected by the state's voters the prior month. Now, if the Circuit Court did not take up the Swift case, Governor Osborn had passed the hot potato off to Ferris.

On December 19th, 1912, the *Charlevoix Sentinel* carried a front-page story titled: "Swift and the Governor" and sub-titled: "Osborn Extends Parole Sixty Days, Passing Case Up to Mr. Ferris." The article reads: "The more we learn of the Swift case the more we are puzzled. The old aphorism that 'justice is blind' should be changed to meet latter day conditions and made to read 'justice is fickle.'

Last Thursday Prosecutor Fitch and J.M. Converse (Converse was a partner in a Boyne City law firm with Leonard Knowles, a man who represented Herman Swift and the Beulah Home at the initial examinations of Swift in Justice Court in Boyne City on December 15th, 1909) were given a hearing by the governor. After hearing their arguments his Excellency jettisoned the whole business by extending Swift's parole sixty days. This throws the case over to Gov. Ferris, and the case will have to be thrashed out again. A new trial may result.

Gov. Osborn writes the editor of this paper that he has received letters from the members of the jury which convicted Swift, expressing a belief in his innocence and that he cannot bring himself up to the point of giving credence to the evidence of a coterie of incorrigible boys.

Added to this is the startling fact that the board of directors of Beulah Home have in writing denoted their confidence in Swift. One of two things is certain—Swift is one of the smoothest scoundrels outside of prison, or he is entitled to a martyr's crown.

We can only wait patiently for the outcome.

A.B. Klise, of Sturgeon Bay, a Beulah Home director, gives the *Petoskey News* the following information: 'An adjourned meeting of the board of directors of Beulah Home was held after the hearing at Hotel Downie. It was decided to proceed at once in an effort for a new trial, and if this fails, to close the home permanently as soon as it can be accomplished. Mr. McIntire was elected a member of the board. While the board has not thought it good policy in the past to give matter for publication, it was decided that the time had arrived that the public and particularly the contributors of the home should know Swift's side of the controversy, and that the whole matter should be given for publication as fast as it can be prepared, it may be understood that it will make quite a volume.

Mr. Swift returned to the bedside of Mrs. Swift in Chicago, where her life is despaired of. Every member of the board has fullest confidence in Mr. Swift's innocence, honesty, and integrity.'"

At the meeting following the conclusion of the hearings the board passed the following resolution that was printed in newspapers across the state of Michigan:

"This board by resolution—hereby places itself on record as being firmly convinced of the innocence and integrity of Mr. Herman Swift, who was convicted on the testimony of one lad, only nine years old, who was pronounced by the governor, after hearing his testimony, as a degenerate. Three other boys, who made complaints, admitted under oath that they were set up to do so by one Jones, that there was not a word of truth in it, and 12 other boys testified that the complaining witness had told them there was no truth in the charge and this lad has written a postal card, stating he was sorry and there was no truth in it. We, therefore, request the public to with-hold their judgment, until this matter can be sifted to the bottom."

The resolution was signed by board members: William H. Hill, John M. Hall, Prof. Morley E. Osborne, Reverend Charles A. Glass, A.B. Klise, and Peter McIntyre. McIntyre had served on the original Beulah Home board. At the December 12th board meeting, he again was elected a board member. H.A. Putnam, a minister from Ludington, Michigan also served on the Beulah Home board. Putnam did not sign the resolution proclaiming support of Swift. On December 26th, the *Charlevoix Sentinel* published the following letter it received from Putnam in response to the December 19th article:

"I notice that it is reported in the papers that all the directors of Beulah Home are personally supportive of Mr. Swift. I do not know how they came by that impression, but whoever has given it out has spoken without keeping within the truth. As one member of the board, I wish it under-stood that I cannot lend my influence to protect Swift from penalty which has been pronounced upon him. I regret to say that I regard him as a very dangerous man to have in any community. And I am disposed to trust the courts in the decision which they have reached."

Most of the newspapers in Charlevoix County dutifully printed the Beulah Home board members resolution in support of Herman Swift. They followed the resolution by reprinting an addendum first included in a *Boyne City Times* article published on December 27th, 1912:

"The above article (the Board Resolution) only reminds the good people of Charlevoix County that Swift made the claim when he was first arrested, saying that a certain person was after his job. These charges were thoroughly investigated at the time and it was found that Swift owned the farm and home which every one supposed belonged to the boys, and that the person whom he claims was after the job certainly had no more chance of getting it than the proverbial snow ball of lasting in —. It is only another joke of that master trixter. From the article which Swift and his friends send out one would think that an investigation had not been held, but we of this community who were present when the skunk was kicked out can hardly draw a deep breath yet because of the stench that greeted our nostrils when the investigation was completed."

The Herman Swift case now represented a fierce publicity battle waged both in southern and northern Michigan. Both sides were attempting to influence public opinion and to provide ammunition for and against a pardon by Governor Ferris.

On January 16th, 1913, the *Boyne City Times* carried the following small article: "The *Elk Rapids Progress* contained nearly a column on the Swift case and in the column Brother Perry quoted from *Progression* a Detroit paper which proclaims his innocence and leads the readers to believe that the fact that W.H. Hill (who 'praise be' was not elected congressman-at-large) has stood by him should be almost proof of his innocence. We believe that there is one thing certain about this matter and that is that Detroit's defeated or elected politicians, or the people of any part of this good old state outside of Charlevoix County, do not know half as much about this matter as the people of Charlevoix County."

On Monday, December 30th, 1912, Judge Mayne received a motion for a new trial from Herman Swift's defense attorneys. The judge agreed to consider the motion.

On New Year's Day 1913, Herman Swift sat in Chicago at the bedside of his wife Grace. During his life, Herman had experienced a number of notable, happy days: the day in 1887 when he became a member of the Methodist-Episcopal Church, the day in 1903 when he acquired the Beulah Home building in Boyne City, the day a few years later when he completed the acquisition of 160 acres of property around that building, the day he completed the accumulation of over $7,000, and the day in 1906 when he married Grace. But January 1st, 1913 for Herman probably was the happiest day of all. On that day Grace gave birth to a son. They named the boy Harold, a name derived from an old English name that means "leader of an army." This is rather interesting, particularly given that Herman is a name meaning "soldier." It seems to me though that Herman and Grace probably were unaware of the old English meaning. Harold Swift was born on New Year's Day and not Christmas Day, but his parents may have named him thinking of the carol "Hark! the Herald Angels Sing," written by Charles Wesley, brother of John Wesley, the founder of the Methodist Church.

Herman Swift was happy that New Years Day, but also very troubled. His parole extended only to February 11th, 1913. He doubted his prospects for receiving either a new trial or a pardon. He feared being returned to state prison. Finally, a physical malady troubled him. He laid it off to stress, but there was a growing fuzzy feeling in his head, as if someone were squeezing his brain and slowly reducing its size. Swift spent a few days in Chicago with his wife and new son. Once those two were placed comfortably in Swift's sister Blenn's home, Swift returned to Michigan, probably to Detroit, to support the efforts to gain him either a new trial or a pardon.

Woodbridge Nathan Ferris, like Chase Salmon Osborn, was born in a log cabin on a farm. Ferris was born January 6th, 1853 in Spencer in Tioga County in the south of New York State. He developed a background in education and in 1884 settled in the town of Big Rapids in Mecosta County in the central part of Michigan. There he founded the Ferris Industrial School that later became Ferris State University. In 1912, Woodbridge Nathan Ferris was elected Governor of Michigan. He was the first Democrat elected Governor in twenty years. Like Osborn, Ferris was a social progressive. During his time in office, among other things, he accomplished the establishments of a farm colony for epileptics and the Central Michigan Tuberculosis Sanitarium.

In terms of religious beliefs, Ferris was a modernist as opposed to a fundamentalist. The "Religious Chapter" in Ferris' autobiography criticizes William Jennings Bryan as a man who could not accept evolution. Bryan was the only person included by true name in Herman Swift's *Victories of a Boy* story. He is mentioned in reverence when: "George recites the Grove is God's First Temple by Mr. Bryan."

On January 23rd, 1913, the *Charlevoix Sentinel* published a small article that began: "In a recent interview concerning the Swift case, Governor Ferris said: 'I am being pestered to death just now by persons trying to get me to pardon Herman Swift.'" Governor Ferris received dozens, if not hundreds, of calls and letters pleading for a pardon for Herman Swift. A number of these came from past Beulah Home contributors and employees:

"I have spent several years working beside Mr. Swift in the effort to save friendless boys, but it proved too great a strain for me to continue. I saw problems there, hereto entirely unsolved, come into the Home, rough, stubborn, uncultivated boys of the most degraded slums, seemingly ready to defy every reformation. I have seen them enter so low and degraded that they would spit in their drinking cups, crawl into bed with their muddy boots still on their feet...and laugh and ridicule when told that their mother was dying, and even call her vile names when they knew she lay a corpse...use language as strong as a pioneer lumberman, later to be brought to respect the rights of others and give their hearts to God. This Mr. Swift has done for many hundreds of boys... Conda J. Ham, District Manager and Reporter, *Detroit News and Tribune*."

"Having been a teacher for twenty-two years and for seventeen years a superintendent of a Boarding School for Boys of good families, and having found it difficult to maintain good discipline, I have often wondered how Mr. Swift managed these untrained boys; but when I found out how he did it I could not help but feel that I had not learned the art. Boys who were untrained at their own home, who lied, smoked, swore, and stole have become trustworthy and examples of good behavior at the Beulah Home. Professor Henry Veysey, Boulder, Colorado."

"Most of us wondered how Mr. Swift kept up under the mental burden of the work, the fathering of over eighty boys, and trips over the state to raise money for expenses. Yet I have seen him after a day's routine in the office and about the Home, throw off all care, run up to the gymnasium after supper with the boys and do stunts on the trapeze, horizontal bar, etc., that I would admire in a college athlete in a rigid training. Mr. Swift has seemed to me unusually fitted by over twenty years of work in what he calls a 'Boys' Character Factory.' Mr. E.H. Brown, a teacher at Benzonia Academy, Benzonia, Michigan and formerly a teacher at the Beulah Home."

"Mr. Swift's regular evening talks to the boys in the Chapel were intensely moral and uplifting, and when any one of them had done wrong such talks as he gave them must have done more good than any punishment could have done. Mr. Swift was an Eaton Rapids boy from our own town. No one can say one word against him, but very much in his praise. Mrs. J.D. Norris, Eaton Rapids, Michigan, formerly did sewing and mending at the Beulah Home."

These letters and others were included in the January/February 1913 issue of *The Youth's Outlook* published by the board of the Beulah Home. That issue ran twelve pages in length and included the board's resolution in support of Herman Swift, the summary of the Governor Osborn hearings, the letter from Floyd Starr, the affidavits and statements from the ten jurors, the recantations of the boy witnesses, and the William Allison statements regarding the Simon Mack and Sidney Jones conspiracy. Allison's statement includes an interesting story that begins on Wednesday, December 1st, 1909, the last day that Allison claimed he worked on the foundation for Herman Swift's grand new building: "Wednesday morning we went out again, the same crew. They took in a load of stone as usual in the forenoon. In the afternoon there were two very small boys who came with the team and Bacon had to load for them. When we got to Beulah Home at night Mr. Swift paid myself and Bacon off with a check. I did not see Mr. Jones from Wednesday until after Mr. Swift's arrest and before the hearing. Between the arrest myself and Bacon met Jones north of the chemical works and got into communication about Mr. Swift. I asked him if he quit work at Beulah Farm. He said that he had. I asked: 'Have you settled up with Mr. Swift?' He said: 'Yes.' I asked if Swift was angry. He replied: 'No, he acted just the same as he always did.' Then I laughed and said: 'Why did you send those two little boys out with the team that last half day I worked?' He replied: 'I sent the others down to make the complaint.' I said: 'Are you going to the hearing?' He replied: 'No, not unless I am forced to.' And he appeared very nervous and agitated. Then I asked him where he was going to work. He replied: 'East Jordan in a stave mill at two dollars a day.' I asked him if he was going to work there all winter. He said: 'He could not tell until he saw how things were going to come out here.' Then his wife came up and they went down town."

Sidney Jones' response to this story appeared in the March 21st, 1913 edition of the *Boyne City Times*. The article reads: "The following letter to a prominent Boyne City man from Mr. S.E. Jones, former farm superintendent of the Beulah Home, and now of Detroit, tells of how one of the sworn statements in that famous number of 'The Youth's Outlook' ('Give the Boy a Chance') is a downright lie. Now if one of these statements wandered from the path of truth to the extent mentioned in the following letter, there is a chance that the others are slightly on the Aminias order. The letter: Detroit, Mich., March 12, 1913: Dear Friend: I just rec'd a copy of the Beulah Home paper, in which Swift has printed a sworn statement from W.J. Allison saying that he heard me planning with the boys to get him (Swift) out of the home, which you know is a lie from start to finish as I knew nothing of it until the boys told you and I. He states in this statement that he heard me tell the boys that with their help I would get him out of the Home, all of which is a lie.

I would like to have you let me know if he has been printing these charges against me in any of the county or town papers, his paper is full of nothing else and he is sending them all over the United States with these charges printed in them against me. I feel as tho I ought to have a denial printed and would like to know how far he has gone with his publishing. Allison also says he and his helper met me on the street north of the Chemical works and had quite a conversation with me, also which is a lie. I never talked a minute with the man in my life and never met him on the street to which my wife can swear as he says she came up while he was talking to me. I would like to hear from you soon. I remain sincerely your friend: Mr. S.E. Jones, 153 Buchanan St. Detroit, Mich."

Sidney Jones probably wrote this letter to either Arthur Urquhart or George Snell.

Citizens in Eaton Rapids signed a petition requesting that Governor Ferris pardon Herman Swift. Citizens in Charlevoix County signed a petition requesting that Governor Ferris not pardon Herman Swift. The January 23rd, 1913 *Charlevoix Sentinel* article reporting on a recent interview with Governor Ferris regarding the Swift case suggested that the Governor favored the Charlevoix County petitioners. The article concluded:

"Now, I (Governor Ferris) won't listen to most of the pleas I receive relative to him. This man had every chance in the world. There is no excuse why he should have committed the crime of which he was convicted, if he committed it. I refuse absolutely to see any mitigating circumstances in his case. If they can prove he never committed the offense that is one thing, but if he committed it, there was no excuse, and he will be obliged to serve his term out for anything I will do to prevent it."

On February 20th, 1913, the Charlevoix County *Evening Journal* printed a front page article titled: "Does Not Blame Him" and subtitled: "For Issuing the Warrant in the Notorious Swift Case." The article reads: "Judge E.H. Shepherd, in reply to a letter written to Governor Ferris on Feb. 6, referring to the Herman Swift matter, has received an answer which is here given in part: 'I am receiving an immense number of letters from Mr. Swift's friends. In the light of what you say in your letter I do not blame you for issuing the warrant. I have already stated again and again that I can't do the work of the judge and the jury. I am not going to try to do it. In my own mind I have selected the path of duty and that path I shall follow.'

This letter would imply that Mr. Swift or his friends need not look to our present governor for help in their persistent search for sympathy."

It seemed that Herman Swift had little hope of gaining a pardon from Governor Ferris, but the governor did extend Swift's parole by forty days, taking the end date from February 11th, 1913 to March 23rd, 1913.

The January/February issue of *The Youth's Outlook* concluded with a brief message from "Professor Henry Veysey of Boulder, Colorado." To Herman Swift the message must have seemed foreboding. Veysey's message reads:

"Why Does God Allow Injustice to Triumph If Mr. Swift is Innocent?

Friends, Mr. Swift will be delivered and God will be glorified. He delivered Joseph, although he first had thirteen years of slavery and terrible suffering and imprisonment on a false charge. 'The iron entered into his soul.' He delivered the Lord Jesus Christ although the Son had to pass through a terrible death on a false charge of blasphemy. He was accused of gluttony and drinking, associating with wine-bibbers and consorting with evil characters. He delivered the apostles, although eleven had to pass through martyrdom in some terrible form of death. John Bunyan was permitted to be in prison for many years, separated from his dear wife and family, but what a blessing he has proved to millions.

No friends, the prison bars cannot cast a stain on an innocent man, but they can prove the outrageous injustice of laws which are supposed to mean the defense of honor and right. It can prove by some clever technicality in the hands of unscrupulous men that even the law which should protect can be made the source of greatest oppression and injustice."

I do not believe that Henry Veysey was either a professor or from Boulder, Colorado. The 1910 Federal Census lists Henry Veysey as a boarder at 1744 Superior Avenue in Toledo, Ohio. His occupation is noted as "traveling evangelist." In 1913, Henry was seventy-four years old and probably still lived in Toledo, Grace Swift's hometown.

Reverend Veysey also served northwest Ohio as a representative for the Children's Home Society. The Children's Home Society's mission was to place orphans in good Christian homes. A late 1800's edition of the *Delphos (Ohio) Herald* carried the following want ad: "Wanted a Home: It is desired to find a home for a bright healthy orphan boy, 9 years old. Has dark brown hair and eyes. Contact Henry Veysey, Children's Home Society." Henry Veysey probably introduced Grace Munson to Herman Swift. And he possibly was responsible for sending a Toledo boy named Garth, a boy discussed later in this story, to the Beulah Home.

XVIII

∽

1913, The Motion for a New Trial

The *Charlevoix Sentinel* edition of January 23rd, 1913 carried another foreboding message for Herman Swift. It came within an article titled: "For the Supreme Bench:"

"Hon. Frederick W. Mayne, of this city, judge of the Thirteenth Judicial Circuit, is a candidate for the supreme bench, and has the support of the bar of the circuit and that of a large and influential element of the laiety.

There are weighty reasons why Judge Mayne's candidacy is logical. First of all, there is no one, either in practice or on the circuit bench, whose ability and legal record have greater force in that direction. Judge Mayne has been on the bench thirteen years. In the trial of causes in his own circuit his decisions and judgments have been marked by a wisdom and impartiality that have placed him in the front rank of Michigan judges, and the affirmation of his record by the Supreme Court will compare favorably with that of the most distinguished of our State jurists.

Secondly, there are strong geographical reasons why Judge Mayne's candidacy should be favorably considered. In this peninsula, north from a line drawn across the State at the latitude of Manistee, a justice has never been chosen. That section, which embraces the Grand Traverse region, is justified in presenting a candidate for the highest office. Judge Mayne is assured of the support of many strong men outside his own circuit."

Judge Mayne worked on the Motion for a New Trial of the Swift case through January, February, and a portion of March of 1913. Only a few records remain of this phase of the case. On February 17th, 1913, Herman Swift's defense attorneys filed a deposition sworn by Dr. L.S. Bartlett. The deposition attacked the credibility of William F. Johnson, probably the key juror in the second Griffin trial. Johnson and Reuben Walton were the only two of the twelve jurors who had not signed either an affidavit or statement calling for a new Swift trial. A number of those juror statements claimed that two of the jurors were prejudiced and determined to convict Swift at the outset of the trial. These claims almost certainly referred to Johnson and Walton. On March 3rd, 1913, the prosecutors filed a response to the court in the form of a sworn deposition from William F. Johnson:

"William Johnson, being duly sworn, deposes and says that at present he is a resident of Charlevoix County, Michigan, and that he was one of the jurors in the case of The People vs. Hermon L. Swift.

Deponent says that he is acquainted with Dr. L.S. Bartlett and that he has read the deposition of Dr. Bartlett...and that at this time he has no recollection of ever having discussed this case with Dr. Bartlett either in Frank Wood's barber shop or in any other place, but that a discussion of this case might have taken place at Wood's barber shop or elsewhere.

...This deponent denies that he had formed an opinion of the guilt of the respondent prior to the trial of said cause, or that he any time stated that if he got on the jury he would soak him (respondent Swift) for all he was worth.

...This deponent further says that, on the trial of said cause, before he was sworn as a juror, he was interrogated as to his qualifications as a juror and that he truthfully answered each and every question, and that he entered as such juror upon the trial of said cause without any preconceived opinion as to the guilt or innocence of the respondent; that he had not, previous to said trial, formed any opinion as to the guilt or innocence of the accused, that, in arriving at the verdict of guilt, he was influenced solely by the testimony presented at the trial; that, after listening to the testimony and the charge of the court, he was convinced of the guilt of the accused, and that the action of this deponent in returning a verdict of guilty was based solely upon the evidence submitted in said case and the law given by the court.

This deponent further says that he had no interest whatever in the result of the suit, and that he has had no occasion since the trial of said cause to alter his mind as to the correctness of the verdict. Signed and notarized: William F. Johnson."

Another remaining record related to the Motion for a New Trial filed by attorney Clink on December 30th, 1912 is a deposition signed by Arthur Urquhart on February 14th, 1913. That deposition begins: "A.G. Urquhart being duly sworn says that at the time Herman L. Swift was first arrested the said Urquhart was city attorney for Boyne City and at the request of Prosecuting Attorney A.B. Nicholas this deponent investigated the charges made by some of the boys at the Beulah Home for Boys against Mr. Swift. Among the boys who told me Mr. Swift had taken indecent liberties with them was James Leys, who at that time told me he was 12 years old and that his home was at 133 Crosby St. Grand Rapids."

Urquhart's deposition is based upon his December 1st, 1909 interview of James Leys and it includes a statement of the details of the indecent liberties Leys claimed in that interview. Urquhart based his deposition on contemporaneous notes he had taken at that time. Those notes included reference to a witness, a Mr. Brown, who was doing repairs at the Home and interrupted the act of abuse against Leys. Judge Mayne presumably utilized this Urquhart deposition when he personally interviewed James Leys later in February or in early March of 1913. Perhaps at this same time Prosecuting Attorney Fitch was threatening Leys and Herman Swift with bringing a case based upon these charges documented in Urquhart's notes.

On March 17th, 1913, Judge Mayne issued his opinion on the Motion for a New Trial. The opinion reads as follows:

"Respondent Hermon L. Swift, having been convicted in this court, appealed to the Supreme Court, where his conviction was affirmed. He now presents a motion for a new trial. On the hearing of this motion the legality of his conviction is not in question. Respondent claims that he is innocent and he has been permitted, without objection, to present any matter that might justify the court in presuming him innocent of the offense charged. The inquiry took a wide range, covering the matters urged by respondent, as follows:

1. The Leoni and Chicago indictments and the Chicago church troubles.
2. The postal card claimed to exonerate respondent.
3. The statements of the jurors.
4. The alleged frame-up or combination of business interests, including county officers and leading businessmen in this county, to ruin Mr. Swift.
5. That the liquor interests of the county had conspired to injure him.
6. That all the boys who had accused Mr. Swift of the crime had retracted.
7. That a fair trial in Charlevoix County could not be had by reason of local prejudice.

In considering these reasons urged for a new trial, we will follow the order named.

1. On the trial, respondent was not a witness in his own behalf, consequently the Leoni and Chicago indictments, and the expulsion of respondent from his church in Chicago for like offenses, were not considered by the jury, and strictly speaking, have no place in this proceeding. The testimony submitted consists of sworn and unsworn statements, newspaper clippings, etc., and relates chiefly to the Leoni matter, although some oral testimony was permitted relating to the church trouble. This testimony has a direct bearing upon respondent's general reputation, and while the witnesses testify to his good reputation, yet no adequate reason is shown why his co-workers in the church and mission should conspire to fasten upon him the crime charged.

2. The postal card presents the most important question. Its authorship is denied by the boy who, it is claimed wrote it and affirmed by another boy who says he saw it written and that it was delivered to him to be forwarded to respondent. Were its authorship admitted by the claimed writer, then the circumstances under which it was written would have to be taken into consideration, but being denied, only the evidence for and against its authenticity may be considered. To my mind the evidence against far outweighs that in favor of its alleged authorship. Much weight is attached to the unreliability and want of veracity of the alleged writer. This should have serious consideration. A similar claim is made against the boy who says he participated in the procuring of the postal card. In addition it is shown that he was one of the first to accuse respondent of a similar practice with himself. While the reputation of both of these boys for truth is now assailed, Mr. Swift in times past, has borne witness as to their truthfulness and reliability. I have personally examined both boys in relation to this postal card and I consider that its authorship has not been proven to any reasonable degree of certainty.

3. On the face of the record the so-called statements of the jurors present an unusual situation. The testimony of the jurors themselves, however, in open court at the hearing somewhat clears the situation. One juror, the last to agree to a verdict of guilty, now believes respondent innocent. There is no question as to his honesty. Juror William Johnson denies the statements of Dr. L.B. Bartlett, that he had an opinion and a prejudice against respondent prior to the trial. His denial is clear and emphatic. Knowing Mr. Johnson intimately, it is impossible to believe that he deliberately committed the crime of perjury, in answering the questions asked him on his voir dire examination, or that he would do this great injustice to respondent. It is much more rea-

sonable to believe that the witness, at this late date, is mistaken than to believe that the juror made the statement alleged. Four jurors are represented as making affidavits. One particular feature in relation to these affidavits presents itself. Each juror, except one, on the witness stand denied making any sworn statements. With one exception, the statements of all the jurors were based upon the representations of counsel or other friends of respondent that the postal card in question was authentic. Believing this, if the postal card had been in evidence, they said their verdict might have been different. These statements were made by the jurors after repeated visits to each of them at their homes or elsewhere by respondent, his counsel or friends, and the statements of the jurors so adroitly worded as to give expression to sentiments not intended by them. Upon the hearing each repudiated the statements as published in the most emphatic terms. Each juror affirms that he acted honestly and based his verdict upon the evidence presented in open court and the law was given. The published statements of the jurors, when read in connection with their testimony given at the hearing of this motion, are deprived of the meaning and force claimed for them by respondent. Taking into consideration the influence that was brought to bear upon each individual juror, the time, place and circumstance under which his statements were made, the intention of the jurors as actually expressed and the statements that later appear in the press in the form of affidavits or letters, there is no ground for the charge that this was a 'fraud verdict' as claimed by respondent.

4. and 5. Reasons 4 and 5 we will consider together. Upon the charge that a frame-up or combination of business or professional men existed or that there was a conspiracy of the liquor interests to injure respondent, no testimony was submitted, and the attention of counsel being called to these charges as made through the public press, he denied that any such claims were made or authorized by him and that there was no foundation for such claims, as far as he knew.

6. It is not a fact that all the boys who have accused respondent of these practices have retracted. In fact, new charges since the first trial, have been made and are now in possession of the officers.

7. As to the fairness of the trial, the answers to the questions asked on the examination of the jurors, touching their qualifications to sit on the trial, conclusively show that the jurors who tried the cause were not prejudiced, and that they were not influenced in their verdict by any public opinion against Mr. Swift, if such existed. The nature of the crime is such as to shock any community. The mere recital of the facts would cause any jury to abhor the perpetrator. It would not, however, cause any person to determine the accused to be guilty. In fact, the accused, with a high reputation for integrity and chastity, would be less apt to be prejudged guilty of this particular offense by those best acquainted with him, than he would be by strangers. The evidence submitted fails to present any ground for these charges.

A careful reading of the testimony will convince anyone conversant with the rules of evidence that, outside of the postal card, respondent could make use of none of the things presented by him, on a new trial, and to my mind, if a verdict of not guilty were rendered, based upon that postal card, there would be a failure of justice. Therefore, motion for new trial is denied.

Dated, Charlevoix, Michigan, March 17, A.D. 1913

Frederick Mayne, Circuit Judge"

A key element of Judge Mayne's opinion is contained in his statement that "any one conversant with the rules of evidence" would be convinced that "outside of the postal card, respondent could make use of none of the things presented by him" to develop a case for a new trial. Defense Attorney Clink probably was well aware of this. He should have learned from the failure of his overly convoluted and complex assignment of errors motion presented to the Michigan Supreme Court. Yet rather than present Judge Mayne with a simple Motion for New Trial based solely upon the postal card, Clink presented a lengthy and complex motion based upon seven claims, all of which the judge had to consider. The judge's opinion indeed makes clear that even attorney Clink saw no merit in the one claim based on the charge that liquor interests had conspired against Herman Swift. So it seems reasonable to ask why attorney Clink made seven claims and the answer to that question may well be that Herman Swift persuaded him to do so.

The number seven is not the most important number in the Bible, but it is the number most frequently cited. And it is a number frequently incorporated in evangelists' sermons. Rev. Henry Veysey's sermons included one titled: "The Seven Precious Peas." Herman Swift was well aware of these facts. He knew that the number seven appears through the whole Bible story from Genesis where God creates the world in seven days and "God blessed the seventh day and sanctified it: because that in it he had rested from all his work which God created and made (Genesis 2:2)" to Revelations, "But in the days of the voice of the seventh angel, when he shall begin to sound, the mystery of God should be finished, as he has declared to his servants the prophets (Revelation 10:5)." The motion for a new trial represented Herman Swift's last real chance to avoid a return to prison and I believe he prayed and leaned on the number seven and maybe he focused upon Mathew 18:21: "Then Peter came and said to him, 'Lord, how often shall my brother sin against me and I forgive him? Up to seven times?'" and Luke 17:4: "And if he sins against you seven times a day, and returns to you seven times, saying: 'I repent,' then forgive him."

On March 27th, 1913 the *Charlevoix Sentinel* published a front page article titled "Mayne Says No" and subtitled "Reasons Not Sufficient For Giving Swift New Trial:"

"Judge Mayne has given his decision in the matter of Herman L. Swift's motion for a new trial in the criminal case in which he was convicted, some months ago. Inasmuch as many copies of a periodical filled with matter intended to make Swift out a martyr to vicious boys and cruel laws, have been circulated in this vicinity, we believe the people at large will be interested in Judge Mayne's decision, the body of which follows."

The *Sentinel* article then included a reprint of the judge's decision in its entirety. This article was followed by an article titled "Prison for Swift." The article reads:

"While justice has not been very swift in the case of Herman L. Swift, it now looks as if it is sure. As will be seen by the decision of Judge Mayne, published in this issue, a new trial for the Beulah Home man has been denied. The only thing that can now keep Swift out of prison is a pardon or parole and Gov. Ferris is not likely to grant either.

The situation is now this: Following the decision of the supreme court Sheriff Robbins delivered his prisoner to the warden of Ionia prison, and Swift was given his number, which stands unfilled, owing to the action of Gov. Osborn in issuing a parole, and the extension of that parole by Gov. Ferris.

It is now up to the prison warden to find his man—Charlevoix County has nothing more to do with him unless, under certain conditions he has to stand trial on one or both of the two counts that still stand against him in the calendar.

The people of Charlevoix County are thoroughly disgusted with this case, and believe, very generally, that Swift is guilty and fully deserving of the penalty that has finally reached him."

XIX

~

The Ending

While Judge Mayne dealt with the Motion for a New Trial in Charlevoix County, Governor Woodridge Nathan Ferris parried it as he ran the government of the State of Michigan from his office in Lansing. Ferris did not give the matter the consideration that Judge Mayne gave it, but the Governor had been inundated with calls and letters related to the Swift case.

One of the letters Governor Ferris received was a lengthy affidavit, a sworn statement of the history of the case from day one written by Arthur Urquhart. Urquhart closed the affidavit with a powerful claim that was reprinted in the *Boyne City Times* on February 21st, 1913:

"At the preliminary examination (before Justice of the Peace Shepherd on December 15th, 1909) Swift was represented by two of Boyne City's most admired attorneys (John M. Harris and Leonard Knowles.) After the hearing one of them was asked 'What he thought of it.' He answered: 'They are mere children. I don't know what to think of it.' Then the city attorney (Urquhart) told him he would send some of the boys up to his office alone and if he could find where they were lying he would apologize to Swift publicly. When he (either Harris or Knowles) was asked what he got out of the boys he said: 'I always need the money but Swift hasn't got the right kind of money to hire me to defend him; that it was a disease that Swift couldn't get away from.'"

Governor Ferris almost certainly received another letter, a letter written from Greenville, Michigan.

Leonora Ferris was the young woman who taught the little boys at the Beulah Home when the initial criminal charges were brought against Herman Swift. She was the lady who encouraged Merrill Griffin to write the December 1st, 1909 postcard to his father in Grand Rapids and she was the lady who delivered the postcard to either Boyne City Police Chief Richard Beach or Arthur Urquhart. Within a day or two of this, she had left the Beulah Home and returned home to Greenville. There she taught public school students and lived with her parents, Agnes and Robert Ferris.

In early 1910, Leonora Ferris received a letter written to her on December 29th, 1909 by Mrs. Miller, a matron at the county jail in Toledo, Ohio. The letter was written under the letterhead of "Office of the Sheriff, Lucas County, J.C. Newton, Sheriff, Toledo, Ohio." The letter reads:

"My dear Miss Ferris: I was very much surprised to hear from you and very much pleased also. You guessed right about my sending for Garth. I was suspicious while there but could not find out one thing. Dear Auntie Foster made me so by saying so many times to me 'Hon, I wish you could take Garth home with you.' Somehow the way she would say it made me uneasy, but I could not get one thing out of Garth. But after I got him home he told me the most horrible story I ever listened to or ever hope to again. Oh, my anguish has been more than I can tell. If his arrest had not come about so soon, I was going to have it done myself. But as you know it is a terrible charge and one that respectable people would like to keep out of and if it is possible to convict this man without Garth's evidence please do it, for he is in a fine school and I wish him to forget it if he can and if it is brought up again I am afraid it will do him harm. But nevertheless I will do my duty. This man must be punished to the full extent of the law. My God why are such men permitted to ruin our boys under the guise of Christianity?

My heart aches for Mrs. Swift but I am convinced in my own mind that she was not ignorant of this thing for she was a very unhappy woman and daughter and I spoke of it while there—that I never saw such a change in any one as I did in her since I had seen her at our house less than one year before she acted as tho she hated him and I am sure she does and no man can have a secret habit like that without his wife knowing it and once knowing it all love and respect must go. I disliked him the moment I saw him and so did my daughter and before I left I hated him for just little things I saw, his voice did not have the true ring and how he has deceived the people so long I cannot understand. Now write me all the news about this and what will be done with the school. I have never seen a paper and if you will send them to me I would be ever so much obliged and when the trial is on let me know and I will send for the papers. I think if you have seven boys to testify it is as good as eight and if they tell their story as Garth did to me any judge or jury could not help but believe. Now good-bye and many thanks for writing and letting me know all and how poor Mrs. Swift is and what she is going to do. Wishing you a Happy New Year and many more of them I remain your friend. Mrs. Miller."

Even though Mrs. Miller wanted to avoid any involvement of Garth in the Herman Swift case, sometime in early 1910 Leonora Ferris forwarded a copy of her letter to Prosecutor Nicholas in Charlevoix County. The letter was of no use to Nicholas. Without seating Garth as a witness, the letter was hearsay and not allowed as evidence in court. In 1913, the Miller letter sat in the voluminous files that Charlevoix County Prosecutor Fitch maintained on the Swift cases. There was no legal reason not to send a copy of the letter to Governor Ferris as he considered the Swift pardon request. Perhaps Prosecutor Fitch did send the letter to the Governor. My guess is that Governor Ferris received a copy of the Miller letter from either Leonora Ferris or her father Robert. Both Governor Woodridge Nathan Ferris and Robert Ferris had come to Michigan from the State of New York. Perhaps they were distant relatives, but clearly they were neighbors, Robert and Leonora living in Greenville only twenty miles south of the Governor's home in Big Rapids.

I imagine Governor Ferris reading Mrs. Miller's letter and pondering a number of things, but mostly reflecting upon the sacrifice and tenacity of Edward Griffin and his son Merrill as they pursued their mission to convict Herman Swift. Governor Ferris neither pardoned Herman Swift nor gave him an extended parole. Swift's last parole extension ended on March 23rd, 1913.

When he arrived at the Ionia Reformatory on December 4th, 1910, Herman Swift was quickly paroled, but not before being assigned prisoner Number 7224. On March 24th, 1913, prisoner Number 7224, Herman L. Swift, was returned to the Ionia Reformatory to serve out his sentence for "Gross Indecent Liberties with a Male Person."

The Ionia State House of Corrections was constructed between 1878 and 1880. Prisoners from Michigan's Jackson State Prison were deployed to assist in the construction and a number of them were transferred to the new prison when it was completed. The Ionia Prison is a large facility. In 1913 it consisted of a number of brick buildings that rose up to a considerable height and were topped by towers and cupolas. The place looked somewhat like an old New England college campus that had been encumbered with bars on the windows and a large brick wall surrounding the perimeter.

The Ionia Prison buildings hold administrative offices, cellblocks, and factories. The grounds include over forty acres of prison farmland. In 1901, they renamed the facility the Michigan Reformatory in Ionia. This represented the influence of progressive politicians who viewed the mission of the facility as reformation as well as punishment. The Reformatory was by no means a minimum-security facility. The prisoner population was large and generally represented a group of tough guys, men convicted of crimes ranging from burglary to arson to murder. The prisoners worked in prison factories and on the farm and were granted few privileges and no luxuries. It was tough time.

Prisons age quickly, just like prisoners. By the time Herman Swift walked through the gates at the Michigan Reformatory in Ionia on March 24th, 1913, the place seemed like a frightening, haunted, bedeviled fortress. There seemed no way out.

The writer of the March 27th, 1913 *Charlevoix Sentinel* article titled "Prison for Swift" apparently did not know that Herman Swift had been imprisoned in Ionia three days earlier. A writer who did know this fact also contributed an article to the same edition of the *Sentinel*. This article was titled "Still At It" and subtitled "Club Organized to Work for Release of Swift." The article reads: "A large number of business and professional men held a meeting at Eaton Rapids Saturday and organized an association to be known of as the Herman Swift Club. Its mission is to put forth every effort possible to obtain the freedom of Herman Swift, manager of the Beulah Home at Boyne City through appeals to Gov. Ferris.

As Mr. Swift's parole has expired a committee of ten appointed by the chairman of the organization accompanied Swift to Lansing for the purpose of holding a personal conference with the governor and asking executive clemency for the convicted man, who, unless the governor grants the request for either a pardon or an extension of parole must enter Ionia Prison.

The committee has interviewed the governor, who refuses to interfere. At last account, Swift was washing dishes at the Ionia Prison."

On April 24th, 1913, Herman Swift had served one month of his sentence in the Ionia Reformatory. That day the *Charlevoix Sentinel* carried a brief article: "Herman L. Swift, manager of the Beulah Home at Boyne City, who went to Ionia on Monday, March 24, 1913, and began serving his sentence in the state reformatory, writes to relatives and friends at Eaton Rapids that he has no fault to find with the tasks that are placed upon him and that he is getting along well. He says he has become a member of the choir, practices twice a week, and teaches a Sunday School class. Mr. Swift is still strong in his declaration of innocence of the charges on which he is convicted and has faith that he will receive a pardon."

One week earlier, the *Sentinel* had carried an article reprinted from the *Boyne City Times* and titled "Has Herman L. Swift Admitted His Guilt in Asking for a Pardon." The article reads: "Now that the governor has indicated that he will not interfere with the judgment of the court and jury of this county in finding Swift guilty and that he will have to take his punishment the same as others are required to, the question has been asked on what construction would be taken in his asking for a pardon.

On investigation we find that a pardon proceeds upon the theory that the person to whom it is granted is guilty of the crime for which the pardon is given and not upon the theory of his innocence, and while a pardon absolves its recipient from guilt and removes the penal consequences of his crime, it doesn't absolve the fact that he has been guilty.

Swift's lawyers must have known the position they were taking in presenting to the governor the request for a pardon for Swift and it would look to the layman as if Swift has finally admitted that he was guilty or he would not have asked for a pardon. The innocent do not ask for pardons."

The archives at the State of Michigan Library in Lansing include a file of the personal records of men who served time at the Michigan Reformatory in Ionia. These records include a one-page document for Inmate Number 7224, Herman L. Swift. This document informs us that when Swift briefly was imprisoned on December 4th, 1912, he was forty-one years old. His recent past occupation was "superintendent Beulah Farm." His former places of residence included: "19 year to Sommerset Center, Mich., 1 year to Chicago at Moody's Institute, 1 yr to New Haven, Conn. On Crown Street, 10 mo. Superintendent Yale University Boy's Club, to Buffalo, N.Y. Superintendent Newsboys Home 5 Yrs., to Chicago 734 Wells St. 2 Yrs., To Leoni, Mich. 5 Yrs. To Boyne City till arrest." His parents were "Hoyt Swift (dead) Farmer, American and Lucy Swift (dead)." His other relatives included "two sisters Hattie, Mrs. Frank Rose, Blenn, Mrs. John Basim, 5510 Iowa Ave. Chicago, and Wife Grace Swift, 5510 Iowa Ave. Chicago." He had received correspondence from "his wife, sisters and Wilbur Fowler." Wilbur Fowler will be identified later in this story. Swift's education was noted as "high school" and he used neither "liquor" nor "tobacco." He identified no "accomplices." Finally, he listed one previous arrest: "Arrested 1900 in Leoni, Mich. on charge of immorality. Was acquitted."

Herman never received a pardon from Governor Ferris, but he did receive one more temporary parole. His Ionia Reformatory record shows two temporary paroles, the first running from December 4th, 1912 to March 24th, 1913 and the second running from May 15th to May 30th, 1913. During this second parole I believe that Swift attended a meeting of the Beulah Home Board held on May 17th in Detroit. The purpose of that meeting was to bring the operations of the Home to an end and dispose of the Beulah Land Farm property.

On May 23rd, 1913, the *Boyne City Times* printed an article titled "New Manager for Beulah Home." The article reads: "Mr. Clement J. Strang, the new manager of the Beulah home arrived in the city Monday to look the ground over and will report for duty about June 1st.

Mr. Strang informs us that Mr. Swift has nothing more to do with home in any way, that the balance of the directors have taken over Swift's interests, and that the establishment will be conducted, hereafter, on lines that will meet the entire approval of the public. The home now contains twelve boys and the same are in charge of Miss Bacon and Mr. Starr, who will remain until Mr. Strang gets acquainted with the surroundings at least.

Mr. Strang is a Congregational minister, and is a man who has had extensive experience with home work. He has conducted homes of over one hundred boys and schools of nearly four hundred. Aside from this record he possesses accomplishments that make him especially desirable, he is an agricultural college graduate and an enthusiastic concerning things of an agricultural and animal nature."

Clement Strang did not report for duty at the Beulah Home on June 1st, 1913. The Board of Directors had decided to close the Home at their May 17th meeting and perhaps at an earlier date. In early 1913, the Board publicly had committed to closing the Home if Herman Swift was placed in prison. Floyd Starr's biography suggests that the Beulah Home board had begun the process of closing the Home in the winter of 1913. They gave Starr the task of placing the Beulah boys in other homes. Starr's biography reads: "Starr confronted a formidable task. Nearly 50 youngsters found themselves without a home. Despite the rigors of winter travel in northern Michigan at that time, Starr managed to make satisfactory arrangements for all but thirteen." By May 23rd, 1913, the number of boys remaining at the Beulah Home reportedly had fallen to twelve.

The Beulah Home board, and more specifically William H. Hill, managed the disposal of the 160-acre Beulah Home property. Herman Swift had conveyed the property to "William H. Hill, trustee of Detroit," through a quit-claim deed dated October 18th, 1911. This conveyance covered "all of the certain pieces or parcels of land, including all buildings thereon, situate in the township of Evangeline, County of Charlevoix, and State of Michigan now owned by the said Herman L. Swift, sole trustee of the Beulah Land Farm for Boys." Herman presumably had completed this property transfer to Hill in exchange for Hill's provision of financial support to his defense against the criminal charges. The transfer occurred just at the time Swift was preparing his expensive appeal to the Supreme Court of Michigan.

A man named E.W. Abbott attended the May 17th, 1913 meeting of the Beulah Home board. Abbott lived in Detroit and was a major land dealer in the State of Michigan. In the early 1900's he ran a prominent advertisement in the annual *Michigan State Business Directory*. The ad ran under the heading "Farms for Sale or Exchange." It reads: "If you own a farm or have the least idea of ever owning one, write me. I will write you information concerning farms and farming lands that will pay you well for your trouble. Do not buy or sell another piece of Real Estate until you have read my latest Real Estate and Farm list. It may save you hundreds of dollars. Forwarded to any address on receipt of 2-cent stamp, E.W. Abbott, Room 10 Whitney Opera House Block, Detroit, Mich." The Whitney Opera House Block was on Woodward Avenue.

E.W. Abbott also worked as land commissioner for the Boyne City, Gaylord, and Alpena Railroad. He traveled frequently to Boyne City and promoted and participated in the purchase and sale of land in Charlevoix County. He and William H. Hill had developed a proposal by which Abbot would exchange property in the City of Detroit for the Beulah Home property. Hill and Abbott negotiated this exchange for several months. During this time an issue arose as to whether Grace Swift was the legal owner of forty acres of the Beulah Home property. Later Grace would bring a lawsuit in Charlevoix County Circuit Court over this matter, but irrespective of this, on September 25th, 1913, through a warranty deed, William H. Hill conveyed the Beulah Land Farm property, all 160 acres, "free of all incumbrances except claims against the farm for taxes" to Jennie Maes Abbott, E.W. Abbott's wife. The transfers of the Beulah Land Farm property from Herman Swift to William H. Hill and from William H. Hill to Jennie Maes Abbott were recorded at the Charlevoix County Court House on April 20th, 1914.

At the May 17th, 1913 meeting I believe Herman Swift advised the Beulah Home Board that he had decided to no longer pursue either a pardon or a parole. He would serve out his sentence at the Ionia Reformatory. Following that Board meeting I believe that Swift traveled to meet with defense attorney Clink and Charlevoix County prosecuting attorney Fitch. Perhaps that meeting took place in Charlevoix County. Swift's Ionia Reformatory personal record showed that he had dark hair speckled with gray and a black beard. He may have traveled in disguise to Boyne City. There he would have visited the Beulah Home for one last time. Sadly he said good-bye to Floyd Starr and the remaining twelve Beulah boys.

Then he met with the attorneys. At that meeting it seems the parties probably signed a three-part agreement. First, Herman Swift agreed to discontinue his efforts to gain a pardon or a parole. Second, Herman agreed to never again set foot in Charlevoix County. Third, Prosecutor Fitch agreed to drop the three remaining criminal cases against Herman Swift and to not pursue other pending cases against Swift. There were other pending cases. One of them is noted in a letter in Prosecutor Fitch's Swift case files. Colonel William T. McGurrin, Commandant of the Michigan Soldiers' Home in Grand Rapids sent that letter to Prosecutor Fitch on November 26th, 1912. The letter reads: "Dear Sir, At the request of James Higgins a member of this Home, I write to ask you what the status of the case at the present time is of James Higgins against a Mr. Swift who is superintendent of the Beulah Home at Boyne City. Awaiting your reply, I remain, Respectfully yours, McGurrin, Commandant." James Higgins served in the 9th Michigan Cavalry and was in a Confederate prison at the end of the Civil War. He received an invalid's pension in 1889 and died at the Grand Rapids Soldiers' Home on April 16th, 1925. I assume this letter refers to a claim he made for his son James (Appendix I.)

On May 28th, 1913, Prosecutor Fitch filed motions for Nolle Prosequi in the three remaining criminal cases against Hermon Swift. Nolle Prosequi represents a commitment by the prosecutor that he will no longer pursue a case. The motion related to the Elliott Fay case reads as follows: "The People vs. Hermon L. Swift, Respondent. Now comes Dwight H. Fitch, prosecuting attorney in and for the County of Charlevoix, and moves the court now here that an order Nolle Prosequi be entered in the above entitled cause, the same being the one upon the complaint of Elliott Fay, for the reason that the said respondent has been heretofore convicted of a similar offense upon the complaint of Merrill Griffin and has been duly sentenced to the State Reformatory at Ionia and the ends of justice thereby attained, Dwight H. Fitch, Prosecuting Attorney."

Prosecutor Fitch on May 28th, 1913 submitted to the court like orders related to the John Hosner and Simon Mack complaints against Swift. The court approved all three of these Nolle Prosequi orders and recorded them on June 2nd, 1913. That same date the court approved and recorded a motion by Prosecutor Fitch to discharge the sureties or bonds in the Merrill Griffin case. The Charlevoix County Circuit Court effectively had gained closure in the matter of the criminal charges against Herman Swift.

Herman Swift was discharged from the Ionia Reformatory on June 17th, 1914. He had served exactly one year in prison. Herman Swift's personal prison record shows that at his commitment to prison on December 4th, 1912 he was measured at five feet five and one-half inches tall and a weight of 140 pounds. When he was discharged from the Ionia Reformatory they measured him at five feet two and one-half inches tall and a weight of only 123 pounds. Herman left Ionia by train. When he arrived in Chicago, Grace may have struggled to recognize him. He celebrated his freedom with Grace, his sister Blenn, and her husband John in the Basim home in Chicago. After a brief stay with his sister, he took his wife Grace and their baby son Harold to a home in Detroit.

R.L. Polk is a Detroit publishing firm that for years has produced city directories. The 1914 *Polk Directory for the City of Detroit* is very large. Detroit's population had surged from 500,000 to 1,000,000 residents between 1900 and 1910, fueled by growth in the automotive and related industries. Polk's directories are arranged in two sections, one that alphabetically lists residents and identifies their addresses, and another that lists addresses by street name and number and then identifies residents at those addresses. In the 1914 City of Detroit Polk Directory, Hermon L. Swift is listed as living at 181 Selden Avenue. Turning to Selden Avenue, we find that the home at 181 Selden was vacant. Herman really lived at 179 Selden Avenue. Obviously, given his conviction, prison time, and particularly the nature of the crime for which he was charged, he did not care for people to know where he lived.

William H. Hill's proprietary medicine manufacturing facilities were located at 55-60 Selden Avenue, two blocks down from the Swift's home. One block up the avenue, Howard Kurtz, I believe a cousin of Grace Swift, lived at 199 Selden.

The prior resident of the Swift home is identified in the *1913 Polk's Detroit Directory* as E.W. Abbot. Abbot probably traded the property as part of the exchange with William H. Hill for the Beulah Land Farm property. Hill undoubtedly owned the 179 Selden Avenue home in 1914 and either rented it or freely provided it as shelter for the Swifts.

Symbolically, Herman Swift's Selden Avenue home was located in the shadows of the Cass Avenue Methodist Episcopal Church. It also was located just west of the palaces constructed in the Woodward Avenue area by wealthy men who Swift had beseeched for assistance during his career. Finally, it was located close to the tough neighborhood "near Woodward Avenue" featured in *The Victories of A Boy* story, the neighborhood where Doddsy was lost and then saved. Herman Swift probably intended to pursue some form of evangelical based social work in the area. He never got the chance.

Swift had experienced a troubling discomfort in his head for several years. The malady progressively grew worse during his time in prison. He hoped and prayed that freedom from prison might bring relief from the condition, but this did not prove to be the case. He lay in bed in the home on Selden Avenue for two weeks. Grace finally prevailed upon him to seek aid from a doctor. On Sunday, July 5th, 1914, Dr. Frank B. Allison arrived at the Swift home and attended to Herman. Dr. Allen was a young general practitioner. He lived on Alexandrine Avenue just one street over from the Swift residence. The following day, Monday, July 6th, 1914, Dr. Allison returned to the home. Herman Swift had died at four o'clock that morning. He had lived only twenty-three days beyond the June 17th date when he was released from the Ionia Reformatory.

I imagine that Howard Kurtz was there to comfort Grace the day that Herman died. Herman's body was taken to the F.B. Brace Funeral Home on Jefferson Avenue in downtown Detroit. There it was prepared for a burial in Eaton Rapids.

Grace was left with the task of providing the required information and signing the death certificate:

"Name: Herman Swift   Address: 179 Selden Avenue, 4th Ward
Birthdate: Nov. 26, 1870   Age: 43 years, 7 months, 10 days
Occupation: Teacher School   Place of Birth: Michigan
Father: Hoyt Swift   Born: Michigan N.Y.
Maiden Name of Mother: Eliza Matison   Born: New York

The Above is True to the Best of My Knowledge: signed, Mrs. Grace Swift, Detroit, Michigan"

Grace carefully filled out the information. She could not recall if Hoyt Swift was born in Michigan or New York. He was born in New York. Grace was sad and nervous. She provided the maiden name of Hoyt's mother and not Herman's mother Lucy Sutton Swift.

On Herman Swift's death certificate, Dr. Allison listed the cause of death as "acute cerebritis." Cerebritus refers to inflammation of the brain. In 1914, cerebritis probably more often represented a diagnosis of symptoms rather than diagnosis of a particular disease. It was a commonly cited cause of death.

On July 10th, 1914, the *Boyne Citizen* published a front page article titled "H.L. Swift Reported Dead At Chicago" and with three subtitles: "Particulars Not Known But Said He Will Be Buried in Eaton Rapids," "Conducted Beulah Home," and "Was Sentenced to One Year at Ionia for Taking Indecent Liberties with Young Boys." The article reads:

"Word was received in this city this morning of the death of Herman L. Swift which occurred in Chicago Monday afternoon. The body will be taken to Eaton Rapids, his old home, where he will be buried.

H.L. Swift was born in Eaton Rapids, where he lived until about twenty-four years ago when he took up the Home for Boys work. He established one home at Leoni, Jackson County and later came to this city where he established the Beulah Land Farm. He conducted the one in this city for a number of years being highly respected throughout the state until an ugly rumor was started concerning his relations with the small boys at the home. An investigation was conducted which greatly incensed the citizens here and throughout the county against the man. Feelings ran high for the opinion of nearly all was that the man was guilty of the offense. He, however, maintained he was innocent and had influential friends at work trying to secure his pardon.

He was sentenced to Ionia for one year from the Circuit Court of Charlevoix County, which he served after a vain attempt to have the governor interfere. He had been living in Chicago the past few months."

On July 17th, 1914, the *Boyne Citizen* reprinted an article from the *Cadillac (Michigan) News*." The article carried the headline "Says Shame and Grief Hasten Death" and the sub-headline "Herman L. Swift's Death Hastened by Punishment for Alleged Crime Committed Here." The article

Swift Family Cemetery Plot (Fig.28)   PHOTO: Vicki Hobey

must have reinforced a belief held by the editor of the *Citizen*. It reads: "Herman L. Swift, who will be remembered as a former secretary and general manager of the Beulah Home for Boys at Boyne City, died at his home on Selden Avenue, Detroit on Monday evening. Mr. Swift had several times visited Cadillac while he was manager for the home for boys at Boyne City, on one or two occasions bringing a number of the boys with him in entertainments.

Mr. Swift was arrested on a serious charge after several years connection with the Boyne City institution and he was found guilty and sent to prison. He was released by the pardon board several months ago. His death is said to have been hastened as the result of shame and grief over the verdict against him and the humiliation over what his friends have referred to as unjust punishment."

While the *Cadillac News* article suggests that Herman Swift received a pardon, Ionia Reformatory records indicate that Swift served his entire one-year sentence and was released on June 17th, 1914.

On Friday, July 10th, 1914, the *Eaton Rapids Journal* published an obituary titled "Herman Swift Dies in Detroit." The obituary reads: " Herman L. Swift, the former secretary and manager of Beulah Home in Boyne City, died Monday at his home in Detroit where had resided the past six weeks having moved his family there from Chicago in May last. His death resulted from an ailment that had been giving him considerable trouble for several years past, but which had kept him confined to his bed for only about two weeks. The body was brought to this city Wednesday and taken to the home of Mrs. Helen Bangs, who is an aunt of the deceased, and the funeral took place from the Methodist church at two o'clock Thursday afternoon, Rev. J.R. Wooten offi-

Beulah and Herman's Final Rest (Fig.29)   PHOTO: Vicki Hobey

ciating, with burial in Rose Hill cemetery. Mr. Swift is survived by his wife and one child. He was born in Eaton Rapids and lived here until he became engaged in the Beulah Home work, about twenty years ago. Mr. Swift was forty-four years of age."

Herman Swift's father Hoyt had two younger sisters, one named Nettie and the other named Helen. Nettie married and became Nettie Green. In 1880, she gave birth to a baby girl and they named the baby Beulah. This was eleven years after the death of Hoyt and Lucy Swift's baby daughter Beulah who died of lung fever at the age of twenty-six days. Helen Swift married a Methodist Minister named Francis Bangs. Helen and Francis never had children, but Helen always looked after the interests of the children and grandchildren of her siblings. For a time Herman Swift's sister Belvia lived with Helen and Francis.

On July 8th, 1914, Herman Swift's body lay for viewing in Helen Bang's home at 531 Hill Street in Eaton Rapids. Helen lived in this home with her niece Beulah Green Fowler, her eight-year old grandniece Helen Fowler, and Beulah's husband Wilbur Fowler. Wilbur was the one man who communicated with Herman Swift while he was in the Ionia Reformatory. I imagine that in doing this Wilbur was responding to the wishes of Helen Bangs.

There are a number of apparently unintentional mistakes in Herman Swift's obituary in the *Eaton Rapids Journal*. One of these is the claim that Herman was buried in the Rose Hill Cemetery. He is not buried in that cemetery. He is buried in the adjacent Hamlin Township Cemetery, a pretty and well-kept resting place, with trees, small hills, and curving drives. Hoyt Swift purchased a plot in this cemetery on January 26th, 1878. "Lucy A. Swift, Wife of H.A. Swift,

1840-1890," is buried in the right front corner of this plot. H.A. Swift is buried in the left front corner. A silver circle marker with the letters U.S. surrounded by five stars sits atop a one-foot tall stake next to Hoyt's grave, commemorating his long service in the Civil War. In the back left of the plot lies a grave marked with a small headstone that reads "Beulah, Daughter of H.A.& Lucy A. Swift." In the back right of the plot, behind Lucy's grave and just next to Beulah's, lies a grave with a headstone marked: "Hermon L. Swift, 1870-1914" (Figs.28&29)

Herman Swift's relatives, his friends, the people of his hometown of Eaton Rapids, and many people in southern Michigan believed he was innocent of the charge that sent him to prison. Most of the people of Charlevoix County believed he was guilty. I think the people of Charlevoix County were correct in their belief.

They wrote the name Herman L. Swift on his death certificate and the name Hermon L. Swift on his tombstone. He had lived the life of a lead player in a Shakespearean Tragedy. Like Doddsy in *The Victories of A Boy* story, he had heard "two voices" one saying "it wouldn't be square" and the other saying "he never said you shouldn't." Hermon had pursued a noble cause. The last time he stood on the porch of the beautiful Beulah Home, perhaps in May of 1913, he looked over at the weeds now sprouting in the abandoned foundation of his new building and he thought of the structure he had planned to house another one-hundred lost boys, the structure he had designed by the famous architect Isaac Erb. We know what the structure would have looked like because this was the building that Doddsy dreamed of in the last chapter of *The Victories of A Boy*, the "large, imposing building of dark blue-gray stone, four stories high, standing on a gently sloping, velvet lawn, overlooking a swiftly moving river."

Like Macbeth, King Lear, and Hamlet, Herman had a fatal flaw. When he left prison, he moved to Detroit intending to start over on his mission, but then he died. He was only forty-three.

Postscript

Grace Swift

In 1915, a chancery or civil complaint was filed on behalf of Grace Swift in the Circuit Court of Charlevoix County. The complaint was filed against Jennie Maes Abbott and The First National Bank of Boyne City. The complaint sought to recover a forty-acre portion of the Beulah Land Farm property that Grace claimed was titled in her name and was not legally included in the Beulah Land Farm property that Herman Swift transferred to William H. Hill on October 18th, 1911. William H. Hill subsequently transferred ownership of the property to E.W. and Jennie Maes Abbott in exchange for property in Detroit. Judge Mayne tried this case.

The judge's decree recognized that on August 12th, 1913: "Mr. Abbott writes Mr. Hill as follows: 'I find upon looking over the abstracts that you have delivered me that the title to one forty is apparently in Grace Swift...Wish you would look among your papers and see what you have that will tell exactly what properties you have here.'

August 14th, 1913, Mr. Hill writes Mr. Abbott: 'Replying to your favor of the 12 instant just received, will say that I never had a deed from Mrs. Swift and was not aware that that forty acres was to be included. I understood that she paid for that with her own money.'

On August 12th, 1913, Mr. Abbott writes Mrs. Swift relative to the land, asking her certain questions, closes with these words: 'Kindly write me fully on this subject so that I may take the matter up with our prospective customer.' To this letter no reply is received."

On November 6th, 1915, Judge Mayne issued his ruling:

"In the letter of August 12th to Mrs. Swift, she is informed by Mr. Abbott that he considers the land in question as a part of the property about which negotiations are being made. While from the evidence it might be found that Mrs. Swift had conveyed the property to Mr. Hill without intending so to do and therefore had not knowingly parted with title to the property, yet I do not consider this as sufficient to sustain the charge of fraud on the part of Mr. Abbott. I therefore find that complainant has not sustained the allegations of fraud made in her bill of complaint and the prayer for relief is hereby denied." Judge Mayne ordered Grace to cover court costs for the defendants.

Following Herman's death, Grace left Detroit and returned to Chicago. Grace and her son Harold lived in a rented home on Indiana Avenue in Chicago until early 1923. At that time Grace began to suffer an ailment with symptoms similar to those that Herman had suffered. She and her son moved back to her hometown of Toledo and lived with Grace's sister Mrs. William R. Gilbert. Grace received medical treatment beginning on February 2nd, 1923. On May 8th, 1923 doctors operated on a tumor in Grace's brain. She died as a result of that tumor on June 25th, 1923. She was only forty-two. The Toledo Blade carried a brief obituary:

"Swift—Grace Munson: Widow of Herman Lee Swift entered into rest Monday, June 25, 1923, at St. Vincent's hospital. Remains will be at Boyer-Kruse mortuary, Monroe and Collingwood until Wednesday at 9 and then removed to home of her sister Mrs. William R. Gilbert, 3518 Willys Parkway. Memorial services at Collingwood M.E. Church, Phillips Avenue, Wednesday afternoon at 2. Internment in Woodlawn cemetery."

Grace's obituary does not mention her son Harold who was thirteen years old and now an orphan. Harold was raised in Washington D.C. by Herman's sister Blenn and her husband John Basim. He died at the age of eighty-three on January 3rd, 1994.

The Beulah Home Building

Edward W. Abbott never was able to find a buyer for the Beulah Home building after he acquired it in his wife's name from William H. Hill in September of 1913. Abbott reportedly converted some of the rooms in the building into flats and rented them out over the period between 1914 and 1919. In September of 1919, the *Boyne Citizen* carried the following want ad: "For Sale: All the furnishings of 'Beulah Home,' consisting of Beds, Springs, Pillows, 75 New Quilts, Commodes, Dressers, Chairs, Tables, 600 Coats and Overcoats for Boys, and Youths, also some Waists, Underwear, and Overalls. Pants 5 cents to 25 cents; Coats 25 cents to $2.00; Overcoats 50 cents to $10.00. Also a lot of Farming, Gardening, Machinist, and Carpenter tools. Your opportunity to secure what you want at a low price as I want to sell all before October 1st. Will sell entire lot in bulk at a special price. Apply 'Beulah Home' North Boyne."

The seller of the Beulah Home furnishings is not identified in this want ad. Jennie Maes Abbott still owned the property, but property taxes had not been paid since 1916.

On August 9th, 1921, Dolly Shay took title to the Beulah Home property by paying four hundred forty eight dollars in overdue property taxes to the Auditor General. Dolly's husband Jesse ran a restaurant in Boyne City and the couple lived on Vogel Street a few blocks away from the Beulah Home. Dolly Shay sold the property to Hylan Heaton. Heaton had operated a saloon in Boyne City. Local authorities had closed the saloon on May 1st, 1909, following the April 1909 voter approval of the Local Option in Charlevoix County. Hylan Heaton sold the Beulah Home property to Cadwell and Sons on March 13th, 1923. This sale did not include the Beulah Home building. During the winter of 1922/1923 Heaton sold the building to a man from the city of Charlevoix named James Saunders. Saunders and his son took the Beulah Home apart board by board. These boards were cut from virgin Michigan timber. The exterior boards were ten inches wide. They were irreplaceable. Saunders transported the boards by truck across frozen Pine Lake from Boyne City to the city of Charlevoix.

Belvedere Club

In 1878, a pioneer Charlevoix businessman named Amos Fox and a group of Baptists from Kalamazoo established the Charlevoix Summer Home Association on a twenty-five acre site on the shores of Pine Lake in Charlevoix. Fox had visited the successful Bay View Association Methodist Camp established in Petoskey and his group set out to develop a similar, but Baptist-based camp in Charlevoix. Their efforts proved very fruitful. In 1923, they changed the name of the Charlevoix Summer Home Association to the Belvedere Club. That year they constructed the Belvedere Casino. This is a wonderful building that still sits on a small bluff right on the lakeshore, looking east over beautiful Lake Charlevoix (Pine Lake in 1923.) The bulk of the Beulah Home building boards were used in the construction of the casino. I believe a few years later they may have utilized the remaining boards in the construction of the Belvedere golf course clubhouse, an attractive old building that sits on a hill looking west over a beautiful golf course. The location of the Belvedere Casino building is ironic in several respects. It seems the Bay View Methodists assisted Herman Swift in establishing the Beulah Home in Boyne City in 1902 and the Belvedere Baptists relocated the body of the Beulah Home building in 1923. Now the building resides in Charlevoix, the town where Herman Swift was convicted. And it no longer is a boys home, but rather is part of a successful resort, just like Hiram Chapman imagined when he constructed the large, rambling hotel in Bay Springs back in the summer of 1883.

The Boyne City Beulah Home sat on lots three and four of block one of the Chapman and Addis Addition. In 1941, Henry Hampton and his wife purchased both lots for thirty dollars. For some time they farmed the land and then it was converted into home-sites.

Police Chief Richard Beach

Richard Beach was terminated from his position as Boyne City Police Chief in 1910. He and his wife moved to Detroit where Richard worked as a foreman in a factory.

Governor Woodbridge Nathan Ferris

Nathan Ferris was elected to a second term as the Governor of Michigan in 1914. In 1922 he was elected to a Michigan seat in the United States Senate. There he was a strong supporter of the establishment of the U.S. Department of Education. He died in his office in Washington D.C. on March 3rd, 1928 and is buried in Big Rapids, Michigan.

Franz Kuhn

Franz Kuhn filled a vacancy on the Michigan Supreme Court in 1912. He served on the Court until 1919 when he resigned and was appointed President of the Michigan Bell Telephone Company. He died on June 16th, 1926.

Governor Chase Salmon Osborn

Following his single term as Governor of the State of Michigan, Chase Osborn traveled the world, authored a number of books, and several times ran unsuccessfully for public office. In

1939, he met with President Franklin Roosevelt to describe his dream of a bridge that would connect the Lower and Upper Peninsulas of Michigan. That dream found fruition with the completion of the Mackinaw Bridge in 1957. Governor Osborn died on April 11th, 1949. He is buried on Duck Island in Lake Huron just south of the city of Sault Ste. Marie. He is memorialized by a historical marker and a bust on the riverfront walk in that city.

Justice Joseph Steere

Justice Joseph Steere resigned his position on the Michigan Supreme Court in 1927. He was seventy-five years old and had served as a judge for forty-six years. He died on December 13th, 1936. He is memorialized in the Judge Joseph Steere room in the Bayliss Public Library in Sault Ste. Marie. That library contains a great portion of Judge Steere's famous collection of historical Upper Peninsula books and documents.

City Attorney Arthur Urquhart

City Attorney Arthur Urquhart left Boyne City sometime between 1913 and 1920. He moved with his wife to Detroit and practiced law in that city.

Sidney E. Jones

Sidney Jones will be remembered as the man in this story who in 1909 worked for six months as farm superintendent at the Beulah Land Farm for Boys and was accused of attempting to steal the farm from Herman Swift. Following his departure from Boyne City in 1910, he worked for a time in Detroit. He also worked turning out wooden handles in a factory in Ann Arbor. In 1920, Sidney and his wife Bertha lived and farmed in Bellevue Township in Eaton County, Michigan. Sidney had returned home. He was born on a farm in Eaton County in 1870, the same year that Herman Swift was born in Eaton County.

APPENDIX I

Lost Boys and Conclusion

Merrill Griffin

Merrill Griffin had lived at the Beulah Home in Boyne City for a little over four months when he was removed from the Home and returned to his father Edward C. and stepmother Nellie in Grand Rapids in December of 1909. After his return his parents never again referred to him as Merrill. Over the years he would go by various first names including Wallis, Wallace M., and perhaps Wesley. Edward C. and Nellie had five children of their own, including a son named Edward Jr. born in 1915.

In 1925, Wallace M. Griffin lived with his father Edward C. Griffin at 533 Hopson in Grand Rapids. It seems that Nellie now lived with her cousin Peter Leys and his wife Gertie in a home at 226 Palmer in Grand Rapids. Nellie worked as a maid and it seems that she had left Edward. In 1931, Edward C. Griffin worked as a plumbing inspector for the City of Grand Rapids. He lived in a nice home at 2108 Palace Avenue in Grand Rapids. More importantly, Nellie had returned and once again lived with Edward.

The *Grand Rapids Press* carried the following obituary on October 31st, 1941: "Edward C. Griffin, 64, of 2108 Palace Avenue S.W., plumbing inspector employed by the city engineer's department for 28 years, died Thursday night at Blodgett Hospital. Griffin was born in Caledonia and lived for a while at Sand Lake. He came to Grand Rapids as a young man. He was a tool and die maker before entering the city's employ. At one time he was a member of the national guard. Burial will be in Woodlawn Cemetery."

Nellie Griffin died in October of 1939. Nellie and Edward's obituaries suggest that Merrill Griffin died sometime between October 1939 and October 1941.

Simon Mack

In 1920, Simon lived as a boarder at 156 Division Avenue in Grand Rapids. He worked as a taxicab driver. In 1931, Simon lived with his wife Irene in a home at 234 Ransom Avenue in Grand Rapids. He worked as a salesman for the Hoover Company. I imagine that Simon made an excellent vacuum sweeper salesman.

On October 6th, 1978, the *Grand Rapids Press* carried the following obituary:

"Mr. Simon Mack, aged 82, formerly of Grand Rapids, passed away Thursday evening at his country residence in Nunica. Mr. Mack is survived by his wife, Irene; one sister, Mrs. Burnice Lampson of Grand Rapids; several nieces and nephews..."

Elliot Fay

I have located only one historical record of an Elliot Fay beyond the 1910 Federal Census. That is a voter registration filed under the name "Elliot Fay" in San Francisco in 1940.

John Hosner

John was a resident of the Charlevoix County Infirmary in the summer of 1910. Beyond this date I don't know what became of Johnnie Hosner.

Inmates Children's Temple Home, 734 Wells Street, Chicago, Illinois

The Federal Census of 1900 listed seventeen inmates at Herman Swift's Chicago Temple Home on June 4th, 1900. Following is a list of those boys, their ages, places of birth, places of father's birth, places of mother's birth, and occupations:

CARL ANDERSON: age 9, Illinois, Sweden, Sweden, at school

ARTHUR ANDERSON: age 13, Illinois, Sweden, Sweden, at school

WALTER BOWERS: age 11, Indiana, Indiana, Indiana, at school

BENJAMIN FISHER: age 9, Canada, Canada, unknown, at school

ANTON KARKREIN: age 14, Illinois, Germany, Germany, messenger

ALBERT LAWRENCE: age 8, Illinois, Sweden, Sweden, at school

BENJAMIN MURPHY: age 15, Illinois, Ireland, Ireland, messenger

JOHN NELSON: age 8, Illinois, Sweden, unknown, at school

ANDREW NELSON: age 12, Illinois, Sweden, unknown, at school

FRANK NOPPER: age 15, Indiana, Germany, Indiana, jewelers trade

OWEN PARKER: age 11, Ohio, Ohio, unknown, at school

GEORGE SCHAEFFER: age 6, Illinois, Germany, Illinois, at school

BENJAMIN SCHAEFFER: age 10, Illinois, Germany, Illinois, at school

WILLIAM SCHAEFFER: age 11, Illinois, Germany, Illinois, at school

GERHARD TABBERT: age 9, Germany, Germany, Germany, at school

OSCAR TONANDER: age 13, Sweden, Sweden, Sweden, at school

HUGO TRIPP: age 13, Illinois, Germany, Germany, at school

Inmates Beulah Home for Boys Leoni Township, Jackson County, Michigan

The Federal Census for 1900 listed twenty-one boys as inmates at Herman Swift's Beulah Home for Boys in Leoni Township (Fig.30). The census indicates: "Nothing known of Parents of These Boys." Following is a list of those boys, their ages, and their places of birth. All of these boys were recorded as "at school."

NELSON ALBERT: age 13, Illinois	FRANK BERRY: age 12, Illinois
WILLIAM BETTS: age 14, Ohio (Fig.6, p.25*)	WILLIE BRADSHAW: age 9, Ireland
FRANK FRANCE: age 12, Michigan	CHARLES GERLACH: age 11, Illinois
WILLIE HENSELL: age 9, Ohio	FRANK HOWELL: age 15, Illinois
GEORGE KEGG: age 11, Illinois	ROBERT KEGG: age 13, Illinois
EDDIE MARTH: age 10, Illinois	CHARLEY MAX: age 13, Illinois
DAVID MITCHELL: age 10, France	HENRY PETERSON: age 12, Illinois

Our first swarm of boys to the Leoni Beulah Land Farm (Fig.30)

FAY RANSOM: age 10, Illinois   HERBERT RANSOM: age 13, Illinois
WALTER SMITH: age 11, Michigan   BURTON WATERS: age 13, Montana
GEORGE WATERS: age 13, Montana   OSCAR WEBER: age 13, Illinois (Fig.7*, p.32)
LEON WINN: age 12, Kansas

Inmates Beulah Home for Boys Boyne City, Michigan (Fig.31)

I am aware of twenty-eight boys who resided as inmates at the Beulah Home in Boyne City and left the Home either during or shortly before the onset of the Boyne City Affair. None of these boys were counted in the Federal census of inmates residing at the Home on April 18th, 1910. Pages noted with an asterisk indicate the location of a biography in this story and pages without an asterisk indicate the location of a reference to a particular boy in this story. Four of the boys are the complainants against Herman Swift: Merrill Griffin (p.65, p.96*); Simon Mack (p.2*, p.78); Elliot Fay (p.78,p.89*); and John Hosner (p.78, p.84*). The remaining twenty-four boys include:

FLOYD BISHOP: Floyd was a member of the Boys Quartette (Fig.27, p.126*)

"BLACKEYES": A member of the Boys Quartette (Fig.27, p.125)

VERL BLESING: Verl Ronald Blesing was born in Tecumseh, a town in southeastern Michigan, on July 27, 1899. In 1900, Verl lived in Tecumseh with his father John, John's wife Laura and an older brother named Russell. John and Laura were married in 1896. John was born in Eaton County in 1873, three years after Herman Swift was born in that county. In the winter of 1908, John sent his son Verl off to the Beulah Home. During the Boyne City Affair he removed Verl from the Home.

The 1910 Federal Census recorded Verl R. Blesing living with John and Laura Blesing in a home at 232 Shawnee Street in Tecumseh. That same census recorded a woman named Emma Blesing living with her sister and brother-in-law in a home at 615 Mill Street in Tecumseh. Emma worked as a laundress. The 1910 census recorded a woman named Alice Cutting living with her parents in a home at 434 Ottawa Street in Tecumseh. Alice worked as a public school teacher.

Were it not for two postcards, we probably would not know that Verl resided as an inmate at the Beulah Home, that Alice Cutting looked after his welfare, and that Emma Blesing was his mother. In July of 1909, Alice Cutting was attending summer school at Michigan Normal University in Ypsilanti when she mailed a postcard to Miss Emma Blesing in Tecumseh, Michigan. The picture side of the postcard was an Edward Beebe photograph of "A Mix-up At Beulah Home Boyne City, Mich." (Fig.16). The message side reads: "I was in such a hurry while at Beulah Home that I did not get any cards at all, but as soon as I got home wrote to Mrs. S. to send me some but this is the only one she sent that showed the outside of the building at all. Had a fine time. Found Verl real well and happy. Mr. S. let him open the box all alone. Am studying hard at 705 Cross St. Ypsilanti. Alice Cutting."

On February 7th, 1909, Verl Blesing mailed a postcard to his mother. The picture side shows fifty-four Beulah boys in front of farm buildings at the Home. It is titled: "A Valuable Property at Beulah Land Farm for Boys, Boyne City, Michigan" (front cover). The postcard reads: "Mama why don't you write to me or are you sick. I ricafed the letter Miss Cutting wrote me. I am not homesick at all. I like it very well. From your loving son Verl."

Verl Blesing may have remembered the cold winters at the Beulah Home. In 1920, he was a private in the United States Army stationed in North Carolina. In 1930, he was stationed with the army at Fort Davis in the Canal Zone in Panama. Verl died in El Paso, Texas on September 17th, 1971. He is buried in the National Cemetery at Fort Bliss.

WILLIE BROWN: On February 23rd, 1906, Herman Swift was traveling on his honeymoon. That day the *Boyne Citizen* reported: "Willie Brown of the Beulah Home, entertained about twenty young people at the home of Mrs. P.J. Howard, with a Valentine party last evening. A gay time is reported, in which pop corn, fudge, marshmallows and lemonade were prominent, as were also various games, etc.—*Petoskey News*." Willie may be a boy who was born in Michigan in January of 1895. In 1900, he lived in South Haven, Michigan with his mother Bertha who was twenty-six and divorced. In 1910, he lived in Dent County, Missouri with his mother and her husband, Harve Babbipp.

EDWY CRANE: Edwy was one of the Ferris Group boys (p.78, p.80*)

EVAN DUNN: Evan was a member of the Boys Quartette (Fig.27, p.126*)

ARTHUR FAY AND EDDIE FAY: Arthur and Eddie were brothers of Elliot Fay. Both boys were removed from the Beulah Home by authorities on February 13th, 1910. In 1930, an Arthur Fay age thirty-one lived in Detroit with his wife Florence and worked as a railroad switchman; while an Edward Fay age twenty-two lived in Detroit and worked as a laborer at a scale company. (p.109)

JIMMIE FAIR: (p.85, p.90): In the Federal Census of 1910, a ten year old boy named James Fair lived as a boarder with Walter and Georgiana Portious in Baldwin Village, Lake County, Michigan. James was born in Michigan and the birthplaces of his father and mother were noted as "unknown."

GARTH: An unidentified boy who left the Beulah Home and returned to his home in Toledo in December of 1909 (p.228).

GEORGE GATES: George was one of the Ferris Group boys (p.57*, p.78, p.90, p.93, p.140).

FRANK GUSTIN: Frank appeared as a witness for the defense in the Swift trial (p.153*).

FRANK HALL: Frank was one of two boys caught stealing candy in November of 1909 (p.67*).

FRANKLIN HALEY: Franklin was the other boy caught stealing candy (p.67*).

JAMES HIGGINS: James was born in Grand Rapids in 1894. In 1900, he lived in Grand Rapids with his father James (age 53), mother Maud (age 27), brother Abraham, and sister Gertrude . The family lived in a home at 26 King Street. The home was four blocks south of Ann Street, in the same neighborhood where Beulah boys Simon Mack, Merrill Griffin, James Leys, Howard Smith, and Gerald and Lloyd Cogswell lived. Early in the 1900s it seems that Maud died. In 1910, Gertrude, now ten, lived with her aunt and uncle. Abraham, now fourteen and named "Lincoln," lived with foster parents. I don't know where young James lived in 1910, but in 1920 he lived in Grand Rapids and worked as a fireman. I believe he was a Beulah boy (p.233).

HOFFMAN: Simon Mack mentioned a Beulah inmate with the last name Hoffman during his examination in the City of Charlevoix Justice Court on June 17th, 1910. Simon claimed Hoffman had charged Herman Swift with abuse sometime prior to 1909 (p.119)

PETER JEWELL: A boy named Peter Jewell was born on July 14th, 1894 in Wisner a small farming town in northeastern Nebraska. Peter's father was from Denmark and worked as a farm laborer. His mother Nellie gave birth to fourteen children, but ten of them died in early childhood. In 1910, Peter worked as a farm laborer and lived with his father Peter and his mother Nellie back in Nebraska. Peter's father had changed the family's last name to Juel. Peter Juel's World War I draft registration indicates that he was of medium height, stout, with dark brown hair.

CHESTER KENT (age 13, Michigan, Unknown, Unknown): Chester almost certainly is the boy who drove the team to the stone quarry when the Boyne City Affair began on November 30th, 1909 (p.1, p.91, p.160). I believe that Chester was born in Gladwin, Michigan and that he was an orphan when he arrived at the Beulah Home. He probably arrived when he was young and lived a long time at the Home. In 1909, he was only twelve yet had the authority to drive the large team of farm horses. The Federal Census records that on April 20th, 1910 Chester Kent lived as a foster son with Benjamin and Carrie McCumber in a home at 131 Groveland Street in Boyne City. Benjamin was a merchant who operated a large general store in the city. In 1920, Chester Kent lived with his wife Nellie in Saginaw. Chester worked: "driving a team."

HAROLD LANE (age 6, Ohio, Ohio, Ohio) AND HOMER LANE (age 14, Ohio, Ohio, Ohio):

Harold and Homer Lane I believe are two boys who were born in Morrow County in central Ohio. Norman and Mary Lane were their parents. Norman worked as a farmer. The two boys were sent to the Beulah Home for some reason. Perhaps Henry Veysey (p.221) played some role. They are mentioned in Simon Mack's Justice Court testimony (p.118). Very early in the Boyne City Affair Norman and Mary brought their two sons home. In the summer of 1910, Harold and Homer Lane lived with their parents and a baby sister Velma back on the farm in Morrow County. In 1930, Homer lived with his wife Eunice in the town of Ashland, Ohio. He worked as a gas and oil driller. Harold married Ida and lived to the age of ninety-four, dying in Morrow County on August 24th, 1997. Harold probably was the last surviving Beulah boy.

HERSHEL MOFFATT (age 14, Michigan, Unknown, Unknown): Hershel Moffatt is mentioned in Simon Mack's Justice Court testimony (p.121). In the summer of 1910, I believe he lived in the town of Greenville in Montcalm County, Michigan. He lived as a boarder with Charles and Nora Miller. Charles was president of the bank in Greenville. Leonora Ferris undoubtedly managed Hershel's move from the Beulah Home to Greenville.

HARRY PERLINE (age 15, Illinois, Russia, Russia): Harry is mentioned in Simon Mack's Justice Court testimony (p.119). I believe he is a boy named Harry Perlin. Harry Perlin was one of nine children. His parents were Moses and Anna Perlin. Moses and Anna were Russian Jews who had immigrated to the United States in 1890. By the summer of 1910 Harry had left the Beulah Home. He lived with his parents and six siblings in a home at 407 St. Antoine in a tough part of Detroit. His father worked as a shoemaker. In 1920, Harry lived in Detroit with his wife Beatrice and a daughter Lillian.

"SUNBEAM": A member of the Boys Quartette (Fig.24, p.127)

EMERY WEAVER: Emery testified as a witness for the defense in the Swift trial (p.155*, p.188).

The 1910 Federal Census of the residents and inmates of the Beulah Land Farm for Boys in Boyne City was completed on April 18th, 1910. The enumerator wrote on the census form: "The boys work at various things at the home, but go to school so large part of the year their work is so varied, no stated work can be given for them." The census listed thirty-one boys as inmates at the home:

GERALD COGSWELL (age 13, Michigan, Michigan, Michigan) AND LLOYD COGSWELL (age 12, Michigan, Michigan, Michigan): Gerald Cogswell was born in Grand Rapids on March 6th, 1896. Gerald's younger brother Lloyd was born in Grand Rapids on February 4th, 1898. In 1900, Gerald and Lloyd lived with their father Harry and their mother Charlotte in a home at 135 Palmer Avenue in Grand Rapids. The home was located one block south of Ann Street. Harry worked as a painter. It seems that at some time between 1906 and 1909 Harry died and Lloyd and Gerald were sent to the Beulah Home. Charlotte married a furniture jobber named John Martin. In 1920, Gerald and Lloyd lived with John and Charlotte Martin in a home at 254 Henry Avenue in Grand Rapids. Gerald worked as a furniture salesman and Lloyd as a machinist. In 1930, Gerald, Lloyd, and Lloyd's wife Carrie lived with Charlotte Martin in a home at 1211 South Jackson Street in Jackson, Michigan. Charlotte was widowed. Gerald was divorced and still worked as a salesman. Lloyd worked as a cable officer for the telephone company.

WALTER CONSINA (age 13, Michigan, Michigan, Michigan): I have found one reference to a Walter Consino who in 1930 was thirty-two, lived with his wife Coletta and two children in a home at 8187 Desoto in Detroit, and worked as an assistant engineer in a laboratory.

EDWARD CRAMER (age 11, Illinois, Illinois, Illinois): Edward Cramer may be the boy referred to as Edwy Crane.

ORA CRAMPTON (age 16, Michigan, Michigan, Michigan): Ora was a member of the Boys Quartette and testified for the defense at the Swift trial (p.125*, p.154).

MARVIN DUBOIS (age 11, Michigan, Michigan, Michigan): A Marvin Dubois was born in Eaton Rapids, Michigan on October 9th, 1897. His mother Nettie was a widow in 1910 and a May 7th, 1910 Federal census entry shows Marvin living in Eaton Rapids with Nettie. I believe that during the Boyne City Affair, Nettie removed Marvin from the Beulah Home. Herman Swift padded his enrollment total by including Marvin in the 1910 census count of boys at the Home. In 1920, Marvin Dubois lived with his wife Elizabeth and two stepchildren in a home at 1909 Francis Street in Jackson, Michigan. He worked as an inspector as Lockwood Ash Meter.

HERSHEL FAIRCHILD (age 12, Michigan, Michigan, Michigan): I believe that Hershel Fairchild is another boy that was counted among the inmates at the Beulah Home in the Federal Census taken at the Home on April 18th, 1910, but who no longer resided there. In the Federal Census taken in Charlotte, Michigan on April 16th, 1910 Hershel Fairchild is recorded living in a home at 40 Lincoln Street with his father John and his mother Ida. This also may be a boy referred to as Archie Fryfield in Simon Mack's testimony (p.119).

ROY FENTON (age 12, Michigan, Michigan, Michigan) AND RAY FENTON (age 16, Michigan, Michigan, Michigan): Roy testified as a witness for the defense in the Swift trial (p.141, p.157*.)

FRED GIBSON (age 14, Michigan, Canadian English, Canadian English): Fred Gibson may be a boy who was born in St. Clair County, Michigan in February of 1896. In 1900, he lived in Wales Township, St. Clair County, Michigan with his parents Archie and Ella.

DONALD GRAHAM (age 14, Indiana, Michigan, Michigan): A Donald Paine Graham was born in South Bend, Indiana on October 1st, 1895. His parents John and Kate divorced and Donald may have been sent to the Beulah Home as a result of this. In 1920, Donald lived with his wife Ethyl and her parents in a home in Hennipin County, Minnesota. Donald worked as a bookkeeper for a milling company.

WILLIAM GRAY (age 10, Michigan, Michigan, Michigan): A William Patrick Gray was born in Saginaw, Michigan on June 30th, 1899. His father William James Gray lost his wife some time before 1910 and perhaps this was the reason that young William was sent off to the Beulah Home. William Patrick Gray registered for the United States draft in 1917. He listed his place of residence as 635 Davison Street in Saginaw. He lived there with his father.

EMIL HARRIS (age 12, Illinois, Illinois, Illinois): This may be a boy named Arthur E. Harris who was born in Chicago on August 22nd, 1897. Arthur's World War I draft registration indicates that he had "black hair and black eyes."

CARLETON LEWIS (age 10, Michigan, Michigan, Michigan): I believe that Carleton Lewis was born in Eaton County, Michigan in July of 1899. His parents were Clyde and Ada Lewis. He is another boy who Herman Swift included in the 1910 census at the Beulah Home, but who had already left the Home. Carleton Lewis was recorded as living with his grandparents Whitman and Phoebe Hall in the 1910 census of Windsor Township in Eaton County. In 1920, Carleton worked as a machinist and lived in Windsor Township with his wife Cava who was a public school teacher.

JAMES LEYS (age 12, Michigan, Michigan, Michigan): James was a member of the Ferris Group and he testified as a witness for the defense in the Swift trial (p.79, p.101*, p.147). In 1930, James lived with his wife Eva and a son James Jr. in a home at 1108 Fisk in Grand Rapids. He worked as an engineer at a furniture factory.

WILBUR LOCKE (age 10, Michigan, Unknown, Unknown): These "unknown" references suggest that Herman Swift either did not know where Wilbur Locke's parents were or that he did not know where they were born. I believe Herman knew both of these facts. Wilbur Locke was born on January 17th, 1899. He died at the age of eighty-five on July 4th, 1984. His obituary in the *Canton Daily Ledger* informs us that he operated an automobile dealership in Fairview, Ohio for thirty-seven years and that his parents' names were William and Flora Locke. The 1910 Federal Census recorded William and Flora living on a farm in Penn Township in Cass County, Michigan. A son Russell age nine and a baby named Sherman lived with them. Their son Wilbur was not recorded living with them because I believe Wilbur lived at the Beulah Home.

PETER MEDJISKA OR MAJESKI (age 11, Michigan, Poland, Poland): Peter may have been a son of Martin and Kate Modeski who immigrated to Michigan from Poland in 1895. The Modeski's had nine children including a son named Peter. They lived in the town of Freesoil in Mason County, Michigan (p.91).

RAYMOND NELSON (age 13, Michigan, Sweden, England): Raymond Nelson may have been a boy born in Detroit on October 20th, 1896. This Raymond Nelson registered for the World War I draft on June 5th, 1918. He had blue eyes and blond hair. In 1920, he lived with his mother Elizabeth Heiser at 283 Second Street in Detroit. His mother was a widow and Raymond worked as a general laborer.

CELESTINO PARADIES (age 16, Cuba, Cuba, Cuba): Celistino testified as a witness for the defense in the Swift trial (p.77*, p.121, p.152)

WILLIS ROBERTS (age 16, Michigan, Michigan, Michigan): A Willis Roberts was born in March of 1894. In 1900, he lived with William and Mary Hogle in the small town of Commins in Oscoda County in northern Michigan. William Hogle worked as a day laborer. By 1910, William and Mary had four of their own children and a daughter-in-law living with them and it seems they had placed Willis in the Beulah Home. In 1920, Willis lived with his wife Edna and a daughter Dorothy in a home at 520 Wilson Street in Flint. Willis worked as a sheet metal worker for a furnace company (p.90, p.96, p.139).

HOWARD SMITH (age 13, Michigan, Michigan, Michigan): Howard Smith is a common name. Taking an educated guess, I believe this Howard Smith was born in Grand Rapids in October of 1896. In 1900, he lived with his mother Jennie and an older sister Gladys at 310 Ann Street in Grand Rapids. Beulah boy James Leys lived right down the street at 166 Ann and Merrill Griffin lived around the corner at 25 7th Avenue. In 1920, Howard may have been a lodger at 207 Legrave Avenue in Grand Rapids who worked as a fireman for a railroad.

ROBERT SPARKS (age 12, Michigan, Michigan, Michigan): Robert Sparks testified as a witness for the defense in the Swift trial (p.149*).

LAMONT SWICK (age 10, Michigan, Michigan, Michigan): I believe that Lamont Swick was born in January of 1900. In 1900, he lived with his mother Alta and his father John in a home owned by Alta's parents in Augusta Township in Washtenaw County, Michigan.

DONALD THOMAS (age 13, Michigan, Michigan, Michigan): Donald Thomas testified for the defense in the Swift trial (p.151*).

SAMUEL VALENTINE (age 13, Ohio, Canadian French, Canadian French): Samuel Valentine testified for the defense in the Swift trial (p.150*).

EARNEST WARDELL (age 15, Michigan, Michigan, Michigan): Earnest was a member of the Ferris Group, a member of the Boys Quartette and he testified for the defense in the Swift trial (p.3*, p.78, p.147, p.158).

THOMAS WEBB (age 14, Michigan, Canadian English, Canadian English) AND NELSON WEBB (age 9, Michigan, Canadian English, Canadian English): I believe Thomas Webb was born on July 29th, 1895 and his younger brother Nelson was born on March 11th, 1901. They lived in the small lumbering town of Frederick in northern Michigan before they were placed into the Beulah Home. In 1930, Thomas Webb and his wife Grace lived in a home at 690 Melrose Avenue in the city of Pontiac, Michigan. Thomas worked as an officer in the city police force. Nelson Webb lived with his wife Gladys in a home at 684 Melrose, right next door to his older brother Thomas. Nelson also worked as an officer in the city police force.

EDWARD WILDE (age 12, Michigan, Canadian English, Wisconsin): I believe that in 1900, Edward Wilde lived in the town of Chrystal Falls in the Upper Peninsula of Michigan. He had three brothers and all four of the boys lived as stepsons with Joseph and Anna Lewis. Ohio death records include a man named Edward Wilde who died in Holmes County at the age of eighty-nine on November 10th, 1987. This man was married and worked as a janitor in a metal forging and stamping plant.

GEORGE WILMOT (age 9, Michigan, Michigan, Michigan): (p.86, p.88): I searched a long time for George and believe I finally found him in Detroit. I figured I'd find him in a larger city, a railroad town, because George on at least one occasion had left the Beulah Home, hopped a train, and traveled to Petoskey with Johnnie Hosner.

A George Wilmot was born in Detroit in May 1900. He grew up in a home on Jefferson Street just east of downtown Detroit. Streetcars ran up and down Jefferson and eastbound trains departed from the Brush Street Station just a few blocks south of George's home. George's mother Mabel died in 1907. I imagine that George was a tough little boy and for some reason his father Joseph sent him to the Beulah Home. In 1914, Joseph enlisted in the Canadian Overseas Expeditionary Force and headed for Europe. He listed George as his "next of kin." George had returned to the home on Jefferson Street.

LEROY WINEGARDEN (age 11, Michigan, Michigan, Michigan): I believe this refers to a boy named Lee Winegarden who was born in February of 1899. In 1900, Lee lived in Spencer Township, near Grand Rapids with his father Adelbert who was fifty-four and his mother Vista who was twenty-one. In 1910, Vista was a widow. She worked as a servant for a farmer who lived in Leoni Township Michigan.

Conclusion

This book began as an effort to portray, with limited narrative, three photographic postcard series that Edward Beebe had created in Boyne Falls, Boyne City, and at the Beulah Home in Boyne City. Soon it became apparent that the story of Herman Swift and the Beulah Home overwhelmed the confines of a postcard book. At times I became concerned that the revelations, the scandal, and the potential embarrassments embodied in the story might overwhelm its historical merit.

The Beulah Home for Boys had wonderful potential. Clearly boys like Floyd Bishop learned, developed, and prospered at the Home. They took those lessons with them and built good lives. And there were happy times for all at the Home. This can be heard when the boys speak of Thanksgiving Day at the Home. It can be seen in Edward Beebe's photographs, in the faces of the boys as they sled, dine, and pose in the large gymnasium and the pool. And it can be believed when reading the letter written by Oscar Weber the first President of the Leoni Beulah Home for Boys.

But I think of the fear that the boys must have held when they left their homes and were sent at the age of eight or nine to live amongst a group of strangers in a large, dark, drafty and spooky home. I think of what they thought at night as they lay there and listened to the chimes of the downtown clock. And I wonder how they felt as they sat in the basement classroom and stared with wide eyes at the man who asked them to raise their hands if he had been good to them.

Herman Swift had started with a noble mission. He modeled himself after Dwight Moody and set out to save forsaken boys in the streets of Chicago and Buffalo. By 1909, it seems to me the mission had become a sham, an excuse to raise money, gain accolades, and recruit selected boys to the Beulah Home in Boyne City. Were it not for the heroics of boys like Merrill Griffin and Simon Mack the sham would have continued.

Many boys probably left the Beulah Home the better for the experience, but I believe a significant number were stressed and traumatized while they were there. After they left the Home, most probably got over the trauma, but perhaps some never did. I believe all the boys at Herman Swift's Chicago Children's Temple Home, his Leoni Beulah Home, and his Beulah Home for Boys in Boyne City must have lived there courageously. Finally, I completed this book so we might remember these boys and I dedicate it to them and their courage, to Leonora Ferris, and to Merrill Griffin's father Edward.

(Fig.31)

Index

~

Bibliography

Books, Pamphlets and Poems

Boyne City: Advantages Offered as a Manufacturing Center Are Unexcelled, (Boyne City, *Boyne Citizen*, July 1907)

John Bunyan, *Pilgrim's Progress*, (1678)

S.J. Clarke, *Modern History of New Haven*, (1918)

Contemporary History of a Michigan Lumber Town That's Booming Again, (Boyne City, Boyne City Rotary Club, 1965)

W.H. Daniels, *Moody, His Words, Work, and Workers*, (1877)

Lyle W. Dorsett, *A Passion for Souls, The Life of D.L. Moody*, (Chicago, Moody Publishers, 1997)

Ethlyn Dyer (Herman L. Swift), *The Victories of a Boy*, (Herman L. Swift, Chicago, 1912)

Elizabeth F. Elliot, *Pioneer Women of the West*, (Scribner, 1852)

John V. Farwell, *Some Recollections of John V. Farwell*, (Chicago, R.R. Donnelly, 1911)

Ihley Bros. & Everhard, *History of Service of Michigan Volunteers in the Civil War, 1861-1865*, (Kalamazoo, 1903)

Julie Ingersoll, *Baptist and Methodist Faiths in America*, (Faith in America Series, 2003)

Frederick C. Martindale, Secretary of State, *Michigan Manual*, (Lansing, 1909)

Hiram Mattison, *The Impending Crisis of 1860 or the Present Connection of the M.E. Church with Slavery and Our Duty in Regard to It*, (1858)

Charles Moore, *History of Michigan*, (Chicago, Lewis Publishing Co., 1915)

Robert Morgridge, *Settlers to Sidewalks in Boyne City*, (Boyne City, Boyne Valley Printing Company, 1981)

J.A. Spalding, *Illustrated Popular Biography of Connecticut*, (Hartford, 1891)

Justice Joseph Steere Opinion—People v. Swift, (188 Northwestern Reporter, Mich., Pages 662-670)

Herman L. Swift, *Give the Boy a Chance*, (Children's Temple, Chicago, 1900)

John A. Weeks, *Beneath the Beeches, The Story of Bay View*, (Erdmanns Printing Company, Grand Rapids, 2000)

John Wesley, *General Rules of the United Society*, (London, 1743)

John Wesley, *Thoughts Upon Slavery*, (London, 1774)

Arthur White, *White's Old Grand Rapids*, (1926)

Newspapers

Beaver Island News, Bellaire Independent, Boyne Citizen, Boyne City Statesman, Boyne City Times, Buffalo News, Cadillac News, Charlevoix County Herald, Charlevoix Courier, Charlevoix Evening Courier, Charlevoix Sentinel, Chicago Times Herald, Detroit Free Press, Detroit News, East Jordan Enterprise, Eaton Rapids Journal, Elk Rapids Progress, Grand Rapids Herald, Grand Rapids Press, Grass Lake News, Jackson Daily Patriot, Jackson Evening Press, Kalkaskian, New York Times, Petoskey Daily Resorter, Petoskey Evening News, Toledo Blade, Traverse City Record Eagle

Periodicals and Articles

Albion Interactive History, *Floyd Elliot Starr, 1883, Founder of Starr Commonwealth*, (Albion, Michigan, albionvision.com/history/starr, April 30th, 1903)

Edmund Kirke, "Rambles in Detroit," (Detroit, *Bay View Magazine*, February, 1903)

Harold Shepstone, "A Commonwealth of Waifs," (London, *The Sunday Magazine*, 1900)

Herman Swift, *The Youth's Outlook*, (August 1907, January 1911, January/February 1913)

Property Records

Charlevoix, Eaton, and Jackson County Register of Deeds Offices

Publications by R.L. Polk & Co., Detroit

Chicago Street Directory (1898, 1900, 1901, 1923), Detroit Street Directory (1887, 1889, 1891, 1893, 1894, 1895, 1900, 1903, 1905, 1909/1910, 1911, 1913, 1914), East Jordan Directory (1911), Petoskey City and Emmet County Directory (1903, 1909), State of Michigan Gazetteers (1899, 1905, 1909)

Records in State of Michigan Archives, Michigan State Library, Lansing

Charlevoix County Criminal Case Records (Cases 218, 219 and 220, December 14th, 1909; Case 226, June 17th, 1910)

Ionia State Reformatory Personal Record No. 7224, Herman L. Swift, December 3rd, 1912

Supreme Court Brief for the People and Brief for Respondent, People v. Swift, November 1911

Trial Transcript, Second Merrill Griffin Trial, December 30th, 1910

United States Federal Census Records, (1850 through 1930)